The Political Economy of NATO

Using simple economic methods while accounting for political and institutional factors, this book puts forward a political economy viewpoint of NATO's current status and its future prospects. A balanced picture of NATO is presented that is sensitive to the perspectives from both sides of the Atlantic. This is accomplished by accounting for the institutional features and the philosophical aspects that distinguish government decision makers and the defense establishment in North America from their counterparts in Europe. A host of NATO policy concerns are addressed, including the optimal membership for the alliance, its role in peacekeeping missions worldwide, the appropriate methods for deterring terrorism, and proper procurement practices for the next generation of weapons. Additional topics concern defense burden sharing, arms trade, NATO's institutional structure, and NATO's role vis-à-vis other international organizations. Although the analysis is rigorous, the book is intended for a wide audience drawn from political science and economics.

Todd Sandler is Distinguished Professor of Economics and Political Science at Iowa State University. He is a NATO fellow for 1998–2000. He was coeditor of the journal *Defence and Peace Economics* and is currently a member of its editorial board. Professor Sandler has taught at numerous universities and has written or coauthored twelve other books including *Global Challenges; Collective Action: Theory and Applications; The Economics of Defense; Handbook of Defense Economics;* and *International Terrorism in the 1980s* (2 vols.). His coauthored book *The Theory of Externalities, Public Goods, and Club Goods* (2nd edition, Cambridge University Press, 1996, with Richard Cornes) is a standard reference in public expenditures analysis.

Keith Hartley is Professor of Economics and founding Director of the Center of Defence Economics at the University of York, England. He is managing editor of the journal *Defence and Peace Economics* and secretary general of the International Defence Economics Association. Professor Hartley has taught at numerous universities and was a NATO research fellow in 1977–79 and 1986–87, and special advisor to the House of Commons Defence Committee in 1985–98. He has been a consultant to the UN, the European Commission, the US Department of Defense, and the UK Ministry of Defence. He has written or coauthored eleven books and more than 250 articles.

Advance Praise for *The Political Economy of NATO*

"As we approach the millennium, NATO faces unprecedented demands, ranging from the challenges it recognizes, the tasks it accepts, the financing it requires, the membership it embraces, the structure of its organization, to its continued operation. This book, by two of the world's premier analysts in the field, is unique for its sweeping grasp of the essentials of NATO's problems, and for the perspective and insight which economics skillfully applied brings to NATO's diverse and pressing questions. The Sandler–Hartley overview of these issues – useful to academic, policy, and operational circles – will endure well into the millennium which it foreshadows."

– Martin McGuire, *University of California, Irvine*

The Political Economy of NATO

Past, present, and into the 21st century

TODD SANDLER KEITH HARTLEY

PUBLISHED BY THE PRESS SYNDICATE OF THE UNIVERSITY OF CAMBRIDGE
The Pitt Building, Trumpington Street, Cambridge, United Kingdom

CAMBRIDGE UNIVERSITY PRESS
The Edinburgh Building, Cambridge CB2 2RU, UK http://www.cup.cam.ac.uk
40 West 20th Street, New York, NY 10011-4211, USA http://www.cup.org
10 Stamford Road, Oakleigh, Melbourne 3166, Australia

First published 1999

Printed in the United States of America

Typeface Times Roman 10.5/13 pt. *System* QuarkXPress™ 4.0 [AG]

*A catalog record for this book is available from
the British Library.*

Library of Congress Cataloging-in-Publication Data
Sandler, Todd.
The political economy of NATO : past, present, and into the 21st
century / by Todd Sandler and Keith Hartley.
p. cm.
Includes bibliographical references and indexes.
ISBN 0-521-63093-2 (hb). – ISBN 0-521-63880-1 (pbk.)
1. North Atlantic Treaty Organization. 2. Europe – Defenses –
Economic aspects. 3. United States – Defenses – Economic aspects.
I. Hartley, Keith. II. Title.
JZ5990.S26 1999
355'.031'091821 – dc21 98-99564

ISBN 0 521 63093 2 hardback
ISBN 0 521 63880 1 paperback

To our children: Tristan Jon Sandler, and
Adam, Lucy, and Cecilia Hartley

Contents

Tables and figures

Tables

Figures

Preface

In April 1999, the North Atlantic Treaty Organization (NATO) will turn fifty. Back in 1949, few political observers would have guessed that the twelve-member alliance would survive for half a century and take in Greece and Turkey on 18 February 1952, West Germany on 6 May 1955, and Spain on 30 May 1982. Even fewer would have predicted that the Czech Republic, Hungary, and Poland – three ex–Warsaw Pact allies – would be scheduled to join on NATO's fiftieth anniversary. NATO played a crucial role in stopping Soviet aggression during the alliance's first few decades. Without question, NATO helped to win the Cold War by outlasting the former Soviet Union and Warsaw Pact in a war of attrition that diverted scarce resources to the defense sector. To keep up with the technically superior Western defense industries, the former Soviet Union had to allocate so many resources into its defense sector that tremendous strains were placed on its economy, which are still being felt today. Economic inefficiencies in the Soviet Union also played a significant role in its Cold War defeat. Of course, the NATO allies also paid for their own diversion of resources in terms of growth and prosperity.

NATO has been a resilient institution that has withstood France's and Spain's exit from the integrated military structure, significant alterations in its military doctrine, hostilities between Greece and Turkey, leadership crises within its allies, policy differences among its members, and major changes in weapon capabilities. Every time NATO approaches a ten-year anniversary, there are those who question its role during the coming decade and who predict its inevitable demise. NATO's upcoming fiftieth birthday is no exception to this ritual. With the end of the Cold War, NATO's original role to face down the Soviet Union and its allies is no longer relevant unless one subscribes to the fear that nationalist elements in Russia will gain control of the government, thus initiating a new Cold War. To justify its continued existence, NATO must demonstrate that the collective security it affords against common threats is worth the transaction costs of maintaining the alliance.

Threats still abound in the late 1990s in numerous forms including the emergence of rogue nations, the proliferation of weapons of mass destruction, the escalation of transnational terrorism, the spread of civil wars, the vulnerability of essential resource supply lines to the West, and the rise of anti-Western superpowers. To address these new challenges, NATO will need to develop novel weapons, alternative military doctrines, additional infrastructure, new reinforcement channels, and different logistics. These security demands come at a time during which most NATO allies are downsizing their defense sectors. This downsizing in itself underscores the need for a collective defense to pool resources so as to maintain NATO's capabilities in the face of shrinking defense budgets. Over the next few years, NATO must redefine its role and strategic doctrine so as to demonstrate that its brand of collective defense is essential to maintain peace during the post–Cold War period.

We shall elucidate how NATO has made headway in accomplishing this redefinition in recent years and what still remains to be done to ensure the alliance's future viability. This book will investigate NATO's past achievements and failures, its current status and challenges, and its likely structure during the coming millennium. Now is an appropriate time to take stock of NATO's past and to speculate on its prospects for the future. A political economy approach is applied in order to meld political and economic considerations with an eye to making policy recommendations. Although economics began as a policy-oriented study of political economy, this classical form of analysis has been too often missing in modern economics. By combining our knowledge of economic methods, institutions, political tools, and political thought, we shall present an up-to-date treatise of the political economy of NATO, accessible to a wide audience of students, practitioners, policy makers, and researchers who want a modern treatment of NATO. We emphasize from the outset that this book presents conclusions based on rigorous analysis rather than ideology. Even though the underlying reasoning is rigorous and based on modern tools and principles of political economy, the presentation is intended to enlighten a reader possessing only a rudimentary knowledge of economic principles. The book has been written so as to stay up to date for a long time; thus, we are less concerned with analyzing a current debate than in studying recurring debates – for example, burden sharing, weapon standardization, NATO's optimal membership size and composition. Our intention is that this book will be useful to readers regardless of whether NATO will one day celebrate a sixtieth anniversary. Whatever is NATO's ultimate fate, military alliances will remain an important supranational structure into the foreseeable future, as they have been for almost four hundred years since the birth of the nation-state. This book has much to say not only about NATO, but also about alliances as an institutional structure.

We owe a great debt of gratitude to collaborators who have worked with us on a host of defense economic issues and NATO-based studies. These people include Jon Cauley, John A. C. Conybeare, Richard Cornes, Andrew Cox, Walter Enders, John F. Forbes, Laurna Hansen, Nick Hooper, Jyoti Khanna, Harvey E. Lapan, Dwight Lee, Elizabeth S. Macnair, Stephen Martin, Edward F. Mickolus, James C. Murdoch, Jean M. Murdock, Gerald F. Parise, Chung-Ron Pi, Keith Sargent, Hirofumi Shimizu, Ron Smith, and John Tschirhart. While assuming full responsibility for any shortcomings of this study, we have greatly profited from comments provided by Charles Anderton, Hans Kammler, James McCormick, Hirofumi Shimizu, and numerous anonymous reviewers of earlier drafts of the chapters. Sincere thanks are also due to Scott Parris, economics editor at Cambridge University Press, who provided encouragement and good counsel throughout the book's preparation. His constant confidence in our project was crucial to the book's success. We also appreciate the efforts of the production staff at Cambridge University Press, who transformed the typescript into a book. We gratefully acknowledge the skills, care, and patience of Anne Hrbek, Margaret Cafferky, and Sue Streeter, who typed the myriad drafts of the book. Finally, we appreciate the support of our wives (Jeannie and Winifred) and our children (Tristan, Adam, Lucy, and Cecilia), who bore the true costs of this venture.

Todd Sandler's research was supported in part by a Faculty Improvement Leave in 1996, at which time he met with Keith Hartley in York, England, on a couple of occasions. It was during these meetings that the book began as an outline and concept. He appreciates this study leave provided by Iowa State University. He also acknowledges the research support of a NATO Fellowship. John Miranowski, Chair of the Department of Economics, Iowa State University, provided financial support to assemble the peacekeeping data used in Chapter 4. Keith Hartley's research was supported by the ESRC's Single European Market Programs (W113251009) and by the Leverhulme Trust.

Ames, Iowa
York, England
August 1998

TODD SANDLER
KEITH HARTLEY

1 NATO at the crossroads: An introduction

Unquestionably, the North Atlantic Treaty Organization (NATO) has been one of the most successful and resilient alliances ever created. NATO has weathered innumerable crises – France's withdrawal from NATO's integrated military structure, Turkey's invasion of Cyprus, coups d'état in Portugal, Greece, and Turkey. Despite these and other exigencies, NATO has outlasted the Soviet Union and the Warsaw Pact, and, in so doing, has contributed to its Cold War victory.[1] As NATO approaches its half-century mark, it stands at a crossroads. The Cold War is over and, with its end, the threat of nuclear East-West confrontation has become, at this writing, an unlikely scenario. Although military budgets of the NATO allies and the ex–Warsaw Pact countries have declined greatly in real spending terms, the world is still a dangerous place.[2] Civil wars in Bosnia, Somalia, Haiti, and the former Soviet republics underscore these dangers. The democratization of the former communist nations has unbridled pent-up ethnic hostilities that have erupted into conflicts that can transcend borders and engulf neighboring nations (Boczek, 1995; Carlier, 1995). Ethnic conflicts continue to threaten the former Soviet republics of Azerbaijan, Armenia, Tajikistan, Georgia, Moldova, and Chechnya. Industrial nations remain dependent on resources imported, in part, from countries in the Middle East, East and Central Africa, and Asia, which face political instability and possible conflict. If resource supplies to the industrial world are to be secure, NATO must be prepared to contend with crises

1. Another contributing factor to this victory was the inherent inefficiency of the Soviet economy – e.g., its reliance on monopolies, its corruption of officials (Lambelet, 1992).
2. NATO allies' real defense spending fell on average by 3.5 percent per year from 1990 to 1995 (US Department of Defense, 1996, p. III-3).

and conflicts outside of Europe. The Gulf War of 1991 and instabilities in East Africa illustrate this need to keep resource supply lines open.

At the current crossroads, NATO must redefine itself in numerous ways. First, NATO must justify its continued existence in the face of critics who argue that NATO has no further political or strategic role to play. To accomplish this, NATO must demonstrate that collective defense is needed to maintain peace during the post–Cold War era, where risks abound and individual allies do not have sufficient resources to confront every challenge. Second, NATO must decide on its membership size and composition given the dissolution of the Warsaw Pact. Should it grow beyond its designated three new entrants (i.e., the Czech Republic, Hungary, and Poland) and admit additional transitional economies and the neutral nations? Third, NATO must identify new strategic missions and alter its military doctrine and force structures accordingly. Changed strategic missions affect myriad activities of the allies including the deployment of forces, the training of military personnel, the composition of forces, the procurement of weapons, and the development of the next generation of weapons. Fourth, NATO must reconsider its institutional structure. Is the institutional structure created to meet Cold War contingencies appropriate to address current and future challenges of a more varied nature? Alterations in institutional design must account for any increase in the alliance size as well as the assumption of any new tasks. Fifth, NATO must assist in the disarmament process that limits conventional, strategic, tactical, and nonconventional (i.e., biological and chemical) weapons. This process began in 1972 with the signing of the Biological Weapons Convention, the Strategic Arms Limitation Treaty Interim Agreement (SALT I), and the Anti-Ballistic Missile (ABM) Treaty. Sixth, the role of the European Union (EU) within the NATO alliance must be determined.

This last consideration questions who will be the basic players within NATO. Since its inception, NATO has been a "loose" alliance, where most defense spending has been decided independently by the allies. As a consequence of this independence, collective action problems abound. In particular, the large, rich allies assumed a disproportionate share of the burdens of the small, poor allies (see Chapter 2; Olson, 1965; Olson and Zeckhauser, 1966; Sandler, 1993). Also, defense spending was judged to be suboptimal. If the European Union were to become more integrated and develop a common defense policy so as to utilize resources more efficiently, then NATO would consist of two major allies – the European Union and the United States – of fairly equal economic size. This development could drastically change burden sharing and resource allocative efficiency. Throughout this book, we will consider the behavior of NATO under two scenarios: many independent allies and two major allies.

The current chapter sets the stage for the rest of the book by enumerating both the challenges ahead for NATO and the alternative means of addressing them. The book's scope, purposes, and content are also presented. Finally, unique features of this book are highlighted and contrasted with the literature.

CHALLENGES AHEAD FOR NATO AND WORLD PEACE

Many of today's challenges for NATO differ fundamentally from the face-off between the two superpowers during the Cold War. Ethnic unrest in Europe is a real threat to peace for NATO allies. The Bosnian situation can develop elsewhere in the Balkans, Central, and Eastern Europe, where ethnic hatreds had been kept in check by once-powerful governments. Whenever ethnic unrest in Europe jeopardizes the peace of the region, NATO must be prepared to take decisive action when the time is right. Sometimes, action is best when it is swift, so as to limit carnage and to minimize peacemaking resource expenditures. As conflicts take hold, they often pose greater risks (e.g., increased threats of mines) and costs to the peacemakers, and leave greater resentment from those who lose loved ones. This resentment may make peace, once achieved, difficult to maintain. But another view maintains that delayed action is best once the two sides have depleted one another's resources and have lost their will to fight in a war of attrition.[3] In this latter scenario, the peacemakers can be deployed and may face little opposition or casualties, as in Bosnia.[4] Regardless of the correct view, it is essential in either case that NATO possesses political procedures and logistical plans for deploying peacekeeping forces rapidly, once they are deemed necessary and must be dispatched. For civil conflict within Europe, NATO allies are most at risk as compared with non-NATO UN members, so that NATO and not the United Nations is the appropriate body to manage the crisis.

Conflict can also develop in out-of-area places, where NATO may have vital economic, political, or strategic interests. The NATO of the twenty-

3. We thank an anonymous referee for this insight.
4. A related timing issue involves actions of the combatants prior to imminent cessation of hostilities. As NATO nears a decision to intervene, each side may fight harder to gain a negotiating advantage. This suggests that once intervention is likely, it should be decided quickly to limit these last-minute escalations of conflict.

first century must be able to project power rapidly to trouble spots where these interests are at risk. Such out-of-area missions are not necessarily covered by the Articles of the North Atlantic Treaty (see Chapter 2). When the Bush administration made its case for Operation Desert Shield to the American people, it pointed to the cutoff of Middle Eastern oil supplies and the dangers of Iraq's alleged weapons of mass destruction. In the future, conflicts may even erupt if a nation's people or property are severely harmed by pollutants from abroad and all diplomatic efforts to curb these deadly pollutants fail. Environmental security may require decisive actions and resolve to deter other nations from polluting the country in the future. As remote sensing and other monitoring technologies have been developed, the transnational dispersion of pollution is becoming better understood and tracked. Borders, once secured through the deployment of military forces, are no longer protected from the daily invasion of pollutants of all kinds.

Within the United Nations, peacekeeping missions have mushroomed since the end of the Cold War in response to conflicts and instabilities that still abound in the world (see Chapter 4). This increase is partly reflected in Table 1.1, which indicates UN members' and NATO allies' *actual* peacekeeping payments to the United Nations in millions of current year's US dollars for the 1980–96 period. In the third column, UN members' total payments are listed. Using UN budgets, we record only the actual payments made by members to UN peacekeeping missions for these years. In most recent years, the actual peacekeeping outlays have exceeded UN members' peacekeeping contributions, with the difference coming out of the regular UN budget. In current dollar terms, the payments during some recent years were at least a *magnitude* greater than those in the years prior to 1989. These outlays do not include the $61 billion spent on the Gulf War in 1991 by the US-led coalition or money spent on other peacekeeping operations, not funded by the UN budget.

In Table 1.1, the second column lists NATO's actual payments for these peacekeeping operations. To put these payments in perspective, we indicate NATO's paid share of UN peacekeeping payments in the last column. After 1984, the fluctuations in this share term are primarily influenced by the extent to which the United States fulfilled its approximate 32 percent pledged share to support UN peacekeeping. The last three US administrations have not always met this obligation.[5] If real peacekeeping burdens are to be in-

5. On the differences between UN members' pledged and actual payments for peacekeeping, see Durch (1993), Hill and Malik (1996), and Mills (1990). Actual cost outlays for 1989–91 are given by Durch (1993, p. 43) for some selected missions.

Table 1.1. *UN peacekeeping expenditures, 1980–96: actual payments in current year's US dollars (in millions)*

Year	NATO outlays[a]	UN members' outlays[a]	NATO's share[b]
1996	816	1339	60.1
1995	1662	2798	59.4
1994	2094	2980	70.3
1993	1706	2312	73.8
1992	1046	1280	81.7
1991	327	452	72.3
1990	191	386	49.5
1989	412	653	63.1
1988	114	208	54.8
1987	111	179	62.0
1986	113	169	66.9
1985	118	162	72.8
1984	123	156	78.8
1983	149	193	77.2
1982	143	182	78.6
1981	119	151	78.8
1980	128	161	79.5

[a]All figures are rounded off to the nearest million. Figures include only assessed payments to UN peacekeeping operations. Hence, expenditures for Operation Desert Storm or for the Implementation Force (IFOR) in Bosnia are not reported.
[b]Shares are in percentage.
Sources: United Nations (1980–1997), *Status of Contributions.*

vestigated, then actual, not pledged, payments to UN peacekeeping must be identified and explained. Peacekeeping activities for both the United Nations and NATO are anticipated to grow in size and importance, and this growth represents a challenge to NATO in terms of resource allocation.

During the Cold War, the enemy was easy to identify: it was either the opposing superpower or its surrogate. In the post–Cold War era, enemies are more difficult to characterize, since they include nonstate agents and rogue nations (Klare, 1995), which may resort to unconventional means of violence. As such, terrorism poses a challenge to modern-day NATO. For example, a terrorist organization can acquire chemical and biological agents, and in so doing, can represent a formidable threat. Aum Shinrikyo's sarin attack on the Tokyo subway system on the morning of 20 March 1995 is an instance (Sopko, 1996/97). During rush hour, eleven sarin-filled bags planted on five subway trains created terror, pandemonium, and injuries at fifteen Tokyo subway stations, resulting in the deaths of twelve people and the hospitalization of more than 5,000. In fact, the cult had purchased a Russian helicopter in order to disperse sarin and other deadly chemical agents at a future date over Tokyo so as to murder thousands. If a rogue state, which operates outside of accepted norms, were to acquire weapons of mass destruction, then its leaders could extort concessions from NATO allies.

In the run-up to the British national elections on 1 May 1997, the Irish Republican Army (IRA) had temporarily halted rail and other forms of transportation with actual and threatened bombings. This terror campaign, relying on phoned threats, disrupted the British economy. Advanced economies are vulnerable to terrorist acts directed at crucial points in their infrastructure (e.g., the transportation system, the power grid, the communication network). The "right" act can temporarily create significant economic consequences. To protect against such scenarios requires security measures that differ greatly from those used during the last forty years. A clear challenge for NATO is to develop such measures.

NATO must also address issues involving weapon development and procurement during the current period of shrinking defense budgets. If production runs of new weapon systems are smaller than in the past, then unit cost of these new systems will be higher as the fixed costs of research and development (R & D) and production are spread over fewer units (see Chapter 5). This raises important economic issues regarding specializing weapon production for various weapons among allies. It also points to political concerns involving a unified procurement process for the European Union. Major industrial powers may have to relinquish the security of being self-sufficient in their arms manufacturing in return for smaller defense budgets. Current trends among weapons manufacturers have been toward merger and fewer competitors. Such trends have implications for efficiency that are examined in Chapter 5.

Another challenge for NATO is associated with the visions of future battlefields where "information warriors," equipped with computers, sensors, and laser-targeting devices, replace traditional foot soldiers. In these future military theaters, being spotted is the difference between life and death. What can be viewed can be targeted and then destroyed. Smaller military units that can hide will have a strategic advantage over larger units on these killing fields. From a strategic vantage, information-gathering assets become the target of choice during a preemptive phase of attack. Thus, satellite and ground-based receptors would require defending. These new technologies are apt to shorten the time or "window" during which a nation must react to a perceived attack, real or imagined. An attacking nation can gain a first-mover advantage by "blinding" its opponent – that is, eliminating its information-gathering assets. These technological developments increase the possibility of an accidental war and may create greater instabilities. Future arms races may involve satellite offensive weapons and countermeasures to defend against such weapons, while future battlefields may require entirely new force structures and military doctrine. New weapons will emerge that will revolutionize warfare and render obsolete current equipment and forces. Also, these sophisticated new weapons may have important burden-sharing implications, because only the richest allies may be able to afford the required investment in developing and upgrading them.

The Pacific Rim presents another challenge to NATO. As China drives toward development, it is anticipated to become a military power with territorial designs on parts of Asia. China's military status is expected to affect Japan and its military spending. As a major economic power, the Japanese economy influences the global economy. If Japan were to divert significant resources into the defense sector, this could have important implications for the industrial world. Potential conflicts between China and Taiwan could affect NATO allies with interests in either place. The Korean peninsula is another potential trouble spot. As economic growth continues among the "Asian Tigers," the NATO allies and Russia will have greater economic, political, and military interests in the Pacific Rim.

Yet another concern of NATO is to continue the disarmament process, which has begun with the ratification of the Biological Weapons Convention in 1975. In Table 1.2, the major treaties limiting arms are listed, along with their signing and ratification (if applicable) dates. Although much progress on reducing tactical, conventional, and strategic weapons has been achieved since 1987, there is still much to be done with respect to outer-space weapons, chemical weapons, and strategic weapons. The major powers still possess massive nuclear armaments that are still sufficient to annihilate populations worldwide even if START II is ratified. It is conceivable that nuclear disarmament, thus far, has only eliminated redundant missiles. Moreover, there is no mechanism for dealing with violators or nonsigners; thus, nuclear proliferation remains a threat to world security with no established procedures for punishing violators.

Perhaps the greatest challenge facing NATO is to convince its members and critics (e.g., Carpenter, 1994) that the alliance still has a role to play in the post–Cold War period. NATO allies must rethink and rationalize the need for an alliance, expanded or otherwise, in light of the strategic, political, and technological developments since the fall of the Berlin Wall. Questions include: Should NATO be abolished? Can either the United Nations

Table 1.2. *Important arms control treaties, 1963–94*

Treaty	Signed	Entered into force	Remarks
Partial Test Ban	5 Aug. 1963	10 Oct. 1963	Banning nuclear weapons tests in the atmosphere, in outer space, and under water.
Outer Space	27 Jan. 1967	10 Oct. 1967	Prohibiting nuclear weapons or weapons of mass destruction in orbit, on the moon, or in outer space.
Nonproliferation of Nuclear Weapons	1 July 1968[a]	5 March 1970	There are 179 states party to the treaty. It was originally of twenty-five years duration, but was extended indefinitely in May 1995.
Seabed	11 Feb. 1971	18 May 1972	Prohibiting nuclear weapons or weapons of mass destruction on the seabed.
Biological Weapons Convention (BWC)	10 April 1972	26 March 1975	Applying to biological weapons and their means of delivery.
SALT I Interim (Limitation of Strategic Offensive Arms)	26 May 1972	3 Oct. 1972	Between the US and USSR. It froze existing levels of these countries' missile launchers and submarines.
Antiballistic Missiles (ABM)	3 July 1974	24 May 1976	Between the US and USSR. Limited each country to a single ABM site.
Threshold Test Ban (TTBT)	3 July 1974	11 Dec. 1990	Prohibiting underground nuclear weapons tests greater than 150 kilotons.
Helsinki Final Act	1 Aug. 1975	1 Aug. 1975	Concluding document of Conference on Security and Cooperation in Europe (CSCE). It mandates advance notice of military maneuvers involving over 25,000 troops.
SALT II	18 June 1979	—	Between the US and USSR for limiting strategic offensive weapons. Superceded by START I in 1991.

INF	8 Dec. 1987	1 June 1988	Between the US and USSR on eliminating intermediate-range and shorter-range missiles. Eliminates and bans cruise missiles and ground-launched missiles with range of 500–5,500 km. Fully implemented 1 June 1991.
CFE	19 Nov. 1990	9 Nov. 1992	Limiting conventional armed forces in Europe. Signed by twenty-two NATO and Warsaw Pact nations to be implemented within forty months of 9 Nov. 1992.
START I[b]	31 July 1991	5 Dec. 1994	Between the US and USSR on reducing and limiting strategic offensive arms. Limits on ICBMs, their launchers and warheads; SLBM launchers and warheads; and heavy bombers.
Chemical Weapons Convention (CWC)	13 Jan. 1993	29 April 1997	Prohibiting the development, production, stockpiling and use of chemical weapons. Signed by 160 nations and entered into force 180 days after the sixty-fifth instrument of ratification was deposited. As of 5 November 1997, 104 nations have ratified the treaty.
START II	3 Jan. 1993	—	Between the US and the Russian Federation concerning further reductions of strategic offense weapons. It eliminates all MIRVed ICBMs. Total number of warheads for each side is reduced to 3,000–3,500. This treaty will enter into force after START I Treaty of 1991 enters into force.
Trilateral Nuclear Agreement	14 Jan. 1994	—	Indicates procedures for transferring Ukrainian nuclear warheads to Russia. It also details compensations for Ukraine and safeguards.

[a]Opened for signature on this date.
[b]The Lisbon START Protocol of 28 May 1992 accounted for the breakup of the Soviet Union. This protocol provides for Russia, Belarus, Ukraine, and Kazakhstan to assume the Soviet Union's obligations under the treaty. Belarus, Ukraine, and Kazakhstan committed themselves to accede to NPT as non-nuclear weapons nations.
Source: NATO Office of Information and Press (1995, pp. 277–82).

Table 1.3. *Taxonomy of transnational interactions for resolving conflict*

	Small number of nations (e.g., 1–16)	Large number of nations (e.g., 16+)
Nonmilitary action	Discussion Informal arrangement Political sanctions Treaty Supranational structure	Discussion Informal arrangement Political sanctions Treaty Supranational structure
Military action	Military-backed threat Sanctions Peacekeeping War	Military-backed threat Sanctions Peacekeeping War

or the European Union assume the role of NATO and confront military threats more successfully? Will EU integration change burden-sharing behavior within NATO? Should NATO be more or less integrated in the post–Cold War period?

ALTERNATIVE MEANS FOR ADDRESSING CHALLENGES

Given the diversity of the challenges on the horizon, the proper group size for confronting instabilities within and beyond Europe is a crucial concern. At times, only a single nation needs to address a crisis, as the United States did in Grenada on 25 October 1983. At other times, a small number of nations will be sufficient to meet the challenge, as in Bosnia or Kuwait. If action is to be taken it is important that the decision-making group is not too large to impede or to dilute action. Larger groups have a more difficult time in reaching decisions, since more nations must agree to go along with an action.

In Table 1.3, we depict a taxonomy for international interactions to resolve differences. In general, one, few, or many nations may be needed to defuse a conflict. The appropriate number depends on the interests affected by the contingencies. Surely, crises in Europe involve the interests of NATO allies and, as such, should be addressed by NATO. If crises outside of Europe have important economic or political implications for European countries, then NATO may still wish to assume a leading role in the resolution. When contingencies are addressed, action may be military or nonmilitary. In each cell of Table 1.3, we indicate the type of action in terms of increasing integration for nonmilitary options and increasing escalation for military options. Discussion is the least binding form of nonmilitary interaction. Next, an informal arrangement can involve a bargained solution between two or more nations. If negotiations fail, political sanctions (e.g., a trade boycott) may follow. A nation may seek a more formal agreement in the form of a treaty between itself and other countries. Treaties may also involve a group of allies and another group of nations, as in the case of the Partnership for Peace, when NATO reached a formal agreement with neutral and ex-communist nations regarding interactions with the NATO alliance.

Supranational structures represent a formal organization linking nations or groups of nations together to accomplish one or more goals. The form of the structure may vary from loose to tight. Loose structures maintain member nations' autonomy, while tight structures fuse nations into a single entity (see Chapter 8). An alliance is an example of a supranational structure.

The mildest form of a military action is a threat, backed up by a show of force with the resolve to use it when the sought-after concession is not granted. If the threat is sufficiently intimidating and credible, then the force will not be applied. When the Bush administration issued its ultimatum to Saddam Hussein to withdraw from Kuwait before 15 January 1991 or else face severe consequences, the United States was delivering such a military-backed threat. This threat and future US threats were made credible by the bombing of Baghdad on the morning of 16 January 1991. Military sanctions are a stronger form of military action that could involve the mining of a nation's harbors, blockading its ships, or bombing an isolated target. If these tactics fail, then one or more nations may resort to deploying a peacemaking force to quell the unrest. For peacekeeping to occur, the peacekeepers must have the consent of the nation(s) where the forces are to be deployed. War represents the most drastic form of military action; no consent is needed from the receiving country when troops are dispatched. Of course, wars can differ greatly in terms of the number of nations involved and the level of warfare. Table 1.3 is not intended to be exhaustive. Additional kinds of military and nonmilitary actions exist and can be fitted into the taxonomy according to their intensity.

Sometimes supranational structure takes the form of a club in which two or more nations *voluntarily* form an association to address one or more common problems requiring collective action. Clubs involve sharing, as when nations form a pollution pact to clean up a waterway so as to share in the costs and benefits of a less polluted environment. Clubs may involve a single product or multiple products. For instance, NATO primarily shares the resulting security that stems from the efforts of the allies to achieve a mutual defense through military arsenals and manpower. The European Armament Agency and the Western European Union (WEU) are representative of single-product clubs, whose primary purpose is to provide security to their members. In contrast, multiproduct clubs share the costs and benefits associated with two or more collectively provided products. For example, the United Nations provides peacekeeping, diplomatic solutions, humanitarian aid, data, and other goods. Similarly, the European Union is associated with a host of products including greater monetary integration, free trade, infrastructure, and reduced pollution.

SCOPE AND PURPOSE OF THE BOOK

A primary purpose of this book is to present an up-to-date assessment of NATO's current position and to address NATO's likely evolution and form for the future. Our intention is to keep the analysis devoid of ideology. To speculate on NATO's future, we take account of the post–Cold War environment (political and economic) and any anticipated contingencies. Modern economic tools and reasoning are applied to investigate allocative and distributive issues that have influenced NATO in the past or that will affect it in the future. By using economic methods while accounting for political and institutional factors, we put forward a political economy viewpoint, where a primary purpose is to examine policy concerns.

A host of policy issues are considered. In particular, patterns of burden sharing are studied to ascertain whether defense burdens have been carried disproportionately by the larger allies (Chapter 2). These patterns are shown to have changed throughout NATO's history and may be anticipated to alter yet again as NATO's missions and threats are transformed. A related policy concern involves the optimal membership size of NATO. Using a simple theory of clubs, we investigate how many allies should comprise NATO (see Chapter 3). Once these factors are uncovered, we are then able to consider the 1994 Partnership for Peace initiative, intended to enlarge NATO to include some Eastern European and neutral countries.[6] Economic considerations are not the only determinants behind alliance size, inasmuch as political concerns are also relevant. Thus, for example, possible Russian re-

6. On the Partnership for Peace see Boczek (1995), Bruce (1995), Gompert and Larrabee (1997), Jordan (1995), and Van Oudenaren (1997).

actions must be weighed against expected gains from expanding NATO. Any change in NATO's membership leads to both transaction costs and benefits that must be compared at the ally and alliance level.

Another policy issue concerns crisis management in the post–Cold War era. This issue raises a number of questions. Should crisis management be assumed by NATO, and, if so, how should NATO reconfigure its forces to manage crises effectively? Recently, NATO allies have assumed significant shares of the military burden for the Gulf War and for peacekeeping missions in Bosnia. Among the NATO members, the United States has assumed a leadership role in both sets of operations. Is this pattern likely to persist? We address this question. The proper composition and deployment of a NATO-based multinational rapid deployment force is another concern. If NATO is expected to field multiple dispatchments of its rapid deployment concurrently, then current forces must be augmented. Worldwide crisis management poses a burden-sharing worry, because non-NATO nations have an incentive to sit back as NATO shoulders these burdens. This follows because the benefits resulting from peacekeeping are received by all nations, whether or not they have supported the operation. A classic free-rider problem emerges. Since the November 1991 Rome summit, NATO has accepted a greater peacekeeping role.

A related policy issue involves the role that NATO should play in enforcing international treaties, such as the nuclear weapons nonproliferation treaty. When, for example, North Korea was in violation of this treaty in 1994, the United States alone had to take a tough stance to get an "agreed framework" from the North Koreans (UN Department of Public Information, 1995), because US appeals to the world community to apply sanctions met with silence. Currently, there is no established enforcement mechanism for such international treaties, so that the international community's response to violations is ad hoc. The 1990s has ushered in an era of global and regional treaty making, ranging from arms-limitation treaties to pollution-control agreements. At some point, some recognized international body with sufficient might will have to enforce these treaties if they are going to accomplish their intended goals.

NATO's role in deterring and imposing sanctions on international terrorism raises yet another policy concern. Although there has been some cooperation among nations in sharing intelligence, there has been less cooperation in coordinating actions to thwart terrorism, even when it has been directed at a number of NATO allies. In fact, this failure to coordinate deterrence often results in overspending as nations attempt to induce the terrorists to shift their activities to less-protected neighboring countries (Sandler and Lapan, 1988). This coordination failure may change in Europe if EU integration moves forward. Terrorism represents a serious threat to the stability of democracies that are expected to protect citizens' lives and property. When terrorists can strike with apparent impunity and cause significant damage, the government is perceived as powerless. An inappropriate response by a democratic government to terrorist acts can diminish its public support and result in its ouster from office. Too strong a response makes the government appear tyrannical, whereas too weak a response makes it seem inept. In 1985, Italian Prime Minister Craxi's government fell after it released two hijackers of the *Achille Lauro.* President Carter's handling of the Iranian embassy takeover in 1979–80 probably cost him a second term in office. As terrorists acquire weapons of mass destruction, their ability to disrupt democracies may increase significantly. A collective, transnational response to terrorism is likely to be more effective and to economize on resources as compared with responses by individual nations; but this collective response is difficult to achieve.

The defense industrial base is also behind some policy questions. For example, the arms trade raises security dilemmas, because weapons sold by one NATO ally may later create security risks for itself or other allies (Levine, Mouzakis, and Smith, 1996). A number of NATO members had sold military hardware and technology to Iraq, which later posed a threat to the coalition forces during Operation Desert Storm. Another policy concern involves weapons development and procurement practices within NATO. Joint ventures, in which two or more allies pool efforts to develop and produce weapons systems, provide a potential means to limit costs. If, alternatively, NATO allies specialize in producing different weapon systems and then trade among themselves, then gains from trade can be achieved. By taking advantage of these gains, NATO can remain strong even during times of shrinking military budgets. A related question involves the extent of competition that should be maintained, as mergers have reduced the number of defense contractors in recent years. Should competitive standards be maintained with respect to NATO as a whole, or with respect to the major arms-producing nations within NATO? Economic analysis can provide answers.

Institutional changes to the alliance represent another policy issue. Currently, NATO is an unintegrated or "loose" international organization that provides its members with a good deal of autonomy in determining their defense expenditures. At times, the alliance has agreed to rough guidelines on military spending (e.g., a 3 percent increase in real spending during the late

1970s and early 1980s), but these guidelines were not enforced or followed (Sandler, 1987). NATO allies continue to pursue defense spending policies independently of the other allies. Greek and Turkish efforts to arm so as to threaten one another graphically illustrate the point. Whether or not this looseness is still appropriate needs to be considered in the post–Cold War era. Alternative institutional configurations should be evaluated, as we do in Chapter 8.

METHODS AND CONTENT

We shall draw upon diverse tools of economics and politics to provide an up-to-date assessment of NATO, its prospects and its policies. Elementary game theory enables us to display strategic interactions among allies, between opposing alliances, and among agents within the procurement process (e.g., Congress, defense contractors, the Pentagon). An interaction is strategic when the choices or the beliefs supporting these choices of two or more agents (e.g., nations) are mutually dependent in a significant fashion. For example, one ally's choice of defense spending depends on the choices of spending levels of the other allies whenever one ally can gain security from another's armed forces. Strategic interaction also involves Congress's funding of weapon procurement, since the quality (or sophistication) of the weapons system put forward by the Pentagon influences the level of R & D and hence the level of fixed costs. By deliberately putting forward sophisticated weapons with high fixed costs, the Pentagon can make a better case at a later date for larger production runs, which, by spreading fixed costs over more units, can reduce per-unit costs (Rogerson, 1990, 1991). As such, strategic behavior is a multiperiod affair, with the Pentagon choosing first so as to influence the subsequent choices of Congress. The Pentagon's choice is predicated on its beliefs regarding how its decision will impact on Congress's later decision.

Two basic kinds of games are germane to our study of NATO: noncooperative and cooperative games. In a noncooperative game, the players make their decisions without consultation or coordination with other players. That is, the players attempt to optimize their objectives independently. A noncooperative game consists of three essential ingredients – the players, their strategies or alternative choices, and the payoffs associated with these choices. By contrast, a cooperative game has two or more players forming partnerships or coalitions so as to maximize jointly their objective. *If each member of the coalition can do better by staying in the coalition than by acting alone or in some alternative coalition, then the coalition will remain stable.* A loose alliance is best represented as a noncooperative game, whereas a tight alliance is best described as a cooperative game.

Microeconomic tools are used throughout our study to display such things as the conduct of firms in the defense industrial base. We ascribe rationality to all agents. As such, agents are represented as optimizing some objective (e.g., national security, profit), subject to one or more constraints (e.g., a budget constraint). Alterations of these constraints (e.g., changing prices in a budget constraint) will lead to predictable changes in behavior. Since optimization underlies the analysis, we are interested in equating the relevant margins. If, for instance, costs are to be minimized in a specific defense industry, then the marginal costs of each firm must be equal at the point of production or else it must be possible to shift production from a high marginal cost firm to a low marginal cost firm and reduce costs in the process.

When explaining the behavior of governmental officials, we frequently rely on tools and concepts drawn from public choice theory, which accounts for the likely motivation and interests of these officials; that is, we do not assume that officials necessarily advance the public interest. For an examination of international organizations, we apply the analysis of the new institutional economics in which transaction costs and informational aspects are taken into account. Wherever possible, we shall report empirical findings from both the political science and economics literature to support our assertions.

Methods and concepts from public economics also figure prominently in the book. In particular, four kinds of market failure, where incentives are lacking for markets to achieve efficient resource allocation, are relevant for our study (see Sandler, 1992; Cornes and Sandler, 1996). First, there is an *externality,* which arises when the action of one agent influences the well-being of another agent and no means of compensation exists. When, for instance, atmospheric tests of nuclear weapons released radioactive fallout that fell on other countries, a transnational externality occurred. With an externality, either private costs do not equal social costs, or private benefits do not equal social benefits, or both. As a result, society does not attain the right mix of goods for maximum well-being. That is, resources could be reallocated so as to make some agents better off without necessarily making anyone else worse off. Externalities may be corrected or "internalized" in a number of ways. A tax or subsidy can be used in the case of an external cost or an external benefit to equate private and social costs or benefits. If only a few agents are involved, they can internalize the externality by bargaining their way to an optimum. In other cases, a supranational structure or a treaty can apply rules to account for the externality. In still other instances, the World Court could assign liabilities regarding the externality so as to equate private and social costs or benefits.

A second market failure may involve public goods. A pure public good possesses benefits that are nonrival among users and nonexcludable. The benefits of a good are nonrival when one agent's consumption of a unit of the good does not detract, in the least, from the consumption opportunities still available for others from that *same unit.* A peacekeeping mission that keeps warring sides apart brings stability to a nation and, in so doing, provides nonrival benefits in the form of increased security to all nations that had been threatened by the fighting. The reduced risk of warfare that Kosovo derives from Bosnian peacekeeping does not detract from the reduced risk that Croatia or Montenegro derives. Benefits of a good, available to all once the good is provided, are called nonexcludable. If, however, the benefits of a good can be withheld costlessly by the provider, then the benefits are excludable. Peacekeeping, like pollution removal, provides nonexcludable benefits to all nations, whether or not they contribute to the mission. Markets fail to function efficiently for nonexcludable goods because there is an incentive to *free ride* on the efforts of others, so that a suboptimal amount of the good is anticipated. Why contribute to something that you can get for free?

A third cause of market failure may be from asymmetric information, where one party is informed while another is not. In the procurement process, for example, the defense contractor has information about its efforts to control costs that Congress cannot observe. Under these circumstances, Congress may have to design a contract so that the defense contractor expends high effort and tries to keep costs in check.

A fourth cause of market failure arises where defense equipment markets are characterized by monopoly, oligopoly, and entry barriers. In some cases, governments might be the cause of market failure through preferential purchasing policies (e.g., the Buy American Act; support for national champions).

Viewpoint

We present a balanced picture, sensitive to the perspectives from both sides of the Atlantic. In so doing, we account for the institutional features and the philosophical factors that distinguish government decision makers and the defense establishment in North America from their counterparts in Europe. Rather than subscribing to an ideological bias from either side of the Atlantic, we apply rigorous economic and political criteria to assess the performance of the allies in fulfilling alternative goals. In the case of burden sharing, for example, we do not take either America's position that it has shouldered the primary defense burdens of its European allies, or the European view that it has always carried precisely the right burden. Similarly, we try fairly to judge the threat posed by rogue nations and terrorism without blindly accepting US allegations or European governments' complacency. Differences in the strategic and political environment between the two sides of the Atlantic are brought into the analysis. For example, civil wars anywhere in Europe would have a greater chance to destabilize European allies of NATO than their non-European counterparts. From a strategic viewpoint, it is easier for the United States to turn its back on a NATO ally in Europe during a nuclear threat than for France, for example, to ignore pleas for protection from a nearby European ally, since in the latter case any collateral damage from an attack is apt to be greater.

Insofar as most European nations are members of the European Union, these nations have greater economic ties to one another than to the United States. These additional ties may eventually result in an integrated defense industrial base developing in Europe that competes with that of North America. Expansion of the European Union to include former communist countries, such as Poland, Hungary, and the Czech Republic, will have implications for Western Europe's defense industrial base. EU expansion will also affect the prospects for the expansion of NATO. To present an up-to-date analysis, we include a discussion on the potential inclusion in NATO of some of the transitional economies and the former Soviet republics as a culmination of the Partnership for Peace started in 1994 (see Chapter 3). Their inclusion has implications for defense burden sharing, the Russian role vis-à-vis NATO, and the nonmilitary missions of NATO.

Our book focuses on a wide range of concerns and scenarios. Because it addresses general factors affecting NATO and examines a large number of scenarios, our book will not become dated too quickly. We do not get much involved with specific proposals and contingencies that tend to change frequently – indeed, even daily.

Content by chapter

The book contains eight additional chapters. Chapter 2 takes stock of NATO's origin, its history, its treaty articles, its strategic doctrines, its missions, and its institutional arrangements. Much of this chapter is devoted to investigating past burden-sharing behavior in NATO. To accomplish this undertaking, we use a public good theory of alliance behavior, which has been popular in both the economics and the international relations literature. Alterations in military doctrine and defense technology are related to changes in burden-sharing behavior. Based on anticipated developments on the horizon, we speculate on NATO's future burden sharing.

In Chapter 3, the expansion of NATO is taken up. The theory of clubs is applied to identify some of the factors that determine an optimal size for an alliance. This chapter also examines the institutional developments encouraging NATO expansion since the fall of the Berlin Wall. These developments included the establishment of the North Atlantic Cooperation Council (NACC) in December 1991 to further economic, diplomatic, and military cooperation among NATO allies and the former communist countries and republics. Within the framework of the NACC, the Partnership for Peace (PFP) in 1994 was designed to further increase cooperation between NATO and the countries of Eastern and Central Europe with the intention of preparing select nations for NATO membership. Chapter 3 also discusses political and economic factors associated with expanding NATO. Issues from both the demand and supply sides are included in the analysis.

Chapter 4 is devoted to the study of peacekeeping and peacemaking by a modern-day NATO. This chapter contrasts burden sharing for peacekeeping missions with burden sharing for defense during the Cold War. In many ways, peacekeeping may usher in an era of unequal burdens, not unlike those of the 1950s when NATO relied on strategic weapons. This chapter reviews the evolution of UN peacekeeping over the last four decades and speculates on future peacekeeping efforts. The peacekeeping role of the United Nations is compared and contrasted with that of the NATO alliance regarding past and future deployments. Principles of collective action are applied to distinguish the effectiveness that these organizations can have in managing world peace. Recent peacekeeping deployments in Bosnia, Haiti, and Kuwait are contrasted and evaluated.

In Chapter 5, an up-to-date overview of NATO's defense industrial base is presented for both the United States and Europe. A host of policy issues are addressed involving competition in the defense sector, alternative industrial practices (e.g., licensing agreements, joint ventures, offsets), a NATO free trade zone for weapons, and weapon development and R & D. For procurement practices, we are particularly interested in the advantages and disadvantages of alternative contractual arrangements (e.g., cost-plus, fixed-price, and incentive-compatible contracts). This chapter also contrasts the EU defense industrial base with that of the United States. In so doing, we consider the effects that EU integration are apt to have on arms production and trade within and outside of NATO in the future. Other issues include the need for and consequences of arms trade, the profitability of the arms industry, and the savings associated with joint ventures (e.g., the Eurofighter aircraft, the Tornado).

Chapter 6 considers the challenges confronting NATO now and in the future. Challenges are many and include civil wars in Europe, nuclear weapon proliferation, transnational terrorism, rogue or "outlaw" nations, environmental security, and instability beyond Europe. Each of these challenges raises interesting questions about force structure, burden sharing, strategic doctrine, and NATO's missions. Some challenges may require greater cooperation than the NATO allies have demonstrated heretofore.

In Chapter 7, we address the relationship between NATO and the European Union. This chapter considers whether or not these two supranational institutions and other European institutions will continue with their overlapping missions in the security area. We are also concerned with the pivotal role that the United States has played and will play in these structures. Anticipated changes in these supranational institutions are presented. For example, the possible effects of the resurrection of the Western European Union on NATO will be addressed. Alliance policies concerning weapons standardization, interoperability, and procurement collaboration are examined, and the division of NATO responsibilities between the United States and the European Union is anticipated.

Chapter 8 provides an in-depth study of both NATO's likely and its ideal institutional structure, based on transaction costs and benefits associated with different institutional arrangements. Using notions from the "new" institutional economics, we explain why NATO has remained a loose structure in which allies maintain their discretion over most of their defense decisions despite the alliance ties. Issues examined include NATO common funding, common logistical practices, Article 5 commitments, and NATO procurement practices. The chapter also speculates on how NATO's institutional arrangement might and should change in light of various contingencies including the imminent expansion of NATO membership.

Chapter 9 concludes the book and contains key conclusions by chapter. Directions for additional research are also presented, along with visions of NATO's future in the near term and the long run.

UNIQUE FEATURES OF THE BOOK

This book is intended for talented undergraduates and graduate students in economics, political science (especially international relations), and public policy. Since the technical rigor of the book is greatly limited, it should also appeal to an audience outside of academia, including practitioners, policy makers, government analysts, journalists, and general readers. There are a number of distinguishing features of the book:

1. Our book is more up-to-date than earlier books that apply economic methods and insights to a study of NATO. These earlier books include Denoon (1986), Kennedy (1979, 1983), and Smith and Smith (1983).[7]
2. The book is accessible to a wide audience even though modern concepts of economics are used. Recent books – Hartley and Sandler (1995), Sandler and Hartley (1995) – are very demanding in terms of theoretical and empirical rigor.
3. The book investigates a wide range of issues concerning the NATO alliance, and does not focus on just disarmament (Kirby and Hooper, 1991; Lall and Marlin, 1992), the arms industry (Drown, Drown, and Campbell, 1990), or the future of NATO (Papacosma and Heiss, 1995; Carlsneaes and Smith, 1994; Leech, 1991; Levine, 1988). By analyzing a host of issues concerning NATO, it goes beyond recent books that stress either budgetary factors (Weidenbaum, 1992) or policy matters (Hartley, 1991).
4. The book applies modern tools of economic analysis, while it takes account of political and institutional considerations. Recent books on NATO focus on just the political and institutional factors, and do not employ economic methods. These include books cited above as well as Gompert and Larrabee (1997), Miall (1994), Sharp (1996), and Sloan (1993).
5. The book presents a balanced view of NATO and does not subscribe to either an American (e.g., Gompert and Larrabee, 1997) or European viewpoint.
6. The chapters are all self-contained and can be read in any order. All chapters contain cross-references to other chapters.

7. Our book is also more up-to-date than earlier political science books devoted to the study of NATO. These include Kaplan (1990) and Myers (1980).

2 NATO burden sharing and related issues

NATO has remained a viable institution from its inception on 24 August 1949, when the North Atlantic Treaty entered into force.[1] Many experts credit NATO with maintaining peace in Europe during the Cold War era and with helping to win the Cold War. For almost fifty years, NATO has endured and responded effectively to alterations in strategic doctrines, changes in economic conditions, advancements in weapon capabilities, and the emergence of political contingencies, while it has sought to deter Soviet aggression in Western Europe. With the end of the Cold War, the dissolution of the Warsaw Pact on 31 March 1991, and the withdrawal of Russian troops some 1,000 kilometers eastward, NATO no longer has the traditional role of deterring aggression from its eastern borders (Asmus, 1997; Bruce, 1995). Although the situation can always change, war with Russia is not a likely scenario these days. It is even less likely because of the downsizing of Russian forces and the severe economic problems challenging Russia today. Russia must allocate its resources to build up its economy if future political upheavals are to be avoided.

In the past, NATO has been an amazingly resilient institution that has grown in size from the original twelve members while it assumed additional chores. At the Madrid summit in July 1997, NATO agreed to accept the Czech Republic, Hungary, and Poland as new allies in 1999. The inclusion of these new allies could have profound political, strategic, and burden-sharing consequences (see Chapter 3). From 13 December 1956, the North Atlantic Council extended NATO missions to involve nonmilitary cooperation among

1. Throughout this chapter, dates are taken from the "Chronology of Events" contained in NATO Office of Information and Press (1995, pp. 295–391).

its allies, including limiting drug trafficking, promoting scientific cooperation, controlling road traffic, furthering economic cooperation, and addressing common environmental problems (NATO Information Service, 1989, pp. 301–15). These nonmilitary missions are anticipated to increase as an expanding alliance continues to develop new ways to justify its existence in the post–Cold War era (e.g., the NATO-based Euro-Atlantic Disaster Response Coordination Center created in June 1998 to respond collectively to disasters). Along with these nonmilitary missions have come new military missions that address threats to allies' interests and security from either nuclear weapon proliferation or conflicts outside of Europe. NATO appears to be prepared to adjust to changing conditions so as to maintain reasons for its continued existence.

Throughout NATO's history, the issue of burden sharing has been in the spotlight.[2] Perhaps no other issue has caused more divisiveness among the allies. Often, the United States has claimed that it has assumed an unfair burden of the defense outlays for the alliance (US Committee on Armed Services, 1988, pp. 11–13). The issue of burden sharing is involved and multidimensional; allies selectively highlight aspects of their defense contributions to put their efforts in the best possible light. Thus, an ally that supports NATO infrastructure to a greater extent than the typical ally will focus on this contribution even if the ally's overall defense spending is well below the mean defense burden, however measured. An evaluation of defense burden sharing is confounded by alternative measures of burdens (Hartley and Sandler, 1998), measurement problems for defense, difficulties associated with international comparisons, and the multiple missions of the alliance. Comparisons are also made difficult because some burdens – hosting US forces, buying US defense equipment – do not show up in the standard defense spending figures. Similarly, Germany's sizable contribution to Desert Storm is not part of its defense budget and hence is not included in burden-sharing measures.

To develop a means for evaluating burden sharing in an alliance, economists and later political scientists have fruitfully applied the theory of public goods to study the distribution of the NATO defense burden since 1949.[3]

2. On burden-sharing concerns, see Beer (1972), Gompert and Larrabee (1997), Olson and Zeckhauser (1966), Pryor (1968), Russett (1970), Sandler and Forbes (1980), US Committee on Armed Services (1988), US Department of Defense (1996), and van Ypersele de Strihou (1967). There is a vast literature on these burden-sharing concerns; the above literature is only representative. Other articles are mentioned later in the chapter. Sandler and Hartley (1995) contains an extensive bibliography.
3. The pioneering articles on burden sharing in economics are by Olson and Zeckhauser (1966,

This theory has been adapted over time to account for changing conditions of the alliance. During its history, NATO burden sharing has changed dramatically as strategy, weapon technology, and perceived threats have altered. Changes on the horizon may again alter burden sharing in the coming millennium, assuming that NATO continues as an institution.

This chapter has a number of purposes. We begin with a review of NATO institutions and their prospects. We next distinguish the pure public good model of alliances from the more general joint product model. Both models are used to derive implications that are applied to the study of NATO. These models and their implications are then employed to take stock of NATO burden sharing and defense demands over the past four decades. Alternative tests of the theories are evaluated. Next, we apply the theory to speculate on burden sharing over the next decade based upon anticipated strategic, institutional, and technological developments. The influence of public choice considerations on burden sharing is then taken into account.

NATO: AN INSTITUTIONAL REVIEW

NATO was originally formed to stop the Soviet Union's westward drive into Europe.[4] After the Soviet Union made satellite states out of a number of countries in Eastern and Central Europe and began its first blockade of West Berlin on 24 June 1948, it was clear to the United States, Canada, and countries in Western Europe that the Soviet threat needed to be countered. This threat was underscored by territorial and political demands directed at Norway and Turkey by the Soviet Union (Rearden, 1995). On 10 December 1948, negotiations began in Washington, D.C., on a North Atlantic Treaty, which would tie participants into a mutual defense alliance (see the appendix to this chapter for an abbreviated chronology). These initial negotiations included representatives from the Brussels Treaty Powers (Belgium, France, Luxembourg, the Netherlands, and the United Kingdom), Canada, and the

1967), Sandler (1977), Sandler and Cauley (1975), and van Ypersele de Strihou (1967). Important papers in political science include Goldstein (1995), Knorr (1985), Oneal (1990a, 1990b, 1992), Oneal and Elrod (1989), Palmer (1990a, 1990b, 1991), Russett (1970), and Starr (1974). Additional papers in economics include Khanna and Sandler (1996, 1997), Murdoch (1995), Murdoch and Sandler (1982, 1984, 1991), Sandler and Murdoch (1990), and Smith (1980, 1987, 1995).

4. Under Stalin, the Soviet Union took over Estonia, Latvia, Lithuania, and portions of Finland, Romania, Poland, Northeast Germany, and Eastern Czechoslovakia. After World War II, it brought Albania, Bulgaria, Eastern Germany, Czechoslovakia, Hungary, Poland, and Romania under its sphere of influence (NATO Information Service, 1989, p. 5)

United States. On 15 March 1949, these seven countries invited Denmark, Iceland, Italy, Norway, and Portugal to join them in negotiating the North Atlantic Treaty, which established NATO on 4 April 1949. On 24 August 1949, the treaty entered into force after each of the above twelve countries had ratified it. The Brussels Treaty Powers alliance was merged into the Western Union, later to become the Western European Union (WEU), which is an organization subordinate to NATO with the security of Europe as its mandate.

Article 9 of the treaty established the North Atlantic Council as the main decision-making body of NATO. The council was empowered with the authority to set up subsidiary bodies including committees (e.g., the Defense Planning Committee) and planning groups (e.g., the Nuclear Planning Group). At least once a week, the permanent representatives to the council from all allies meet; usually twice a year, the council holds meetings at either the foreign ministers or heads of government level to make policy decisions. When the heads of states are in attendance, the council is said to conduct a summit. All decisions of the council must be unanimous among its member states. On 17 September 1949, the first session of the North Atlantic Council was held in Washington, D.C.

In Table 2.1, we list brief descriptions of the fourteen articles of the North Atlantic Treaty. Article 1 binds the alliance members to resolve disputes in a peaceful fashion, if possible, in accordance with Article 51 of the United Nations (UN) Charter, which allows UN members to defend themselves, either individually or collectively, against potential armed attacks. Actions of the Soviet Union both before and after the conclusion of World War II threatened Western Europe, thus motivating action under Article 51. Although the United States, the United Kingdom, and Canada reduced their collective armed forces from over 3.7 million men in 1945 to under 900 thousand in 1946, the Soviet Union maintained its armed forces at the wartime strength of 6 million men in 1946, with its war industries running at capacity. Article 2 provides for strengthening members' free institutions and encouraging economic cooperation, while Article 3 allows for augmenting allies' military forces independently and collectively.

The essential articles of the treaty are Articles 4 through 6. Article 4 provides for allies to consult one another when a threat is posed to either their independence or their territorial interests. Any armed attack on one ally is characterized as an attack against them all by Article 5. In the event of an attack, *the allies are only pledged to consult as a group by Article 5 prior to determining the necessary response.* Most notable, Article 5 does not

Table 2.1. *NATO Articles in brief*

Article 1:	Parties will settle international disputes in a peaceful manner in accordance with the UN Charter.
Article 2:	Parties will promote stability and well-being by strengthening their free institutions and by encouraging economic collaboration among themselves.
Article 3:	Parties will develop, separately and jointly, their ability to resist armed attacks.
Article 4:	Parties will consult one another whenever any of them views its territorial interests or political independence is at risk.
Article 5:	Parties will consider an armed attack on one or more of them as an attack against the collective and will assist individually or collectively as they determine necessary. This assistance may include the use of force.
Article 6:	Defines an armed attack under Article 5 as an attack on the territory of any of the allies in Europe or North America, or on these allies' territorial holdings or interests.
Article 7:	Indicates that the treaty does not affect the rights and obligations of the UN Charter or the Security Council.
Article 8:	Pledges the parties not to enter into international agreements that conflict with the treaty.
Article 9:	Establishes the North Atlantic Council as the decision-making body of NATO.
Article 10:	By unanimous agreement, any other European state can join NATO.
Article 11:	Sets out ratification procedures for the treaty.
Article 12:	After the treaty is in effect for ten years, any ally can request that members consult to review the treaty.
Article 13:	After the treaty is in effect for twenty years, any ally may quit the alliance after giving a year's notice.
Article 14:	Indicates that the official text of the treaty be in English and French.

Note: The treaty was framed on 4 April 1949 in Washington, D.C., and entered into force on 24 August 1949.
Source: NATO Office of Information and Press (1995, pp. 231–4).

commit the allies to an automatic military response, or any necessary response. Article 6 extends an ally's territory to include territorial holdings or interests. It is Article 6 that must be broadened or else loosely interpreted to permit out-of-area operations under NATO's post–Cold War strategic doctrines (Thomson, 1997).

The remaining eight articles set some of the institutional rules for NATO. Article 7 indicates that the North Atlantic Treaty does not affect an ally's obligations to either the UN Charter or the Security Council, while Article 8 mandates that the allies cannot consummate other international agreements inconsistent with the treaty. The North Atlantic Council is made the decision-making body of NATO by Article 9. Articles 10 and 13 allow allies to enter or exit, respectively, under stated conditions. Treaty ratification procedures are covered by Article 11; treaty review procedures are set out in Article 12. Finally, Article 14 allows the official text to be in English and French.

During the Cold War, the alliance increased in size on three occasions. On 18 February 1952, Greece and Turkey joined; on 6 May 1955, West Germany joined; and on 30 May 1982, Spain joined. Most recently, unified Germany replaced West Germany as a member of NATO. During the January 1994 summit in Brussels, NATO adopted in principle a decision to expand to the east by including some ex–Warsaw Pact nations. This expansion was made official in July 1997 with the decision to include the Czech Republic, Hungary, and Poland as NATO members in 1999. At a later time, former Soviet republics (e.g., Estonia, Latvia, Lithuania) and other ex–Warsaw Pact nations (e.g., Romania) may be allowed to join NATO. Even the neutral nations – Sweden, Austria, Finland – are potential allies.

NATO operates as a "loose" or unintegrated structure in which sovereign allies maintain both policy independence and discretionary power over military expenditures.[5] Any action by the North Atlantic Council must be unanimous, so that member states have *not* committed themselves to go along with any decision that they disagree with. Meetings of the council at the ministerial level or higher are fairly infrequent – about twice a year. Most important, the allies decide the overwhelming portion of their defense spending independently. Collective or common funding is used to finance three major areas: the civil budget supporting NATO headquarters, its staff, committees, and planning groups; the military budget supporting NATO's military commands, its staff and committees; and the infrastructure (e.g., pipelines, satellites, communication networks, airfields). For the 1970s, common funding was a little less than 1 percent of NATO's total defense spending, so that over 99 percent of NATO's defense spending is at the discretion of the allies, and much of the spending is transacted across markets (Sandler and Forbes, 1980). In 1997, estimates given for the US share of this common funding would place the aggregate of such funding at just 0.4 percent of NATO's total defense spending (US General Accounting Office, 1997c, p. 1). Although allies discuss defense strategies, weapon requirements, and defense planning, actual defense outlays are primarily decided at the country level, where domestic trade-offs and political influences affect

5. For a detailed institutional description of NATO, see NATO Information Service (1989) and NATO Office of Information and Press (1995).

the outcome. Even when agreements to increase defense spending are consummated – for example, the pledged 3 percent increase in real defense spending given at a 1978 Council meeting – there is no provision to enforce such agreements.[6] Whether or not this unintegrated structure is desirable is discussed in Chapter 8.

NATO's civil structure consists of six primary entities. The North Atlantic Council is the supreme political authority in terms of decision-making power. The Defense Planning Committee handles most collective defense matters, while the Nuclear Planning Group addresses issues concerning nuclear forces in NATO. Both bodies meet at the ministerial level about twice a year. Except for France, the allies participate in some capacity in both of these bodies. As a senior statesman elected by the allies, the secretary general is the chairman of the North Atlantic Council, the Defense Planning Committee, the Nuclear Planning Group, and other important committees. The secretary general is also the spokesperson for NATO. Subordinate to the above three bodies is the Military Committee, which advises the political authorities of NATO on issues involving common defense, and which also oversees the two NATO military commands. Finally, a host of committees round out the civil structure and address myriad issues including weapons standardization, defense reviews, nuclear weapons proliferation, NATO infrastructure, NATO budgets, NATO security, arms control, and treaty verification. The international staff for the civil structure is drawn from member nations.

NATO military structure consists of the integrated command structure, which now includes just two primary commands – Supreme Allied Command Europe (SACEUR) and Supreme Allied Command Atlantic (SACLANT).[7] SACEUR has three subcommands that represent the designated three subregions of Europe: the South, the Central, and the North West. These military commands are responsible for determining force requirements, defense planning, defense exercises, and force deployment in their respective regions. SACEUR and SACLANT are responsible for preserving peace in Europe and the North Atlantic, respectively. In 1994, SACEUR assumed the responsibility for out-of-area crisis management, peacekeeping, and humanitarian aid projects. The Headquarters of the Allied Command Europe

6. See Sandler (1987) for an evaluation of this 3 percent rule. Except for the United States and the United Kingdom, the allies did not meet this pledge. No sanctions were imposed on allies failing to meet the pledge.
7. A third military command – Allied Command Channel (ACCHAN) – was eliminated on 1 June 1994. SACEUR assumed the responsibilities of ACCHAN.

(ACE) is the Supreme Headquarters Allied Powers Europe (SHAPE) at Casteau, Belgium. If a military operation were to take place in Europe or an out-of-area locale, it would be commanded by SHAPE. Whenever the need arises, SACEUR and SACLANT have access to the chiefs of staff, defense ministers and heads of state of the NATO nations. SACLANT protects the region between the North Pole and the Tropic of Cancer, and includes North America as well as the area between the North American coast and the European/North African coasts. Within SACLANT, the Canada-US Regional Planning Group provides for the defense of Canada and the United States. Rapid deployment forces are developed, trained, and commanded by SACEUR and SACLANT.

PURE PUBLIC GOOD MODEL: DETERRENCE

Starting with the seminal studies by Olson and Zeckhauser (1966, 1967), military alliances have been characterized as sharing a public good. If defense is purely public for the allies, then the benefits associated with defense must be nonrival and nonexcludable. The benefits of a good are nonrival among users when a unit of the good can be consumed by one agent – say, an ally – without diminishing in the slightest the consumption benefits still available to others from that same unit of the good. Deterrence, as provided by strategic nuclear weapons, is nonrival among allies because, once deployed, these weapons' ability to deter enemy aggression is independent of the number of allies on whose behalf the retaliatory threat is made, provided that the promised retaliatory response is automatic and credible. A retaliatory threat is credible to a would-be aggressor if the aggressor believes that its actions against an ally will automatically trigger the promised response. If sufficient retaliatory weapons exist to deal a devastating punishment to an aggressor, this threat of punishment is not diminished if it is made on behalf of fifteen or sixteen allies. Given that there is no rivalry or marginal cost from extending a pure public good's benefits to another agent, there is no reason to limit the size of the group sharing the good. In the case of nuclear deterrence, marginal cost might be positive if the country providing the threatened retaliation will suffer from carrying through with it. When, however, an ally can retaliate with impunity on behalf of any of its allies, the marginal cost of including another ally under the deterrence umbrella is zero.

The benefits of a good are nonexcludable if they cannot be withheld at an affordable cost by the good's provider. For strategic forces, benefits are nonexcludable whenever the defense provider(s) cannot fail to deliver the promised retaliatory response against an invader of another ally. If, for instance, an invasion of one ally creates significant collateral damage to the provider of the deterrent forces, then the retaliatory reaction is expected to be executed. Consider Canada, where a nuclear attack would cause widespread and unacceptable carnage and destruction from fallout and stray bombs to its downwind neighbor to the south; surely, the United States could not sit by and do nothing if Canada were attacked. Collateral damage may also arise from stationing troops on another ally's soil (e.g., US troops in Western Europe), the residency of citizens of one ally in another ally, or the flow of investment among allies. Clearly, these three factors tied the United States' interests to those of the Europeans during the Cold War, thus giving some credence to the US threat of a retaliatory response if its European allies were attacked.

In contrast, a private good possesses benefits that are rival and excludable at a negligible cost. Food and clothing yield excludable benefits whenever property rights are protected by law enforcement authorities or private means. When one person consumes a unit of these private goods, no one else can consume that same unit at the same time, so that the benefits of the goods are fully rival.

Private goods can be parceled out and sold in markets. Agents can only receive the benefits of a private good if they pay for them, since benefits can be withheld. On the other hand, nonpayers cannot be denied the benefits of a pure public good since, once the good is provided, the benefits are received by everyone regardless of whether or not a payment has been made. Those agents who value a public good most will provide it, while others will rely or *free ride* on the provision efforts of others. If, as in the case of deterrence, the value derived from the public good depends directly on the wealth of the agent (e.g., the value of defense depends on how much one has to lose), then the wealthy agents will provide the public good and the others will free ride. Defense tends to be income normal – that is, the demand for defense increases with income.

When defense is purely public among a set of allies, some important testable implications follow.[8] First, defense spending burdens are anticipated to be shared unevenly; large, wealthy allies will shoulder the defense burdens for smaller, poorer allies. This is known as the *exploitation hy-*

8. These testable hypotheses are derived in Khanna and Sandler (1996), Murdoch and Sandler (1984), Olson and Zeckhauser (1966, 1967), and Sandler and Forbes (1980).

pothesis. If the "optimal" amount[9] of defense for the rich ally (where an ally's marginal benefits equal its marginal costs) is $300 billion, while this optimal amount for the poor ally is $10 billion, then the defense outlay of the rich ally may satisfy the poor ally's defense needs without any spending on the latter's part. Of course, this scenario hinges on the purely public nature of defense, so that one ally's defense provision is *perfectly substitutable* for that of the other ally. Second, defense spending will be allocated inefficiently from an alliance standpoint, inasmuch as the *sum* of marginal benefits of defense provision will not be equated to the marginal cost of this provision (Sandler and Hartley, 1995, chapter 2). This sum is over the number of allies, so that aggregate marginal benefits over all allies equal marginal cost. In the two-ally example, the rich (poor) ally will not include the marginal benefits that its provision confers on the other ally.[10] Third, there is no need to restrict alliance size when defense is purely public. This follows because additional allies do not reduce current allies' defense benefits, derived from a given army and arsenals, when nonrivalry is present. Fourth, some central authority in the alliance is required to coordinate spending to overcome suboptimal provision.

A couple of implications are also associated with an ally's demand for defense when this defense is purely public among the allies. This demand equation is based on a unitary decision maker (e.g., the Joint Chiefs of Staff, a median voter, the Department of Defense) in each ally optimizing its welfare subject to a budget constraint and to the defense spillins that a nation receives from its allies. This demand function typically has the following general form:[11]

$$\text{DEF} = f(\text{PRICE}, \text{INCOME}, \text{SPILLINS}, \text{THREAT}, \text{STRATEGIC}). \quad (1)$$

In (1), DEF denotes military spending in real terms; PRICE is the relative price of defense goods to nondefense goods; INCOME is the national income

9. Optimal is in quotation marks because it is optimal only from the single ally's viewpoint and not for the alliance as a whole, where the sum of marginal benefits must be equated to marginal cost.
10. The standard prediction about suboptimality ignores two factors that can counterbalance somewhat this tendency toward suboptimality. First, bureaucrats within the defense sector can maximize their budgets, thus leading to some overspending. Second, an arms race dynamic between the alliance and an opponent can also lead to greater spending tendencies. In the latter case, the within-alliance spending on defense may still be suboptimal, given the perceived level of threat, owing to free riding. If, however, the arms race is between two allies (e.g., Greece and Turkey), then this rivalry can lead to defense spending levels that counterbalance the free-riding tendency for these two allies – hence, the high burdens carried by these allies.
11. For an analysis of an ally's demand for defense, see Hartley and Sandler (1990), Murdoch and Sandler (1984), Sandler and Hartley (1995) and Smith (1980, 1987, 1989, 1995). Seiglie (1993) provides a particularly interesting dynamic analysis.

of the relevant decision maker; SPILLINS are the defense outlays of the other allies; THREAT represents the enemy's defense spending; and STRATEGIC indicates changes in the military doctrine of the alliance. When defense is purely public, INCOME and the value of SPILLINS can be added together to form a *full income* variable (Cornes and Sandler, 1996, p. 495).

In (1), an increase in the relative price of defense is expected to decrease the quantity of defense demanded, while an increase in either the nation's income or its perceived threat is expected to increase the ally's defense demand. The negative influence of relative prices on the quantity of defense demanded follows from the law of downward sloping demand, according to which the quantity demanded falls with a price rise, holding all other prices constant. This law depends on two underlying factors: a substitution and an income effect. The substitution effect implies that buyers will substitute away from goods that are relatively dearer after a price rise. An income effect occurs because a price rise (fall) will decrease (increase) purchasing power from a given money income level, thus causing the buyer to purchase less (more) of all goods. If a nation's income rises, then the country has more to protect and the means to do so, and this heightened income should stimulate the demand for defense. Defense demand is also anticipated to increase with enhanced threat. Given that one ally's defense substitutes for another's efforts in the case of pure public goods, an increase in defense spillins should then decrease the ally's demand for its own defense. This negative relationship is the basis of free riding. Lastly, the effect of a change in strategic doctrine on the demand for defense depends on the nature of the strategic change.

Interactions among allies' defense decisions can be displayed with the help of reaction paths. In Figure 2.1, ally 2's defense provision (q^2) is measured on the vertical axis, whereas ally 1's defense provision (q^1) is shown on the horizontal axis. Curve N_1N_1 depicts the reaction path for ally 1, and curve N_2N_2 represents the reaction path for ally 2. Each reaction path shows the ally's best choice for its defense spending, given the defense spending of the other ally and holding the other independent variables – such as income and relative prices – constant. For reaction paths N_1N_1 and N_2N_2, the equilibrium is at point E where nation 1 supplies q^1_e and nation 2 provides q^2_e. This equilibrium is stable provided that N_1N_1 (N_2N_2) is steeper (flatter) than a downward-sloping line making an angle of 45° with the horizontal axis. Equilibrium E is stable in Figure 2.1, since both reaction paths fulfill these requirements. If, therefore, a point on either N_1N_1 or N_2N_2 is reached

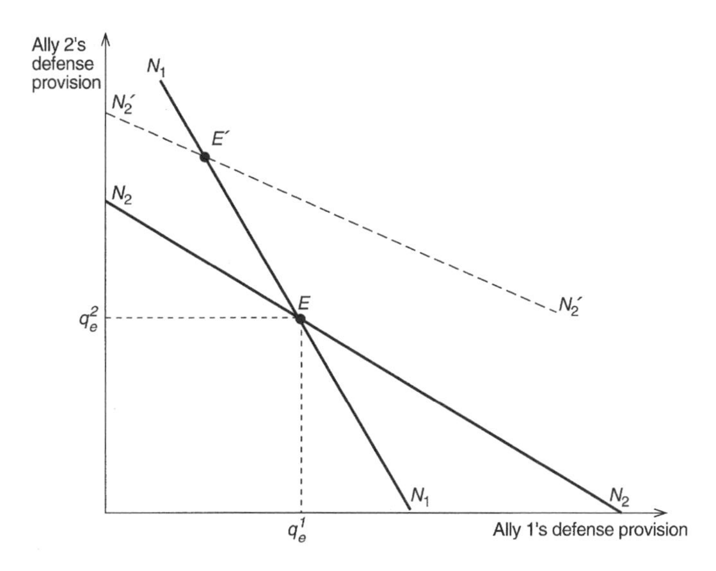

Figure 2.1. Allies' reaction paths: pure public defense model

below (above) E, then ally 1 will decrease (increase) its defense spending while ally 2 will increase (decrease) its defense spending until E is reached. Now suppose that income (e.g., GDP) in ally 2 increases from the level associated with N_2N_2. If defense is a normal good so that a rise in income results in an increase in defense demand, then N_2N_2 shifts to $N_2'\,N_2'$ (the dashed line in Figure 2.1) and, at the new equilibrium E', ally 2 spends more on defense, while ally 1 spends less on defense as compared with point E. Changes in relative prices, income, threat, or strategic factors can lead to shifts in the reaction path.

The exploitation hypothesis can also be illustrated with Figure 2.1. Suppose that ally 2 is much richer than ally 1, so that its defense reaction path lies even above $N_2'N_2'$. In this case, the resulting equilibrium (not displayed) would have ally 2 supplying most, if not all, of the defense. If the equilibrium were to lie on the vertical axis, then ally 1 would be granted a free ride on ally 2's defense efforts. This diagrammatic treatment is really only useful for illustrating the two-ally case. For n allies, we would have to rely on reaction equations where each ally's demand for defense depends on the provision levels of the other allies (Murdoch, 1995). As the number of allies increases, the resulting equilibrium is apt to be more suboptimal as free-riding opportunities are enhanced through greater spillins (Hardin, 1982; Olson, 1965; Sandler, 1992). With larger alliances, each ally is *ignoring a greater sum of marginal benefits* that their defense provision confers on others when the ally equates its own marginal benefits to the marginal costs of provision.

In the purely public defense scenario, these general tendencies towards suboptimality, exploitation, and free riding hinge on a number of crucial implicit assumptions, whose relaxation may lead to different outcomes. For example, the marginal costs or relative price of defense is often assumed to be the same for the allies,[12] so that differences in allies' demand for defense can be traced to variations in either income or taste. Suppose that the poor ally has a large cost advantage in defense over its richer ally. If a poor ally has a cost advantage in producing defense, then its defense reaction path will be further to the right than it would be in the absence of the advantage, thus implying a greater defense provision for any level of spillins. When equating its marginal defense benefits with its relatively low marginal defense costs, the poor ally may then provide more of the defense than its rich counterpart. This same outcome may arise if the small ally's taste for defense exceeds that of the large ally. For example, Israel has allocated a higher portion of its GDP to defense than the United States, because the former is more at risk given its proximity to numerous enemies.

JOINT PRODUCT MODEL OF ALLIANCES

The joint product model of alliances generalizes the pure public good model, because it encompasses the latter as a special instance when only a single pure public output is derived from the defense activity. If defense provision gives rise to multiple outputs, then joint products exist. An arsenal may, for example, deter aggression while allowing the provider to pursue its own territorial ambitions. In this case, the joint products are deterrence and imperialism. The joint product model allows an alliance arsenal to fulfill at least three general functions: (1) deterrence, (2) damage limitation or protection, and (3) private or ally-specific goals (Knorr, 1985; Russett, 1970; van Ypersele de Strihou, 1967). Benefits derived from defense activities are impurely public among allies when these benefits are either partially excludable by the providing ally or else partially rival among the allies. Conventional forces and weapons yield both deterrence and damage-limiting protection, needed when deterrence fails and conflict begins. Conventional forces are subject

12. Two notable exceptions are Olson and Zeckhauser (1967) and McGuire (1990).

to consumption rivalry in the form of force thinning as a given commitment of forces is spread to defend a longer perimeter (exposed border) or a greater surface area. This follows because increasing the concentration of troops and materiel along one ally's border may increase the vulnerability of another ally's borders. Insofar as deployment decisions can exclude one or more allies, damage-limiting conventional armaments and troops possess partially excludable benefits.

Private or ally-specific benefits occur when a jointly produced defense output assists the provider, but the output's benefits are not received by other allies. These ally-specific benefits may assume a variety of forms: quelling domestic unrest, pursuing territorial expansion, threatening a neighboring state, managing domestic terrorism, controlling drug trafficking, responding to national disasters, and patrolling coastal waters. All allies are motivated, to some extent, in their defense provision decisions by these private benefits. Although these defense outputs are private to a specific ally, they are public *within* the ally doing the providing. For example, the control of drug trafficking provides nonrival and nonexcludable benefits to the nation's citizens.

Generally, a defense activity may give rise to diverse benefits that vary in their degree of publicness depending on technological, strategic, and other considerations. Thus, conventional forces may yield impurely public damage control during conflict along with various country-specific private benefits, depending on how these forces are deployed. Additionally, these same conventional forces can deter an attack on the alliance, and, in so doing, provide some alliancewide pure public benefits. Typically, the relative amount of private and impurely public outputs associated with conventional forces is anticipated to be greater than the amount of alliancewide purely public outputs derived from such forces. In contrast, strategic nuclear forces are anticipated to give relatively more purely public benefits in the form of deterrence than private and impurely public outputs (Hansen, Murdoch, and Sandler, 1990; Sandler, 1977). These strategic forces are not prone to thinning or spatial rivalry as allies confront a common enemy. Modern arsenals and armies yield defense outputs that can vary greatly from one another in terms of *the ratio of excludable benefits* (private and impurely public outputs) *to total benefits*. A change in strategy – which, say, emphasizes the building of weapons of mass destruction to deter attacks – can reduce this ratio. This same view can be applied to changes in weapon technology that augment some capabilities of weapons at the expense of others – for example, the development of precision-guided munitions has increased the effectiveness and importance of conventional weapons, thus increasing the share of excludable benefits.

Many implications of the joint product model are at odds with those of the deterrence model and serve to distinguish between the two models. First, the joint product model implies that defense burdens can be shared based on the benefits received. The greater the ratio of excludable benefits to total benefits, the larger should be the concordance between benefits received and burdens shared, because these excludable benefits can only be acquired by providing one's own defense. When this ratio is high, the economic size of the ally is expected to have less influence upon defense burden sharing, so that the exploitation hypothesis should have little relevance. Second, the extent of suboptimality also depends on the share of excludable benefits to total benefits. As this ratio approaches 1, markets and club arrangements can exclude nonpayers and force preference revelation, thereby matching marginal benefits and marginal costs – the condition for optimal provision of defense. The opposite is true as the ratio approaches 0 and all benefits become purely public. If, for example, a change in strategic doctrine were to stress conventional forces over strategic forces, then this event should increase the share of excludable benefits and augment efficient resource allocations. A club arrangement could monitor force deployment and charge recipients accordingly. Third, alliance size restrictions are relevant based on the thinning of forces associated with damage-limiting protection (Sandler, 1977). Neither private nor purely public outputs require any size restrictions, because private defense outputs are not shared among allies, while pure public defense outputs have zero marginal cost from extending services to another ally.

The demand for defense can also differ between the joint product model and the pure public model. Sandler and Murdoch (1990) demonstrated that the following demand equation characterizes the joint product model:

$$\text{ALLDEF} = f(\text{PRICE, FULL, SPILLINS, THREAT, STRATEGIC}), \quad (2)$$

where ALLDEF represents *alliancewide* defense spending and FULL denotes full income or the ally's income plus the value of defense spillins. The other terms in equation (2) have been defined previously. If the defense output only provides a single alliancewide pure public good of deterrence, then (2) becomes

$$\text{ALLDEF} = f(\text{PRICE, FULL, THREAT, STRATEGIC}), \quad (3)$$

where SPILLINS no longer appears as a separate argument. Since (3) is nested (contained) in (2), a test that examines the significance of the coefficient of the SPILLINS variable in the empirical representation of (2) can distinguish between the two models. For a sample of ten NATO allies, Sandler and Murdoch (1990) found that the coefficient on SPILLINS was significantly different than zero for all sample allies, thus supporting the joint product model for the 1956–87 period.[13] This is an important finding that suggests that the exploitation of the large allies by the small as well as suboptimality are likely to have been attenuated in recent times. Simply stated, this finding indicates that defense provisions by the allies are not perfectly substitutable.

Another distinguishing feature of the joint product model concerns the reaction paths, shown previously in Figure 2.1. When defense activities give rise to multiple outputs, two or more of them may be *complementary,* so that they enhance one another's derived marginal benefits when consumed together. If, say, the ally's private defense benefit is complementary to alliancewide deterrence, then greater spillins of deterrence may increase the ally's interest in providing defense, thus leading to a positively sloped reaction path (Cornes and Sandler, 1994, 1996). When this occurs, the coefficient on the SPILLINS term in the demand equation in (1) would have a positive value. Consequently, free riding is greatly limited. If a change in strategic doctrine alters the consumption relationship among two or more defense outputs, then changes in the SPILLINS coefficient may result.

MILITARY DOCTRINES OF NATO

Mutual Assured Destruction: 1949–66

During the 1950s and the first half of the 1960s, NATO relied on US strategic force superiority to deter Soviet exercise of its conventional force superiority in Western Europe. NATO became outmatched by Soviet conventional forces because the Soviet Union had continued to run its defense industries at wartime levels, while NATO allies had converted their defense industries, in large part, to peacetime uses. During this period, the threat of Soviet westward expansion was held in check by NATO's adherence to a deterrence strategy of mutual assured destruction (MAD), whereby any Soviet territorial expansion involving NATO allies would be met with a devastating nuclear attack. This strategic doctrine was supported by MC48, a

13. This same methodology was employed by Khanna, Huffman, and Sandler (1994) to test for publicness in the case of agricultural research expenditures.

document approved by the North Atlantic Council in 1954, which allowed NATO to use nuclear weapons from the start of any conflict with the Soviet Union (Rearden, 1995, p. 73). The promised attack would be so heinous that its threat would make such aggression simply unthinkable. Moreover, this retaliatory threat was initially credible, because, up until the mid 1960s, the Soviet nuclear forces were vulnerable to a preemptive strike, so that US strategic nuclear forces could attack with impunity. Since the United States had little to fear from unleashing a preemptive nuclear strike, the US threat to retaliate on behalf of its European NATO allies was credible and more or less automatic. In consequence, a large share of the defense output derived from the allies' defense efforts was deterrence, which was essentially nonrival and nonexcludable. This, in turn, implied the likelihood of the exploitation of the large by the small, suboptimal resource allocation, and free riding.

Flexible response: 1967–91

Starting in the early 1960s, the United States began pressing for a *doctrine of flexible response* that required strategic nuclear forces, tactical nuclear forces, and conventional forces to work together. NATO's heavy reliance on US forces and nuclear deterrence gave it little choice but to go along with the new doctrine, which attempted to limit escalation toward a nuclear exchange. In 1967, NATO adopted directive MC14/3, which set out the principles of flexible response as a strategic doctrine. This doctrine permitted NATO to respond in alternative ways to a Warsaw Pact challenge; conventional forces or strategic forces could be used and, in the latter case, a missile exchange could be limited or complete. Under the new doctrine, aggression would be countered with a measured response based on the nature of the provocation. To fulfill this doctrine, NATO needed to strengthen both its conventional and tactical forces. Since the initial stages of warfare were anticipated to involve conventional and tactical exchanges within the European theatre, the European allies needed to prepare themselves to defend against conventional aggression. These allies could no longer rely on the nuclear deterrent umbrella for their external security. An ally that did not increase its military activities might invite aggression, since the Warsaw Pact might have a better opportunity to gain an advantage in a conventional exchange on that ally's soil.

This new reliance on conventional weapons meant that a greater share of NATO's defense benefits was either ally-specific or impurely public as compared with the MAD era. Defense burdens should thus be shared more equally within the alliance, and there should be less reliance on the large allies to underwrite security. The new doctrine also created a *complementarity* between strategic and conventional weapons. There was yet another reason why the Europeans would assume a greater share of NATO defense burdens. The Soviet Union had built up its strategic nuclear arsenal and, by doing so, had eliminated any US first-strike advantage by the late 1960s. A significant implication of this buildup concerned the credibility of the US pledge to retaliate on behalf of its European allies. Even though the United States still possessed a sufficient second-strike capability, any such retaliation would cost the United States dearly in terms of lives and property. Given the punitive costs associated with retaliation, the US-pledged retaliatory response was less credible and no longer automatic (Goldstein, 1995). US troops, citizens, and investment in Europe then assumed an even greater importance, for they ensured collateral damage on US interests from a European invasion.

In the 1980s, important events influenced NATO burden sharing even though the doctrine of flexible response still ruled (Khanna and Sandler, 1996). These events included Reagan's buildup of US forces, with its emphasis on weapon procurement and strategic nuclear forces (Salmon, 1997). Reagan's refurbishment of strategic weapons involved the entire nuclear triad – land-based MX missiles, Trident submarines, and B-1 and B-2 bombers. This buildup afforded the European allies some of the free ride back that had been lost during the first decade and a half of flexible response. Another significant event concerned the modernization of French and British strategic forces beginning in the 1980s and scheduled to end in the late 1990s. In Britain, this modernization was anticipated to cost about 5% of the defense budget and 10% of the procurement budget (Hartley, 1997a). France's modernization increased the nuclear force share of the military budget from 13.42% in 1976 to 17.52% in 1988 (Fontanel and Hebert, 1997, p. 40). This share was still at 15.97% in 1991. By 1988, French strategic nuclear force expenditures accounted for 0.65% of GDP, up from 0.48% in 1980 (Fontanel and Hebert, 1997). As these strategic modernizations are achieved, NATO burden sharing may be drastically affected within Europe. Both France and Britain will be providing nearly pure public benefits, vis-à-vis their strategic forces, to their European allies. Excludability of these deterrent benefits is much more problematic than in the case of the United States. A nuclear attack on almost any European ally could *not* be ignored by these smaller nuclear powers owing to France's and Britain's proximity to the attack and the resulting collateral damage. Hence, the non-nuclear allies are anticipated to free ride somewhat and rely on Britain and France for their security.

A third defining event for burden sharing in the 1980s was the US pursuit of the Strategic Defense Initiative (SDI), intended in its grandest view to provide an impenetrable shield over the United States and its NATO allies to repel any incoming missiles. A comprehensive SDI umbrella would confer purely public benefits to US allies. Ironically, the Reagan vision, if feasible, would have eliminated any incentives for the European allies to contribute to NATO's defense. The more likely SDI plan was a limited defense of US intercontinental ballistic missiles (ICBMs) or other military assets. This latter vision would have the opposite influence on burden sharing, since the European allies would have to buy in if they wanted to protect their own assets, military and civilian.

As an upgrade to flexible response, NATO adopted the *forward-defense strategy* or "deep strike" in 1984. This new strategy shifted the fighting focus away from NATO's eastern front by relying on precision-guided munitions to target and destroy the Warsaw Pact's rear-echelon forces before they could be brought up to reinforce the front. This strategy upgrade still stresses the importance of conventional forces and should result in similar burden-sharing behavior as that of flexible response. Interestingly, this forward-defense strategy was used by the coalition to defeat Iraqi forces during the Gulf War of 1991.

Post–Cold War doctrine: 1991 on

With the end of the Cold War, NATO embarked on its quest for a new defense doctrine. A number of crucial events were associated with the end to the Cold War. These included the following: the ratification of the intermediate-range treaty (INF) on 31 May 1988; the fall of the Berlin War on 9–10 November 1989; the formation of a coalition government in Czechoslovakia on 7 December 1989; the end of Ceausescu's rule in Romania on 22 December 1989; the conducting of free elections in East Germany on 18 March 1990; the entry of unified Germany into NATO on 3 October 1990; the withdrawal of Pershing II and cruise missiles from Europe on 26 March 1991; and the dissolution of the Warsaw Pact and the Soviet Union on 1 July 1991 and 20 December 1991, respectively.

At a Rome summit on 7–8 November 1991, a new defense doctrine began to take shape as NATO assumed responsibility for ensuring Europe's safety from threats both within and beyond NATO boundaries (Asmus, 1997, p. 37). In the future, NATO would be less concerned with guarding its perimeter than with addressing exigencies that adversely affect European economic and military security. This new defense doctrine of crisis management required the development of more mobile forces that could be projected where needed (Jordan, 1995). Surely, the 1991 Gulf War with Iraq motivated this new defense doctrine. At the Oslo summit in June 1992, NATO added peacekeeping as an official NATO mission, thus increasing still further the requirement for rapid-deployment forces and power-projection capabilities. During the December 1993 Brussels meeting, NATO defense ministers discussed the need for Combined Joint Task Forces (CJTFs), multilateral forces that include air, land, and maritime capabilities (Thomson, 1997). CJTFs must possess the transport to be sent to address crisis management wherever needed, whether in North Africa, the Middle East, or the Balkans. NATO later agreed officially to develop these CJTFs at the January 1994 Brussels summit.

This crisis-management doctrine has alliance burden-sharing implications. One of the greatest expenditures for these CJTFs is the investment in air and sea transports to project forces to any trouble spot. If the Gulf War of 1991 is any indication, then NATO will rely on the United States for power projection (also see Chapter 6) unless the other allies enhance their transport capabilities (Carlier, 1995). This reliance will place significant burdens on the United States to underwrite and support the new doctrine. Additional burdens of this nature will fall on Britain, France, and Germany. As a consequence, the new doctrine may resurrect exploitation concerns. Currently, the United States is considering massive future investments in its projection capabilities (Congressional Budget Office, 1997a). France and Germany are also making investments to augment their ability to project forces (Fontanel and Hebert, 1997).

BURDEN SHARING IN NATO: THE PAST AND PRESENT

To examine the burden-sharing record, we must choose an appropriate measure. The most commonly used burden-sharing measure is defense expenditures as a percent of GDP, which shows the within-country burden of defense spending. This and other defense burden measures share some common problems since they rely on defense spending, which does not adjust for conscription. Countries with conscripted forces – France and Germany, for example – do not pay the true opportunity costs for their troops, so that these countries' defense burdens are somewhat underrepresented (Khanna and Sandler, 1997; Oneal, 1992). Moreover, defense spending definitions are not entirely consistent among allies depending on how some items (e.g., pensions) are treated. In Table 2.2, defense expenditures as a percent of GDP are displayed for various time periods for all NATO allies except Iceland, which has negligible defense spending. These burdens are listed for six separate years, 1990, 1992–95, and 1997. In addition, the average values of this burden measure are given for four five-year intervals prior to 1990. By the 1975–79 period, the doctrine of flexible response had taken hold in NATO. Table 2.2 shows that the defense burden for the United States had dropped following the introduction of this doctrine, while those of the other allies had typically stayed about the same, thus narrowing the burden-sharing gap. During the Reagan defense buildup in the 1980s, this gap widened as the US procurement efforts increased purely public defense benefits.

US defense outlays have decreased in real terms from 1985 to 1995 by nearly $100 billion, or 25 percent of its defense budget. During the 1990–95 period, US real defense spending fell on average by 4.4 percent per year, compared with an average drop of 2.3 percent per year for the rest of NATO (US Department of Defense, 1996, p. III-3). Although military downsizing has occurred in both the United States and its NATO allies, downsizing has been more pronounced in the United States, meaning that more of the NATO defense burden is being shifted from the United States to its NATO allies during the post–Cold War era. This closing of the burden gap also shows up for 1990–97 (see table). The downward drift in British and French defense burdens in the 1990s has been attenuated by their strategic force modernization. Both allies have reallocated defense spending among various defense categories in order to focus on strategic forces, while finding ways to reduce their defense burdens. This downward trend has been more pronounced in Britain than in France.

The first test of defense burden-sharing behavior in NATO was conducted by Olson and Zeckhauser (1966). For 1964, these researchers found a significant positive correlation between NATO allies gross national product (GNP) and their defense burden as measured by the ratio of military expenditures to GNP. This result is consistent with the exploitation hypothesis, whereby the rich allies shoulder the largest defense burdens. During 1964, the NATO alliance adhered to MAD, whereby purely public deterrence was

Table 2.2. *Defense expenditures as a percent of GDP (in constant prices)*

Country	Average 1970–74	Average 1975–79	Average 1980–84	Average 1985–89	1990	1992	1993	1994	1995	1997
Belgium	2.8	3.2	3.2	3.0	2.6	2.0	1.9	1.9	1.7	1.6
Canada	2.4	2.0	2.1	2.1	2.0	1.9	1.9	1.7	1.6	1.3
Denmark	2.6	2.5	2.4	2.1	2.1	2.0	2.0	1.9	1.8	1.7
France	3.9	3.8	4.1	3.8	3.6	3.4	3.4	3.3	3.1	3.0
Germany	3.5	3.4	3.4	3.0	2.8	2.2	1.9	1.8	1.7	1.6
Greece	4.7	6.7	6.6	6.2	5.8	5.6	5.5	5.6	4.4	4.6
Italy	2.6	2.2	2.1	2.2	2.0	1.9	2.0	2.0	1.8	1.9
Luxembourg	0.8	0.9	1.2	1.2	1.1	1.2	1.1	1.2	0.9	0.8
Netherlands	3.2	3.0	3.0	3.0	2.7	2.5	2.4	2.3	2.0	1.9
Norway	3.7	3.1	3.0	3.1	3.1	3.1	2.9	2.9	2.3	2.2
Portugal	6.9	3.9	3.4	3.2	3.1	3.0	2.9	2.9	2.6	2.6
Spain	—	2.1	2.4	2.2	1.8	1.6	1.7	1.6	1.5	1.4
Turkey	2.3	3.9	3.8	3.5	3.9	4.0	4.0	4.0	3.4	3.3
UK	5.8	5.1	5.3	4.5	4.0	3.8	3.6	3.4	2.9	2.7
US	7.1	5.4	5.9	6.3	5.7	5.2	4.8	4.4	3.9	3.4
NATO-Europe	—	—	3.6	3.3	3.0	2.7	2.6	2.5	2.3	2.2
NATO-N. America	6.8	5.1	5.6	6.0	5.4	5.0	4.6	4.2	3.7	3.3
NATO total	—	—	4.8	5.0	4.5	4.1	3.8	3.5	3.0	2.7

Note: Unified Germany is listed for 1991–94.
Source: NATO Office of Information and Press (1995, Table 3, p. 359). The figures for 1995 come from NATO Press Release (1996). We should note that a different price deflator is used than that of the source for the other figures. Except for Greece and Portugal, this different price deflator did not have much effect. It lowered the ratio for Greece and Portugal considerably. The estimated figures for 1997 come from NATO Press Release (1997b).

the primary defense output. We would therefore anticipate exploitation and suboptimal defense spending.

Following the introduction of flexible response in the late 1960s, burden-sharing behavior changed. Russett (1970) noticed that the correlation between GNP and defense burden weakened drastically in the late 1960s, thus suggesting that the exploitation had also weakened. This finding is consistent with the predictions of the joint product model. A number of subsequent studies examined this correlation in greater detail. Sandler and Forbes (1980) examined the rank correlation between GDP and defense burdens (DEF/GDP) for all years between 1960 and 1975. Their findings showed that this rank correlation was statistically significant (at the .05 level) *only until the mid-1960s.* When the rank correlation also accounted for per-capita GDP and force thinning, a similar finding resulted: after 1966, the positive rank correlations between GDP and defense burdens were not significant (Sandler and Forbes, 1980, pp. 435–8).[14]

Recently, Khanna and Sandler (1996) updated this earlier study through 1992 and found that there were no statistically significant positive rank correlations between an ally's income and its defense burden after 1966. There was, however, some increase in the positive correlation during the Reagan buildup and then a subsequent decrease at the start of the 1990s. In a follow-up study, Khanna and Sandler (1997) adjusted the defense data to account for conscription. Allies (e.g., Belgium, Denmark, France, Germany) that rely, in whole or in part, on conscripted troops assume a larger defense burden than their defense spending indicates, because military personnel are paid below their true opportunity cost. Using Oneal's (1992) opportunity-cost adjustments, Khanna and Sandler (1997) uncovered no statistically positive rank correlation between an ally's income and its conscription-adjusted defense burden. For 1993 and 1994, these researchers found insignificant negative rank correlations between these two variables.

Thus far, these empirical tests support the applicability of the pure public deterrence model for the MAD era, and the joint product model for both the flexible-response and the post–Cold War eras. To provide further support for our hypotheses concerning burden sharing, we turn to an alternative burden-sharing measure that allows for a comparison between defense benefits received and defense burdens paid. This alternative defense burden measure equals *the ally's share of NATO total defense expenditures,* and in-

14. A marginally significant positive correlation for 1973 was, however, found for one of the correlation tests. This single aberrant result was not representative. For other similar tests, consult Oneal (1990a, 1990b), Pryor (1968), and van Ypersele de Strihou (1967).

Table 2.3. *Relative defense burdens and benefits in NATO using population, GDP, and exposed border shares as proxies: 1975, 1980, 1985 (conscription-adjusted data)*

Country	1975 Average benefit share	1975 Defense burden	1980 Average benefit share	1980 Defense burden	1985 Average benefit share	1985 Defense burden
Belgium	1.24	1.34	1.25	1.61	0.91	0.70
Canada	25.92	2.05	25.64	1.76	25.53	1.98
Denmark	1.00	0.66	0.99	0.69	0.85	0.38
France	7.12	9.44	7.21	10.74	5.75	6.03
W. Germany	8.34	10.39	8.56	10.96	6.56	5.84
Greece	2.14	0.99	2.16	0.93	2.04	0.68
Italy	6.01	3.16	6.19	3.62	5.86	2.25
Luxembourg	0.05	0.02	0.05	0.02	0.04	0.27
Netherlands	1.77	1.98	1.85	2.23	1.40	1.12
Norway	2.83	0.64	2.86	0.69	2.76	0.53
Portugal	1.00	0.59	0.98	0.35	0.78	0.19
Spain	NA	NA	NA	NA	3.26	1.16
Turkey	3.68	1.53	3.80	0.99	3.78	0.69
UK	6.94	7.52	7.44	10.25	6.30	6.43
US	31.96	59.64	31.06	55.13	34.19	71.99
NATO-Europe	42.12	38.31	43.30	43.11	40.28	26.03
NATO-North America	57.88	61.69	56.70	56.89	59.72	73.97

Notes: Figures represent percentage shares of NATO's totals. Defense burdens are calculated from SIPRI (1977, 1983, 1994) defense expenditures, valued in US dollars at current exchange rates. The underlying figures for GDP and POP used to compute average benefit shares are calculated from IMF (1990) data. GDP is converted to US dollars in current prices using current exchange rates. Exposed borders are calculated from border and coastline measurements given by the Central Intelligence Agency (1991). NA indicates not applicable.

dicates burden sharing *among* allies. In Tables 2.3 and 2.4, we indicate these defense burdens using conscription-adjusted data for fifteen NATO allies for five snapshots in time – 1975, 1980, 1985, 1990, 1994 – in the right-hand columns beneath each year (see Khanna and Sandler, 1997). If NATO-Europe defense burden is compared with that of NATO–North America, we see a dramatic shift of defense burdens to Europe in the late 1970s. A reverse trend occurs in 1985 during the Reagan defense buildup. In the 1990s, burdens again shifted to Europe. Thus, this defense burden behavior is consistent with that of the earlier ratio measure (DEF/GDP). Although many

Table 2.4. *Relative defense burdens and benefits in NATO using population, GDP, and exposed border shares as proxies: 1990, 1994 (conscription-adjusted data)*

	1990		1994	
Country	Average benefit share	Defense burden	Average benefit share	Defense burden
Belgium	1.03	0.99	1.01	0.87
Canada	25.45	2.25	25.08	1.95
Denmark	0.92	0.54	0.89	0.57
France	6.42	9.06	6.20	9.75
Germany	7.66	9.14	8.57	8.07
Greece	2.05	0.84	2.01	0.98
Italy	6.63	2.42	6.91	4.75
Luxembourg	0.04	0.02	0.05	0.02
Netherlands	1.57	1.67	1.54	1.49
Norway	2.77	0.74	2.72	0.78
Portugal	0.82	0.40	0.94	0.50
Spain	3.76	1.98	3.43	1.73
Turkey	4.02	1.14	3.92	1.11
UK	6.70	8.00	6.26	7.26
US	30.16	60.81	30.48	60.18
NATO-Europe	44.39	36.94	44.44	37.87
NATO-North America	55.61	63.06	55.56	62.13

Notes: See the notes to Table 2.3. GDP and POP data for 1990 and 1994 come from IMF (1993, 1995). Defense burdens for 1994 are calculated from SIPRI (1995). Exposed borders for 1990 and 1994 are taken from Central Intelligence Agency (1991, 1993).

defense burden measures can be used, alternative measures' behavior over time has given consistent results, thus making it less important which measure is used.

To give further evidence of the applicability of the joint product model, we compare defense benefits received to actual defense burdens paid. We must, however, stress the normative nature of any attempt to come up with a single index of defense benefits, when these benefits derive from multiple activities. Unless we know an ally's utility function, we have no way to know precisely how to weight the various defense benefits received. Following Sandler and Forbes (1980), we identify three benefit measures of defense: (1) an ally's share of NATO's population, (2) an ally's share of NATO's GDP, and (3) an ally's share of NATO's exposed borders (i.e., borders not adjacent to an ally or a friendly country). The population share is a proxy for lives protected, while the GDP share is a proxy for the industrial base defended. The exposed-border share is a proxy indicating territory protected. Given our ignorance about an ally's underlying utility function, we weight the three benefit proxies equally and report these "average benefit shares" in the left-hand column under each year in Tables 2.3 and 2.4. For example, Belgium received 1.24 percent of NATO average benefits in 1975 when its shares of NATO's population, GDP, and exposed borders are averaged (Khanna and Sandler, 1997). During that year, Belgium assumed 1.34 percent of NATO's defense spending burden.

Khanna and Sandler (1997) compared allies' average benefit shares with their actual defense burdens using a Wilcoxon test that indicates whether or not these two measures are statistically equivalent. At the .05 level of significance, they found that actual defense benefits matched average defense benefits received for 1975, 1980, 1990, and 1994. In 1985, however, at the height of the Reagan defense buildup, these benefits and burdens were not statistically the same. These results provide further support for the joint product model during the flexible response period, since this model is consistent with burdens being matched with defense benefits to the extent that excludable defense benefits are prevalent. Perfect agreement between burdens and benefits is not anticipated, because some purely public benefits still characterized defense even after the adoption of flexible response. As the Reagan buildup increased these nonexcludable deterrence benefits, the agreement between benefits and burdens disappeared in 1985. In 1994, the match declined in significance as France and Britain augmented their strategic forces and as peacekeeping missions assumed greater importance.

Thus we see that as NATO altered its strategic doctrine, predictable changes characterized burden sharing among the allies. These burden-sharing changes are based on the influence that alterations in strategic doctrine have on the mix of excludable and nonexcludable defense benefits shared by the allies. Similarly, changes in weapon technology can, if they affect this mix, influence burden sharing.

Studies of the demand for defense also support the finding that the joint product model best represented the post-MAD period.[15] Sandler and Murdoch (1990) offered the most direct comparison of the two models by estimating a linear representation of equation (2) for each of ten sample allies

15. Also see Gonzales and Mehay (1990), Hansen, Murdoch, and Sandler (1990), Hilton and Vu (1991), Murdoch, Sandler, and Hansen (1991), Oneal (1990a, 1990b, 1992), Oneal and Elrod (1989), Palmer (1990a, 1990b), and Smith (1989) for other demand studies of NATO.

for the 1956–87 period. For all sample allies, the coefficients on the SPILLINS term were significantly different than zero, thus indicating that the pure public good model did not apply for this period. Another demand study showed that an implied complementarity between strategic and conventional weapons imparted a positive slope to some of the allies' defense reaction paths, following the introduction of flexible response (Murdoch and Sandler, 1984). Most studies of NATO demand for defense supported the joint product model during the period of flexible response (see Sandler and Hartley, 1995, Table 2.1, pp. 47–50).

BURDEN SHARING IN NATO: THE FUTURE

Over the next decade, the crisis-management doctrine will affect NATO burden sharing, much as earlier doctrines have influenced burden sharing. Crisis management will involve instabilities both inside and outside of Europe. For those instabilities within Europe, the larger allies – France, the United Kingdom, Germany, the United States – will likely assume much of the burden, thus giving rise to greater exploitation than in the two earlier decades. An increase in exploitation is already evident in 1993–94, as shown in Khanna and Sandler (1997). Crisis management outside of Europe poses even greater tendencies toward exploitation, since only the large NATO allies are taking steps to acquire sufficient transport to project peacekeeping forces to places where they might be needed. Allies without the means to project forces will support crisis management by contributing troops and materiel to the CJTFs, currently under development.

Peacekeeping activities, like defense, give rise to joint products that vary in their degree of publicness. The actual peace or stability achieved by peacekeeping efforts is an alliancewide pure public output, which motivates free riding. Peacekeeping also yields private, ally-specific outputs. For example, allies nearest to the site of the instability or with economic interests at the site may derive benefits not experienced by others. Moreover, nations that assume active peacekeeping roles may gain private benefits in terms of enhanced status or reputation (i.e., recognition as a world leader). Such private benefits will motivate an ally to engage in peacekeeping activities, so long as expected benefits equal or exceed expected costs. The greater are the nonexcludable public benefits relative to the private benefits from peacekeeping, the less sharing of these peacekeeping missions will ensue. The large, rich allies will assume the lion's share of peacekeeping support as purely public benefits increase in proportion to total benefits. In a recent study, Khanna, Sandler, and Shimizu (1998) showed that there was a significant positive rank correlation between an ally's GDP and its burden of peacekeeping in the 1990s, thus implying disproportionate burden sharing. Peacekeeping and burden sharing are examined in greater detail in Chapter 4.

Another new mission of NATO involves enforcement of the Nuclear Non-Proliferation Treaty (NPT), which entered into force on 5 March 1970. Any ally that polices nuclear non-proliferation gives rise to increased security that is purely public to NATO allies and others. The affair with North Korea during 1994 is instructive. Although the United States tried to enlist other NATO members to assist it in pressing the North Koreans to open their nuclear plants to inspection, the US ultimately had to act alone to induce the North Koreans to comply with the treaty. If NATO continues to address more of these worldwide security concerns, there is a real possibility that the largest NATO allies will be shouldering greater burdens of defense (see Chapters 4 and 6).

New weapon technology may also impact burden sharing. War is becoming a high-technology contest where "information warriors" and their computers are replacing foot soldiers. In future conflicts, the difference between victory or defeat may hinge on being hidden or seen. To develop these high-technology defenses and offenses will require massive R & D budgets and huge investments in weapon systems. Associated command, control, and communication systems possess a mix of country-specific private and alliancewide public good elements. For example, information gathered from satellite surveillance is excludable but nonrival among allies. To date, it is the United States, the United Kingdom, and France that spend the most on weapon R & D. In 1993, the United States, France, and the United Kingdom spent 0.66%, 0.43%, and 0.36% of GDP, respectively, on government-sponsored defense R & D (Hartley, 1997a, Table 3, p. 31).[16] In the United States, 59% of government-funded R & D was spent on defense in 1993, compared with 42.5% in the United Kingdom and 34% in France. Germany spent only 0.08% of GDP on defense R & D in 1993, which was just 8.5% of government-funded R & D. Government-supported defense research has a significant opportunity cost, since this money could be directed toward

16. As pointed out by one reader, one must wonder why such sizable R & D programs are still necessary in the 1990s with the end to the Cold War. Some of these budgets are allocated to developing the next generation of fighter jets, helicopters, anti-missile systems, and tanks. Such weapons may be needed to confront threats from rogue nations or to engage in peace-enforcement operations.

developing innovations in the private sector that could result in competitive gains. As weapons become more technologically sophisticated, R & D may come to account for an ever-increasing portion of defense spending. Once a technological breakthrough is made, the discovery can be applied to enhance the weaponry of the other allies. Such breakthroughs provide nonrival but excludable benefits (e.g., stealth technology). The discoverer may, however, be willing to share the discovery with its allies whenever this sharing augments the discoverer's own security.

The ally expending the largest R & D effort is apt to make the breakthrough. Since this ally is often the richest, with the most to allocate to the research project, a worsening exploitation of the large by the small may result as weapon technologies become ever more complex. A potential escape from this exploitation outcome would be for the EU countries to pool their R & D efforts on defense, so that the United States and the European Union would have comparable R & D programs. Currently, this type of cooperation has not materialized in the European Union. Cooperation has, instead, taken the form of joint ventures to develop *specific* weapon systems – for example, Tornado combat aircraft, Eurofighter multipurpose aircraft, and Jaguar strike aircraft (see Sandler and Hartley, 1995, chapter 9). As weapon R & D becomes more burdensome, EU allies may have to resort to a common R & D effort regarding defense technology development (see Chapter 5).

PUBLIC CHOICE CONSIDERATIONS

Throughout our analysis of burden sharing, defense-spending interactions among allies have been emphasized to the exclusion of the consideration of factors that influence these spending decisions *within* an ally. Since defense-derived outputs are purely public within an ally, there are grounds for state provision to correct for potential market failures. Within NATO allies, defense decisions are made by bureaucracies (e.g., the Pentagon) and elected politicians who are apt to pursue their own self-interest at the expense of their constituencies. These pursuits can lead to government failures as stressed by public choice analysis, which applies economic methods to the study of political decision making. As such, political agents are characterized as maximizing an objective subject to constraints, which in the case of an elected official might involve support needed for reelection. These objectives do not necessarily reflect the good of the electorate. Thus, for example, a defense bureaucracy, such as the Ministry of Defence, may seek to maximize its budget and, in so doing, may encourage larger than ideal budgets.

Budget-maximizing tendencies result in augmenting defense budgets as opposed to the free-rider behavior associated with inter-allied interactions. Thus, public choice considerations suggest that government officials' actions to increase their responsibilities and remuneration may offset free-riding tendencies (Lee, 1990). From an empirical standpoint, it is difficult to measure this offsetting tendency, since it is impossible to know officials' objective functions. In Chapter 5, public choice aspects of defense budgets are discussed in greater detail.

CONCLUDING REMARKS

NATO has come through a number of different experiences with respect to burden sharing. Until the mid-1950s, the United States assumed a disproportionate share of NATO defense spending. Over the following decade, the alliance shared a defense activity that had a large portion of purely public benefits in the form of deterrence. During the 1955–66 period, the richer allies – the United States, the United Kingdom, France, West Germany – shouldered a disproportionate share of defense burdens. Once the doctrine of flexible response was adopted in principle, defense burdens became more evenly spread among the allies, more in accordance with the benefits received. With flexible response, defense activities produced multiple outputs, some of which were consistent with allies revealing their preferences through defense provision. This improved match between defense burdens and benefits weakened temporarily during the Reagan defense buildup of the early 1980s.

With the end of the Cold War, NATO has searched for new missions to justify its continued existence and proposed expansion. Since 1991, NATO has assumed a crisis-management doctrine aimed at preserving world peace and economic security. This new doctrine's emphasis on peacekeeping and power projection of NATO forces to trouble spots may involve more purely public outputs than those derived from NATO's defense activities in the previous two decades. From this, a new era of disproportionate defense burden sharing may follow. The continued trend to information-based armaments may also reinforce this predicted burden-sharing trend. If the past is any guide, changes in NATO doctrines and/or weapon technology will have profound impacts on burden sharing. NATO membership size and composition are also anticipated to influence burden sharing and the demand for defense among NATO allies.

APPENDIX: NATO ABBREVIATED CHRONOLOGY, 1945–97

26 June 1945:	UN Charter signed in San Francisco.
5 June 1947:	Announcement of Marshall Plan to rebuild Europe.
24 June 1948:	Start of Berlin blockade by Soviet Union.
10 Dec. 1948:	Negotiations on North Atlantic Treaty opened in Washington, D.C. Representatives were from Brussels Treaty Powers (Belgium, France, Luxembourg, the Netherlands, and the United Kingdom), Canada, and the United States.
15 March 1949:	Negotiators of the North Atlantic Treaty extended invitations to Denmark, Iceland, Italy, Norway, and Portugal to join.
4 April 1949:	North Atlantic Treaty was signed in Washington, D.C., by Belgium, Canada, Denmark, France, Iceland, Italy, Luxembourg, the Netherlands, Norway, Portugal, the United Kingdom, and the United States.
9 May 1949:	Berlin blockade ended.
24 Aug. 1949:	North Atlantic Treaty entered into force.
17 Sept. 1949:	In Washington, D.C., the first session of the North Atlantic Council was held.
25 June 1950:	North Korea attacked the Republic of South Korea.
20 Dec. 1950:	The Brussels Treaty Powers merged the military organization of the Western Union into NATO.
18 Feb. 1952:	Greece and Turkey joined NATO.
23 July 1953:	Korean Armistice signed.
23 Oct. 1954:	Italy and West Germany became members of the Western European Union (WEU).
6 May 1955:	West Germany joined NATO.
14 May 1955:	Warsaw Pact formed, containing Albania, Bulgaria, Czechoslovakia, East Germany, Hungary, Poland, and Romania.
13 Dec. 1956:	North Atlantic Council extended NATO mission to include nonmilitary cooperation.
25 March 1957:	European Economic Community (EEC) was set up by the Rome Treaty.
1 Jan. 1958:	The treaty establishing the EEC entered into force.
20 Nov. 1959:	Stockholm Convention established the European Free Trade Asso-

	ciation (EFTA), including Austria, Denmark, Norway, Portugal, Sweden, Switzerland, and the United Kingdom.
14 Dec. 1960:	Convention established the Organization for Economic Cooperation and Development (OECD).
13 Aug. 1961:	Berlin Wall was erected.
10 March 1966:	France announced its intention of withdrawing from the integrated military structure of NATO.
14 Dec. 1966:	Defense Planning Committee established the Nuclear Defense Affairs Committee and the Nuclear Planning Group.
16 Oct. 1967:	NATO Headquarters opened in Brussels.
13–14 Dec. 1967:	Defense Planning Committee adopted the doctrine of flexible response as the strategic doctrine of NATO.
20–21 Aug. 1968:	Soviet Union and Warsaw Pact invaded Czechoslovakia.
12 Sept. 1968:	Albania ended its membership in the Warsaw Pact.
5 March 1970:	Nuclear Non-Proliferation Treaty (NPT) entered into force.
1 Jan. 1973:	Denmark, Ireland, and the United Kingdom joined the EEC.
14 Aug. 1974:	Greece withdrew its forces from NATO's integrated military structure.
2 Feb. 1976:	The Independent European Programme Group was established to foster cooperation in R & D and production of defense weapons.
20 Oct. 1980:	Greece rejoined NATO's integrated military structure.
1 Jan. 1981:	Greece joined the EEC.
30 May 1982:	Spain became the sixteenth NATO ally.
1 Jan. 1986:	Portugal and Spain became members of the EEC.
8 Dec. 1987:	INF treaty was signed, eliminating land-based intermediate-range nuclear missiles. (INF treaty implemented on 31 May 1988.)
14 Nov. 1988:	Portugal and Spain signed their intention to enter the WEU.
9–10 Nov. 1989:	Berlin Wall was opened.
7 Dec. 1989:	Coalition government was formed in Czechoslovakia.
22 Dec. 1989:	Ceausescu's regime was overthrown in Romania.
18 March 1990:	First free elections in East Germany in forty years.
27 March 1990:	Portugal and Spain entered WEU.
2 July 1990:	Monetary union was established between West and East Germany.
22 Aug. 1990:	East German legislation approved unification with West Germany.
3 Oct. 1990:	Unified Germany became a member of NATO.
17 Jan. 1991:	Air attacks began the Gulf War between coalition forces and Iraq.
25 Feb. 1991:	The Warsaw Pact was voted by its members to be disbanded.
28 Feb. 1991:	Iraq surrendered to coalition forces.

26 March 1991:	Pershing II and cruise missiles were withdrawn from Europe as mandated by the INF treaty.
31 March 1991:	Formal dissolution of the military structure of the Warsaw Pact was accomplished.
12 May 1991:	Soviet Union eliminated its remaining SS20 missiles as mandated by the INF treaty.
1 July 1991:	Warsaw Pact was officially disbanded.
30–31 July 1991:	START treaty was signed, thereby reducing strategic nuclear weapons.
6 Oct. 1991:	In Cracow, the foreign ministers of Poland, Hungary, and Czechoslovakia expressed their wish to join NATO.
7–8 Nov. 1991:	Rome summit adopted a new strategic doctrine of peacekeeping.
8 Dec. 1991:	In Minsk, representatives of Russia, Belarus, and Ukraine agreed to establish a Commonwealth of Independent States (CIS) to replace the Soviet Union.
9–10 Dec. 1991:	EC heads of state adopted treaties on economic and monetary union and political union. Ratification of the treaties was still pending.
20 Dec. 1991:	The end of the Soviet Union. In Brussels, the first meeting of the North Atlantic Council included foreign ministers from the sixteen NATO countries and from nine Central and Eastern European countries.
21 Dec. 1991:	In Alma Ata, eleven republics of the former Soviet Union signed an agreement forming the CIS.
16 June 1992:	US President Bush and Russian President Yeltsin agreed to reduce strategic missiles well beyond the limits of the START treaty.
17 July 1992:	CFE treaty, signed on 19 Nov. 1990, provisionally entered into force.
2 Sept. 1992:	The North Atlantic Council pledged resources to support efforts by the UN, CSCE, and EC to bring peace to the former Yugoslavia.
1 Oct. 1992:	US Senate ratified the START I treaty, which reduced US and Russian nuclear forces by one-third.
2 Oct. 1992:	NATO's Allied Command Europe (ACE) rapid deployment force was deployed at Bielefield, Germany.
14 Oct. 1992:	The North Atlantic Council permitted NATO's airborne warning and control systems (AWACS) to be used to monitor the UN "no-fly" zone in Bosnia.
9 Nov. 1992:	The CFE treaty officially entered into force.
11 Dec. 1992:	At a Defense Planning Committee meeting, NATO defense ministers supported UN and CSCE peacekeeping among NATO including missions.
17 Dec. 1992:	North Atlantic Council's foreign ministers indicated their resolve to bolster UN action in the former Yugoslavia. Furthermore, these min-

	isters pledged to increase NATO's means to assist in peacekeeping wherever needed.
3 Jan. 1993:	Presidents Bush and Yeltsin signed the START II treaty, which eliminated all multiple warhead ICBMs and reduced nuclear stockpiles by two-thirds.
13 Jan. 1993:	The Chemical Weapons Convention, banning chemical weapons, was signed by 127 nations.
4 Feb. 1993:	Belarus ratified the START I treaty.
15 March 1993:	North Korea ejected inspectors from the International Atomic Energy Agency and indicated its intention to withdraw from NPT.
2 April 1993:	The North Atlantic Council directed SACEUR to prepare to implement UN Resolution 816 regarding a no-fly zone over Bosnia.
12 April 1993:	NATO began its operation to maintain the no-fly zone.
9 Aug. 1993:	The North Atlantic Council approved the use of air strikes in Bosnia.
8–9 Dec. 1993:	In Brussels, NATO Defense ministers examined new tasks for NATO, including support of peacekeeping missions and the development of Combined Joint Task Forces (CJTFs). The Partnership for Peace program was also supported.
10–11 Jan. 1994:	At the Brussels Summit, the Partnership for Peace program was launched with invitations to North Atlantic Cooperation Council (NACC) partner states and CSCE nations to join.
14 Jan. 1994:	Procedures were established for the transfer of Ukrainian nuclear warheads to Russia. These procedures were agreed to by the United States, Russia, and Ukraine.
28 Feb. 1994:	NATO airplanes shot down four warplanes that violated the UN-mandated no-fly zone over Bosnia.
22 April 1994:	The North Atlantic Council authorized air power to protect UN personnel in Bosnia. Air strikes were authorized unless Serbian artillery were withdrawn by 27 April from Gorazde.
12 July 1994:	Constitutional restrictions on the use of German forces in peacekeeping missions abroad were removed by German courts.
5 Aug. 1994:	NATO airplanes attacked targets within Sarajevo in support of UN troops.
12–16 Sept. 1994:	In Poland, the first joint exercises under the Partnership for Peace program are held.
22 Sept. 1994:	NATO authorized air strikes on Serbian tanks, after a UN vehicle was attacked.
11 Dec. 1994:	Russian President Yeltsin deployed troops to Chechnya to quash rebellion.
1 Jan. 1995:	Start of a four-month cease-fire in Bosnia. Austria, Finland, and Sweden became members of European Union.

23 Feb. 1995:	In violation of the CFE treaty, Belarus halted its weapon destruction program.
31 March 1995:	Russia accepted in principle the Individual Partnership Program.
1 May 1995:	UN peacekeepers were used as human shields in Bosnia by the Serbs.
11 May 1995:	Indefinite extension of the Non-Proliferation Treaty (NPT) was approved by participating countries.
25–26 May 1995:	NATO air attacks on a Bosnian Serb ammunition depot near Pale.
11 July 1995:	NATO air strikes unleashed on targets near Srebrenica.
1 Aug. 1995:	NATO's Operation Deliberate Force commenced with air and artillery attacks as a response to Serbian shelling of Sarajevo.
1 Sept. 1995:	Operation Deliberate Force suspended after Bosnian Serbs promised to remove heavy weapons from a twenty-km zone of exclusion.
5 Sept. 1995:	NATO air strikes resumed in Bosnia.
14 Sept. 1995:	Bosnian Serbs signed an agreement acknowledging the exclusion zone.
28 Sept. 1995:	The NACC and PFP were briefed on NATO Enlargement Study.
2 Oct. 1995:	Start of cease-fire in Bosnia.
27 Oct. 1995:	In a memorandum of understanding, NATO and the Western European Union agreed to a communication linkage.
1 Nov. 1995:	Bosnian peace talks began in Dayton, Ohio.
5 Dec. 1995:	NATO endorsed troop deployment to Bosnia. UN troops handed over command in Bosnia to NATO troops.
14 Dec. 1995:	Bosnia Peace Agreement was signed in Paris.
20 Dec. 1995:	NATO-led IFOR replaced UNPROFOR in the former Yugoslavia.
2 May 1996:	NATO and WEU signed security pact, protecting classified and sensitive materials provided to one another.
18 June 1996:	Operation Sharp Guard was suspended in the former Yugoslavia.
22 Oct. 1996:	US President Clinton announced that the first wave of new NATO allies will be admitted by 1999.
20 Dec. 1996:	SFOR replaced IFOR troops in Bosnia.
18 Feb. 1997:	NATO agreed to recently negotiated changes to the CFE Treaty.
27 May 1997:	Founding Act on Mutual Relations Cooperation & Security between NATO and the Russian Federation is signed.
29–30 May 1997:	NATO members and twenty-six partnership nations convened the first meeting of the Euro-Atlantic Partnership Council (EAPC), which combined the PFP military cooperation program and the NACC.
8–9 July 1997:	Madrid summit on NATO expansion. Hungary, the Czech Repub-

lic, and Poland were given the go-ahead to prepare for membership in 1999. Charter of Distinctive Partnership between NATO and Ukraine signed.

18 Dec. 1997: US President Clinton announced that US troops would remain in Bosnia indefinitely.

Source: NATO Office of Information and Press (1995, pp. 295–351) was consulted for 1945–94. The chronology for 1995–97 was based on the author's research from magazines and newspaper items. Only those developments most germane to our book are listed.

3 On NATO expansion

There is probably no current issue concerning NATO that elicits stronger emotions and more divergent viewpoints than that of NATO expansion. One group of analysts depicts NATO expansion as fostering collective defense capabilities, improving alliance burden sharing, imposing affordable costs, furthering democratic reforms in Europe, promoting European stability, and adapting NATO to the post–Cold War environment.[1] Another group views NATO expansion as isolating Russia, limiting the cohesiveness of NATO, jeopardizing arms-reduction treaties (e.g., the CFE treaty and START II), placing greater financial burdens on NATO allies, and exposing NATO to new risks.[2] Despite these vast differences in viewpoint, NATO expansion is slated to occur sometime in the first half of 1999 with the addition of the Czech Republic, Hungary, and Poland. This first wave of entrants was announced at the 7–8 July 1997 summit in Madrid. Although no announcement has been made, a second set of entrants might include Romania and Slovenia. Seven further applicants – Slovakia, Macedonia, Bulgaria, Albania, Estonia, Latvia, Lithuania – have expressed an interest in joining NATO (RUSI, 1996; US GAO, 1997a, 1997b).

Our intention here is not to take either side of this debate, but rather to

1. These positive aspects of NATO expansion are discussed in Boczek (1995), Bruce (1995), Bureau of European and Canadian Affairs (BECA) (1997), Congressional Budget Office (CBO) (1996), Gompert and Larrabee (1997), NATO (1995), and Royal United Services Institute for Defence Studies (RUSI) (1996).
2. Bogomolov (1996), Brown (1995), and Carpenter (1994) address the isolation of Russia, whereas Ilke (1995) considers the limiting influences of the cohesiveness of NATO. Possible financial burdens are analyzed by CBO (1996), Perlmutter and Carpenter (1998), and US General Accounting Office (US GAO) (1997b, 1997c).

delineate the issues involved. Some of these issues have not been brought to light in the literature. Additionally, we shall discuss some of the methodological aspects of this debate. A skilled analyst can find support for either position, depending on the assumptions upon which to calculate the associated benefits and costs of NATO expansion. To date, cost estimates have varied greatly due to differences in these underlying assumptions among analyses.

The purpose of this chapter is sixfold. First, the process for extending NATO membership is reviewed along with important events that have paved the way for this expansion. Second, the potential *benefits and costs* associated with membership expansion are identified. Most analyses have focused exclusively on the cost side, even though alternative underlying assumptions have implications for both benefits and costs. Third, relevant factors left out of the debate thus far are identified and included. Fourth, a club theory analysis for determining optimal membership size is put forward as a conceptual device for determining the appropriate extent of NATO expansion. Fifth, earlier cost estimates by the Department of Defense (DOD), the CBO (1996), and RAND (Asmus, Kugler, and Larrabee, 1995, 1996) are contrasted and evaluated. Sixth, some policy recommendations are offered.

NATO EXPANSION: ISSUES, INSTITUTIONS, AND PROCEDURES

Issues associated with NATO expansion abound. Key questions include whom to invite and the timetable for admitting new members. Other concerns involve the preconditions for membership in terms of military strength, force interoperability with NATO, political stability, economic well-being, democratic control of the military, the transparency of the military processes, and the absence of ethnic and territorial disputes (Asmus, 1997; BECA, 1997; CBO, 1996; Larrabee, 1997; NATO, 1995; Partnership for Peace, 1996). Yet another crucial issue concerns the Russian Federation and its views of an expanded NATO that includes ex–Warsaw Pact nations and even republics of the former Soviet Union. Although NATO has taken in new allies in the past, never has such a large expansion been considered. The only previous occasion on which more than one ally was admitted was 18 February 1952, when Greece and Turkey joined the original twelve members. Subsequent expansions included West Germany on 6 May 1955, Spain on 30 May 1982, and unified Germany replacing West Germany on 3 October 1990. Article

10 of the NATO treaty provides for new members when current members unanimously approve of the entrant (see Chapter 2). Hence, all allies must either perceive a net gain from expanding the alliance or else be compensated by proponents if expansion is to be supported.

With the fall of the Berlin Wall, the dissolution of the Warsaw Pact, and the collapse of the Soviet Union, NATO's existence was called into question (Leech, 1991). The first significant precursor to NATO expansion occurred on 6 July 1990, when NATO heads of state issued the London Declaration, which called for increased military and political cooperation between the NATO allies and the nations of Central and Eastern Europe (Thomson, 1997). This declaration directed that there be established diplomatic liaison between NATO and these Central and Eastern European nations. At a summit of the North Atlantic Council in Rome on 7–8 November 1991, a subsequent declaration outlined NATO's new strategic concept of peacekeeping and crisis management, according to which NATO pledged to protect European security beyond NATO's borders with rapid reaction forces. The Rome Declaration initiated a more formal consultation process between Central and Eastern European countries and NATO in the form of the North Atlantic Cooperation Council (NACC) (Asmus, 1997, p. 37), which met for the first time on 20 December 1991. In many ways, the NACC complements the work of the Organization for Security and Cooperation in Europe (OSCE), formerly the Conference on Security and Cooperation (CSCE), to promote trust and cooperation among nations in Europe, Central Asia, and North America.[3] Unlike the OSCE, the NACC also addresses security-related issues that would permit NACC members to coordinate some of their defense activities with those of NATO. In Table 3.1, the four key organizations behind NATO expansion – OSCE, NACC, the Partnership for Peace (PFP), and the Euro-Atlantic Partnership Council (EAPC) – are listed along with some important facts about each.

At the Oslo summit of NATO on 4 June 1992, peacekeeping became an official NATO mission and, as such, signaled NATO's strategic commitment to underwrite European security beyond NATO's borders. Arguably, the most significant event paving the way for NATO expansion was the Brussels summit on 10–11 January 1994 (Jordan, 1995), where NATO nations' leaders launched the PFP within the framework of the NACC (see Table 3.1). When the PFP was originally proposed during the 1994 summit,

3. The CSCE changed its name to the OSCE on 1 January 1995. NATO Office of Information and Press (1995) is an excellent source of information on the NACC, the OSCE, and the Partnership for Peace (PFP). Chapter 7 considers these institutions in greater detail.

Table 3.1. *Four key organizations for NATO expansion*

Organization for Security and Cooperation in Europe (OSCE)

- formerly the Conference on Security and Cooperation (CSCE) until 1 January 1995. CSCE, which began in 1972, resulted in the Helsinki Final Act of 1975, which indicates measures to build trust among nations, to foster human rights, and to provide cooperation.
- the sole forum that brings together nations from Europe, Central Asia, and North America for discussions on political, economic, legal, and security matters.

North Atlantic Cooperation Council (NACC)

- established on 20 December 1991.
- a forum for constructive political dialogue and cooperation on security-related issues (e.g., defense conversion, defense budgets, disarmament, weapon standardization, airspace coordination, and NATO expansion).
- as of February 1995, members consist of NATO allies and Albania, Armenia, Azerbaijan, Belarus, Bulgaria, the Czech Republic, Estonia, Georgia, Hungary, Kazakhstan, Kyrgyzstan, Latvia, Lithuania, Moldova, Poland, Romania, Russia, Slovakia, Tajikistan, Turkmenistan, Ukraine, and Uzbekistan. Austria, Finland, Slovenia, and Sweden are observers.

Partnership for Peace (PFP)

- established within the framework of NACC on 10–11 January 1994.
- promotes civilian control of armed forces and transparency of military processes in PFP members.
- consists of bilateral relationships between PFP members and NATO. Through PFP, participating nations can strengthen their security ties to NATO.
- NATO pledges to consult with any PFP member that perceives a threat to its territory or security.
- PFP facilitates eventual NATO membership for selected nations. Joint exercises and an Individual Partnership Program (IPP) increase interoperability of forces between NATO and PFP nations.
- As of 17 December 1996, PFP members include Albania, Armenia, Austria, Azerbaijan, Belarus, Bulgaria, the Czech Republic, Estonia, Finland, Georgia, Hungary, Kazakhstan, Kyrghz Republic, Latvia, Lithunia, Macedonia, Moldova, Poland, Romania, Russia, Slovakia, Slovenia, Sweden, Switzerland, Turkmenistan, Ukraine, and Uzbekistan.

Euro-Atlantic Partnership Council (EAPC)

- successor of NACC, intended to raise the level of political and security cooperation between NATO and PFP countries. Began on 24 May 1997.
- provides for a more direct political linkage between NATO and PFP nations. EAPC countries can tailor their interactions.
- membership consists of NACC members and PFP participating countries.

Sources: NATO Office of Information and Press (1995), NATO Press Release (1997a), and Partnership for Peace (1996) on Internet at gopher://marvin.nc3a.nato.int:70/00/partners/pfpintro.txt and gopher://marvin.nc3a.nato.int:70/00/partners/pfpalfa.

the Clinton administration viewed it merely as a means to improve security links between NATO and the former communist countries. PFP members established bilateral relationships with NATO to accomplish this enhanced security. The PFP later evolved to allow prospective NATO allies to prepare their armed forces to interact with those of NATO. This interaction is directed at fostering interoperability of forces, standardization of weapons, commonality of logistical procedures, and modernization of PFP members' defense forces. Joint exercises also promote these goals, as does PFP nations' participation in peacekeeping missions in Bosnia. As part of the PFP program, the United States provides training in English, information on US defense programming and budgeting practices, and support for upgrading PFP members' air traffic control systems (US GAO, 1997a, p. 2). The Brussels summit was also noteworthy because it formalized NATO's new strategic doctrine of peacekeeping and nonproliferation. To support this doctrine, NATO outlined its plan to develop combined joint task forces (CJTFs) to provide a multiservice, multilateral rapid deployment force (Thomson, 1997, p. 86).

PFP members now include ex–Warsaw Pact members, former Soviet republics, and some neutral countries as listed in Table 3.1. Civilian control of PFP members' armed forces is emphasized. In addition, PFP members are expected to maintain a transparency of military processes and to promote democratic ideals and institutions. Each partnership country consults with NATO to tailor its own annual Individual Partnership Program (IPP) as a means of fostering security cooperation and interface with NATO. In the event of a threat to a PFP member, NATO is obliged to confer with the member, but the extent of a response on NATO's part is left unspecified. PFP members are encouraged to participate in a biennial Planning and Review Process (PARP), whereby a member shares defense budget information and plans with NATO so as to augment interoperability of its forces with those of NATO. IPP and PARP are two crucial procedures that help prepare NATO aspirants for membership.

Another important event behind NATO expansion took place on 22 June 1994 when Russian Foreign Minister Andrei Kozyrev signed the PFP Framework Document, which set in motion Russian-NATO cooperation on a wide range of security matters. Later that year the first joint PFP exercises between NATO and PFP nations were held during 21–28 October 1994. Thereafter, the number of these PFP exercises has increased each year. PFP nations provided troops to support the NATO-led Implementation Force (IFOR) and the subsequent Stabilization Force (SFOR) (see Chapter 4), and thereby furthered their ability to operate beside NATO forces.

On 1 December 1994, US Secretary of State Warren Christopher made the opening statement at the meeting of the NAC in Brussels. This speech marked a turning point in US policy toward NATO expansion. Christopher (1994) stated that, "Central to building a comprehensive security architecture for Europe is a measured process of NATO expansion, along with continued European integration and a determination to strengthen the Conference on Security and Cooperation in Europe." With this speech, the United States began to view the PFP as a way to prepare nations, willing to embrace NATO obligations and ideals, for NATO membership. At this point, the stage was set for NATO expansion. The Clinton administration's support for NATO expansion emerged during 1993–94. This emergence is documented by Goldgeier (1998), who shows that the Clinton administration's view was transformed during this period from mild opposition to fast-track encouragement of admitting selected PFP members. Passage of the NATO Participation Act of 1994 and the NATO Enlargement Facilitation Act of 1996 by Congress authorized the president to provide security assistance to the Czech Republic, Hungary, Poland, Slovenia, and other countries meeting PFP goals (US GAO, 1997a, p. 8) as a means of readying them for membership in NATO.[4]

On 14 May 1997, NATO and Russia reached a tentative agreement on a Russia-NATO Partnership Pact that assured Russia that NATO expansion would have no adverse military implications for Russian security interests. A final agreement, signed in Paris on 27 May 1997 by NATO heads of state and Boris Yeltsin, is the Founding Act on Mutual Relations, Cooperation, and Security. By signing the Founding Act, Russia lifted its opposition to NATO expansion. To entice Russia into signing, NATO promised that "it has no intention, no plan and no reason to deploy nuclear weapons, or to station permanently substantial combat forces on the territory of new members" (*The Economist,* 1997a, p. 55). Furthermore, this act established a NATO-Russia Permanent Joint Council for addressing security matters (e.g., terrorism, weapons deployment, strategic doctrine) of mutual interest. Under the Founding Act, NATO is free to establish headquarters and infrastructure on these new allies' soil. With Russian objections overcome, invitations to join NATO by April 1999 were extended to the Czech Republic, Hungary, and Poland on 7–8 July 1997. These countries, with

4. During the 1995–97 fiscal years, the United States allocated $308.6 million to assist twenty-three PFP members, with almost half of this assistance going to the Czech Republic, Hungary, Poland, Romania, Slovakia, and Slovenia. Over half of this money was earmarked for air traffic control equipment and other dual-use equipment (US GAO, 1997a, pp. 2–3).

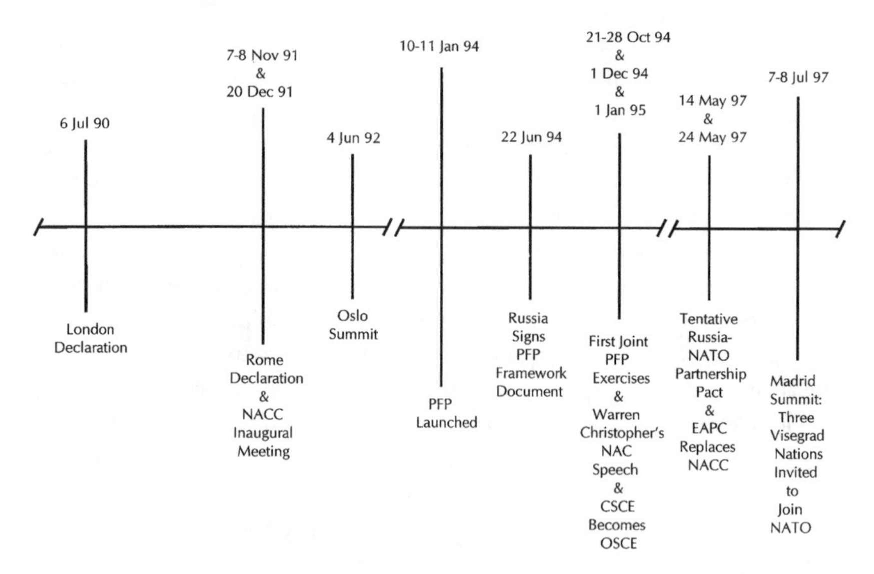

Figure 3.1. NATO expansion time line

NATO help, are expected to prepare their armed forces for membership over the coming years.[5]

A fourth institution germane to NATO augmentation is the Euro-Atlantic Partnership Council (EAPC), which replaced the NACC on 24 May 1997 (see Table 3.1). The EAPC is designed to enhance political and military cooperation between NATO and PFP countries. Under EAPC, a member country or a small group of EAPC members can develop a direct political relationship with NATO (NATO Press Release, 1997a). In essence, political and security consultations are held on a more regular basis and are more tailored to the individual needs of the EAPC members as compared to the NACC.

By way of summary, Figure 3.1 presents a time line containing many of the most noteworthy events leading up to the invitations to three of the Visegrad nations to join NATO. Although the Clinton administration has been a driving force for NATO expansion since the end of 1994, the time line indicates the initial stimulus was given prior to his administration by actions of NATO heads of state in 1990 and 1991 as a response to the ending of the Cold War.

5. According to the US GAO (1997a, p. 8): "The fiscal year 1997 Foreign Operations Appropriations Act also earmarked $30 million for foreign military financing grants for the Czech Republic, Hungary, and Poland and allocated $20 million to subsidize lending up to $242.5 million for purchases of US defense articles, services, and training by these three countries."

Remaining issues

Many questions remain to be resolved prior to the admittance of the prospective entrants. For example, how much interoperability and modernization of the entrants' forces must be achieved prior to their entry? This issue is important because if most of the upgrading of military personnel and equipment comes after admission, then other aspirants for membership can argue that stricter standards should not be applied to them. NATO could be weakened by taking in nations whose armed forces are poorly prepared and not interoperable with allied forces. If NATO were to expand to include most of Europe, then one must wonder whether such a large body would possess sufficient unity of purpose to respond quickly in times of crisis. This is particularly worrisome for NATO, which relies on a unanimous decision rule when reacting to a threat under Article 5. There is also the problem of integrating diverse military command and control elements from many different entrants into NATO's military structure. Entrants will be inexperienced in NATO's logistics and operations, which could inhibit a swift response in times of crisis. Additionally, a trans-European NATO may become less a security pact and more a political consultative committee indistinguishable from OSCE.

Another lingering concern involves the Russian Federation. Despite the Founding Act, Russian opposition to NATO may resurface. Present-day Russia presents a fluid political climate that can change drastically, especially if economic conditions do not improve rapidly enough. As NATO prepares its new members, Russian nationalists may convince voters that an eastward expanding NATO represents a security threat to Russia, and thereby rally support for invigorating Russian forces (Asmus, Kugler, and Larrabee, 1995; Kugler, 1996). This, in turn, could initiate a new arms race. A threatened Russia may abrogate its commitments to the CFE and START II treaties and withdraw its support for NATO-sponsored peacekeeping operations in Bosnia and elsewhere. In order not to marginalize and isolate Russia, some analysts have even recommended that an expanded NATO include the Russian Federation (see references in CBO [1996, p. 11] and Gompert and Larrabee [1997]). With Russia in NATO, China would become a greater risk owing to animosities between the two countries. Given the ethnic rivalries and political uncertainties in Russia, its membership would expose NATO to myriad risks. Allowing for any degree of interoperability and standardization for Russian and NATO forces would be very expensive. In sum, there are so many roadblocks and pitfalls to Russian membership that any reasonable scenario must discount this possibility. If Russia is not to be part of NATO, then NATO expansion must be made nonthreatening to Russia. Actions by NATO *must correspond* to its assurances to Russia that an enlarged NATO is not directed at counterbalancing a potential Russian threat. This nonthreatening posture to Russia becomes more difficult to achieve when CBO (1996) cost estimates for NATO enlargement, to be discussed later, are based on a renewed Russian threat. NATO denials of its interest in countering a future Russian challenge become rather incredible when preparation of *prospective* allies includes the ability to project NATO forces to their eastern borders. Only Russia poses a threat to those borders!

The inclusion of the ex–Warsaw Pact countries and nonaligned nations is not anticipated to present the same threats to Russia as the entry of former Soviet republics such as Estonia or Ukraine. The admission of the Baltic states represents a potential threat to Russia, because these countries have unresolved border disputes with the Russian Federation and many Russians reside in them (Larrabee, 1997, p. 177). Furthermore, the Baltic countries are more strategically located vis-à-vis vital Russian interests than the Visegrad countries – Hungary, Poland, the Czech Republic, Slovakia. Ukraine's membership in NATO poses a threat to Russia, insofar as Ukraine is economically linked to Russia and, like the Baltic states, is home to many Russians. While Ukraine appears to have no interest in joining NATO (Asmus, Kugler, and Larrabee, 1995), the Baltic countries very much want to be part of NATO (Birkavs, 1996). Surely, the entry of some new allies presents greater risks and costs to NATO security and European stability than that of others. For example, the Baltic states represent greater risks to NATO, since they are difficult to defend, given their location, and Russia is so opposed to their membership. Thus, not all potential club members should be viewed equally. Any determination of an optimal alliance size, as presented below, must account for nations' strategic, political, and military heterogeneity.

BENEFITS AND COSTS OF MEMBERSHIP

If all existing NATO allies perceive a net benefit from accepting another ally and if, furthermore, the entrant perceives a net benefit from membership, then NATO's admission of this ally would appear to make sense. This unobjectionable statement, however, masks a number of subtle issues behind the determination of whether or not a proposed expansion should be undertaken. Any computation of these net benefits is dependent on the assumptions upon which the cost and benefit calculations are drawn. A crucial assumption involves the identification of the status quo position used as a benchmark from which to calculate the true additional costs and benefits of membership. At the end of the Cold War, many of the ex–Warsaw Pact nations' armed forces were ill-equipped and poorly trained. These forces were probably due for some modernization even if these nations did not join NATO. Only the modernization costs beyond the expenses that these allies would have to make anyway should be included. For example, costs associated with transponders that identify tanks as friendly give rise to additional costs of membership. If fuel depots have to be refitted with nozzles used by NATO allies, then these standardization expenses are a price of NATO membership. Other NATO-entry costs may involve training new allies' commanders and troops in the NATO languages of English and French. Entry costs may also arise when a prospective ally's forces must be modified to make them interoperable with NATO forces in terms of communications, logistics, and command.

Another key assumption concerns the strategic environment that underlies an analyst's estimates of entry costs and benefits. Since the 1994 Brussels summit, the appropriate strategic environment from which to compute costs and benefits from alliance enlargement must stress peacekeeping, crisis management, and nonproliferation. Under the current strategic doctrine, force mobility and interoperability are essential factors if the new allies are to contribute to NATO defense burdens. An entrant must consider costs associated with "out-of-area" missions as mandated by this doctrine. Bosnia is an initial instance of these out-of-area missions, but others may involve more distant theaters and even greater risks. For costs and benefits to be properly identified, an appropriate level of threat must be assumed. If, for example, costs are calculated based on ethnic unrest within Central and Eastern Europe, but the real threats occur in the more distant Middle East or even North Korea, then the true costs needed to integrate the new members' forces will be poorly represented.

The extent of commitment and integration expected of the new allies is also an important consideration when ascertaining the costs and benefits of membership. In general, the institutional arrangements of the post-entry alliance must be known in order to compute the costs and benefits of expansion. Obviously, the identity of the entrant(s) also makes a difference in this computation. To adjust for temporal factors, the dates when costs and benefits are incurred must be taken into account. When costs are more immediate but benefits are experienced only after a considerable lag, the *present value* of net benefits would be smaller than when benefits are immediate and costs are put off until a later date. One striking shortfall of all cost estimates to date is a failure to address the intertemporal pattern of costs. As a consequence, present value calculations are not made so that the dollar figures reported treat a dollar spent in 1997 as the same as a dollar spent in 2006;[6] moreover, there is no attempt to display the likely spending pattern by year.

When determining the expansion burdens on the allies, an analyst must make an assumption about cost sharing. The same cost of expansion can have vastly different impacts on the current allies and the entrants depending on how these costs are shared. Today's cost estimates are based on alternative cost-sharing assumptions. A pattern of cost sharing that is sufficiently burdensome to one ally may make that ally perceive a negative net benefit from enlargement, thus motivating it to oppose expansion. Under Article 10's unanimity membership-entry rule, even a single dissatisfied ally can block a prospective entrant.

Benefits

Although alternate sources stress different benefits, there appears to be consensus on what types of potential gains may stem from NATO expansion.[7] According to US Secretary of State Madeleine Albright, "the new NATO can do for Europe's east what the old NATO did for Europe's west: vanquish old hatreds, promote integration, create a secure environment for prosperity, and deter violence" (*The Economist,* 1997b, p. 22). Secretary Albright and the Clinton administration view an enlarged NATO as furthering democratic reforms and political stability for the entrants and the would-be entrants. If membership in NATO and the European Union are tied, then economic and political integration are, indeed, linked to security integration. In the case of Turkey, however, membership in NATO has not yet led to membership in the European Union; hence, caution should be exercised when assuming this linkage. Increasing the size of NATO is seen by Secretary Albright as eliminating hatreds, because potential entrants are expected to settle territorial disputes with their neighbors and quell ethnic divisions prior

6. This is true of the US DOD figures reported in BECA (1997). It also applies to the RAND study (Asmus, Kugler, and Larrabee, 1996) and to the CBO (1996) report.
7. Benefits presented here draw from a variety of sources including Asmus (1997), Asmus, Kugler, and Larrabee (1996), BECA (1997), CBO (1996), *The Economist* (1997b, pp. 21–23), Gompert and Larrabee (1997), NATO (1995), NATO Office of Information and Press (1995), RUSI (1996), SIPRI (1997), and US GAO (1997b, 1997c).

to attaining NATO membership (NATO, 1995). PFP membership requires that these issues be addressed. In response to this requirement, Hungary and Slovakia have settled their differences concerning their common borders, and Slovakia has agreed to protect the rights of its Hungarian minority (CBO, 1996, p. 10). Similarly, Hungary and Romania are negotiating a settlement of border disputes and minority issues. If political stability can be achieved in these prospective NATO allies, then foreign direct investments, an important source of savings and growth, will be attracted to them, which in turn will bolster their economic prosperity and stability.

Alliance expansion is also intended to enhance collective defense capabilities and thus to deter aggression. This alleged benefit may be problematic, since the addition of a weak ally may reduce collective security for all allies under some scenarios. Suppose that allies are assigned to protect a front. The strength of this protection depends on the weakest defenders, because it is with them that an aggressor has the best opportunity to penetrate the perimeter, putting allied forces in jeopardy (Conybeare, Murdoch, and Sandler, 1994). When Secretary Albright mentions deterring violence, one must wonder whom she has in mind, since assurances have been given to the Russian Federation that NATO expansion is not directed at a Russian threat. Furthermore, deterrence depends on credibility and an automatic response to aggression (Schelling, 1960). NATO's failure to act quickly in Bosnia when there were just sixteen members does not bode well for its ability to act rapidly with nineteen members, who must unanimously approve and support any NATO-led response.

Yet another benefit from increasing NATO membership may involve adapting NATO to the post–Cold War environment, with its absence of a superpower confrontation and the need to keep local crises from escalating. This environment also carries the risk of the proliferation of nuclear and other weapons of mass destruction. For this benefit to apply, new allies must acquire the means to support peacekeeping and enforcement operations in Europe and beyond. While these allies have been contributing to Bosnian peacekeeping efforts (US Department of Defense, 1996), this contribution has been rather modest. For out-of-area missions, the prospective allies neither possess nor are anticipated to acquire power projection capabilities, and must rely on the United States, the United Kingdom, France, and (possibly) Germany for these capabilities. This realization also severely limits these entrants' ability for the foreseeable future to improve NATO burden sharing, another alleged benefit of expansion.

Another potential benefit, not mentioned in the literature, arises from increased weapon sales by NATO arms-producing allies. If NATO entrants are to acquire interoperable and standardized weapons, then these weapons must be bought from other NATO allies. These new sales may increase production runs sufficiently to bring down unit costs, thus recapturing some economies of scale lost in downsizing (see Chapter 5).[8] It is understandable that the United States, which stands to gain the most from these sales, has not highlighted this potential benefit from enlarging NATO. Nevertheless, there can be significant economic gains to the large arms suppliers of NATO.

At the top of Table 3.2, potential expansion benefits are summarized. All of these benefits suffer from a common problem – quantification difficulties. For example, how does one put a dollar value on the furthering of democratic reforms, or on supporting political integration? Ironically, the benefits that are the easiest to quantify – for example, improving NATO burden sharing or increasing weapon sales – may be either very limited or else not mentioned for obvious political reasons. To judge whether NATO burden sharing is to be improved through expansion, we should examine recent defense burdens among the invitees and among NATO allies. In terms of the percentage of GDP devoted to defense in 1995, Poland spent 2.4%, the Czech Republic spent 2.5%, and Hungary spent 1.5% (CBO, 1996, p. 71), which, except for Hungary, is on a par with comparable burdens in NATO-Europe, where 2.3% was spent on average (see Chapter 2, Table 2.2). According to the CBO (1996, p. 40) estimates of enlargement costs – which many view as too high (see, e.g., US GAO, 1997b) – Poland would have to increase its defense burden to 3.8% of GDP, the Czech Republic to 3.6%, and Hungary to 2.6%. Even if these increases occurred, these nations' defense spending amounts are relatively small compared with those of the major NATO allies, thus implying very little burden-sharing relief.

If expanding NATO is to be justified on economic grounds, then these expansion benefits must be estimated and must outweigh the associated expansion costs. To date, studies concerned with the economic implications of NATO expansion have made no attempt to quantify the associated benefits so as to compute a net benefit measure from NATO expansion, which is the value that really matters. This practice might be acceptable if all alternative membership configurations had the same benefits, but this is clearly not the case. When only costs are computed, then these costs can be viewed as the minimum level of membership benefits to justify expansion.

8. This increased arms trade within the alliance does not necessarily imply that NATO's overall arsenal will increase. However, some tendency for this arsenal to increase stems from the new members' arsenals rather than from increased arms trade within NATO.

Table 3.2. *Potential benefits and costs of NATO expansion*

Potential expansion benefits
- foster collective defense capabilities
- further democratic reforms and political stability in entrants
- support economic and political integration
- improve relations among neighboring nations
- adapt NATO to the post–Cold War environment
- improve NATO burden sharing
- increase weapons sales in NATO
- cost savings from scale economies in weapons production

Potential expansion costs
- direct enlargement costs (e.g., C^3I, infrastructure, logistical considerations, interoperability, expanded civil structure, reinforcement reception facilities)
- added risks from entrants' ethnic and territorial disputes
- joint exercises
- PFP expansion associated assistance
- thinning of forces
- limits on NATO decision making under consensus
- **entrants' force modernization for self-defense** (e.g., military forces modernization, weapon upgrades, weapon standardization, ammunition storage facilities, infrastructure, surface-to-air defenses)
- **reinforcement capability enhancement** (e.g., rapid-reaction force)

Costs

The bottom half of Table 3.2 displays the most important expansion costs.[9] As indicated earlier, only those costs that result from NATO expansion should be included. In Table 3.2, the two boldfaced costs – entrants' force modernization, reinforcement capability enhancement – are calculated in the DOD, CBO, and RAND studies (US GAO, 1997b), but would have to be met regardless of expansion. The Visegrad nations would have to improve and upgrade their forces whether or not they join NATO. One or two items, such as weapon standardization, in this category of costs may be attributable to NATO membership. Given its strategic doctrine of 1994, NATO needed to enhance its reinforcement capabilities in Eastern and Central Europe irrespective of whether it accepted new allies. The presence of new allies may increase the likely deployment of the rapid reaction forces if one of the entrants confronts a security challenge.

From our perspective, the first six costs categories in Table 3.2 are relevant for NATO expansion. The most important category of expansion costs

9. These costs are contained in Asmus, Kugler, and Larrabee (1995, 1996), BECA (1997), CBO (1996), SIPRI (1997), and US GAO (1997b).

consists of direct enlargement costs and includes upgrading command, control, communications, and intelligence (C^3I) facilities, extending NATO infrastructure (e.g., pipelines, airfields), standardizing logistics among the entrants, expanding NATO civil structure, making entrants' forces interoperable, and building reception facilities for reinforcements. Two other easily measurable costs include those associated with joint exercises. Not all of the expense of joint exercises can be attributable to NATO expansion, because NATO needs to conduct these exercises with PFP members in order to pursue crisis-management preparedness even if those members do not join NATO. NATO expansion may require augmenting the assistance given to PFP nations not initially invited to join (e.g., Romania), so as to ease disappointment.

The three remaining costs in Table 3.2 are more difficult to measure, but may be the most important. Costs may stem from the added risks of conflict that a new ally brings to the alliance. To limit these risks, NATO and the United States intend the PFP framework to be an intermediate step toward membership, during which prospective allies address their ethnic and irredentist concerns. Because ethnic tensions may be based on longstanding hatreds and past atrocities, there may be no way completely to eliminate such risks. By admitting more ethnically homogeneous allies, NATO can minimize this cost greatly. The three allies given the first invitations in July 1997 are among the most ethnically homogeneous of the applicants. Both Romania and Slovakia are less ethnically homogeneous, and this might explain the failure of their initial bid to join.

A vital cost of expansion that has, heretofore, been absent from the literature concerns the *thinning of forces* associated with a spatial rivalry as a given deployment of conventional forces is stretched across a longer perimeter or a greater surface area (Sandler, 1977, 1993). The fixity of forces is an appropriate assumption given the CFE treaty. This thinning applies differently to two distinct kinds of warfare: conventional wars with battles along a front, and insurgencies with battles waged anywhere in the country. For conventional wars, thinning of forces applies to the nation's exposed borders or the perimeter, not contiguous with an ally or a friendly power. For insurgencies, the country's entire area must be patrolled and thus determines thinning, insofar as rebels can stage attacks anywhere. The addition of the Czech Republic, Hungary, and Poland does little to alter the size of NATO's eastern front – it just displaces it eastward – but these entrants do add perimeter to the north along Poland's coast, and to the south along Hungary's southern border with Croatia and Serbia.[10] If protecting against a conventional conflict, launched from another nation, is the relevant concern, then thinning costs arise from protecting NATO's expanded northern and southern flanks. If, however, troops are stationed in the rear in Germany, the United Kingdom, France, and elsewhere and must be projected to the east during threats, then some of this projection expense could be, in part, attributable to NATO expansion. Nevertheless, for a conventional war scenario, thinning costs arising from NATO's planned expansion are really quite modest. The same conclusion does not hold, however, regarding the inclusion of Romania, Bulgaria, and the three Baltic states, whose inclusion would increase NATO's eastern perimeter greatly, resulting in large thinning costs. In, say, the case of the Baltic states, the entire perimeter around this cluster of countries would require protection, making thinning an important consideration. NATO's eastern perimeter would not merely be displaced to the east. Given their location, projecting NATO troops to these countries during a crisis would also be more logistically complex than reinforcing NATO's neighboring Visegrad countries.

A much different picture of thinning emerges for insurgencies, guerrilla warfare, and terrorism where targets are countrywide wherever people and property are vulnerable. Among the current prospective entrants, Poland poses the greatest potential thinning costs from these concerns because of its large area. Fortunately, the three invitees to NATO are not currently at risk from these three kind of conflicts, and hence we again conclude that thinning costs will be modest for the first wave of applicants.

Although proponents of NATO expansion have recognized that decisions may be slower and more difficult to reach in an enlarged NATO (see references in CBO, 1996), the increased costs of decision making associated with NATO's expansion have not been properly addressed or incorporated into the analysis. To rectify this omission, we shall draw on the seminal analysis of Buchanan and Tullock (1962), in which an optimal decision rule is determined. Two kinds of costs must be included, and then their sums minimized, if an optimal decision rule or majority is to be identified. Suppose that a constitutional stage for NATO is considered where members' heads of state meet to decide what size majority is required during consultations to respond to a future Article 4 or Article 5 contingency, in which one or more allies' interests are threatened. When less than unanimity

10. The Czech Republic's southern borders are with Austria and Germany – two friendly countries – and are, therefore, not exposed.

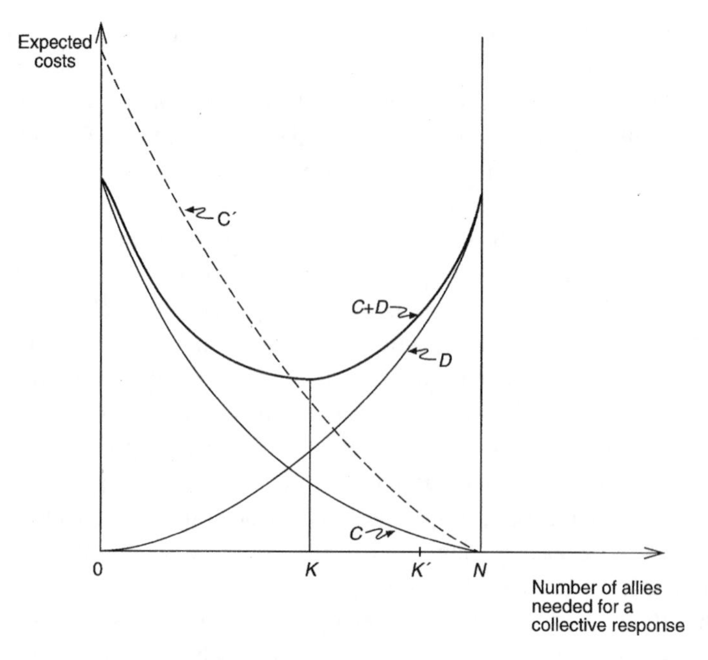

Figure 3.2. Optimal majority

decides an appropriate response, *political external costs* are imposed by the majority on the minority. Ceteris paribus, the larger is the minority, the larger are these political external costs. A decision, say, to go to war would impose enormous external costs on any ally who is against the war but is made to contribute troops and materiel. Enemy attacks will be directed at all allies regardless of an ally's vote on whether or not to go to war.

In Figure 3.2, the curve labeled *C* depicts these political external costs. On the horizontal axis is the number of allies whose agreement is needed for a collective response. Expected costs are measured on the vertical axis. Political external costs are largest when the decision is imposed from the outside, and these costs decline as more of the *N* allies must concur with an action. When all must agree at point *N,* political external costs are zero. If there are no additional costs in deciding a response, then the optimal majority is clearly unanimity; however, time and effort must be expended to identify a response beneficial to all allies. During the negotiating process, the allies incur decision-making costs, indicated by *D.* If just a single ally is required to decide a response, then decision-making costs should be modest. As more allies must be part of the majority, decision-making costs will rise at an increasing rate, as represented by *D* in Figure 3.2.

To find the optimal majority, we vertically sum the political external costs and the decision-making costs and find the number of allies – K in Figure 3.2 – that minimizes this sum. At K, the marginal decision-making costs of increasing the required majority equals the negative of the corresponding marginal political external costs.[11] In other words, at the optimal majority, the increase in decision-making costs from adding an ally to the decisive majority must match the associated decrease in political external costs. Now suppose that, for each K, the political externality costs are greater than those of C owing to greater burdens being imposed on each minority, so that the dashed curve C' applies in Figure 3.2. If decision-making costs are unchanged from those of D, then the optimal majority is displaced to the right at group size K', requiring a larger decision-making proportion K'/N.[12] Article 5 decisions that commit allies' armed forces to combat surely create large political external costs and, as such, should result in a large optimal majority. In Figure 3.3, we have drawn a scenario where the C curve is discontinuous at N; it drops from a positive value just prior to N to zero at N, while the decision-making cost curve rises more slowly than C falls at all Ks and is below C throughout. As shown, the lowest possible sum of decision-making and political external costs occurs at unanimity, where $K = N$. In this case, the optimality majority should be unanimity as set out by Article 5. Even though unanimity may be justifiable under some scenarios, it may not necessarily be optimal for other scenarios. With the Article 5 decision rule institutionally given at unanimity, the decision-making costs are expected to be high owing to a nonoptimally determined majority.

As an alliance grows, the decision-making curve is apt to shift rightward and downward *for each absolute majority* up to the original N, because larger alliances are anticipated to have more allies with similar tastes. This implies that any fixed number of supporters is easier to achieve from a larger pool of allies; however, this anticipated fall in decision-making costs *is not expected to be proportional to the increase in group size.* If, say, alliance size increases by 10 percent, the anticipated fall in decision-making costs for each majority is apt to be less than 10 percent, so that the optimal percentage of

11. The underlying problem is to find the K that solves

$$\min_{K}[C(K) + D(K)].$$

The optimizing K occurs where $-dC/dK = dD/dK$ or the slope of D equals the negative of the slope of C.

12. To keep the diagram uncluttered, we have left out the $(C' + D)$ curve from Figure 3.2. K' corresponds to the majority where the absolute value of the slope of the C' curve equals the slope of the D curve.

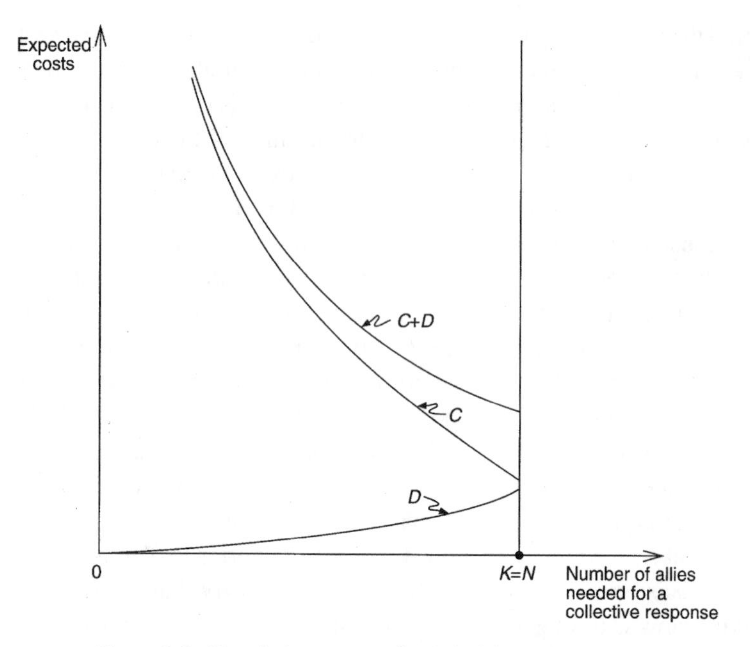

Figure 3.3. Unanimity as an optimal decision rule

N needed for decision making decreases (see Buchanan and Tullock, 1962, pp. 111–16; Mueller, 1989, pp. 54–5). Consequently, unanimity decision rules, when maintained in light of alliance expansion, will imply more onerous levels of decision-making costs. Another negative implication of all this is that an expanded NATO is likely to become less able to act. This problem can be partly rectified if the decision rule is renegotiated as NATO membership increases; but that is not slated to happen. Even though decision-making costs are given almost no attention in studies of NATO expansion, they are apt to grow in importance with NATO enlargement.

To illustrate this decision-making difficulty for NATO, we consider events of the spring of 1997. Prior to the Madrid summit, two viewpoints on NATO expansion prevailed. One group, led by France, wanted NATO expansion to include Romania and Slovenia along with the three later-designated entrants, while another group, led by the United States, wanted just the three Visegrad entrants. This disagreement necessitated delicate negotiations, and perhaps side payments to France, to achieve unanimity. If further expansion beyond nineteen allies is considered after 1999, more diverse opinions are likely to be aired, thus requiring even more extensive negotiations and larger side payments, if unanimity prevails as the decision rule. As a consequence, a reduced majority may be recommendable.

A larger alliance membership can also cause problems for effective crisis management as NATO attempts to reach a consensus about peace-enforcement missions. As negotiations among NATO allies drag out over dispatching troops, opposing combatants may escalate their fighting to gain territory as a negotiating advantage when and if NATO intervenes. This scenario characterized the lengthy deliberations over NATO's intervention in Bosnia, during which the fighting often intensified. A larger alliance could lead to even longer intense battles for territories prior to peacekeeping operations.

A CLUB THEORY APPROACH TO NATO EXPANSION

In Chapter 2, allied defense spending activities were shown to yield joint products that varied in their degree of publicness. That is, a unit of a defense activity can produce ally-specific outputs, alliancewide deterrence, and damage-limiting protection. These three classes of benefits are private, purely public, and impurely public, respectively, among allies. We shall use these concepts to define an optimal-sized alliance based on club theory.[13] In essence, club theory permits an additional ally to join if the entrant's benefits derived from alliance membership are greater than or equal to the entrant's costs of membership. These membership costs must compensate the existing members for any diminishment of their security caused by the entrant. The following scenarios are intended to elucidate the membership decision.

Scenario 1: Homogeneous allies, a single shared club good of fixed size

Suppose that n identical allies, possessing the same tastes and income, contemplate whether or not to accept another identical ally. Further suppose that defense levels remain unchanged after entry owing to a treaty-imposed limit. In the presence of conventional forces, the addition of an ally has two opposing effects that must be balanced for an optimal membership. An entrant will thin the given forces, which will make the allies worse off; and an entrant will reduce each ally's provision costs through cost sharing, which will make the allies better off. When the values of these opposing marginal effects are precisely offsetting for a representative ally, an optimal alliance

13. On club theory, see Sandler and Tschirhart (1980) and Cornes and Sandler (1996).

size has been obtained. As more allies are added, the cost-sharing benefit diminishes because one's cost share falls more slowly,[14] while thinning costs increase rapidly as force strength per mile along a front declines.

Force thinning is an important consideration for conventional weapons. For strategic weapons, deterrence is not subject to thinning (see Chapter 2); hence, there are no requisite restrictions on club size if deterrence is the only concern. NATO's new strategic doctrine of peacekeeping, crisis management, and nonproliferation is, however, dependent on conventional armaments and troops, and as such is subject to the phenomenon of force thinning. This is clear when the number of engagements that a given force can support simultaneously is addressed. The NATO-Russian Founding Act limits the armed forces that can be deployed forward along NATO's new eastern perimeter in the absence of threats, but does not really affect thinning. The latter only occurs when these forces are deployed forward to address a crisis. Constraints on arsenals and armies, as imposed by the CFE treaty, can accelerate thinning costs as new allies join whenever their entry means that the same treaty-imposed limit now applies to the expanded alliance. This suggests that arms-control treaties may need to be renegotiated following alliance expansion.

Scenario 2: Homogeneous allies, joint products

Next suppose that *n* identical allies provide a defense activity that yields deterrence and damage-limiting protection. Only the latter is subject to thinning considerations. Further suppose that the level of this deterrence depends on the number of allies, with there being increased strength in numbers (Murdoch and Sandler, 1982). Also assume that a new ally's forces need some standardizing at the time of membership.[15] This second scenario implies that two costs must be balanced against two benefits if an optimal alliance size is to be attained. On the cost side, an entrant thins the alliance's forces and also requires entry costs in the form of standardization. On the benefit side, the entrant reduces per-ally costs through cost sharing and enhances the alliancewide deterrence. This scenario comes closer to the present-day membership choices of NATO.

This basic framework can easily be adapted to accommodate further considerations. If, for example, an additional ally brings its own risk factors of

14. In going from two to three allies, one's cost share goes from one-half to one-third; however, in going from nine to ten allies, one's cost share goes from one-ninth to one-tenth.
15. That is, there is a "hook-up cost" to membership.

war to the alliance, then these risks represent an added cost that must be included with the other costs of membership expansion, which are balanced against membership benefits. Membership expansion may be unwise if such risks are sufficiently great. When identifying costs and benefits associated with the membership choice, *we should balance only those costs and benefits that change with the number of members.* Ally-specific benefits derived from the defense activity are independent of alliance size and thus are not germane to the membership decision. Additional membership costs arise from transaction costs associated with increasing NATO's civil structure and infrastructure. These transaction costs also involve decision-making costs, as discussed in the preceding section. Each additional ally is anticipated to contribute more to decision-making costs than the preceding ally as unanimity becomes increasingly difficult to achieve. Given that membership costs increase at an increasing rate, while membership benefits increase at a decreasing rate, there will be a finite optimal size of membership. NATO must not pursue enlargement as though there are no limits to size; real limits exist based on membership benefits and costs, and these should not be surpassed.

What might be the limit to NATO membership? Surely Slovenia would add very little to thinning, with Hungary to its east, Austria to its north, and Italy to its west. Only Slovenia's southern border with Croatia is exposed and presents a problem of thinning. Nevertheless, there can be a case made to include it. Similarly, Slovakia also implies modest increases in thinning costs so that its inclusion could be warranted provided that ethnic uncertainties are resolved. Romania, however, is a different story in terms of thinning costs owing to its large exposed border in many directions. It is, therefore, doubtful that NATO should grow beyond twenty-one members, based solely on thinning cost considerations; but other factors could outweigh thinning costs.

Scenario 3: Heterogeneous allies, joint products

A final scenario allows the allies to differ by tastes, income, and location. Also, *armed forces are no longer assumed to be fixed.* An important source of heterogeneity concerns the thinning of forces that a prospective entrant creates. Surely, a potential ally with more exposed borders or land area, such as Poland and Romania, creates more thinning costs than one with fewer exposed borders, such as the Czech Republic. To compensate for the greater degree of thinning they cause, larger allies would have to bring greater forces to the alliance upon joining. Allies should be considered for inclusion based on their taste for membership: those with the greatest demand for membership should be considered first, since they are better able to compensate for the thinning and other costs that their inclusion imposes on the rest of the alliance, and still gain a net benefit from joining. Another factor that can determine a prospective ally's place in the alliance queue would be the extent of benefits that the alliance would derive from its membership. A strategically located candidate would enhance alliance security more than a poorly located one. The additional security benefits derived from the former make it a better prospect for membership, since the existing allies would have a greater likelihood of gain despite the thinning and other costs associated with expansion.

Heterogeneity considerations also have a bearing on decision-making costs associated with alliance enlargement. As the diversity of tastes and endowments among allies increases with expansion, decision-making costs will increase, thereby limiting the ability of the alliance to act decisively in times of crisis. In its July 1997 Madrid summit announcement, it is not surprising that NATO selected from among the aspirants those that are, in many ways, the most similar to the current members.

In a complex alliance like NATO, there are many costs and benefits that must be traded off when admitting one or more allies. Surprisingly, recent studies of the implications of NATO expansion, reviewed in the next section, quantify only *some* of these costs and makes no attempt to quantify the associated benefits. Without quantifying both expansion costs and benefits, an informed membership decision cannot be made. Moreover, these tradeoffs will have to be ascertained if the optimal club size of NATO is to be determined.

COSTS OF NATO EXPANSION: SOME RECENT STUDIES

There have been three recent US studies to estimate the likely costs of NATO expansion. Given the different assumptions upon which these estimates were drawn, it is not surprising that estimates vary greatly among studies. Two of the three studies presented alternative options for expansion and thus contained a wide range of cost estimates.

The DOD estimates are in an internal government memo, not available to the public; however, they are presented and discussed in two US government reports – US GAO (1997b) and BECA (1997). To derive its estimates, DOD assumed that a limited number of countries would be invited to be among the first set of entrants. Although the identities of these nations were classified, they probably included the three actual invitees, insofar as the Clinton administration would have informed the DOD on which applicants the administration was planning to support. DOD estimates were based on NATO facing no real conventional threat in Europe for the foreseeable future, so that military forces are primarily needed for crisis management and peacekeeping. Thus, NATO's 1994 strategic doctrine formed the basis for the estimates. In DOD estimates of NATO expansion costs, the United States was viewed as paying 24 percent of NATO expansion-related infrastructure costs. Only the direct costs of NATO enlargement were shared by the United States in the DOD estimates. Current NATO allies were assumed by DOD to maintain current defense spending in real terms for 1997–2009 (US GAO, 1997b). Given recent downward trends in these allies' real defense spending and their announced future spending, this assumption is certainly suspect. NATO entrants were anticipated by DOD to increase their real defense spending at an average annual rate of 1–2 percent of GDP in order to support the required modernization of their forces. This assumption is also questionable, given the fragility of these economies and their need for private-sector investment. In the event of crisis, DOD assumed that four armed divisions and six fighter wings would be deployed forward to any entrant in jeopardy (US GAO, 1997b, Table 1).[16] Unlike the other two studies, DOD assumed that entrants would purchase some refurbished equipment to bolster their armed forces. For instance, a refurbished I-Hawk air-defense system was assumed rather than a new Patriot air-defense system. DOD's assumption of refurbished equipment limited cost estimates greatly but would not imply the same level of security as that underlying the other two studies, which were based on more up-to-date equipment and facilities. A time frame of 1997–2009 was used for the DOD estimates of NATO expansion costs.

In Table 3.3, a few of DOD's key assumptions and cost estimates are listed in the second column. Three categories of costs were delineated (US GAO, 1997b):

- $10–13 billion for modernizing entrants' military forces. Modernization would be directed at a quarter of each entrant's ground forces.

16. A division consists of 17,500–20,000 soldiers, while a fighter wing includes 72 combat planes. In Appendix I of the same US GAO (1997b) report, reinforcements were given as three allied divisions and five allied wings.

Associated costs also involved procurement of refurbished combat planes, ammunition upgrades, an air-defense system, and improved troop training.
- $8–10 billion for NATO allies' reinforcement improvement. Associated costs involved power-projection enhancement and rapid-reaction forces.
- $9–10 billion for "direct enlargement costs." In the DOD estimates, these costs included C^3I improvements, infrastructure enhancement, and additional exercise facilities.

The entrants were assumed to pay all of the modernization costs, while current NATO allies (excluding the United States) were slated to pay all of the reinforcement expense. Direct enlargement costs would be shared as follows: entrants, $3–4.5 billion; current (non-US) NATO allies, $4.5–5.5 billion; and the United States, $1.5–2 billion. The United States was expected to pay an average annual amount of $150–200 million from 2000 to 2009. According to US GAO (1997b, 1997c), DOD estimates were difficult to evaluate owing to a lack of details. There is also an issue as to whether non-US allies and the entrants will actually be willing and able to cover these costs. If they do not meet these expenses, then the United States is likely to be the residual claimant, since it has pushed so hard for the expansion. Many of the costs associated with modernization of the entrant's forces will be needed regardless of whether or not NATO expansion occurs. Furthermore, if NATO is to pursue its 1994 strategic doctrine, then many of the reinforcement expenses would result even without NATO enlargement. Clearly, DOD estimates have not properly distinguished those costs explicitly linked to NATO expansion. US GAO (1997b) identified additional costs not in the DOD calculations – for example, "consolation" assistance to countries not in the first set of entrants.

At this juncture, we must caution that the figures in Table 3.3 appear large because they aggregate over groups of allies and years – thirteen to sixteen depending on the estimates. For the United States and current NATO allies, the annual expense is not that large. A different story emerges for the three entrants, since there are fewer of them to share the burdens. Also, we must emphasize that the real expansion costs are less than those listed when spending that must be made in the absence of expansion – that is, $10–13 billion for force modernization under the DOD proposal – is eliminated.

A second but no less controversial (see, e.g., SIPRI, 1997) set of estimates was presented by CBO (1996). Table 3.3 indicates some of the key assumptions of the CBO study. The $109 billion total cost figure in Table 3.3 came the nearest to the strategic mission of the DOD and RAND studies.

Table 3.3. *Alternative cost estimates for NATO enlargement*

	Alternative reports		
Assumptions	DOD	CBO	RAND
New allies	Classified[a]	Poland Hungary Czech Republic Slovakia	Poland Hungary Czech Republic Slovakia
Strategic Doctrine	NATO's 1994 doctrine	NATO's 1994 doctrine	NATO's 1994 doctrine
Time period	1997–2009	1996–2010	1995–2010
Threat envisioned	Low	A resurgent Russia	Low
Reinforcement forces	4 divisions 6 wings	11.7 divisions 11.5 wings	5 divisions 10 wings
Total costs	$27–35 billion[b]	$109 billion[c]	$42 billion[d]
US cost share	16.7% of direct enlargement costs	11.9% of all cost categories	13% of all cost categories
US costs	$1.5–2 billion	$13 billion	$5–6 billion

[a]Probably includes the three "invitees": the Czech Republic, Hungary, and Poland.
[b]In constant 1997 US dollars. Costs are broken down as follows: new members' force restructuring and modernization, $10–13 billion; rapid reinforcement force enhancement by existing European NATO allies, $8–10 billion; and direct enlargement expense, $9–12 billion. Many of the procurement items involve the purchase of refurbished equipment (US GAO, 1997b, Appendix II).
[c]In constant 1997 dollars. Estimates of costs for the five options range from $61 billion to $125 billion. Option 3 with a cost of $109 billion comes nearest to the strategic missions envisioned by DOD and RAND. Procurement involves the purchase of new equipment.
[d]In constant 1996 dollars. Estimates of costs run from $10 billion to $100 billion based on four alternative missions. The $42 billion price tag corresponds to the option that provides for entrants' self-defense and NATO joint-power projection of air and ground troops during crisis. Procurement involves the purchase of new equipment.
Sources: Asmus, Kugler, and Larrabee (1995, 1996), Congressional Budget Office (1996), and US GAO (1997b). DOD assumptions and estimates are contained in the latter report.

CBO (1996) presented cost estimates for five strategic options or missions that built on the previous one in terms of scope. There are some notable differences between the CBO and DOD assumptions. Most important, CBO (1996) assumed a more significant threat from a resurgent Russia. To respond to this greater threat, 11.7 troop divisions and 11.5 fighter wings were used in the reinforcement scenario. Another difference concerned the component missions of the options which were: (1) enhancement of Visegrad

Table 3.4. *Cumulative cost estimates and shares for CBO's five options (in billions of 1997 dollars)*

	Costs to US	Costs to NATO allies[a]	Costs to entrants	Total cost
Option 1	4.8	13.8	42.0	60.6
Option 2	9.4	24.1	45.6	79.2
Option 3	13.0	44.4	51.8	109.3
Option 4	13.3	45.3	51.9	110.5
Option 5	18.8	54.0	51.9	124.7

[a]Excludes the United States.
Source: CBO (1996, p. xiv).

defense and NATO supplemental reinforcements; (2) projection of NATO air power eastward to ward off threats to Visegrad states; (3) projection of NATO ground troops, based in Germany, to respond to threats to the Visegrad states; (4) preposition of weapon stocks in Visegrad states; and (5) and deployment of 2.66 troop divisions and 2 fighter wings in the Visegrad states (CBO, 1996). Each option builds on all previous options; for example, option 3 achieves the missions of options 1, 2, and 3. CBO (1996, p. xiv) calculated the costs of the five options as follows: option 1, $60.4 billion; option 2, $79.2 billion; option 3, $109.3 billion; option 4, $110.5 billion; and option 5, $124.7 billion.

Much of the expense listed under option 1 falls under the category of modernization of entrants' armed forces and, as such, is not really an expansion cost. There are, however, some infrastructure expenses in option 1 for C^3I and other expenses for exercises that can qualify as expansion costs. A portion of the power-projection costs associated with options 2 and 3 corresponds to reinforcement enhancement under the DOD estimates. Once again, a significant portion of the power projection costs can be attributable to NATO's crisis management doctrine and not to NATO expansion per se. The large differences between the CBO and the DOD estimates highlight the point made at the outset that the underlying assumptions have a large impact on the hypothesized costs of NATO expansion. A reasonable scenario for defense costs for Visegrad nations in the absence of NATO expansion is required if the true incremental costs of NATO enlargement are to be ascertained.

Table 3.4 provides a breakdown of the five options' cost shares for the United States, the non-US NATO allies, and the four prospective entrants, as set out in CBO (1996, p. xiv). To approximate per-country average annual expense for these CBO options, each cost in a column must be divided by fifteen (i.e., the number of years) and the relevant number of sharers. The bulk of these alleged expansion costs are imposed on either the non-US NATO allies or the Visegrad nations. Expansion cost estimates computed by the Visegrad nations come nowhere near those of even option 1 of the CBO report (SIPRI, 1997). Clearly, options 4 and 5 are in the entrants' interests, because they reap the added security with virtually no increased costs, as the existing NATO allies foot the bill.

In Table 3.3, the fourth column lists the expansion cost calculation of RAND, where the underlying mission associated with the $42 billion price tag comes the closest to option 3 of the CBO report. Like the DOD estimates, the RAND estimates were based on a low threat level with no large-scale conventional conflicts in Europe on the horizon (Asmus, Kugler, and Larrabee, 1996). RAND assumed reinforcement levels somewhere between those of CBO and DOD, with an allocation of five troop divisions and ten fighter wings. RAND specified four options, which like those of the CBO study, built up a larger degree of NATO support.

The self-defense support option is the most modest and involves improvements in the entrants' C^3I, logistics, and military forces. The underlying defense strategy is to build up the Visegrad forces so that they can fend off a threat. A surface-to-air missile defense system is part of this option. Moreover, NATO's command structure would be modified to include linkages with the new members. Combat planes from the entrants would be refitted with communication systems linked to other NATO defense systems and planes. RAND estimated the cost of this option at $10–20 billion. The next two RAND options allow for NATO air-power projection and NATO ground and air-power projection, respectively, to the entrants during crises. Air power consists of five to ten fighter wings, stationed in Western Europe, for deployment when needed. This option was estimated to cost $20–30 billion, which included the $10–20 billion of self-support expense. If NATO prepares for both air and ground troop rapid-deployment capability, then the bill can run between $30–52 billion, depending on the number of troop divisions and fighter wings reconfigured and held in readiness. RAND estimated a cost of $42 billion if five ground divisions and ten fighter wings were assigned to the task.[17] The high-end figure of $52 billion is made up of $20 billion for self-defense, $10 billion for ten fighter wings, and $22 billion for

17. According to RAND, the $42 billion would be funded as follows: $13 billion by the entrants; $17 billion by a core group (i.e., the United States, the United Kingdom, France, and Germany); and $12 billion by other NATO allies (Asmus, Kugler, and Larrabee, 1996).

ten ground divisions. The most expensive RAND option involved the deployment of NATO air and ground forces on the soil of the new members. This so-called "forward-presence" option was calculated to cost between $55 billion and $110 billion, based on the number of fighter wings and ground divisions deployed forward. According to the RAND estimates, self-defense when coupled with the development and forward deployment of ten divisions and ten fighter wings would cost $110 billion. Much of this forward deployment is inconsistent with the understanding embodied in the Russia-NATO Partnership Pact and can be dismissed out of hand. At this time, there is no eastward threat that would warrant this kind of deployment.

The RAND estimates appear to suffer from many of the same problems as those of the DOD and CBO. There is, for example, no attempt to distinguish expenses associated with the modernization of Visegrad forces, which would occur anyway, from the *additional* modernization expenses tied to NATO membership per se. A similar problem involves attributing costs for developing rapid-reaction forces to the expense of an enlarged alliance. Surely, NATO's new strategic doctrine requires the enhancement of its mobile forces if the alliance is to fulfill the crisis-management tasks set out in the 1994 doctrine. And, as with the other expansion studies, the time frame for enlargement costs is not specified, so that these costs cannot be put into present value terms.

In order to indicate a more realistic estimate of expansion costs under RAND's $42 billion package, we made some educated adjustments to RAND's price tag. First, we deducted new members' contributions to self-defense of $8 billion, leaving $34 billion.[18] Next, we reduced the $25.6 billion figure for air and land power projection, since some of this projection expense must be met regardless of expansion under NATO's new strategic doctrine. We supposed that half of this latter expense was assigned to fulfilling this doctrine, so that expansion cost was only $21.2 billion for sixteen years, shared over sixteen allies, which represents a fairly modest average annual burden, particularly if these costs are discounted to present value terms. Surely, new expansion costs estimates will appear; it is our feeling that these new estimates will revise expansionary costs downward as nonexpansionary costs are deducted.

Overall evaluation

If the decision among alternatives is to be based on cost efficiency grounds, then these alternatives must contain the same benefits. However, two ex-

18. Figures in this paragraph come for Asmus, Kugler, and Larrabee, (1996, p. 24).

pansion options may, because of different assumed troop levels, produce diverse benefits, so that cost comparisons alone do not provide sufficient information to make informed judgments. Thus far, no study of NATO expansion has attempted to quantify these benefits. Each report mentions the benefits in very general terms without putting a value on them. That being the case, we must view the expansion costs, net of nonexpansion-related spending, as the *minimum benefits required to justify an expansion proposal.* Thus, the present value of the $21.2 billion calculated for RAND's proposal represents the smallest benefits required for the sixteen allies to warrant this expansion option. Current estimations of the impact of NATO expansion must also go further and distinguish costs tied to NATO enlargement from costs that would be incurred even if NATO membership remains unchanged, as illustrated earlier.

There are also relevant expansion costs that have been left out of current studies. Obvious instances are the costs associated with the thinning of forces, the risks of conflict, and decision-making efforts of consensus building. Much more work needs to be done if we are to evaluate the net gains from NATO expansion at either the alliance or the ally level. Given the sensitivity of these net benefits to the underlying assumptions, cost estimates to date may be far from the mark when the actual structure of the expanded alliance takes shape. The wide range of estimates for three exercises highlights the difficulty in determining these expansion costs with any precision.

POLICY IMPLICATIONS AND CONCLUDING REMARKS

Given the wide range of cost estimates and the absence of benefit calculations, there is no way of knowing whether or not NATO expansion is an appropriate policy from an economic standpoint. Since NATO is committed to go ahead with the first announced expansion, prudence would dictate that further enlargements should wait until analysts can better calibrate the net benefits from this first expansion. The benefit side should not be ignored when trying to determine whether expansion is "affordable" (see Asmus, Kugler, and Larrabee, 1996, pp. 25–6). There is, clearly, more to making the appropriate decision than merely ascertaining whether or not NATO allies and entrants can carry the costs. Why pay the costs if the benefits do not measure up? A related issue concerns the distribution of these benefits and costs among entrants given geographical considerations. For example, Poland will have to bear a relatively greater burden than other entrants, given Poland's large land area. NATO may have to consider differential subsidies among the entrants so that none is burdened too greatly. There is also the concern about who will pay any costs not covered by the entrants. Will these unpaid expenses be shared among all allies or will only some allies be saddled with them? Whoever covers any shortfall will affect how the proposed expansion will be viewed by member countries over time, and how future expansions will be viewed.

As NATO enlargement goes forward, NATO's degree of integration is apt to increase owing to a number of factors. First, the extent of defense common funding, which is an important measure of alliance integration (see Chapter 8), is anticipated to increase. Commonly funded infrastructure spending will increase greatly due to expansion. In fact, RAND predicted that the $42 billion option would double NATO's current infrastructure budget (Asmus, Kugler, and Larrabee, 1996, p. 23). Expansion-linked augmentation of NATO's civil and military structures will also raise common funding. Second, some decisions may have to be based on a less-than-unanimous decision rule if the alliance is to act decisively. Third, the push toward greater weapons standardization and interoperability may result in increased cooperation and hence greater integration. Finally, the development of CJTFs and other multilateral troop divisions will mean that allies will have to meld their forces into common force structures, thereby sacrificing autonomy over their own troops. This contribution of troops to a centralized authority or command is likely to create concern over a political backlash from either failed operations or a high casualty count. By changing the pattern of linkage costs and benefits, alliance expansion will affect the linkage form among the allies.

NATO expansion may also have significant implications for current and future arms-control agreements. If, say, NATO expansion puts the alliance over agreed-upon limits for some conventional forces, then the least effective weapons must be retired regardless of whether they are possessed by the entrant or an existing ally. Consequently, allies will have to cooperate in retiring weapons systems. Some weapon limits may need to be renegotiated in light of NATO expansion, and this opens up the possibility that Russia will use NATO expansion as an opportunity to argue for more favorable terms.

Given the difficulty to quantify costs and benefits, no study to date has really thrown enough light on NATO expansion. Clearly, NATO should be cautious about opening the flood gates to new members until more is known about expansion costs and benefits and how they compare. Much can be learned from the first set of entrants if future expansions are put off until the three entrants have been integrated into the alliance. Our analysis indicates that there are limits to NATO expansion when thinning and other expansion costs arise. Insofar as the initial set of designated entrants are probably the least costly to admit, future entrants must provide even greater alliancewide benefits to justify their inclusion. With nineteen allies, there is concern that unanimity may be too demanding a decision rule if NATO is to act decisively when the need arises. NATO's entire structure needs to be examined in light of the 1999 planned expansion.

4 NATO and peacekeeping

In recent years, peacekeeping missions have multiplied: from 1988 to 1992 there were more missions than during the first four decades of the United Nations. This pattern has continued with nineteen new operations initiated between 1 January 1993 and 13 February 1998. The nature of peacekeeping has drastically changed since the end of the Cold War with many new missions providing humanitarian aid, political transition assistance (e.g., training police, monitoring elections), or, in a few instances, peace enforcement. The cost of UN peacekeeping has increased dramatically in recent years: prior to 1989, the United Nations usually spent about $200 million per year on peacekeeping; after 1989, the peacekeeping cost was over $3 billion during a couple of years (Durch, 1993; Hill and Malik, 1996, p. 127).[1] These increases have created a financial crisis for the United Nations, which has put increased monetary and military demands on NATO allies. UN peacekeeping spending peaked in 1994 and 1995 at $3.5 billion and $3.2 billion, respectively. Peacekeeping expenditures then fell precipitously to $1.35 billion in 1996,[2] due in part to NATO's assuming the financial responsibilities for Bosnian peacekeeping and to the UN's limiting its adoption of ambitious

1. In a private communication from the UN Information Center, actual UN expenditures on peacekeeping were estimated by Sam David in millions of current year dollars as follows:

1975	101.8	1981	212.4	1987	180.4	1993	2,900
1976	134.6	1982	248.9	1988	205.5	1994	3,500
1977	120.5	1983	229.5	1989	568.5	1995	3,200
1978	213.9	1984	212.4	1990	388.9	1996	1,350
1979	221.9	1985	213.6	1991	421.3		
1980	190.0	1986	183.7	1992	1,676		

2. UN peacekeeping expenditures for 1997 are similar to the figure for 1996.

new missions. With NATO's strategic doctrine of peacekeeping and non-proliferation, NATO is developing highly mobile Combined Joint Task Forces (CJTFs) that can be dispatched to the world's trouble spots (see Chapters 2 and 6).

From 1976 to 1996, NATO allies' shares of *actual assessed payments* to UN peacekeeping operations have varied from 49.4 percent to 82.5 percent yearly, with an average annual value of about 70.6 percent. Thus, the NATO allies have assumed a relatively large share of UN peacekeeping financial burdens over the last two decades. These payments to support official UN peacekeeping activities underestimate NATO's full peacekeeping burden by excluding non-UN-financed operations, such as the Bosnian actions by the NATO Implementation Force (IFOR), which consisted of 72,245 troops, with the United States contributing 20,000 and the rest of NATO contributing 39,903, of which 14,000 were from the United Kingdom and 10,000 were from France (US Department of Defense, 1996, p. III-8). Since December 1996, the NATO Stabilization Force (SFOR) has been maintaining peace in Bosnia, financed by NATO allies and NATO aspirants. UN-assessed payments also exclude the billions contributed by the United States, Germany, the United Kingdom, and France to fighting the Gulf War of 1991 (see Department of Defense, 1992).[3] Another non-UN-financed operation was the US-led Operation Provide Comfort in northern Iraq in 1991 to assist the Kurds (Reed, Vaccaro, and Durch, 1995).

NATO is anticipated to continue to assume a sizable portion of UN and non-UN-financed peacekeeping burdens in the years to come. In fact, these burdens are anticipated to increase as the alliance expands. Unless the United Nations improves its intelligence, procurement practices, troop training, equipment, and logistics, the UN will have little choice but to rely on NATO forces to address large-scale peace-enforcement missions, such as Bosnia and Kuwait (Palin, 1995).[4] As NATO develops its mobile multilateral forces, it will be in a unique position to handle challenges to regional and out-of-area peace and stability. With the end to the Cold War, ethnic rivalries and hatreds, once held in check by strong central governments, have been unleashed in Central and Eastern Europe. In Africa, tribalism has created civil wars and instability that have led to human tragedies of immense

3. In financial terms, the largest contributors to the Gulf War were Saudi Arabia and Kuwait, which paid $16 billion apiece in cash and in-kind payments (US Department of Defense, 1992).
4. On UN peacekeeping and its inadequacies, see Fetherston (1994), Kolodziej and Kanet (1996), Mokhtari (1994), Ratner (1995) and Reed, Vaccaro, and Durch (1995); also see Latawski (1996) and Heidenrich (1994). Some improvements in UN infrastructure for these operations is being accomplished (Bobrow and Boyer, 1997).

proportions in Zaire, Rwanda, Somalia, and elsewhere. The current need for humanitarian assistance and peacekeeping is expected to continue into the foreseeable future.

The purpose of this chapter is to assess NATO's peacekeeping role in the past, present, and future. Since NATO's role is integrally connected to that of the United Nations, UN peacekeeping is also investigated and contrasted to that of NATO. A main purpose is to examine burden-sharing behavior for NATO peacekeeping during the last two decades.[5] In doing so, we are interested in discovering to what extent peacekeeping is either a pure public good or an impure public good. If the latter applies, then peacekeeping can be characterized as an activity that gives rise to both indivisible benefits for NATO allies and ally-specific benefits to the provider. Another purpose is to investigate how peacekeeping burden shares within NATO have changed since the end of the Cold War and the rapid expansion of peacekeeping activities. Finally, this chapter presents an outlook for the future of NATO peacekeeping efforts.

PEACEKEEPING AND PEACEMAKING

Peacekeeping involves military personnel used as monitors or observers (Cerjan, 1994). In this role, the observers watch whether or not the "rules of engagement," associated with a cease-fire, are being obeyed. Traditional peacekeeping personnel are lightly armed and powerless to do much if either opposing side chooses to resume hostilities. To fulfill their assignment, peacekeepers require the consent of the opposing sides. Peacemaking, by contrast, consists of actions to resolve a conflict or to bring about a cease-fire; these actions include negotiations, diplomacy, and arbitration. Finally, peace enforcement involves applying military force and other available means to end hostilities between warring sides, as the enforcement of the no-fly zone in Bosnia during 1993–95 attempted to do. Until recently, the United Nations and NATO have been involved with peacekeeping and peacemaking; but missions in Bosnia, Somalia, and Haiti are best characterized as peace enforcement. Even though these alternative terms for various peace-promoting activities can be distinguished, peacekeeping is often used in a generic sense, which we will do here unless a particular type of activity requires emphasis.

5. Recent studies on peacekeeping burden sharing include Bobrow and Boyer (1997), Khanna and Sandler (1997), and Khanna, Sandler, and Shimizu (1998).

Background: UN peacekeeping

Article 41 of the UN Charter provides the Security Council with means, not involving force, to preserve world peace (Hill and Malik, 1996). These means can include economic boycotts, severance of diplomatic relations, and disruption of communications. If force is required to maintain peace or resolve conflict, then Articles 42 and 43 assign the authority to the Security Council to take the necessary actions. Although the five permanent members of the Security Council have this mandate, incessant use of the veto severely limited this body's peacekeeping abilities during the 1946–86 period. The veto was exercised 242 times as follows: China, 22; France, 16; United Kingdom, 26; United States, 57; and USSR, 121 (Hill and Malik, 1996). Even though only a small portion of these 242 vetoes involved peacekeeping per se, the Security Council was nonetheless unable to fulfill its peacekeeping mission on some occasions.

In Table 4.1, official UN peacekeeping missions for 1947–97 are listed. Missions highlighted in italics were ongoing as of 13 February 1998. For each operation, we indicate its name, acronym, duration, purpose, and authorization. Authorizations beginning with an S refer to the Security Council, whereas those with an A refer to the General Assembly. The latter had to step in during some Cold War years when the superpowers exercised the veto. Some peacekeeping operations were completed quickly (e.g., UNOGIL in 1958 or DOMREP in 1965), while others lasted a long time (e.g., UNTSO for fifty years, UNFICYP for almost thirty-five years). In a few cases, the UN's first attempt to achieve its goal was not realized and the operation had to be later reinstated – for example, UNEF and UNAVEM.

UN-financed peacekeeping operations have evolved through four distinct phases (Hill and Malik, 1996; Ratner, 1995). First, there was the initial period, 1947–56, when there were four missions mostly of the monitoring type, with the exception of UNEF I in the Sinai, where UN peacekeepers created a buffer zone to separate Israeli and Egyptian forces.[6] This was a complex and risky operation of peacemaking, which eventually failed. Next, there was the active period, 1957–74, during which nine new missions were undertaken, mostly of the observer type. One mission stands out from the others: the failed attempt to end hostilities in the Congo – ONUC – which

6. In 1950, the Security Council authorized nations to take military enforcement actions against North Korea following its invasion of South Korea. Although the ensuing military operation was sanctioned by the United Nations, the operation was not under UN command and is not classified as an official UN peacekeeping operation (UN Department of Public Information, 1996, p. 6).

Table 4.1. *UN peacekeeping missions, 1947–97*

Operation	Duration	Purpose and authorization
UN Special Committee on the Balkans (UNSCOB)[a]	1947–52	Investigate foreign support of guerrillas in Greece. (A/RES/109)
UN Truce Supervision Organization (UNTSO)	1948 to date	Monitor cease-fire lines between Israel and neighbors. (S/RES/50)
UN Military Observer Group in India and Pakistan (UNMOGIP)	1949 to date	Monitor cease-fire in Kashmir. (S/RES/47)
UN Emergency Force I (UNEF I)	1956–67	Create a buffer between Israeli and Egyptian forces in the Sinai. (A/RES/998)
UN Observation Group in Lebanon (UNOGIL)	1958	Monitor military forces in Lebanon. (S/RES/128)
UN Operation in the Congo (ONUC)	1960–64	Aid the Congolese government in restoring order. (S/RES/143)
UN Security Force in West New Guinea (UNSF, also known as UNTEA)	1962–63	Administer West Irian prior to transfer of territory to Indonesia. (A/RES/1752)
UN Yemen Observation Mission (UNYOM)	1963–64	Monitor military forces into Yemen from Saudi Arabia. (S/RES/179)
UN Peacekeeping Force in Cyprus (UNFICYP)	1964 to date	Maintain order from March 1964 until 1974. Thereafter monitor buffer zone between Turkish and Greek partitions. (S/RES/186)
Mission of the Representative of the Secretary-General in the Dominican Republic (DOMREP)	1965	Observe cease-fire between opposing de facto authorities. (S/RES/203)
UN India-Pakistan Observation Mission (UNIPOM)	1965–66	Monitor cease-fire in the aftermath of the 1965 war. (S/RES/211)
UN Emergency Force II (UNEF II)	1973–79	Provide a buffer between Israeli and Egyptian forces in the Sinai. (S/RES/340)
UN Disengagement Observer Force (UNDOF)	1974 to date	Monitor the separation of Israeli and Syrian forces on the Golan Heights. (S/RES/350)
UN Interim Force in Lebanon (UNIFIL)	1978 to date	Provide a buffer between Israel and Lebanon. (S/RES/425)
UN Good Offices Mission in Afghanistan and Pakistan (UNGOMAP)	1988–90	Monitor Soviet troop withdrawal from Afghanistan. (S/19836 and S/RES/622)
UN Iran-Iraq Military Observer Group (UNIIMOG)	1988–91	Monitor cease-fire following Iran-Iraq War. (S/RES/598)
UN Angola Verification Mission I (UNAVEM I)	1989–91	Monitor Cuban troop withdrawal from Angola. (S/RES/626)

Table 4.1. *(cont.)*

Operation	Duration	Purpose and authorization
UN Transition Assistance Group (UNTAG) in Namibia	1989–90	Supervise transition from South African rule to independence. (S/RES/632)
UN Observer Group in Central America (ONUCA)	1989–92	Monitor compliance with Esquipulas II agreement and facilitate the demobilization of Nicaraguan Contras. (S/RES/644)
UN Iraq-Kuwait Observation Mission (UNIKOM)	1991 to date	Monitor buffer zone between Iraq and Kuwait following the Gulf War. (S/RES/689)
UN Angola Verification Mission II (UNAVEM II)	1991–95	Monitor the cease-fire, the creation of a new army, and the holding of elections. (S/RES/696)
UN Observer Mission in El Salvador (ONUSAL)	1991–95	Monitor the cease-fire, human rights, elections, and the demobilization and reintegration of forces. (S/RES/693)
UN Mission for the Referendum in Western Sahara (MINURSO)	1991 to date	Organize, conduct, and monitor referendum on independence from Morocco. (S/RES/690)
UN Advance Mission in Cambodia (UNAMIC)	1991–92	Advance planning for UNTAC. (S/RES/717)
UN Protection Force (UNPROFOR)	1992–95	Initially create conditions for peace by ensuring demilitarization of three zones in Croatia. Monitor cease-fire in Croatia and elsewhere in the former Yugoslavia. (S/RES/743)
UN Transitional Authority in Cambodia (UNTAC)	1992–93	Supervise elections, disarmament, and demobilization of forces. Ensure the repatriation of refugees. (S/RES/745)
UN Operation in Somalia I (UNOSOM I)	1992–93	Provide humanitarian relief operations; monitor cease-fire. (S/RES/751)
UN Operation in Mozambique (ONUMOZ)	1992–94	Monitor and verify demobilization and disarmament; verify withdrawal of foreign troops; assist in monitoring elections; coordinate humanitarian aid. (S/RES/797)
UN Operation in Somalia II (UNOSOM II)	1993–95	Maintain secure environment for humanitarian relief efforts. End hostilities and bring about reconciliation. First UN peace-enforcing mission. (S/RES/814)

Table 4.1. *(cont.)*

Operation	Duration	Purpose and authorization
UN Observer Mission Uganda/ Rwanda (UNOMUR)	1993–94	Monitor the border between Rwanda and Uganda; confirm end of military aid to Rwanda. (S/RES/846)
UN Observer Mission in Georgia (UNOMIG)	1993 to date	Monitor military forces in Georgia and Abkhazia. (S/RES/858)
UN Observer Mission in Liberia (UNOMIL)	1993–97	Monitor military forces in Liberia. (S/RES/866)
UN Mission in Haiti (UNMIH)	1993–96	Bring peace to Haiti. Reinstate elected president; train a police force; hold general elections. (S/RES/867)
UN Assistance Mission for Rwanda (UNAMIR)	1993–96	Monitor cease-fire and compliance with Arusha Peace Agreements; provide security for Kigali; monitor repatriation of refugees. (S/RES/872).
UN Aouzou Strip Observer Group (UNASOG)	1994	Monitor Aouzou Strip between Libya and Chad. Lasted under two months, May 94-June 94. (S/RES/915)
UN Mission of Observers in Tajikistan (UNMOT)	1994 to date	Monitor military forces in the civil war. (S/RES/968)
UN Angola Verification Mission III (UNAVEM III)	1995–97	Monitor the elections and the neutrality of the Angolan National Police. Help in the implementation of the Lusaka Protocol. (S/RES/976)
UN Confidence Restoration Operation in Croatia (UNCRO)	1995–96	An offshoot of UNPROFOR. Provide proper environment for a negotiated settlement in Croatia. (S/RES/981)
UN Preventive Deployment Force (UNPREDEP)	1995 to date	Prevent expansion of the conflict in Bosnia to Macedonia. (S/RES/983)
UN Mission in Bosnia and Herzegovina (UNMIBH)	1995 to date	Assist in the transition to peace. (S/RES/1035)
UN Transitional Administration for Eastern Slavonia, Baranja and Western Sirmium (UNTAES)	1996–98	Assist in maintaining peace; supervise the demilitarization; train police. (S/RES/1037)
UN Mission of Observers in Prevlaka (UNMOP)	1996 to date	Monitor the peace in Croatia. (S/RES/1038)

Table 4.1. *(cont.)*

Operation	Duration	Purpose and authorization
UN Support Mission in Haiti (UNSMIH)	1996–97	Assist in transition to democratic rule; train and monitor the new police force; monitor the elections. Ended July 1997. (S/RES/1063)
UN Verification Mission in Guatemala (MINUGUA)	1997	Verify implementation of the Comprehensive Agreement on Human Rights signed on 29 March 1994. (S/RES/1094) (A/RES/48/267)
UN Observer Mission in Angola (MONUA)	1997 to date	A follow-up to UNAVEM III. Intended to assist UNITA and the Angolan government to establish a lasting peace. Promote human rights, verify the integration of UNITA elements into the government, and provide offices for mediation. (S/RES/1118)
UN Transition Mission in Haiti (UNTMIH)	1997	A follow-up to UNSMIH to finish the transition process to democratic rule. Started on 30 July 1997 and ended in November 1997. (S/RES/1123)
UN Civilian Police Mission in Haiti (MIPONUH)	1997 to date	Successor of UNTMIH to professionalize the Haitian National Police as part of the transition process to democratic rule. (S/RES/1141)

Note: "to date" refers to 13 February 1998. Current missions are in italic.
[a]Not always considered an official UN peacekeeping mission.
Sources: Hill and Malik (1996) and Web page "Comprehensive List of UN Peacekeeping Operations," Center for International Relations, Swiss Federal Institute of Technology, Zurich, Switzerland, http://www.fib.ethz.ch/fib/pko/allops.html

resulted in the deaths of 250 peacekeepers and demonstrated that the United Nations would be ill-equipped for such missions unless it improved its peace-enforcing capabilities in terms of troops, weaponry, command, intelligence, and response time (Hill and Malik, 1996; Rikhye and Skjelsback, 1990; UN Department of Public Information, 1996). ONUC involved 20,000 peacekeepers with an unclear mandate; it remained the most ambitious official UN peacekeeping mission for many years. Next came a dormant period that lasted from 1975 to 1987, during which only the UNIFIL mission,

Table 4.2. *UN peacekeeping mission taxonomy*

Observing and monitoring:		
UNTSO (1948 on)	UNDOF (1974 on)	UNOMUR (1993–94)
UNMOGIP (1949 on)	UNGOMAP (1988–90)	UNOMIG (1993 on)
UNOGIL (1958)	UNIIMOG (1988–91)	UNOMIL (1993–97)
UNYOM (1963–64)	UNAVEM I (1989–91)	UNAMIR (1993–96)*
UNIPOM (1965–66)	UNPROFOR (1992–95)*	UNASOG (1994)
DOMREP (1965)	UNOSOM I(1992–93)*	UNMOT (1994 on)
UNFICYP (1974 on)*	ONUMOZ (1992–94)*	UNMOP (1996 on)
Buffer between forces:		
UNEF I(1956–67)	UNEF II (1973–79)	UNIKOM (1991 on)
UNFICYP (1964–74)*	UNIFIL (1978 on)	
Humanitarian:		
UNOSOM I (1992–93)*	ONUMOZ (1992–94)*	UNOSOM II (1993–95)*
Political help during transition:		
UNTEA (1962–63)	UNAMIC (1991–92)	UNMIBH (1995 on)
UNTAG (1989–90)	UNTAC (1992–93)	UNTAES (1996–98)
ONUCA (1989–92)	ONUMOZ (1992–94)*	UNSMIH (1996–97)
UNAVEM II (1991–95)	UNMIH (1993–96)	MINUGUA (1997)
ONUSAL (1991–95)	UNAMIR (1993–96)*	MONUA (1997 on)
MINURSO (1991–on)	UNAVEM III (1995–97)	UNTMIH (1997)
	UNCRO (1995–96)	MIPONUH (1997 on)
Peace enforcing:		
UNPROFOR (1992–95)*	UNOSOM II (1993–95)*	UNMIH (1993–96)*
Others:		
UNSCOB (1947–52)	ONUC (1960–64)*	UNPREDEP (1995 on)

*indicates that the mission is listed under more than one category.
Mission's names and descriptions are in Table 4.1.

designed to provide a buffer between Israeli forces and hostile elements in Lebanon, was begun. In the final period, from 1988 to the present, UN peacekeeping operations expanded greatly with thirty-three missions of varying complexity. There were also peace-enforcing operations, not indicated on Table 4.1, including Desert Shield/Desert Storm and IFOR in Bosnia, that were not funded by the United Nations.

Missions are categorized in Table 4.2 into six classes. Traditional peacekeeping operations, involving observing and monitoring cease-fires, are the most common ones, with twenty-one listed in the top cell. When peacekeeping troops provide a buffer between opposing forces, a more active role is being played by the peacemakers, inasmuch as neither side may yet be committed to ceasing hostilities. In this role, the UN troops must possess the requisite firepower to turn back either side or else they represent only a symbolic buffer that can be breached at any time. Humanitarian operations involve the use of peacekeeping troops to deliver and distribute food, clothing, and shelter to refugees, typically caught in a civil war. A fourth class of missions provides assistance in the form of training police, holding elections, rebuilding political institutions, or ensuring demilitarization during a transition to democracy. The logistically most complex and risky activities involve peace enforcement. In Table 4.2, missions that are difficult to categorize are characterized as "others." For example, ONUC involved sending peacekeeping troops to the Congo in the early 1960s to assist the government in restoring order.

Although UN missions since 1988 have included many traditional peacekeeping operations, a trend toward greater involvement and risk has characterized recent efforts. In Table 4.2, twenty missions concerned providing political assistance during transition; three involved humanitarian aid; and three consisted of peace-enforcing activities. This added complexity of recent operations will increase financial burdens; hence, these burdens will be higher than in earlier periods, because both the number of operations and their complexity have increased.

Financial arrangements

Until 1974, peacekeeping costs were covered by the UN regular budget, so that a member's peacekeeping burden corresponded to its assessed budget share. During the 1960s, the United Nations experienced a financial crisis owing to insufficient funds to cover its interventions in the Congo (ONUC) and Cyprus (UNFICYP). Bonds were issued to pay for ONUC, while a voluntary contribution fund was established to finance UNFICYP (Mills, 1990, p. 97). To create a more permanent funding source to cover the annual expense of peacekeeping, the General Assembly passed Resolution 1310 (11 December 1973), which established *assessment accounts* for peacekeeping missions. These accounts assigned each member a fixed share of the annual costs for each peacekeeping mission. After December 1973, such payments were in addition to the regular budget assessments for members.[7] A few missions were still supported by the regular budget. Under the new arrangements, members could protest a specific deployment by withholding

7. Regular budget assessments were based on a country's income, its membership (if applicable) in the Security Council, and its standing in the world community.

payment of their assigned costs for that operation, while still meeting regular budget and other assessment account charges. Such actions, when exercised, were in violation of UN rules.

Insofar as nations did refuse, at times, to support one or more peacekeeping operations, the shortfall had to be made up either from the regular budget or from voluntary contributions, which a few nations made on occasion. These voluntary contributions went into a special account. With respect to the assessment accounts for peacekeeping, members are required to pay their assessments within thirty days of receiving a statement of their obligations from the secretary general. Once a UN member is in arrears for its assessed amounts for the two full preceding years, Article 19 of the UN Charter provides that it can lose its voting privilege in the General Assembly (Mills, 1990, pp. 92–3). For a Security Council member, the General Assembly vote is not nearly as important as its Security Council vote, with which it can singlehandedly block an action. Notably, Article 19 does not threaten this latter voting privilege. Many UN nations, including the United States in the latter 1980s, have been in arrears with respect to their assessed payments for peacekeeping. Given the insignificance of one vote in the General Assembly, the sanction of Article 19, used on occasion, is not much of a deterrent.[8]

Four classes of nations are distinguished by the assessment account. These include: the five permanent members of the Security Council (A); twenty-two developed countries, not permanent members of the Council (B); wealthy developing countries (C); and specifically identified less-developed countries (D).[9] The bulk of peacekeeping is financed by the nations in groups A and B, with permanent members of the Security Council paying over 63% and developed countries in group B paying almost 35% (Mills, 1990, p. 101). This leaves a mere 2% to be picked up by all of the countries in groups C and D. Group A countries pay about 22% more than

8. According to the Office of the Spokesman for the Secretary General of the United Nations, peacekeeping payments in arrears (in millions of US dollars) amounted to:

1975	19.2	1981	214.0	1987	363.0	1993	992.8
1976	34.3	1982	208.4	1988	355.2	1994	1,286.4
1977	49.0	1983	291.6	1989	444.2	1995	1,723.9
1978	132.2	1984	323.5	1990	346.2	1996	1,633.0
1979	134.6	1985	262.1	1991	357.8	1997	1,574.1
1980	260.8	1986	312.3	1992	664.3		

These figures may be found on the worldwide web at www.globalpolicy.org/finance/tables/pkoarr.htm.

9. Financial arrangements for UN peacekeeping are discussed in Durch (1993), Mills (1990), Rikhye (1990), and UN Department of Public Information (1996). Durch (1993, pp. 55–8) contains a list of the countries' assessed peacekeeping shares.

their regular budget assessment scale to peacekeeping, while group B nations pay their regular budget assessment scale. Group C countries pay just one-fifth of their regular budget assessment scale, and group D countries pay a mere one-tenth of their regular budget assessments (Durch, 1993, p. 46). Assessed peacekeeping burdens are intended to be disproportionate in terms of income. Although assessed percentages changed slightly in 1991 and at other times (Durch, 1993, pp. 45–58), the overall burden-sharing picture has remained essentially unchanged: just over thirty countries pay about 98 percent of peacekeeping expenses.

Assessed payments for peacekeeping must be distinguished from actual payments, because nations do not always satisfy their obligations. Although assessed shares vary infrequently, actual shares paid vary greatly over time. To analyze financial burden sharing for UN peacekeeping, we must gather data on *actual* payments each year, using data provided in the *UN Status of Contributions as at 31 December 19_,* which is published annually.[10] These amounts are reported and analyzed for the NATO countries later in this chapter.

Another crucial distinction involves troop versus money contributors to peacekeeping. Troop contributors are reimbursed at a flat rate of about $1,000 per month for each soldier, regardless of rank (Durch, 1993, pp. 39–40). Countries providing well-trained troops do not come close to recovering their opportunity costs, which can run upwards of $4,500 per month; while those sending poorly trained troops may receive 3.5 times their opportunity costs (Durch, 1993, p. 50). Thus, it is not surprising that countries such as India, Pakistan, and Bangladesh were among the largest troop contributors in recent years (see the UN web page at www.un.org/Depts/dpko/troop/troop.htm). During 1994, the ten largest troop contributors were, in descending order, as follows: Pakistan, France, India, Bangladesh, the United Kingdom, Jordan, Malaysia, Canada, Egypt, and Poland (Reed, Vaccaro, and Durch, 1995, Figure A-1, p. A-9). From January to April 1997, the top ten troop providers were Pakistan, India, Russia, Bangladesh, Jordan, Poland, Canada, Brazil, Finland, and Austria (www.globalpolicy.org/security/peacekpg/pkotrp97.htm).[11] For the United States and other developed

10. Bobrow and Boyer (1997) use assessed, not paid, shares of GDP devoted to peacekeeping to analyze burden sharing. Owing to this different measure, some of their results differ greatly from the ones reported in this chapter. Since peacekeeping assessment scales change little and infrequently over time, any alteration in Bobrow and Boyer's assessment shares of GDP is likely due to fluctuations in GDP rather than a deliberate choice of peacekeeping efforts. Thus, we prefer GDP shares based on actual payments.

11. From January to April 1998, the top ten troop providers were Poland, Bangladesh, Austria, Ghana, Ireland, Norway, Argentina, Nepal, Fiji, and the United States (www.globalpolicy.org/security/peacekpg/pkotrp98.htm.)

countries, unreimbursed opportunity costs for troop contributions represent yet another peacekeeping burden not captured by actual payments.

Ideally, to measure *all* peacekeeping burdens, we would have to translate troop burdens, whether negative or positive, into nominal value and add them to peacekeeping payments. This adjustment to our peacekeeping measure cannot be calculated, since troop figures are only available for a few recent years. Moreover, we would have to know every sample country's cost per troop for each year during 1976–96. The difference between this figure, summed over a country's UN peacekeeping troops, and the actual UN reimbursement (when received) represents the additional annual financial burden of supplying troops. Insofar as the requisite data are currently unavailable, we must necessarily focus on financial or paid burden sharing and caution the reader that the whole burden-sharing story is not being revealed. If this fuller story could be told, we speculate that the disproportionality of burdens displayed later might be increased, because many rich troop-contributing countries receive from the United Nations only a fraction of what they pay their soldiers when on a UN peacekeeping operation.

PEACEKEEPING AS A PUBLIC GOOD

There are two alternative collective action–based theories that can be applied to explain peacekeeping burden-sharing behavior.[12] The simplest theory characterizes peacekeeping as providing a purely public good in the form of world peace, which benefits all nations. According to this theory, the peace and stability achieved through peacekeeping activities produce nonexcludable and nonrival benefits to all nations. By improving the well-being of those in need, humanitarian aid similarly yields nonexcludable and nonrival benefits for the world community. Nonexcludability of benefits gives rise to free riding, in which nations rely on the peacekeeping payments of others by withholding some or all of their assessed charges, with shortfalls being covered when possible by the regular UN budget. Why pay for a good, whose benefits can be received practically free? Free riding releases scarce resources that can be used for other things.

Three important predictions derive from this theory. First, rich nations are anticipated to shoulder a disproportionate burden of peacekeeping for

12. Alternative theories of collective action are surveyed by Hardin (1982), Olson (1965), and Sandler (1992).

the poor nations in terms of the share of GDP devoted to peacekeeping.[13] This is the so-called *exploitation hypothesis.* Second, peacekeeping reimbursements, whether mandated or otherwise, will be suboptimal, because a contributor will not account for the "spillover" benefits that their contributions confer on others. Presumably, the United Nations can partly make up for this shortfall-induced suboptimality by redirecting money from the regular UN budget, but at the cost of alternative activities. Third, free riding and suboptimality will worsen as the size of the group supporting peacekeeping increases.

An alternative, more general theory is the joint product explanation of peacekeeping, whereby these activities are characterized as yielding both purely public benefits for the world community and contributor-specific benefits. These latter benefits may arise from *status enhancement,* being recognized as a major promoter of world peace (Kammler, 1997; Khanna and Sandler, 1997). If a contributor is near the region of instability where peacekeeping forces are deployed, then nation-specific benefits may stem from the reduced risk that the conflict will spread to them. Certainly, Bosnia posed these risks to NATO allies near the Balkans. Additionally, nation-specific benefits may derive from the political value of doing more than one's fair share for peacekeeping. Given the relative magnitudes involved in defense spending and peacekeeping, this overcontribution to peacekeeping might be expedient. In 1994, European NATO allies devoted about 2.5 percent of GDP on average to defense (NATO Office of Information and Press, 1995, p. 358). A contribution as small as 0.0002 percent of GDP would allow a NATO ally a claim to carry the largest peacekeeping burden in terms of GDP (see Khanna and Sandler, 1997, Table 4, p. 115). Thus, an ally can argue that its exemplary behavior with respect to peacekeeping offsets or makes up for its parsimonious spending on defense. Even if this argument does not carry weight with other NATO allies, it may be politically expedient within the country. Nation-specific benefits may also be derived from providing humanitarian aid if the donor nation uses its efforts to gain favorable world opinion or if the donor's citizens take pleasure in their nation's altruism. Additional nation-specific benefits may derive from arms sales such as followed the Gulf War or from increased trade stemming from enhanced regional security.

The joint-product representation of peacekeeping leads to collective

13. These predictions are shown for defense as a pure public good by Olson and Zeckhauser (1966) and Sandler (1977, 1993).

action implications that differ from those of the pure public good scenario. For example, disproportionate burden shares need not result, so that peacekeeping burdens do not have to be correlated with an income measure. If a poorer ally receives a large amount of nation-specific benefits, such as status enhancement, from its peacekeeping, then it may carry a relatively heavy peacekeeping burden – for example, Norway. Furthermore, suboptimality will be attenuated as the share of nation-specific benefits increases. If, for example, all derived benefits are nation-specific, then an efficient allocation may ensue since benefits should match costs at the margin. Additionally, increases in the size of the group supporting peacekeeping need not affect either free riding or suboptimality if there is a significant portion of ally-specific benefits associated with peacekeeping.

NATO PEACEKEEPING BURDEN SHARING: 1976–96

To investigate burden sharing with respect to peacekeeping, we must devise an appropriate burden measure. The actual payments to peacekeeping by themselves would not be a proper measure, since such expenditures do not really capture the hardship or burden imposed. This follows because the nation's GDP or ability to pay has not been taken into account. Following the literature on defense burden sharing, we use actual peacekeeping spending (PK) as a share of GDP – that is, PK/GDP. Alternative burden-sharing measures will be discussed later.

In Table 4.3, each NATO ally's actual peacekeeping payments to the United Nations are displayed for every year starting in 1996 and going back in time to 1989. These data are taken from the annual United Nations (1990–97) *Status of Contributions* by adding each ally's actual payments toward its assessment account for all active missions in a given year. To this total annual payment, we added the actual voluntary payment made in a given year for the UNFICYP operation, which is solely funded by voluntary contributions.[14] For each country, expenditure figures are given in millions of current year US dollars, rounded to the nearest $100,000. Table 4.4 also displays these actual peacekeeping payments by NATO allies for even years during the earlier 1976–88 period.

A number of interesting features can be inferred from Tables 4.3 and 4.4.

14. Voluntary contributions to UNFICYP are taken from United Nations (various years), *Financial Report and Audited Financial Statements for the Biennium Ended 31 December 19_ and Report of the Board of Auditors.*

Table 4.3. *NATO allies actual peacekeeping payments to the United Nations, 1989–96* (in millions of current year US dollars)*[a]

	1996	1995	1994	1993	1992	1991	1990	1989
Belgium	25.5	21.6	36.8	22.7	16.9	3.6	3.3	8.6
Canada	39.3	97.2	99.4	81.5	47.7	14.8	9.3	21.1
Denmark	9.1	22.1	20.6	17.8	9.3	3.4	2.0	5.1
France	110.0	317.1	159.0	205.4	114.6	33.4	22.8	50.3
Germany[b]	124.3	285.0	275.2	247.1	131.0	46.5	26.7	59.5
Greece	1.4	2.4	2.1	2.4	2.1	1.1	1.4	1.2
Iceland	0.4	0.7	0.8	1.1	0.2	0.1	0.1	0.2
Italy	61.4	144.6	147.0	131.8	37.1	16.7	9.6	27.7
Luxembourg	0.9	2.2	1.9	1.7	0.9	0.3	0.2	0.4
Netherlands	19.9	50.3	46.1	39.3	23.1	7.9	4.4	11.8
Norway	6.8	17.4	18.6	13.8	8.9	3.2	2.1	4.5
Portugal	1.7	1.9	1.5	1.0	0.4	0.1	0.1	0.2
Spain	46.4	69.8	83.3	29.2	14.2	7.6	2.8	2.9
Turkey	3.4	0.8	0.5	0.8	0.4	0.2	0.1	0.5
UK	89.3	207.2	194.7	175.2	93.5	34.3	18.1	43.1
US	278.1	407.4	991.7	732.8	542.7	153.1	87.1	174.7
NATO total	815.7	1647.7	2079.2	1703.5	1043.2	326.2	190.0	412.1
UN Total[c]	1338.6	2738.6	2920.6	2306.4	1274.6	450.8	384.9	650.9
NATO percent of UN Total	*60.9*	*60.2*	*71.2*	*73.9*	*81.8*	*72.4*	*49.4*	*63.3*

*Includes actual yearly payments on assessed contributions to special peacekeeping accounts and actual voluntary payments to UNFICYP.
[a]Figures are rounded to nearest $100,000.
[b]Unified Germany 1990–96, Federal Republic of Germany in 1989 and before.
[c]Actual payments received, not cost of peacekeeping. Totals may not add owing to rounding.
Sources: United Nations (1990–97), *Status of Contributions as at 31 December 19__*, and authors' calculations. Voluntary payments for UNFICYP are from United Nations (various years), *Financial Report and Audited Financial Statements for the Biennium ended 31 December 19__ and Report of the Board of Auditors.* Two-year payments are divided equally between the two years.

NATO's share of UN total contributions ranged from a low of 49.4 percent in 1990, when the United States was in arrears, to a high of 82.5 percent in 1980. In Tables 4.3 and 4.4, NATO shares are in italics in the bottom row. These shares display a good deal of variability since changes in the payment behavior of the United States, France, Germany, or the United Kingdom can have a large impact. During the 1980s and early 1990s, the United States often withheld part of its assessment. NATO's aggregate paid share fell to about 60 percent of UN totals in 1995 and 1996. These tables also show the precipitous rise in peacekeeping expense in 1989, followed by the peak in

Table 4.4. *NATO allies actual peacekeeping payments to the United Nations, Selected Years 1976–88* (in millions of current year US dollars)*[a]

	1988	1986	1984	1982	1980	1978	1976
Belgium	2.59	2.74	2.96	1.28	2.95	2.03	0.06
Canada	6.04	6.14	5.34	6.92	7.55	4.41	3.50
Denmark	1.41	1.57	1.42	1.68	1.40	1.38	0.99
France	16.08	17.99	13.74	10.19	11.28	5.71	8.38
German, FR[b]	16.47	18.08	15.66	18.47	13.94	16.16	6.44
Greece	1.18	0.77	0.94	0.96	0.88	0.86	0.87
Iceland	0.07	0.07	0.06	0.07	0.06	0.02	0.03
Italy	10.46	6.03	4.24	8.26	8.06	5.40	5.91
Luxembourg	0.12	0.11	0.11	0.11	0.10	0.09	0.05
Netherlands	3.44	3.81	3.63	2.95	2.94	3.01	1.69
Norway	1.68	1.84	1.22	1.66	1.59	1.33	1.10
Portugal	0.11	0.00	0.12	0.06	0.04	0.07	0.09
Spain[b]	0.77	0.80	0.95	0.54	—	—	—
Turkey	0.12	0.14	0.11	0.18	0.02	0.04	0.08
UK	15.43	12.78	12.51	14.10	11.64	7.95	10.05
US	38.12	40.05	60.19	75.34	64.87	49.39	43.85
NATO Total	114.08	112.93	123.21	142.80	128.44	97.84	83.10
UN Total	206.65	169.23	155.54	182.24	155.68	129.05	113.17
NATO Percent of UN Total	*55.2*	*66.7*	*79.2*	*78.4*	*82.5*	*75.8*	*73.4*

*Includes actual yearly payments on assessed contributions to special peacekeeping accounts and actual voluntary payments to UNFICYP.
[a]Figures are rounded to nearest $10,000.
[b]German, FR denotes West Germany; Spain was not part of NATO before 1982.
[c]Actual payments received, not cost of peacekeeping. Totals may not add owing to rounding.
Sources: United Nations (1977–89), *Status of Contributions as at 31 December 19_,* and authors' calculations. Voluntary payments received for UNFICYP are from United Nations (various years), *Financial Report and Audited Financial Statements for the Biennium Ended 31 December 19_ and Report of the Board of Auditors.*

1994. Because UN collections are less than the actual outlays for peacekeeping (see footnotes 1 and 8), the true rise in such spending is somewhat higher than shown. The difference between UN peacekeeping expenditures and actual payments to the assessment accounts is made up by membership dues in the UN regular budget. Another noteworthy feature is the variability of the actual payments made by the individual allies; allies have a difficult time anticipating what their peacekeeping liabilities will be each year, since these vary according to exigencies.

We also require data on GDP to derive the peacekeeping burden measure of PK/GDP. Data for GDP at market prices in current US dollars are taken from the 1995 World Bank CD-ROM for the 1976–93 period. For 1994 and 1995, we drew data for this GDP measure from the International Monetary Fund (IMF) (1996, 1997). The IMF *International Financial Statistics* data were virtually identical to those of the World Bank for years prior to 1994; hence, we were confident that using a different data source for recent years would not bias our findings. The GDP figures for unified Germany for 1990 are taken from the UN (1996) *Statistical Yearbook 1994* and agree in size with figures for the early 1990s taken from the World Bank CD-ROM for unified Germany.[15] In 1995, missing values for Luxembourg and Portugal were filled in by computing a growth rate for 1991–94 and then applying this rate to the GDP in 1994. We estimated the 1994 GDP figure for Turkey, since IMF's (1996) GDP for that year did not correspond well to the World Bank GDP in 1993. For Turkey only, we used the growth of GDP between 1990 and 1992 to estimate GDP in 1994, 1995, and 1996. The 1991–94 growth rate was applied to 1995 GDP values to estimate 1996 GDP for all NATO allies except Turkey.

To test for the pure publicness of peacekeeping, we examined the correlation between peacekeeping burdens and GDP. This correlation will indicate whether or not the large allies are paying a disproportionate share of their income on peacekeeping (Khanna and Sandler, 1996; Olson and Zeckhauser, 1966; Sandler and Forbes, 1980). We used a Spearman rank-correlation test to ascertain if economic size (as measured by GDP) is rank correlated with peacekeeping burdens (as measured by PK/GDP).[16] The underlying alternative (H_1) and null (H_0) hypotheses are:

$$H_1: r_s \neq 0,$$
$$H_0: r_s = 0,$$

where r_s is the population's rank correlation between GDP and peacekeeping burdens. The higher the absolute value of the rank-correlation, the greater the association between GDP and peacekeeping burdens as a share of GDP. The pure public good scenario of peacekeeping is predicted to be

15. The World Bank CD-ROM contained only the GDP figure for West Germany for 1990. Peacekeeping expenditures reported in the UN budget for 1990 are for unified Germany; hence we had to get a comparable GDP figure.
16. In Khanna, Sandler, and Shimizu (1998), Kendall rank-correlation tests are performed for a NATO sample and larger samples of UN members. The clearest results applied to the NATO sample. More sophisticated nonparametric tests confirmed the findings of the less sophisticated Spearman rank-correlation test.

Table 4.5. *NATO GDP and PK/GDP ranks for four selected years*

	1980		1985		1992		1994	
Country	GDP rank	PK/ GDP rank	GDP rank	PK/ GDP rank	GDP rank	PK/ GDP rank	GDP rank	PK/ GDP rank
Belgium	8	3	9	2	9	6	9	4
Canada	6	1	6	11	7	4	6	2
Denmark	9	7	11	6	11	10	10	9
France	3	13	3	13	3	3	3	12
Germany[a]	2	11	2	4	2	9	2	6
Greece	12	5	13	3	14	13	13	14
Iceland	15	10	16	9	16	11	16	11
Italy	5	9	5	10	4	12	5	7
Luxembourg	14	8	15	1	15	8	15	13
Netherlands	7	12	8	8	8	7	8	10
Norway	10	2	10	7	12	5	12	5
Portugal	13	14	14	15	13	15	14	15
Spain	NA	NA	7	14	6	14	7	3
Turkey	11	15	12	16	10	16	11	16
UK	4	6	4	5	5	2	4	1
US	1	4	1	12	1	1	1	8

[a]West Germany in 1980 and 1985; unified Germany in 1992 and 1994.
NA denotes not applicable; since Spain was not a member of NATO in 1980.

associated with disproportionate burden sharing, in which the rich allies allocate a larger percentage of their income to peacekeeping – that is, r_s is positive and significant. If, however, the joint product scenario applies, then burdens are shared in closer agreement with benefits received, which may be less correlated with GDP. In this latter case, r_s does not necessarily have to be positive and significant.

In Table 4.5, NATO allies' GDP ranks and PK/GDP ranks are displayed for four representative years: 1980, 1985, 1992, and 1994. The highest rank is assigned a value of 1, while the lowest rank is assigned a value of 16. A glance at the relative ranks for the years displayed suggests that there is greater agreement between an ally's income and its peacekeeping burden for sample years in the 1990s than for those in the 1980s. Exploitation, while absent in the 1980s, appears to be present to some extent in the 1990s. For a test of this hypothesis, the Spearman rank correlation, r_s, between GDP and peacekeeping burdens was computed for each year from 1976 to 1996.

Three distinct periods characterize the results for r_s, reported in Table 4.6. In the 1970s, there was some positive rank correlation, but r_s is insignifi-

Table 4.6. *Spearman rank correlation between GDP and the share of GDP devoted to peacekeeping: NATO, 1976–96 (z-value in parentheses)*

Year	r_s	Year	r_s
1976	0.250 (0.94)	1987	0.126 (0.49)
1977	0.254 (0.95)	1988	–0.038 (0.15)
1978	0.139 (0.52)	1989	0.079 (0.31)
1979	0.339 (1.27)	1990	0.097 (0.38)
1980	0.143 (0.54)	1991	0.324 (1.26)
1981	0.021 (0.08)	1992	0.456 (1.77)*
1982	0.009 (0.03)	1993	0.106 (0.41)
1983	0.115 (0.45)	1994	0.500 (1.93)*
1984	0.003 (0.01)	1995	0.462 (1.79)*
1985	–0.132 (0.51)	1996	0.341 (1.32)
1986	0.147 (0.57)		

*Significant at the .10 level.

cant throughout, so that we were unable to reject the null hypothesis, H_0, and concluded that any disproportionality or exploitation is very weak. Throughout the 1980s there is little, if any, rank correlation. We were again unable to reject H_0; given the small correlations, we concluded that there is no disproportionality in this period. Following the end of the Cold War and the expansion in peacekeeping operations in the 1990s, a larger positive correlation begins to appear after 1991. This rank correlation is significant at the .10 level for 1992, 1994, and 1995. During these years, we were able to reject the null hypothesis at the .10 level and must accept the alternative hypothesis of positive correlation. Thus there is evidence of disproportionality surfacing for the first time with respect to peacekeeping burden sharing, in keeping with greater pure publicness of peacekeeping operations in the 1990s.

In Figure 4.1, the rank correlations for 1976–96 are displayed. The solid horizontal line at a critical r_s of 0.423 indicates the .10 level of significance, while the dashed line at a critical r_s of 0.506 denotes the .05 level of significance. Starting from the time in 1988 when UN peacekeeping budgets rose, the positive rank correlation increased along with the budgets through 1992. The rank correlation dropped in 1993, but then rose again in 1994, the peak spending year, and stayed significant during 1994 and 1995. As UN peacekeeping spending fell by more than 50 percent in 1996, the correlation dropped and became insignificant again. This behavior suggests that *the exploitation of the large by the small is tied to the size of the peacekeeping effort:* large budgets tend to be associated with disproportionate burden sharing with respect to GDP. The sole exception is 1993, when the two smallest allies, Iceland and Luxembourg, assumed high peacekeeping burden ranks of 2 and 5, respectively, owing to large drops in their GDP. Furthermore, the high growth of US GDP in that year, relative to other allies, gave it a low peacekeeping burden. Thus, 1993 was quite unusual because of some recessionary influences.

These results support the joint product model as characterizing peacekeeping until 1991. Apparently, ally-specific benefits motivated contributors, so that an ally's size was not a primary determinant of peacekeeping burdens during the 1976–90 period. For some of the 1990s, economic size is a determinant, consistent with an increased importance of the share of purely public benefits. This finding has important policy implications for the future, since this trend towards heightened peacekeeping activities and nonproliferation efforts is expected to continue.[17] If this prediction holds true, and if, moreover, spending on these activities also rises, then the large allies will be shouldering disproportionately large burdens for the small. Furthermore, the normative implications are unfavorable, since suboptimality is expected to worsen. Of course, an offset to the efficiency consequence of exploitation is the distributional outcome; such exploitation engineers a redistribution of income from the rich to the poor. This redistribution may have normative merits.

Other considerations

Of necessity, our data were drawn from UN peacekeeping payments as reported in the UN budget. NATO has, however, financed UN-sanctioned

17. This predicted increase in peacekeeping expenditures will include UN *and* NATO efforts. NATO is likely to take on more activities of this kind, so that the UN peacekeeping budgets may not return to the $3 billion mark for some years to come.

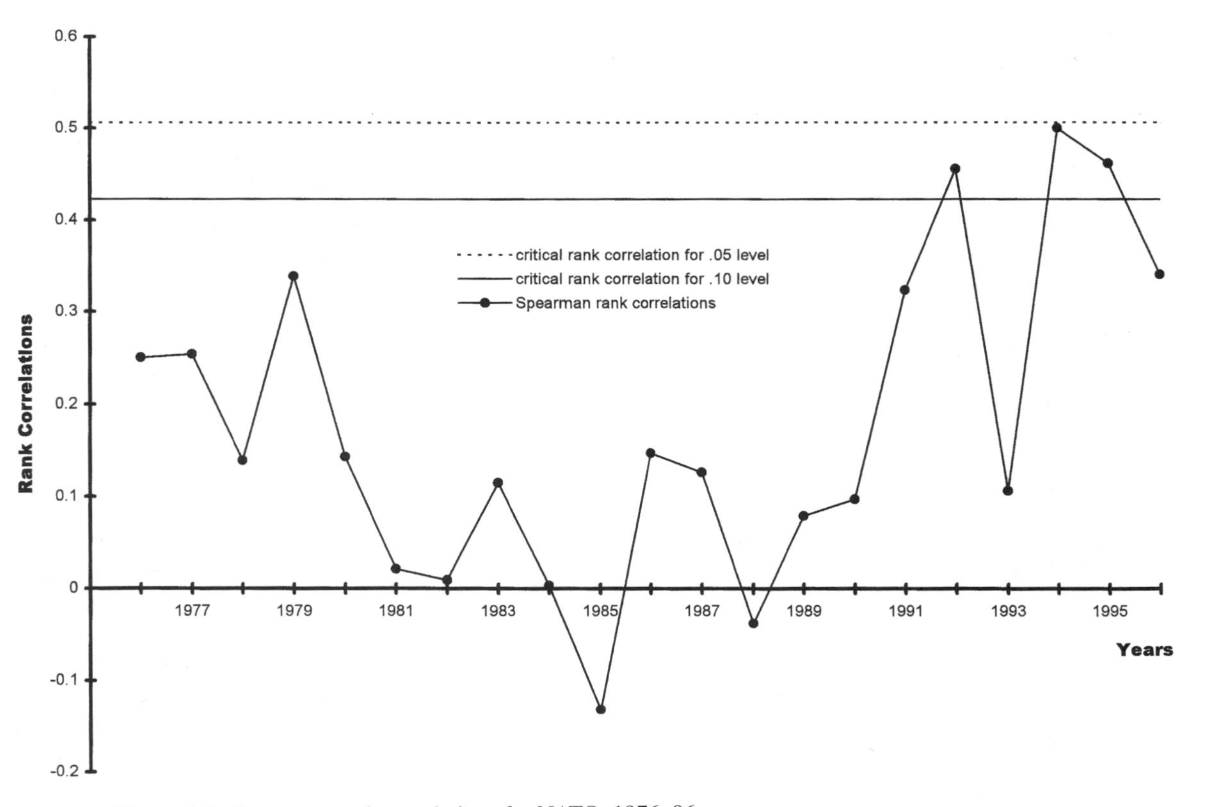

Figure 4.1. Spearman rank correlations for NATO, 1976–96

peacekeeping operations in the 1990s, including Deny Flight (April 1993 to December 1995), Operation Provide Comfort (1991), and the IFOR and SFOR operations in Bosnia. These operations were not financed through the United Nations. IFOR consisted of over 70,000 troops, with the major NATO allies providing troops as follows: the United States, 20,000; the United Kingdom, 14,000; France, 10,000, and Germany, 5,000 (US Department of Defense, 1996, pp. III-17–III-19). Much of the spending burden for IFOR and SFOR fell on these large allies (US Department of Defense, 1996, Table A29). If we could get an annual per-ally breakdown of non-UN-financed peacekeeping spending, analogous to the data used here, and add these expenditures to the ones reported in Table 4.3, then an even stronger indication of disproportionate burden sharing would result. As an attempt to confirm this conjecture, we shall make some informed adjustments to the peacekeeping data and then compute the Spearman rank correlations between GDP and PK/GDP for the 1990s during the era when non-UN-financed peacekeeping missions were important.

For 1990–91, we accounted for the additional costs of the Gulf War for NATO allies. Germany paid $955 million toward the expense of Desert Shield in 1990, while it paid $5.5 billion towards the cost of Desert Storm in 1991 (US Department of Defense, 1992, pp. P-5, P-6). The remainder of the $61 billion expense for these operations came from the United States ($8 billion), Japan ($8.3 billion), Saudi Arabia ($16 billion), and Kuwait ($16 billion) (US Department of Defense, 1992). France and the United Kingdom contributed troops and equipment to the coalition in the Gulf. To adjust for the Gulf War effort, we added German and US contributions for the Gulf to their respective UN peacekeeping payments. For 1990–91 this adjustment gave the United States a rank of 1 for PK/GDP and Germany a rank of 2. We then assigned a peacekeeping rank of 3 to the United Kingdom and a rank of 4 to France, based on their troop contributions and UN peacekeeping burdens. The remaining allies were then re-ranked from 5 to 16 based on their UN peacekeeping burdens.

For 1992–96, we had less detailed evidence on the precise spending efforts in Bosnia on non-UN-financed peacekeeping operations. The four largest NATO allies were involved in these operations to a heavy extent. To adjust roughly for this involvement, we assigned ranks according to their troop contributions, so that the United States received a rank of 1, the United Kingdom a 2, France a 3, and Germany a 4 for these years for aggregate peacekeeping efforts. The remaining NATO allies were again re-ranked from 5 to 16 according to their UN peacekeeping burdens.

Once these adjustments were made, we found the following adjusted Spearman rank correlations for NATO (with z-values in parentheses):

1990	0.476 (1.84)	1994	0.832 (3.22)
1991	0.479 (1.86)	1995	0.821 (3.18)
1992	0.576 (2.23)	1996	0.779 (3.02)
1993	0.509 (1.97)		

For five of the seven years, these rank correlations are significant at the .05 level or better, and the remaining two are significant at the .10 level. In Figure 4.2, we display the adjusted Spearman rank correlations as the dashed portion of earlier-drawn time series. The evidence is quite convincing that peacekeeping burden sharing displayed exploitative behavior in the 1990s, consistent with free riding by the poor on the rich. If UN and NATO peacekeeping spending continues to grow as anticipated, this exploitation will worsen in the years to come.

Even this adjustment to the data does not go far enough, since the four largest allies are also spending greatly on transport to improve their power projection capabilities (see Chapter 6). Power projection is needed to support out-of-area peacekeeping and peace-enforcing missions, so that some of this transport investment should be added to UN peacekeeping spending if a more accurate spending measure is to be devised. Insofar as only the largest NATO allies are investing in power projection, this adjustment would add still further support to the disproportionate burden sharing trend uncovered.

Other measures of burden sharing

Earlier we argued that peacekeeping spending would not by itself provide an adequate measure of peacekeeping burdens, because the relative hardship of this spending is not taken into account. To demonstrate how this burden-sharing measure might be quite misleading, we went ahead and found the associated Spearman rank correlations for all years during 1976–96.[18] Not surprisingly, the measure was 0.841 (with a z-value of 3.67) or higher for every year. Virtually every value was 0.920 or above, indicating almost perfect correlation between ranks. This correlation was high throughout the entire period with no discernible trend. Since peacekeeping assessments were based primarily on GDP rankings, a strong correlation must follow

18. These correlations are available upon request from Sandler.

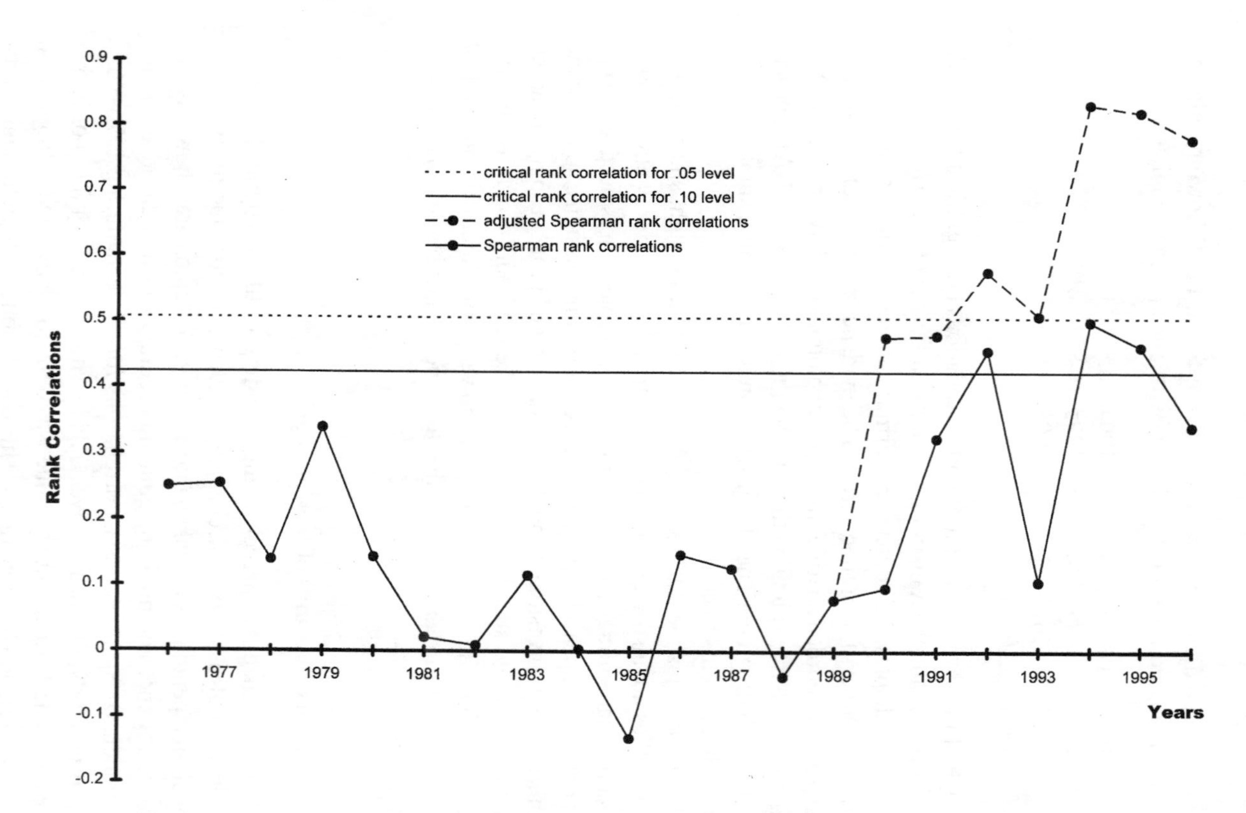

Figure 4.2. Adjusted Spearman rank correlations for NATO, 1976–96

and did.[19] Most important, this correlation did not really tell us whether or not the smaller nations were assuming a greater or lesser *burden* in terms of spending abilities.

Yet another burden-sharing measure is peacekeeping per capita. Data on population for 1976–94 came from the 1995 World Bank CD-ROM. For West Germany, we drew data from IMF (1996), since the former source did not break down the population of West and East Germany prior to 1990. Population figures for NATO allies showed virtually no difference between IMF (1996) and World Bank (1995). To get population figures for 1995 and 1996, we estimated values forward by applying the population growth rate for 1991–94 to the 1994 population figures. We computed the Spearman rank correlation between peacekeeping spending per person and GDP, and found no significant rank correlation whatsoever. In 1982, peacekeeping spending per person averaged just 23 cents; in 1993, it averaged only $2.84 per person. The absence of any correlation is probably due to the minuscule burden per person even in the 1990s. Hence, PK/GDP appears to outperform this alternative.

As a final exercise, we investigated the rank correlation between an ally's peacekeeping share of NATO's peacekeeping [Pk_i/(NATO PK)] and its GDP share of NATO's GDP [GDP_i /(NATO GDP)], where i denotes the ally. This measure is a "fairness" measure that attempts to match allies' peacekeeping burdens relative to other NATO allies with their ability to pay relative to other NATO allies. A Wilcoxon signed difference test was used to ascertain whether or not the underlying population distributions for these two measures were identical. The null hypothesis is that the two distributions are the same. We computed the associated z statistic of this test for 1976, 1980, 1984, 1988, and 1990–96. In all years, the z statistic was insignificant at any reasonable level and in nine of eleven years it was less than 0.9 in absolute value, where a z of 1.64 is required for significance at the .10 level for a two-tailed test. For all years, we could not reject the null hypothesis and concluded that the distribution of relative peacekeeping shares were identical to that of relative GDP shares. This finding is misleading, however, and must be viewed with caution. To show this, we also found the Spearman rank correlation between these two share measures and uncovered the same kind of rank correlations as those associated with GDP and PK. Because the denominators of PK/(NATO PK) and GDP/(NATO GDP)

19. The same result would follow if we checked the rank correlation between peacekeeping per capita and GDP per capita, since the correlation is again only between PK and GDP, inasmuch as the denominators are the same.

do not differ between allies, Spearman rank correlations are essentially picking up the correlation between PK and GDP and, as such, are not really showing useful burden-sharing comparisons. This insight has not been recognized in the defense burden-sharing literature. Once again, we must conclude that the comparison between PK/GDP and GDP is the most appropriate test for burden sharing.

Different burden-sharing measures can yield different results. The clearest findings are associated with the traditional burden-sharing measure, where an expenditure activity is normalized with respect to GDP. The findings for this measure agree best with a collective action explanation of peacekeeping.

WHO SHOULD DIRECT PEACEKEEPING, THE UN OR NATO?

In Bosnia, NATO has played a pivotal role, which is likely to continue for other peacekeeping missions in Europe for a number of reasons. First, NATO has begun to develop a sizable multinational rapid deployment force that will be highly mobile, well-trained, interoperable, and capable. In contrast, the United Nations must draw its forces from a host of countries and this takes time, which can compromise the entire mission. Even after the United Nations manages to assemble the requisite force, other problems exist in terms of logistics, planning, procurement, training, and force effectiveness (Palin, 1995; Fetherston, 1994). Second, NATO allies have greater interests in Europe than the typical UN member, and this should motivate NATO's action to a greater extent than that of the United Nations. Third, NATO allies are more homogeneous politically than the members of the United Nations, and this should also promote action when needed. Fourth, the United Nations has become involved in so many affairs since 1988 that it does not have the support staff to take on new missions unless it either abandons old missions or increases its infrastructure. Efforts to accomplish the latter have begun recently (Reed, Vaccaro, and Durch, 1995). Until this is accomplished, NATO is probably the only body capable of addressing the instabilities and threats to world peace in Europe. Fifth, NATO troops, command, and weapons stockpiles are located near any crises that might develop in Europe. Sixth, NATO possesses air bases and air power to protect its ground forces sent on peacekeeping operations in the region. Seventh, NATO will, within the next five years, have the necessary transport for power projection. Eighth, NATO has a current comparative advantage in procurement over the United Nations.

NATO's planned expansion can provide more resources and reduce some of the burdens of peacekeeping for the largest NATO allies if the entrants continue to support peacekeeping as they have done for IFOR and SFOR (Bureau of European and Canadian Affairs, 1997, p. 4). These NATO aspirants' payments for UN peacekeeping have, however, been quite modest owing to their current small assessments. In 1994, for example, the Czech Republic paid $5.9 million and Poland paid $1.5 million of the $2.9 *billion* collected for UN peacekeeping (United Nations, 1995, *Status of Contributions*). Unless these assessments are increased significantly, the *trend toward the exploitation of the large NATO allies regarding UN peacekeeping will be reinforced with NATO expansion.* Given the requirement that NATO entrants build up their armed forces as a condition of NATO membership, it is doubtful that they will have either the resources or the inclination to further their support of peacekeeping outside Europe. The admittance of Hungary, the Czech Republic, and Poland is anticipated to require between $800 million and $1 billion annually from 1997 to 2009, with these entrants underwriting the greatest share of these modernization expenses (Bureau of European and Canadian Affairs, 1997). To satisfy US expectations, the entrants will have to increase their defense spending from an average of 2.2 percent of GDP in 1995 to approximately 3.6 percent. This effort, if followed, will tax resources greatly, leaving little left to increase their contributions to peacekeeping – thus, our prediction that NATO expansion will worsen exploitation.

OUTLOOK AND CONCLUDING REMARKS

In NATO, the peacekeeping trend toward the large allies assuming a disproportionately large share of peacekeeping burdens is predicted to strengthen. If NATO abides by its new doctrine of crisis management and peacekeeping, then peacekeeping spending will grow greatly. As the United States, the United Kingdom, France, and Germany expand their power-projecting capabilities (see Chapter 6), associated spending will further add to disproportionate burden sharing. Given the United Nations' recent financial crisis, it is anticipated that complex peace-enforcing missions, like Bosnia, will be taken up by NATO, which will acquire in the next five years the requisite resources to respond quickly. Less involved operations in Africa, where NATO interests may not be as great, will remain with the United Nations. If population continues to grow as projected in the tropical countries (Sandler, 1997), then famine, health crises, and political upheavals may become more frequent. Consequently, UN peacekeeping may involve ever-increasing numbers of humanitarian-aid missions, as local factions battle over control of scarce resources. Unless the United Nations invests in sufficient transport vehicles, NATO's efforts to increase its transport capabilities may result in the UN's habitually drawing on these resources. This UN reliance would place even greater peacekeeping burdens on NATO and its largest allies.

This trend towards disproportionate burden sharing with respect to peacekeeping is in stark contrast to the burden-sharing behavior regarding defense spending in the 1990s (see Chapter 2). Since the end of the Cold War, there has been no evidence of this kind of disproportionality regarding traditional defense spending (Khanna and Sandler, 1996, 1997). Peacekeeping appears to produce a greater share of alliancewide pure public benefits, and, as such, leads to greater disproportionality. With current peacekeeping budgets, this exploitation of the large by the small is not yet that important, but this is expected to change with NATO's new commitment to crisis management and peacekeeping. In the future, new demands for peacekeeping may involve combating terrorism and taking preventative action before conflict begins.

5 NATO and the defense industrial base: EU and USA

NATO's defense industries are adjusting to the disarmament following the end of the Cold War. Industrial adjustment has been reflected in job losses, plant closures, a search for new military and civil markets at home and overseas (e.g., arms exports and diversification), national and international mergers, and strategic alliances. By 1998, industrial restructuring had been most evident in the US, where a series of major mergers had created three giant defense companies – Boeing, Lockheed-Martin, and Raytheon. In Europe in late 1996 there was a major initiative towards joint procurement with the formation of a quadrilateral armaments agency comprising France, Germany, Italy, and the United Kingdom, known as OCCAR. This agency aims to achieve a more efficient, effective approach to the management of collaborative defense programs. By 1998, the major European nations had announced plans to restructure their aerospace and defense electronics industries.

There are few authoritative economic studies on the size, structure, conduct, and performance of NATO's defense industries. What is known, what is not known, and what is it necessary to know for an informed debate and sensible public choices concerning NATO's defense industries? The performance of these industries is important in an era of expensive equipment, rising weapons costs, and disarmament. The efficiency with which equipment is supplied is an important determinant of national and alliance defense output, so that member states cannot avoid questioning the efficiency and competitiveness of their national defense industries and their market arrangements for the procurement of weapons. Nations need to reexamine the benefits and costs of maintaining a national defense industrial base and how much importance should be attached to its wider economic benefits.

Critics point to protected domestic markets and support for national champions resulting in inefficient monopolies protected from competition and characterized by costly equipment, cost escalation, delays in delivery, gold plating, inadequate performance and unreliability of weapons, poor labor productivity, labor hoarding, project cancellations, and excessive profits. Criticism is particularly leveled against Europe's defense industries for being "fragmented" and undertaking "too many" similar projects leading to the "wasteful duplication" of costly R & D and relatively short production runs reflecting the smallness of European national markets. As a result, it is claimed that Europe's defense industries are inefficient and uncompetitive, especially in relation to the US defense industry, which has the economic advantages of a large home market. Here, though, it has to be recognized that the US defense industry is not a model of perfection: it is protected by the so-called Buy America Act, and its weapons are subject to delays, cost escalation, gold plating, unreliability, poor performance, and cancellations. Critics also point to the failure to create a NATO free trade area for weapons, where entry barriers into national markets would be abolished for firms from member states and defense contracts would be awarded on the basis of competition reflecting a nation's comparative advantage.

This chapter focuses on defense industries and the market arrangements for equipment procurement. It starts by outlining the economics of defense markets and then defines the defense industrial base (DIB) and presents the stylized facts on size, structure, and performance for NATO's defense industries. The role of competition in procurement is assessed and alternative industrial policies are reviewed with supporting case studies. There is an evaluation of the costs and benefits of extending the Single European Market to defense equipment and the possible creation of a NATO free trade area. The conclusion considers the affordability of modern defense equipment.

THE ECONOMICS AND POLITICS OF DEFENSE MARKETS

Defense markets have both demand and supply sides. The demand side is dominated by government in its role as a purchaser of all the inputs of labor, capital, land, other resources, and services needed for its armed forces. Some of these are purchased from industries which might be specialist suppliers of defense equipment (e.g., missiles, submarines, tanks) or which are suppliers of civil goods and services (e.g., food, office equipment: Hartley and Hooper, 1995). This combination of government, the armed forces, defense contractors, together with politicians and other lobbying interest groups forms the military-industrial-political complex.

Defense procurement

Government is central to understanding defense equipment markets. It is a major buyer (for some equipment, it is the only buyer) and regulator of the market. Governments purchase a variety of equipment, goods and services for their armed forces. Equipment purchases range from simple items such as motor cars, batteries, and clothing to highly complex and high technology items such as combat aircraft, missiles, and nuclear-powered warships. These items might be purchased from state-owned or privately owned firms. State-owned defense companies characterize France, Greece, Italy, and Spain; privately owned defense industries are characteristic of Germany, the United Kingdom, and the United States (Markowski and Hall, 1998).

In defense procurement, government can use its buying power to determine all the major features of its national defense industries, namely, industry size, structure, ownership, location, conduct, and performance. For example, disarmament following the end of the Cold War has resulted in major "downsizing" of defense industries in NATO and the former Warsaw Pact. Governments can promote or prevent entry and exit (e.g., support for national champions); they can support or prevent mergers; and they can influence the form of competition (i.e., conduct reflected in price or nonprice competition). The government can also use its buying and regulatory powers to determine industry performance reflected in technical progress (e.g., via the performance requirements of weapons), exports (e.g., via licenses), and profitability (e.g., via profit controls: Martin and Hartley, 1997; Sandler and Hartley, 1995). The importance of government in defense markets means that political factors cannot be ignored.

Defense industries

A number of economic features are important for understanding defense industries:

1. *The importance of research and development (R & D).* Equipment acquisition costs consist of R & D and production costs. The requirements of the armed forces for high technology and high performance equipment has resulted in high and increasing R & D costs. For example, the

total development costs for the four-nation Eurofighter 2000 combat aircraft were estimated at almost $21 billion (1996–7 prices: HCP 238, 1997), and development costs for the American F-22 combat aircraft were estimated at almost $23 billion (1997 prices: CBO, 1997b, table 5.8). As a result, it is important to spread such total fixed costs over a large output so as to reduce the average per unit R & D component in acquisition unit costs.

2. *The importance of quantity.* Quantity is a determinant of average costs through the spreading of fixed R & D costs over a larger output and its impact on unit production costs (i.e., average costs comprise unit R & D and unit production costs). In the production stage, greater output leads to economies of scale and learning and hence to lower average production costs. For example, learning economies in the aerospace industry result in a reduction of about 10 percent in unit production costs for each doubling of cumulative output (Sandler and Hartley, 1995, p. 124). Similarly, on short production runs for aircraft, learning economies mean that the average cost of 10 units might be 60 percent of the cost of the first unit; whereas with large quantity production, the average cost over 900 units might be some 30 percent of the cost of the first unit (Pugh, 1986, p. 112).
3. *Development costs are usually proportional to unit production costs for each type of equipment.* There are relationships between total development costs and unit production costs. For example, the ratio of development to unit production costs is 100–200:1 for combat aircraft and 1,500–5,000:1 for missiles, compared with 0.4:1 for warship hulls and 50–100:1 for armored fighting vehicles (e.g., tanks: Pugh, 1986; Kirkpatrick, 1995).
4. *Life cycle costs.* Acquisition forms only one element in the total cost of equipment throughout its life (i.e., from "cradle to grave"). Life cycle costs comprise acquisition (R & D and production) and ownership costs (e.g., operating costs, training, maintenance, modifications, and disposal). Life cycle costs for aircraft might be divided into 20% for development, 18% for production, and 62% for support; and the corresponding shares for air-launched guided weapons might be 52%, 30%, and 18%, respectively, whereas the shares for warships might be 2% for development, 23% for procurement, and 75% for support (Pugh, 1986, p. 124; Holder, 1995). It has been shown that equipment with high performance and a correspondingly high unit production cost generally has a high unit life cycle cost: hence, the growth in the unit production costs of defense equipment is associated with similar growth in unit life cycle costs (Kirkpatrick, 1997). Also, quantity involves a trade-off between average fixed costs and life cycle costs.

Larger quantities will reduce average fixed costs (R & D) but at the expense of higher total life cycle costs.

5. *Cost trends.* Defense equipment is costly, and, in real terms, the unit production cost trends of successive generations of equipment are upward (i.e., after correcting for inflation and production quantities). Typically, over a range of US and UK equipment such as combat aircraft, guided missiles, helicopters, and warships, real unit production costs have increased at about 10 percent per annum, resulting in a doubling in cost every 7.25 years (Kirkpatrick, 1995; Pugh, 1993). For example, over the period 1950–2005, the unit production cost of combat aircraft has risen from £1.2 million for the US F-86 Sabre (1950), to £3.55 million for the British Lightning (1960), to £15.6 million for the F-15 Eagle (1974), to an estimated £65 million (2005) for the F-22 Raptor (1990 prices: Kirkpatrick, 1997). Inevitably, defense budgets have failed to keep pace with this cost escalation in new equipment. As a result, there has been a long-run decline in numbers purchased for the armed forces, with corresponding impacts on the size and structure of defense industries. For example, in the 1960s, the US forces purchased some 3,900 Phantom combat aircraft and 745 B-52 bombers; by the late 1990s, the corresponding numbers were 339 F-22s and 21 B-2 bombers (hence, some commentators have forecast a single-aircraft air force – Starship Enterprise – and a single-ship navy). Policies to improve the efficiency of procurement will help to delay the impact of rising unit costs. Cost savings of some 20 percent as occurred after the introduction of competition in the United Kingdom might achieve relief from cost escalation for almost two years. But eventually, the trend of rising equipment costs and stable or falling defense budgets means that policy makers will not be able to avoid some difficult choices in national defense policy. Independence in the form of a complete range of balanced armed forces and a domestic defense industrial base is costly and becoming costlier. In such circumstances, international alliance options based on NATO or within Europe become attractive as a means of providing modern, well-equipped armed forces able to deter potential aggressors even when equipment costs have risen beyond the affordability of nation states (Kirkpatrick, 1997).
6. *The cost penalties of stretching programs.* Budget limitations often result in procurement programs being "stretched out" over a longer period, thus slowing down production. A US study of a sample of air and land systems estimated that a 50% reduction in annual production rates compared with the basic rate would increase real unit costs by between 7% and 60%, with a median figure of some 20%. Interestingly, the median cost penalty differed significantly between equipment types,

varying from a median of 32% for armored fighting vehicles to 30% for missiles and 17% for aircraft and helicopters (CBO, 1987).

7. *US competitiveness and domination.* Large American defense companies able to achieve economies of scale and scope are a major competitive threat to European and other countries' defense industries. Following the end of the Cold War, there has been major restructuring in the US defense industry resulting in a smaller number of larger firms, especially in the aerospace and electronics industries.
8. *Defense industries as economically strategic industries.* In addition to their military-strategic significance, defense industries have the features of an economically strategic industry. Such industries are characterized by decreasing per-unit costs reflecting economies of scale and learning, high technology reflected in major and costly R & D, together with technical spillovers to the rest of the economy (e.g., aerospace, electronics, nuclear). Typically, competition in these industries is imperfect based on national monopolies and oligopolies leading to monopoly profits. As a result, they are the focal point for government strategic trade policy whereby government support for these industries (e.g., via subsidies or anticompetitive behavior) is seen as a means of promoting technical spillovers for the economy and of enabling a nation to obtain a share of monopoly profits in world markets (e.g., Airbus: Hartley, 1997b).

The military-industrial-political complex: A public choice analysis

Traditional economic analysis assumed that state intervention through bureaucracies and government was required to correct for market failure, with elected politicians and bureaucracies pursuing the so-called public interest and implementing the will of the people. Defense is the classic example of a public good where government intervention is designed to produce a socially desirable outcome. By contrast, public choice analysis recognizes that governments and state intervention can also fail.

Public choice analysis focuses on various agents in the political marketplace and involves the application of the principles of self-interest and the benefits of trade and exchange to collective nonmarket decision making. The agents in the political market comprise voters, political parties, governments, bureaucracies, and other interest groups, each pursuing their self-interest. In democracies, voters want the best set of policies offered by rival political parties (e.g., taxation, public spending); political parties seek votes to win elections; governments aim to remain in office; bureaucracies desire the largest possible budget; and producer interest groups will pursue opportunities for rents and profits. Such analysis can be applied to NATO during the Cold War and especially since the end of the Cold War.

The main agents in the NATO military-industrial-political complex are the NATO headquarters and organizations, earmarked NATO forces, NATO-supported defense equipment programs, together with national defense ministries, their armed forces, and defense contractors. The bureaucracies within this complex will aim to maximize their budgets and they will do so by overestimating the benefits of their preferred policies and underestimating the costs of these policies. As a result, a budget-maximizing bureaucracy will be inefficient, providing too large an output which will be justified as an optimum by exaggerating demand and underestimating costs.

During the Cold War, NATO organizations, national defense ministries, and their armed forces had every incentive to overestimate the threat from the Warsaw Pact. They could point to the size of conventional forces and the range of nuclear forces deployed by the potential enemy; and they could focus on the numerical superiority of the Warsaw Pact forces compared with those of NATO. The alleged superiority of the Soviet forces was then used as a key argument by NATO and the United States as alliance leader to maintain defense spending and armed forces in NATO member states. Often it was claimed that adequate NATO defense required equivalent matching of Soviet forces and that NATO needed to maintain a technical superiority to offset the numerical superiority of the Warsaw Pact forces. The threat of a massive surprise attack by Soviet forces in Central Europe was also used to justify keeping NATO forces at a high state of readiness – a posture which appealed to the armed forces, who could then use the readiness argument for appropriate funding. Such arguments were supported by defense industries which benefited from the contracts awarded to maintain the technical superiority of NATO equipment, thus resulting in a technological arms race between the two superpowers.

Defense contractors also had every incentive to underestimate the costs of new equipment programs. Once started, projects were difficult to stop: they attracted interest groups of scientists, managers, and workers whose livelihood and votes depended on the continuation of the project. The inevitable cost escalation on high technology defense programs (e.g., aerospace) was funded by cost-based contracts, but defense contractors could always "justify" such outcomes as the necessary price of maintaining democracy and providing national economic benefits in the form of jobs, technology, and exports. Defense industries and central staffs in NATO could also point to the apparent cost advantages from standardization and long production runs of one type of equipment achieved by Warsaw Pact defense industries – 10,158 Mig-21 combat aircraft, for example, were built in three Soviet factories.

Not surprisingly, there was little critical appraisal of these arguments used by the military-industrial-political complex in NATO (similar arguments are likely to have been used in the Kremlin). The focus on the size of Warsaw Pact forces ignored their effectiveness and the economic principles of comparative advantage and substitution. A nation's armed forces will reflect its resource endowment, so that nations well-endowed with physical and human capital resources will be expected to have capital-intensive forces (e.g., compare the capital-intensive US forces and the labor-intensive forces of Turkey). Similarly, the economic principle of substitution suggests that there are alternative methods of achieving protection. For example, equipment can be substituted for personnel (as in the Gulf War, where capital and technology-intensive air power replaced ground forces), attack helicopters can replace tanks, nuclear forces can replace conventional forces, and reserves can replace professional soldiers. Such substitutions can have radical implications for the traditional monopoly property rights of each of the armed forces. The army, for example, by operating surface-to-air missiles could replace manned combat aircraft operated by the air force in the air defense role; while maritime patrol aircraft operated by the air force could replace naval frigates in the antisubmarine role.

Nor was there much critical evaluation of the belief that the Warsaw Pact's defense industries were achieving cost advantages from standardization and economies of scale from long production runs of each type of equipment. The former USSR preferred single producers of a given type of weapon, which, in theory, were able to exploit fully scale economies and spread overhead and management costs over a large output. Within NATO such examples and arguments were used to promote standardization. However, no consideration was given to the efficiency with which the Warsaw Pact's defense industries were organized and operated. It was often assumed that the experience of capitalist industries with scale economies would apply equally to the command economies of the Warsaw Pact. Such an assumption ignored the role of incentives, profitability, and rivalry in promoting efficiency in capitalist economies, features which were absent from centrally planned socialist economies. NATO nations generally preferred to maintain some competition in defense equipment procurement. In contrast, defense firms in the former USSR were not subject to efficiency incentives and competitive pressures and their pursuit of large-scale output might also have pushed them into regions where they encountered diseconomies of scale. Experience since the end of the Cold War has confirmed the failings and inefficiencies of Soviet industry under central planning.

Public choice models continue to provide an explanation of NATO since the end of the Cold War. Interest groups of defense ministries, the armed forces, and defense industries seeking to maintain their budgets, incomes, and rents have a continued incentive to identify new threats and formulate new roles for NATO and its armed forces. So the end of the Cold War now means that the world is regarded as "more dangerous," with a variety of regional instabilities (e.g., the Middle East, the Far East) and a new set of threats (e.g., terrorism, drugs, environmental problems: see Chapter 6). New roles have emerged to justify a certain level of NATO forces and their continued requirement for modern defense equipment capable of operating in a variety of combat situations in areas outside the traditional NATO boundaries. Thus there is an emphasis on peacekeeping, peace-enforcing, and humanitarian roles in support of the UN (e.g., Bosnia), with such roles requiring rapid reaction forces with supporting strategic airlift and sealift capabilities (see Chapter 4). These roles are likely to attract public support for continued defense funding following the end of the Cold War. They are a further example of the efforts by bureaucracies and interest groups to affect favorably the demand for their services while underestimating or ignoring the costs of these policies. Similar behavior occurred over the expansion of NATO, where the emphasis was on the likely benefits of adding new members from the former Warsaw Pact with little focus on the risks and costs associated with expanded membership (e.g., force thinning; the need to defend Budapest, Prague, and Warsaw). Of course, the pursuit of new roles and new members provides extensive opportunities for government ministers and their officials to enjoy the international travel and prestige associated with participating in NATO summit meetings; similar benefits accrue to these groups and to industrialists from participating in collaborative defense projects and from potential arms sales to the new members; and the armed forces enjoy the opportunities for foreign travel associated with overseas postings.

A public choice analysis appears attractive and is supported by casual empiricism, but such features of an analytical framework are no substitute for clearly specified hypotheses and predictions capable of being tested, refuted, and compared with alternative models. Certainly, the public choice "story" sounds persuasive and seems to fit the facts of the military-industrial-political complex and its behavior. Also, most democracies have voting systems which are extremely restricted in allowing voters opportunities for expressing their preferences for various defense and NATO policies. Voters usually vote for a package of policies of which defense policies and especially policies towards NATO are only one element in the range of alternatives offered to the electorate. Secrecy also means that voters are poorly informed and have only limited information about defense issues and the nature of military threats. On this basis, there must be serious doubt that the defense policies of NATO represent a preferred position for the electorate and hence a social welfare maximum. Indeed, the public goods nature of defense and military alliances provides considerable opportunities for various interest groups in the military-industrial-political complex to pursue their own ends, but to do so by presenting themselves as well-informed agencies able to interpret society's preferences and to act in its best interest (by defending the national interest).

NATO DEFENSE INDUSTRIES

Defining the defense industrial base

Any analysis of defense industries in NATO countries needs to start by defining the defense industrial base. In countries such as the United States, the United Kingdom, and France, the domestic defense industrial base (DIB) is a significant component of the economy through its contribution to output, R & D, exports, and employment (Hartley and Hooper, 1995). However, the concept of the DIB has been the victim of various definitions. Examples are "the DIB consists of those industrial assets which provide key elements of military power and national security: such assets demand special consideration by the government" (HCP 518, 1986, p. xxxvii); and "the DIB embraces industrial sectors that unequivocally manufacture military goods (e.g., artillery, missiles, submarines) as well as sectors which produce civil goods"; and "designation as a defense industry depends upon the destination of the bulk of the industry's output: should most of it be earmarked for defense markets, the industry is classified as a defense industry" (Todd, 1988, pp. 14–15).

Often definitions of the DIB focus on the major prime contractors supplying defense equipment (aircraft, ships, tanks) to the national Defense Department. Such a definition neglects the supply chain and the range of subcontractors; it neglects the suppliers of other goods and services (e.g.,

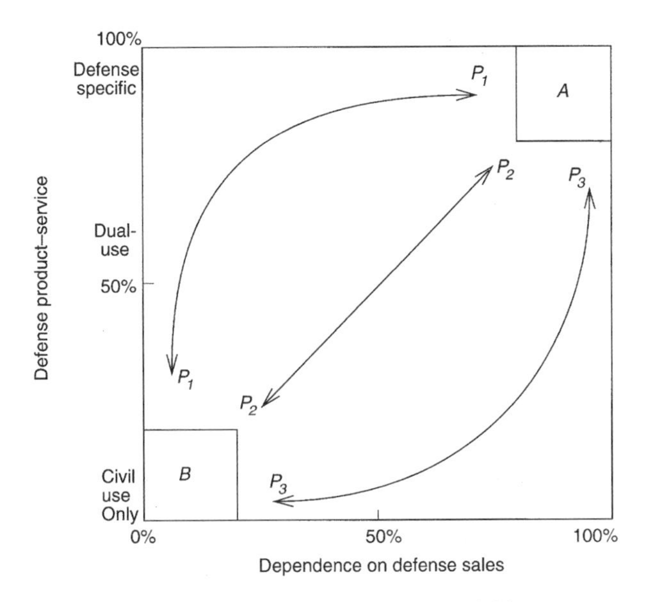

Figure 5.1. A taxonomy for the defense industrial base

construction, clothing) to the Defense Department, to overseas defense ministries, and to overseas defense industries; and it neglects exports of defense equipment and services. Some suppliers might not be aware that they are involved in defense production (e.g., manufacturers of ball bearings and switch gear). Further problems arise because there is usually a lack of an official standard industrial classification heading for the DIB. It is also misleading to refer to the DIB as a single, homogeneous entity. On the supply side, the defense market comprises varying numbers of small to large firms, either privately owned or publicly owned, involved in the design, development, production, servicing, support, and disposal of nuclear and conventional air, land, and sea systems. Problems of defining the DIB make it difficult to estimate its precise contribution to the national economy and to undertake international comparisons. For example, international comparisons of employment estimates could be based on different definitions of both the DIB and its labor force (i.e., direct, indirect, and induced employment impacts of the DIB: Hartley, 1996; Dunne, 1995).

A taxonomy for defining and classifying the DIB is shown in Figure 5.1. This distinguishes between dependence on defense sales and the type of defense product, embracing complete weapons systems, subsystems, components, materials, and services. In Figure 5.1, boxes *A* and *B* show two extreme cases. Firms in box *A* are clearly in the DIB (i.e., completely dependent on defense sales and supplying defense specific products or services). By contrast, firms in box *B* are in the civilian economy, with zero defense sales and supplying purely civil goods. The problems of classification arise with movements in either direction along illustrative paths P_1 to P_3 (paths P_1 and P_3 could be linear, parallel to the axes with right angles at the 100% points). On this basis, the key question in defining the DIB becomes one of selecting a cut-off point: 50% on both axes seems a reasonable starting point, although stronger criteria might require a higher cut-off point of, say, 80% or more. However, such an approach omits certain civilian sectors, such as civil airlines and merchant shipping (box B), which can be important components of a nation's DIB during a conflict. Nor does Figure 5.1 allow for the absolute size of the arms firm as measured by arms sales, which is the variable often used to rank the world's leading defense contractors (see Table 5.1). Changing technology and the convergence of some commercial and military production technologies creates further complications in defining the DIB (e.g., dual-use technologies). This convergence suggests that the production of some military equipment, together with some maintenance and logistic support, could increasingly occur outside of the traditional DIB. Budget pressures will accentuate such developments and the result could be weapons systems and components of high quality but lower cost compared to those provided by current procurement (Gansler, 1995; Gummett and Stein, 1997).

The economic characteristics of the world's top twenty defense companies in 1995 are shown in Table 5.1. Thirteen of the top twenty are US companies; almost all are in the aerospace and electronics industries; and the degree of defense dependency varied between 4% and 98%. If subsidiaries are included, only nine of the twenty-three leading arms companies shown in Table 5.1 were 50% or more defense dependent, and only four were over 90% defense dependent (three of which were involved in shipbuilding). The size advantage of the leading US defense companies compared to their European rivals enables the American firms to benefit from economies of scale, learning, and scope.

Scale of output and size of firms

The economic characteristics of defense procurement are a major determinant of industry structure as reflected in the number and size of firms and concentration ratios. The size of orders for a nation's armed forces and the

Table 5.1. *Top twenty defense companies, 1995*

Rank	Company	Country	Sector	Arms sales (millions of US dollars)	Total sales (millions of US dollars)	Arms sales as share of total sales	Total employment
1	Lockheed-Martin	US	Ac, El, Mi	13,800	22,853	60	160,000
2	McDonnell Douglas	US	Ac, El, Mi	9,620	14,332	67	63,610
3	British Aerospace	UK	A, Ac, El, Mi, SA/O	6,720	9,062	74	44,000
4	Loral	US	El, Mi	6,500	6,700	97	38,000
5	General Motors	US	El, Eng, Mi	6,250	168,000	4	709,000
S	Hughes Electronics (GM)	US	El, Mi	5,950	14,772	40	84,000
6	Northrop Grumman	US	Ac, El, Mi, SA/O	5,700	6,818	84	37,300
7	Thomson	France	El	4,630	14,388	32	96,040
S	Thomson-CSF	France	El	4,620	7,111	65	48,860
8	Boeing	US	Ac, El, Mi	4,200	19,515	22	109,400
9	GEC	UK	El, Sh	4,100	17,348	24	82,970
10	Raytheon	US	El, Mi	3,960	11,716	34	73,200
11	United Technologies	US	El, Eng	3,650	22,624	16	170,600
12	Daimler Benz	Germany	Ac, El, Eng, MV, Mi	3,350	72,255	5	310,990
13	DCN	France	Sh	3,280	3,352	98	22,400
S	Daimler Benz Aerospace	Germany	Ac, El, Eng, Mi	3,250	10,493	31	50,780
14	Litton	US	El, Sh	3,030	3,320	91	29,100
15	General Dynamics	US	MV, Sh	2,930	3,067	96	27,700
16	TRW	US	Oth	2,800	10,172	28	66,520
17	IRI	Italy	Ac, El, Eng, Mi, Sh	2,620	41,904	6	263,060
18	Westinghouse Electric	US	El	2,600	9,605	27	77,810
19	Aerospatiale Groupe	France	Ac, Mi	2,550	9,862	26	38,670
20	Mitsubishi HI	Japan	Ac, MV, Mi, Sh	2,430	32,067	8	67,370

Notes: A = artillery; Ac = aircraft; El = electronics; Eng = engines; Mi = missiles; MV = military vehicles; SA/O = small arms/ordnance; Sh = ships; Oth = other; S = subsidiary

Ranking based on arms sales; total employment refers to all group employment.

Rankings are for OECD and developing countries.

Source: SIPRI (1997).

Table 5.2. *Equipment expenditures (in millions of US dollars, 1990 prices)*

Country	1985	1990	1996	Percentage change 1990–96 (%)
Belgium	608	367	172	–53
Denmark	361	395	323	–18
France	6,387	8,518	7,686	–10
Germany	5,746	7,491	3,661	–51
Greece	656	827	859	+4
Italy	3,673	4,091	3,067	–25
Luxembourg	3	3	5	+66
Netherlands	1,720	1,328	1,149	–13
Norway	831	767	960	+25
Portugal	44	193	267	+38
Spain	2,083	1,150	1,125	–2
Turkey	545	1,063	2,213	+108
UK	11,758	7,120	6,956	–2
NATO Europe	34,415	33,313	28,443	–15
Canada	2,038	1,963	1,666	–15
USA	80,520	75,930	58,630	–23
NATO Total	116,973	111,206	88,739	–20

Notes: Figures are in millions of US dollars at 1990 prices and exchange rates.
France does not return these figures to NATO: hence, its equipment spending is estimated by using Germany's share figures for 1985 and 1990; 1996 is assumed to be the same as 1990.
Spain: 1985 figures are for 1986.
Sources: SIPRI (1995, 1996, 1997).

extent of competition and contestability for defense contracts are the features of defense procurement which affect the size of firms and their ability to achieve economies of scale and learning with implications for labor productivity and unit costs. There are major differences in the scale of output and the size of firms between the US and European defense indusries. Compared with Europe, the US has the benefit of a large home market.

Table 5.2 shows the differences in the scale of expenditure on defense equipment in the United States and Europe. Typically, aggregate NATO Europe expenditure on weapons varied between 43% and 49% of the US total over the period 1985–96. However, this is misleading, since the NATO member states pursue their own national procurement policies and there is no single procurement agency for either NATO Europe or the EU. As a result, in 1996, equipment spending in France and the United Kingdom was about

Table 5.3. *Military R & D expenditures*

Country	Annual figures: US $ million (1990 prices)	Annual figures: Percent of total military expenditure (%)	1989–94: Cumulative total of government-funded military R & D (US $ million, 1990 prices)
US	32,000	14	228,000
France	4,800	12	34,400
UK	3,200	9.1	17,900
Germany	1,500	4.8	10,600
Sweden	560	10.3	3,910
Italy	320	1.4	3,880
Spain	280	3.5	2,380
Canada	150	1.6	1,230
Switzerland	140	2.0	na
Netherlands	78	1.3	na
Norway	61	1.8	na
Finland	27	1.3	na
Poland	18	1.5	na
Czech Republic	8.6	1.2	na
Turkey	5.6	0.1	na
Denmark	5.3	0.2	na
Portugal	5.1	0.2	na
Slovakia	3.9	1.2	na
Belgium	3.9	0.1	na
Greece	3.4	0.1	na
Hungary	1.1	0.2	na

Notes: Figures for Czech Republic and Slovakia are in 1993 US $ million.
Annual data based on 1994, or 1995, or 1996.
Figures in US dollars at 1990 prices and exchange rates.
Source: SIPRI (1997).

12%–13% each compared to the US total. In Europe, national expenditures are so widely dispersed that no European nation approaches the US scale of equipment spending. Table 5.2 also shows that over the period 1985–96, the big four nations of France, Germany, Italy, and the United Kingdom accounted for 75% to 82% of NATO Europe equipment spending.

Military R & D spending determines technical progress in weapons and can favorably affect international competitiveness. Table 5.3 shows the dominant position of the US in the military R & D "league table": its annual total was almost seven times that of France and ten times that of the United Kingdom. The scale difference between the US and Europe is confirmed by the fact that the combined total of annual military R & D spending by all the European states shown in Table 5.3 is 35% of the US figure.

Expenditure figures are only one indicator of the scale difference between the United States and European nations. Volume figures for the total stock of military holdings together with total and annual rates of output for major air, land, and sea equipment are equally striking. The total stock of military holdings of major weapons is an indicator of scale differences. In 1993, US military holdings of major defense equipment were 2.5 to 7 times the largest holding in a European state; and such scale differences were confirmed by the data on national procurement. For example, for combat aircraft, US holdings were 6.6 times the holdings in France, and US annual procurement of combat aircraft was about ten times French annual aircraft procurement (Chalmers and Greene, 1995).

Table 5.4 shows the differences in the scale of national procurement and total output between the US and European nations for combat aircraft. For the smaller European nations, such as Belgium, Denmark, Greece, and Norway, typical national orders for combat aircraft for their air forces are in the region of 70 to 160 aircraft (e.g., the F-16). The larger European nations, such as France, Germany, and the United Kingdom, might buy 200 to 400 units of advanced combat aircraft for their air forces (e.g., Rafale, Mirage, Tornado). In contrast, US procurement of combat aircraft for its armed forces ranged from 1,000 to almost 3,000 units (e.g., F-15, F-16, F-18, JSF). As a result, US aerospace firms achieve significant learning economies with favorable impacts on labor productivity. For example, assuming a 90% unit production cost curve (learning curve), increasing output from 200 units to 1,600 units of one type leads to savings in unit production costs of almost 30% (i.e., unit costs fall by 10% for each doubling in cumulative output). Consider the potential cost savings if NATO states were to agree upon one standard type of combat aircraft to replace the current duplication of new types (F-18E/F, F-22, JSF, Rafale, EF2000, Gripen). The result would be an order for some 5,000 units of a single type (based on current orders; other NATO states might also demand the same aircraft). In theory, such standardization should result in savings from reduced duplication of costly R & D programs (see Table 5.8) and lower unit production costs from economies of scale and learning. Of course, European nations can seek to reduce their scale disadvantage compared with the US through collaborative programs and exports (see Table 5.4).

Differences in the scale of national procurement and in total output are reflected in the size of defense industries as measured by employment. Table 5.5 confirms the difference in *industry size* between the United States

Table 5.4. *National procurement and output of combat aircraft*

Aircraft	National procurement		Total output
US			
F-15	1001		1437
F-16	2250		3970
F-18 A/D	1049		1437
F-18 E/F	548		548
F-22	339		339
Joint Strike Fighter (JSF)	2885		2945
France			
Mirage F-1	269		704
Mirage 2000	380		609
Rafale	316		316
UK			
Hawk	175		782
Sweden			
Gripen	204+		204+
Collaborative Programs			
Alpha Jet (France-Germany)	France	= 176	554
	Germany	= 175	
Harrier II (UK-USA)	USA	= 262	396
	UK	= 96	
Tornado (Germany; Italy; UK)	UK	= 398	974
	Germany	= 357	
	Italy	= 99	
EF2000 (Germany; Italy; Spain; UK)	UK	= 232	620
	Germany	= 180	
	Italy	= 121	
	Spain	= 87	
European F-16 Purchases	Belgium	= 160	
	Denmark	= 70	
	Netherlands	= 214	
	Norway	= 74	

Note: Total output includes licensed production.
Source: Flight International (1997).

and the other national defense industries in NATO and the rest of Europe. In 1995, the number employed in the US defense industries was almost eight times the number employed in the largest European industry, namely, the United Kingdom. Even aggregate employment in the EU was under 40% of US employment, and the EU total was spread among all member states. Table 5.5 also shows the employment reductions in defense industries over the period 1985 to 1995, especially since the end of the Cold War in 1990;

Table 5.5. *Employment in defense industries*

	Index 1995 = 100			
Country	1985	1990	1995	Numbers in 1995 (000s)
Belgium	350	250	100	10
Czech Republic	120	120	100	25
Denmark	120	140	100	5
Finland	100	100	100	10
France	136	120	100	250
Germany	256	167	100	120
Greece	100	100	100	15
Hungary	600	600	100	5
Italy	215	200	100	40
Netherlands	120	133	100	15
Norway	150	100	100	10
Poland	295	205	100	88
Portugal	100	100	100	10
Spain	220	333	100	30
Sweden	117	100	100	30
Switzerland	200	167	100	15
Turkey	67	83	100	30
UK	162	152	100	290
Canada	143	143	100	35
US	141	136	100	2,200
NATO	148	140	100	3,060
EU	170	150	100	830
World	152	148	100	10,900

Source: BICC (1997).

as well as the concentration of employment in the world's defense industries, with NATO accounting for almost 30% of the world total.

Firm size is a further indicator of scale differences between the United States and Europe. An analysis of the size of major defense firms surviving in the United States and Europe provides an indication of the "ideal" or optimum size of firm (survivor method). However, in defense industries, it has to be recognized that government policy and its "willingness to pay" for an independent source of supply is an important determinant of firm size. Moreover, the continued industrial restructuring in the US and especially in Europe, means that the details of firm size and ownership are subject to continuous change. Nonetheless, the data presented in this chapter are the latest available and are sufficient to illustrate the policy issues.

The list of the top 100 arms-producing companies in the OECD and Third

World countries in 1995 was dominated by US firms and by companies in the aerospace and electronics industries. Within the top 100 in 1995, American companies accounted for twelve of the top twenty firms and 40 percent of the top 100. Also within the 1995 top 100 there were twelve French firms, eleven UK firms, eight German firms, and two Italian firms.

The end of the Cold War resulted in major restructuring of NATO's defense industries, reflected in mergers, exits, and downsizing. In the US, three giant companies have been created: *Lockheed-Martin,* which was a merger between Lockheed and Martin Marietta and included the General Dynamics combat aircraft division and GE Aerospace and the subsequent acquisition of Loral, so creating a military aerospace and defense electronics group; *Boeing,* which acquired Rockwell Aerospace and McDonnell Douglas, so creating a military and civil aircraft, space and defense electronics group; and *Raytheon,* which created a large defense electronics group by acquiring the Hughes Electronics defense division, Texas Instruments' defense electronics activities, and Chrysler's electronics business. Mergers in the US defense industry have been subsidized by the US Department of Defense (DOD), the aim being to achieve lower costs and lower prices to the benefit of the DOD (SIPRI, 1997, p. 242). In theory, larger firms can achieve economies from reduced duplication, and from the increased scale and scope of their operations. But such economies might involve a trade-off through reduced competition and possible monopoly reflected in higher prices, monopoly profits, organizational slack (inefficiency), and a reduced incentive to innovate.

European defense companies have also been involved in mergers both within and between nations. The UK defense industry was privatized in the 1980s, resulting in some restructuring (e.g., British Aerospace acquired the land systems business of Royal Ordnance; Vickers acquired the tank business of Royal Ordnance; GEC bought Yarrow, the warship builder; and Short Bros. was bought by the Canadian group of Bombardier). Since 1990, GKN (armored fighting vehicles) has acquired Westland (helicopters); GEC has acquired VSEL (nuclear-powered submarines); Alvis merged with Sweden's Hagglunds (armored fighting vehicles); and British Aerospace has acquired a 35 percent interest in Saab, and in partnership with Daimler-Benz has acquired the defense electronics business of Siemens-Plessey. In France, there are plans to merge Aerospatiale and Dassault, as well as Aerospatiale and Lagardère (Matra); and Thomson-CSF has been partly privatized and acquired by the French companies Alcatel Alsthom and Dassault Industries. French companies have a substantial involvement in the Belgian defense

Table 5.6. *World's top defense companies, 1997*

Company	Nation	Defense sales ($ billion)
Lockheed-Martin	US	19.39
Boeing (McDonnell Douglas)	US	17.90
Raytheon (Hughes/TI)	US	11.67
British Aerospace	UK	6.47
Thomson	France	4.68
Aerospatiale/Dassault	France	4.15
GEC	UK	4.12
United Technologies	US	3.65
Lagardère Groupe (Matra)	France	3.29
Daimler-Benz Aerospace	Germany	3.25
DCN	France	3.07
General Dynamics	US	2.90
Finmeccanica	Italy	2.59
Litton Industries	US	2.40
Mitsubishi Heavy Industries	Japan	2.22
General Electric	US	2.15
Tenneco	US	1.80
TRW	US	1.71
ITT Industries	US	1.56

Note: Sales based on 1995 figures. This table differs from Table 5.1 in showing the impact of recent mergers. Table 5.1 provides more comprehensive data, but based on 1995.
Source: The Economist (1997c).

industry, including GIAT ownership of the Belgian firm FN Herstal (small arms, ammunition). In Germany, the Daimler-Benz group owns DASA (aerospace), MTU (aero-engines), and Siemens Defense Electronics. Some European joint venture companies have been created, such as Matra-BAe Dynamics missile group (which in 1997 purchased 30 percent of DASA's LFK missile businsess), Matra-Marconi Space, the Airbus Military Company, Eurofighter, Eurocopter, and EH Industries. There are plans to restructure Airbus Industrie (civil jet airliners) from an international consortium into a stand-alone company, known as the single corporate entity, during 1999. In addition to mergers within Europe and within the US, there have also been some transatlantic acquisitions. Examples include the Fairchild Aerospace (US) purchase of Dornier (Germany); the Rolls-Royce (UK) acquisition of the Allison Engine Company (US); and the GEC 1998 takeover of Tracor, a US defense electronics company.

Table 5.6 shows the world's top defense companies in 1997 (cf. top companies in 1995: see Table 5.1). Assume that the current scale of output is an indicator of the scale needed to survive. Lockheed Martin in 1997 was almost three times the size of the largest EU defense firm. The average size of the top three US firms in 1997 was 3.2 times the average size of the top three European firms. On this basis, the combined output of the top three European firms could be produced by one firm of the average size in the US top three. The scope for restructuring Europe's defense industries can be illustrated by a further example. In 1997, the combined output of the top eight EU defense firms was some 65 percent of the aggregate output of the top three US defense companies; this suggests that the EU's top eight could be reduced to two firms of US size (see Table 5.6). Here it is important to remember that the scale of output is a major determinant of unit costs in defense industries and hence of prices, competitiveness, and profitability. However, large size does not guarantee success: there are potential diseconomies of size (e.g., reflecting the management problems of giant companies), and there are also specialist (niche) market opportunities for smaller firms.

Too many different European types

In addition to the small scale of national procurement in Europe, there are too many rival projects compared with the US. The result is the duplication of costly R & D projects and a failure to obtain economies of scale and learning. In Europe, there is considerable duplication of industrial development and production facilities for combat aircraft, helicopters, missiles, tanks, and warships. Table 5.7 shows the results of government support for national defense industries reflected in the European development of large numbers of different types of equipment compared with the United States. Tanks, armored fighting vehicles, rifles, ground-attack aircraft, missiles, and warships all illustrate the European inefficiency, providing a further indicator of the opportunities for restructuring Europe's defense industries. The selection of a smaller number of types, as in the United States, would lead to savings from less duplication of costly R & D and longer production runs of each type, with the resulting economies of scale and learning.

The costs of duplication are illustrated in Table 5.8. Six EU nations are developing three different types of advanced combat aircraft, and the combined production order for the three types is over 1,100 units. If the six EU nations could agree on one type there would be savings in R & D costs, and an order for some 1,100 units of one type would lead to reductions in unit production costs in the region of 10–20 percent. Even greater cost savings

Table 5.7. *Number of different types of equipment, 1993*

Equipment	Number of types: Europe	Number of types: USA	European producer nations
Land systems			
Main battle tank	4	1	UK, F, G, It
Armored infantry fighting vehicle	16	3	F(x3); G; UK(x2); It(x3); Sw; Gr(x2); Sp (x2); Au; Sz
Howitzer (155mm)	3	1	F; G; UK
Assault rifle	7	1	B; F; UK; Sp; G; It; Au
Air systems			
Fighter-strike	7	5	F(x2); UK; Sw; G-It-UK; G-It-Sp-UK
Ground-attack/trainer	6	1	UK; Sp; It(x2); G-F; It-Brazil
Attack helicopter	7	5	F(x2); UK; It(x2); G; G-F
Air-to-air missile	8	4	F(x3); UK(x2); It(x2); Sw
Anti-tank missile	8	5	F-G(x2); UK; It-Brazil; Sw; Sp-USA
Naval systems			
Frigate	11	1	F(x3); UK; G(x3); Nl; Sp; Dk; It
Anti-submarine torpedo	9	2	UK(x2); Sw(x3); F(x2); It; G
VSTOL and helicopter carrier	3	1	UK; It; Sp
Diesel submarine	7	0	G(x3); It; Nl; Sw; UK
Nuclear attack submarine	2	1	F; UK
Total (all)	*125*	*53*	

Notes: F = France; G = Germany; It = Italy; Gr = Greece; Sp = Spain; Sw = Sweden; Sz = Switzerland; Au = Austria; Nl = Netherlands; Dk = Denmark.
All types includes some not shown in the Table.
Source: De Vestel (1995).

would result if the EU nations agreed to standardize the purchase of the American JSF aircraft, leading to a combined order for over 4,000 units.

NATO arms trade

The arms trade reflects both economic and political factors. Economic factors take the form of price and product competitiveness, while political factors depend on international relations and the willingness of nations to trade with each other, alliance and treaty commitments, UN arms sanctions, and human rights policies. A nation's arms exports and its share of the world arms market is an indicator of its international competitiveness. Over the period

Table 5.8. *Major combat aircraft programs*

Country	Program	Start of full-scale development	Expected in-service date	Estimated government R & D funds (US $ billion, constant prices)	Estimated numbers	Unit procurement cost (US $ million, 1997 prices)
US	F-22	1991	2004	17	339	91–108
US	JSF		2010	(22.8)	2,885	45–68
US	F/A-18E/F	1991	2001	2	548	61
UK, G, It, Sp	EF2000	1988	2001	12	620	64
France	Rafale	1987	2002	7	316	(58)
Sweden	Gripen	1982	1996	2	200+	(24)

Notes: Development costs for JSF and F-18E/F are in $ billions, 1997 prices; all remaining figures in constant prices from SIPRI (1997); but base year not specified.

Unit procurement costs are based on US definitions for US aircraft and unit production costs for EF2000.

EF2000 is a four-nation project involving the UK, Germany, Italy, and Spain.

Unit costs for Rafale and Gripen are flyaway costs in 1994 prices.

Sources: SIPRI (1997); Flight International (1997); CBO (1997b); Lorrell et al. (1995).

1992–96, the US was the world's leading supplier of arms exports, accounting for over 50 percent of the total supplied by the top thirty suppliers (SIPRI, 1997, p. 268). In this top thirty list, Germany, the UK, France, Netherlands, and Italy were ranked third, fourth, fifth, seventh, and eighth, respectively.

The arms trade between buyers and sellers in NATO over the period 1993–95 is summarized in Table 5.9. The United States dominates NATO arms exports. It is the major supplier to NATO Europe, while the United States, Turkey, Greece, Spain, and Germany are the major NATO importers. Not surprisingly, the US has a sizeable balance of trade surplus with NATO Europe; but among the European nations, the UK achieved a balance of trade surplus with the US.

ALTERNATIVE INDUSTRIAL POLICIES

The policy options

There are alternative industrial policies for purchasing defense equipment. Each option involves the purchasing nation in different amounts of industrial involvement or work sharing in the development and/or production and/or support of the equipment being acquired. Also, the various options have different implications for costs, delivery, control over equipment specifications, and risks, as well as wider economic and industrial benefits for the purchasing nation. Broadly, there are four industrial policy options ranging between the extremes of buying from national sources of supply (national champions) and importing foreign equipment:

1. *National independence,* where a nation buys its defense equipment from domestic firms. Buying from national suppliers appears to offer military, strategic, and wider economic benefits (e.g., jobs, technology, exports); but there are no free gifts, and these benefits are achieved at a cost. For example, foreign equipment might be cheaper, available earlier, and have demonstrated the ability to meet the performance requirements of the armed forces. There are also alternative, and often better, ways of achieving national economic benefits (e.g., more jobs might be created if a given public expenditure were used on construction projects such as roads, schools, and hospitals, rather than on defense projects).
2. *International collaboration.* The rising costs of national development programs (e.g., aerospace) together with the relatively small production

Table 5.9. *Arms trade: suppliers and buyers, 1993–95 (in millions of US dollars, current prices)*

	Suppliers					
Buyers	US	UK	France	Germany	Other NATO	Total
NATO-Europe						
Belgium	300	0	280	0	170	775
Denmark	190	0	0	0	0	220
France	260	0	0	0	40	370
Germany	1,000	0	0	0	230	1,270
Greece	1,200	0	60	525	20	2,195
Italy	250	60	0	0	0	330
Luxembourg	5	0	0	0	0	5
Netherlands	525	0	0	0	0	560
Norway	210	0	120	0	0	390
Portugal	410	60	0	0	0	515
Spain	1,300	0	0	0	0	1,580
Turkey	2,300	0	170	90	60	3,020
UK	725	0	0	0	0	735
NATO Europe Total	8,675	120	630	615	520	11,965
NATO–N. America						
Canada	400	0	290	0	0	710
USA	0	1,200	130	310	950	3,575
NATO Total	9,075	1,320	1,050	925	1,470	16,250
Other Western Europe						
Austria	10	0	160	0	0	185
Finland	40	100	160	0	0	375
Ireland	0	0	0	0	60	60
Sweden	100	0	0	280	0	395
Switzerland	60	0	0	160	0	290
Other W. Europe Total	210	100	320	440	60	1,305
Total: NATO + W. Europe	9,285	1,420	1,370	1,365	1,530	17,555

Note: Figures are rounded.
Source: ACDA (1997).

runs for domestic markets has provided economic incentives for international collaboration. France, Germany, Italy, and the UK have been variously involved in programs involving shared development and production for aircraft, helicopters, aero-engines, and missiles, while the UK and US have been involved in collaborative work on combat aircraft (Hartley and Martin, 1993).

3. *Licensed production and coproduction,* where a purchasing nation builds foreign-designed equipment under license in its own country for its national order only; or undertakes the domestic production of a foreign design but shares in the production work of two or more purchasing nations.
4. *Importing military equipment either with or without some form of offset arrangement.* But imports have their problems and costs. For example, foreign equipment might have to be modified to meet national requirements, and such modifications can be expensive; large stocks of spares might have to be bought to cover unforeseen contingencies; exchange rates might change; and the foreign supplier might exploit any monopoly position (e.g., the pricing of spares).

The economics of international collaboration: The European experience

International collaboration involving two or more allies in the development and production of defense equipment provides opportunities for cost savings in both R & D and production. In the ideal case, costly development programs are shared between two or more partner nations, and a pooling of production orders enables economies of scale and learning to result in lower unit production costs and output levels, thus allowing European nations to be more competitive with the United States. Table 5.10 shows a simple example of perfect collaboration. The upper part of the table shows two nations pursuing the independent development of similar aircraft, each purchasing 200 units; the lower half of the table shows the results of the two nations collaborating equally on the development and production of one type of aircraft.

European collaboration has resulted in the creation of a number of international organizations, mostly in the aerospace industry and typically involving national champions from France, Germany, Italy, Spain, and the United Kingdom. The major EU international companies could form the basis for the creation of a European aerospace industry, and they provide a model for the extension of collaboration to land and sea systems. Examples of the

Table 5.10. *Perfect collaboration*

Independent venture	Number of weapons purchased	Development cost (£ billions) Total	Development cost (£ billions) Each nation	Production cost Total (£ billion)	Production cost Unit production cost (£ million)
Nation A	200	10	10	2	10
Nation B	200	10	10	2	10
Collaboration (2 nations, A&B)	400	10	5	3.6	9
Collaborative savings		10	5	0.4	1

major international organizations are shown in Table 5.11. A number of these organizations have associated international companies for aero-engines and avionics (e.g., EJ 200 is the international company building the engine for EF2000).

While aerospace projects have dominated European collaboration, there have been some collaborative initiatives in sea and land systems. The Common New Generation Frigate is a three-nation collaborative program involving France, Italy, and the UK (the agreement was signed in July 1994) for the procurement of a new class of anti-air warfare frigates. Joint development and first-of-class construction costs will be shared equally by the three nations. Production costs will be shared on the basis of offtake and, unlike other collaborative projects, there is no predetermined work share. Where practicable, work will be competed, but the partner nations are seeking work-share to broadly follow cost share (HCP 238, 1997). There are also examples of collaborative land systems involving battlefield radar and the "battlefield taxi." The battlefield radar (COBRA) is a three-nation project involving Britain, France, and Germany, with development work starting in 1990 and the production contract signed in March 1998. Similarly, in April 1998, Britain, France, and Germany announced their decision to purchase 5,000 to 6,000 units of a new European armored personnel carrier (the battlefield taxi) to be supplied by a consortium of European companies comprising Krauss-Maffei, MaK and Wegman (Germany), GIAT (France), and GKN (UK). The project will be managed by the new European procurement agency known as OCCAR.

International collaboration is not without its problems, all of which lead

Table 5.11. *EU international companies*

Joint company	Project	Participants	Work shares
Panavia	Tornado (CA)	BAe (UK)	42.5%
		DB/DASA (G)	42.5%
		Alenia (It)	15.0%
Eurofighter	EF2000 (CA)	BAe (UK)	33%
		DB/DASA (G)	33%
		Alenia (It)	21%
		CASA (Sp)	13%
Eurocopter	Tiger (AH)	Aerospatiale (F)	50%
		DB/DASA (G)	50%
EH Industries	EH 101 (MRH)	Agusta (It)	50%
		Westland (UK)	50%
NH 90	NH 90 (MRH)	Eurocopter (F,G)	67% (F = 43%)
		Agusta (It)	26%
		Fokker (N)	7%
Airbus Military Company (AMC)	Future Large Aircraft, FLA (TA)	Aerospatiale (F)	To be determined
		Alenia (It)	
		BAe (UK)	
		CASA (Sp)	
		DB/DASA (G)	
AIRBUS	Civil jet airliners	Aerospatiale (F)	37.9%
		BAe (UK)	20%
		CASA (Sp)	4.2%
		DB/DASA (G)	37.9%
Euromissile	TRIGAT (ATM)	Aerospatiale (F)	33%
		BAe (UK)	33%
		DB/DASA (G)	33%
European Space Agency (ESA)	Civil space research and satellites	13 member states	Member states contribute to mandatory budgets based on national income.
International Joint Venture Company (IJVC)	Common New Generation Frigate (CNGF)	BAe (UK)	Equal sharing of development costs
		GEC Marine (UK)	
		Vosper Thornycroft (UK)	
		Orrizonte (It)	
		DCN (F)	
Euro-Art	Battlefield radar (COBRA)	Siemens (G)	29%
		Thomson-CSF (F)	29%
		Racal (UK)	16%
		Lockheed Martin	26%

Notes: F = France; G= Germany; It = Italy; Sp = Spain; UK = United Kingdom.
AH = attack helicopter; ATM = antitank missile; CA = combat aircraft; MRH = multirole helicopter; TA = transport aircraft.
BAe = British Aerospace; DB/DASA = Daimler Benz/Deutsche Aerospace; CASA = Construeciones Aeronauticas.

to departures from the ideal model. The governments, military staffs, scientists, and industrialists in each partner nation form interest groups which will pursue their self-interest concerning leadership, design requirements, technology, and work shares. Compromise is inevitable, and nations will join the collaborative club and remain members so long as membership is expected to be worthwhile (compared with the alternatives of a national program or imports). Within the collaborative club, nations will reach agreement about a given project's military specifications, the delivery dates for each partner's armed forces, work shares, and the arrangements for project management. Reaching agreement on such a *complex international contract* involves substantial transaction costs in specifying, negotiating, agreeing, and monitoring where there are differences in information between buyers and contractors (information asymmetries) and opportunities for strategic behavior (e.g., bargaining, threats, bluffing). Typically, such contracts involve specific break or withdrawal points at which the partner nations can withdraw from the collaborative program: these points are usually the feasibility and design study stages, full-scale development, and full-scale production, each of which involves increasing resource commitments. Separate contracts are usually negotiated for development and production. For example, on Eurofighter 2000, development costs for the United Kingdom are estimated at £4.3 billion (33 percent share) and production costs at £11.1 billion (1996–97 prices, with a UK production of 232 aircraft: HCP 238, 1997).

The international agreement reflected in a collaborative program specifies the broad terms under which trading takes place. Given the political, economic, and technological uncertainties involved in two or more nations developing and purchasing advanced defense equipment over long time horizons (e.g., ten to twenty-five or more years), the international contract for collaboration is necessarily incomplete, but it will specify broad parameters concerned with payments for specific assets (technology and production) and governance structures for the transactions. Nations might be expected to learn from previous experience with collaboration, but such learning benefits might be reduced if new partners are added to the club. Nonetheless, one rule has dominated collaboration, namely, *juste retour,* where the emphasis is on a "fair share" of the work between partner nations, which usually means work allocated on the basis of each nation's planned production orders (where planned production can change between the development and production phases of the program). For example, on collaborative aircraft development work, *juste retour* means that each nation will demand its fair share of high technology work on the airframe, engine, and avionics as well as demanding its own flight testing center. Similarly, with collaborative production work, each nation demands a final assembly line. Thus, work is allocated on the basis of equity and political bargaining rather than on the basis of efficiency criteria (i.e., competition and comparative advantage).

Nor are the partner governments models of efficient decision making. Governments and their officials create elaborate and complex committee structures which seek consensus at every level and require unanimity for key decisions; some decisions can only be made by the most senior committees or by ministers. For example, on the EF2000 project there is a four-level hierarchy of committees (originally thirty-nine committees were established), with a steering committee providing overall guidance and meetings attended by national officials and other interested parties (up to sixty people can be present at a meeting). Program management is further complicated by the need for extensive monitoring arrangements as partner nations seek to police costs and progress on incomplete contracts for costly and complex projects. An international agency is usually created for the day-to-day management of a collaborative program (e.g., NEFMA, the NATO EF2000 Management Agency). However, such agencies often lack a clear mandate; they sometimes duplicate the work of national project management offices; and staff posts are filled by each nation in line with the cost-sharing arrangements on the program (HCP 724, 1995, p. 33). The result is excessive bureaucracy and slow decision making, which can be a further source of delays and inefficiency in collaboration.

The arrangements for work sharing and government decision making lead to departures from the ideal model of collaboration resulting in cost penalties and delays. On development work, the costs of collaboration are sometimes approximated by the *square root rule:* collaborative development costs can be estimated by the square root of the number of nations involved in the project (Sandler and Hartley, 1995, p. 236). For example, with four nations, collaborative development actually costs twice as much as an equivalent national program. On production work, the official UK view is that collaboration results in "little savings" and there are indications that the unit production costs of a collaborative program may be higher than a national equivalent – a view which suggests substantial inefficiencies in production arrangements (up to a 10 percent cost penalty: HCP 247, 1991). Collaborative production inefficiencies are illustrated in Figure 5.2. In the ideal case, collaboration which increases output from Q_1 to $2Q_1$ should reduce unit production costs from C_1 to C_0 on the average cost curve AC_0; but collab-

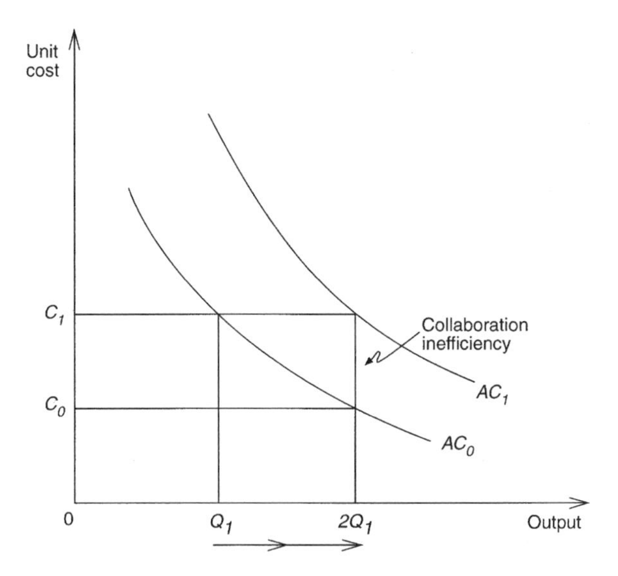

Figure 5.2. Collaboration inefficiencies

oration inefficiencies may result in a higher cost curve of AC_1 and no reduction in unit costs (i.e., C_1). There is also a general belief that collaborative development programs take longer to develop and deliver to the armed forces, with delays being approximated by the *cube root* of the number of partner nations involved. Some estimates suggest that collaborative development could take an extra two years or over 50 percent longer than a national project; but generally such claims are not supported by statistical tests (Hartley and Martin, 1993).

The four-nation Eurofighter 2000 project illustrates the problems of collaborative programs (see Table 5.11). Between 1988, when it started, and 1996, the costs to the United Kingdom of the EF2000 development program had risen by 46 percent (£1,360 million, 1996–97 prices) and the project was at least three years late (HCP 238, 1997). These cost increases and delays reflected the rigid work-sharing requirements and the political and financial uncertainties surrounding the program, rather than any major technical difficulties (HCP 724, 1995). The rigid work-sharing arrangements are specified by the partner nations in the main development contracts and are designed "to provide a balanced spread of technology between the participating nations," and "have often resulted in industry placing work with specially formed consortia with complex managerial and working structures and variable levels of technical expertise rather than on grounds of value for money" (HCP 724, 1995, p. 25). In each of these specially created consortia there are complex industrial interfaces to manage, which places a premium on industry to establish suitable systems to coordinate the work of companies located in different nations. The Flight Control System (FCS) for the EF2000 is a classic example of all the worst features of collaborative work sharing and a major source of program delays. One parliamentary view is that the industrial arrangements for the FCS had all the characteristics of an "accident waiting to happen. Even though British companies . . . had demonstrated their competence to carry out the work, other companies became involved who were either not up to the job or whose involvement made arrangements unduly cumbersome" (HCP 222, 1994, p. xiv). GEC-Marconi has estimated that a solo bid for the work would have been one-third cheaper than the consortium bid. Nonetheless, estimates suggest that on EF2000 the UK will have paid two-thirds of the total costs of a national program (i.e., total project costs for all four partners were twice the costs of a national program).

The EF2000 project has also been subject to considerable political and financial uncertainty. For example, such uncertainty delayed for more than one year the formal agreement by the partner nations on the 1992 reorientation of the program, with Germany being a major source of the uncertainty and delay. Further uncertainty arose in the mid-1990s as the partner nations reviewed their future budgetary positions, their likely orders, and their work-sharing requirements prior to a contractual commitment to production. Germany was a source of delay in proceeding to the production phase, mainly due to its desire to meet the Maastricht criteria for the creation of a single European currency. By 1997, it was estimated that these procurement delays had accounted for sixteen of the thirty-six months' slippage in the program (HCP 238, 1997, p. 111). In January 1998, the four partner nations on the EF2000 project signed production contracts for an initial planned purchase of 620 aircraft, with first deliveries scheduled for June 2002 (i.e., a total delay of forty-two months). In September 1998, EF2000 was named Eurofighter for European partner nations and Eurofighter Typhoon for export markets.

There are at least two lessons to be learned from the EF2000 program. First, care is needed in identifying the criteria used in evaluating collaborative programs. Perfect problem-free projects do not exist. Most high technology defense projects, whether they be national or collaborative, are characterized by problems reflecting poor procurement management and ambitious technical requirements leading to cost overruns, delays, and sometimes cancellation. Interestingly, though, while EF2000 is a third-generation collaboration (after Jaguar and Tornado), it is characterized by the traditional problems of work sharing and government decision making. Of course, it could be claimed that these problems and inefficiencies would be even greater without the benefits of previous collaborative experience.

Second, there remain considerable opportunities for improving the efficiency of collaborative programs. Efficiency could be improved by allocating work on the basis of each nation's comparative advantage, using competition to determine work shares; by selecting a single prime contractor for the program and ensuring that the prime contractor is subject to contractual incentives placing it at risk (via competitively determined fixed price or target price incentive contracts); and by applying the principle of compensation. Adequate arrangements are needed to compensate the losers from policies designed to improve efficiency in collaborative programs. Compensation need not be organized within the program but could involve offsets on other defense projects or more general regional aid and manpower policies (e.g., training and retraining, labor mobility, occupational guidance).

Licensed production and coproduction

Rather than purchasing directly "off the shelf," nations buying foreign defense equipment often demand that some form of "offsetting" economic activity be placed by the supplier in the importing country. Offsets form part of the product and its price. Licensed production is the traditional form of direct offset, where the purchasing nation builds foreign-designed equipment under license in its own country (e.g., European and Japanese production of the US F-104 aircraft; European coproduction of US F-16 aircraft). For the licensed producer, the aim might be to build all the equipment locally or to build some parts and undertake final assembly.

Coproduction has been variously defined. A RAND study defined it as "any international collaboration during the production phase of a major weapon system acquisition program" (Rich et al., 1981, p. 1). The classic case is fully integrated coproduction, in which all participating nations purchase the same equipment and produce parts of each other's orders. An example was the original four-nation European consortium purchase of US F-16 aircraft, whereby European industry was initially awarded work on 10% of the 650 F-16s bought by the USAF, 40% of the 348 F-16s bought by the Europeans, and 15% of export sales. Initially, this guaranteed European industry 58% of the value of the European order. The Japanese FSX aircraft program is a further variant of coproduction involving some codevelopment. In this case, Mitsubishi Heavy Industries (MHI) and Lockheed-Martin (previously General Dynamics) are codeveloping and coproducing a substantially modified F-16 aircraft. MHI is the prime contractor; Lockheed and other US companies will receive 40% of the development and 40% of the production work.

Licensed production and coproduction generally involve *cost penalties* compared with buying directly from the main manufacturer. These cost penalties reflect entry costs, the costs of transferring technology, relatively short production runs, and the absence of learning economies. Interview-questionnaire studies estimate cost penalties of up to 50% for licensed and coproduction, with a typical penalty of 10–15% (Chinworth, 1992; Hartley, 1983; Hartley and Cox, 1995). On the US-European coproduction of the F-16 it has been estimated that the Europeans incurred a 34% cost penalty compared with a direct buy from General Dynamics. On the same program, it was estimated that coproduction added about 5% to the USAF program costs for its first 650 F-16s (Rich et al., 1981). On the Japanese FSX aircraft, it has been claimed that its costs are some three to four times those of a basic F-16 aircraft (Flight International, 1997, p. 66). There are some exceptions. A RAND study of Japanese experience with the licensed production of the Lockheed F-104 aircraft estimated that the unit costs of the Japanese aircraft were 88% of US costs for a comparable aircraft (Hall and Johnson, 1967). The savings arose because Lockheed transferred a significant portion of its accumulated learning on the F-104 to Mitsubishi; since US firms were paid for data, data rights, and technical assistance, "they had clear incentives to provide Japanese firms with the fruits of US experience" (Hall and Johnson, 1967, p. 187).

Licensed production and coproduction are believed to have their wider industrial and economic benefits. These include support for a nation's defense industrial base, technology transfer (e.g., in management and production manufacturing), employment, import savings, and military standardization. In addition, manufacturing under license saves substantial R & D resources which would have been required for an independent national venture. Unfortunately, there is little quantitative evidence on the likely magnitude of these benefits. A case study of Japanese experience with licensed production estimated that Japanese work content ranged from 60% on the Patriot missile to 70% on the F-15 to 90% on the F-4 (Chinworth, 1992). An alternative policy is to seek other forms of offsets.

Offsets

Offsets are associated with the import of foreign defense equipment. They are a form of work sharing whereby the nation purchasing foreign defense equipment requires the supplier to allocate some work to the industries of the purchasing nation (Martin, 1996). Offsets are a growing feature of the international trade in defense equipment, particularly aerospace equipment, and this is a field which is relatively unexplored by economists. Offsets impose conditions on the foreign seller of defense equipment, enabling the purchasing government to recover or offset some or all of its purchase price (Martin, 1996). Offset schemes are usually designed to achieve a relocation of economic activity – namely, from the country of the equipment supplier to the purchasing nation. Such relocation resembles trade diversion and has been criticized by economists as welfare reducing. For the seller, offsets reflect the desire of profit-seeking firms to do business with governments: they can be regarded as part of the sales package and as an alternative to price discounts. For the supplying nation (particularly the United States), there are concerns about the impact of offsets on domestic defense industries, on employment, and on technology transfer to potential rivals (although international competition usually means that other companies will offer work-sharing deals). For the buying nation, offsets appear to provide industrial benefits in the form of jobs, technology transfer, support for the defense industrial base, and foreign currency savings (Martin, 1996).

Offsets may be direct or indirect and embrace defense and/or civil goods and services. *Direct* offsets involve participation of the buying nation's industry in some aspect of the contract for supplying foreign defense equipment. For example, if a nation purchases a foreign aircraft, its firms might be involved as subcontractors and suppliers, or there might be a fully integrated coproduction program, or it might manufacture the foreign aircraft under license. *Indirect* offsets involve goods and services unrelated to the purchase of the specific foreign defense equipment. For example, an indirect offset might involve work on some other defense project. The sale of American F-18 aircraft to Spain allowed aid to Spanish tourism to count as part of the offset agreement (a civil offset). Indirect offsets can include foreign investment and counter-trade transactions such as barter, counter-purchase and buy-back (Martin, 1996). Each type of offset can be assessed in terms of its contribution to the national economy in the form of technology (i.e., high, low, or no technology) and its employment impacts reflected in the number of jobs, their skill content, and their location over the time period of the offset.

Because they interfere with normal commercial market transactions, it might be thought that offsets are inefficient. However, in some circumstances, offsets can contribute to efficiency improvements if they remove nontariff barriers and lead prime contractors to search for, and to discover, more efficient subcontractors located overseas. They can lead to an extension of market information and knowledge and remove barriers to the use of foreign subcontractors, thus allowing entry into previously closed markets.

Clearly, in competitive bidding for foreign defense contracts, overseas firms have every incentive to offer an attractive offset package as part of the bid: maximizing offsets becomes part of the competitive process, with firms seeking new and ingenious methods of satisfying their contractual obligations. They might, for example, use specialist agencies, such as banks, as well as their suppliers to achieve their offset targets; and they will try to claim as much business as possible as offset. At the same time, vote-sensitive governments have every inducement to claim the maximum offset deal so that they can justify the import of defense equipment in terms of protecting the national defense industrial base, jobs, and technology.

But while offsets *appear* attractive, there are a number of associated pitfalls and reservations:

1. *New work.* Major reservations arise about the extent to which offset business represents genuinely new work which would not otherwise have been obtained without the offset agreement. Some experts have suggested that genuinely new business might be some 25 percent to 50 percent of the total offset (Martin and Hartley, 1995).
2. *Civil work.* On the AWACS contract for the UK, Boeing was allowed to count its purchase of Rolls-Royce civil aero-engines for its commercial aircraft as part of its offset obligation (up to a maximum of $800 million). This meant *civil* aerospace work counted against a *defense* offset commitment; the arrangement was generous to Boeing, representing more than 50 percent of Boeing's offset commitment; and Rolls-Royce aero-engines would have been purchased without the offset agreement. Hence, they were not new work resulting from the offset obligation.
3. *High technology work.* Problems will always arise in defining high technology work. Moreover, on projects purchased directly off the shelf, opportunities for involvement in high technology work are likely to be restricted to the production domain. Inevitably, in the long term, offsets have implications for the future technological capability and continued international competitiveness of the buying nation's defense industry.

4. *Estimated employment impacts.* Offsets can always be shown to generate large employment impacts if they involve low-wage jobs. Numbers can be further inflated by adding together full-time and part-time jobs (rather than full-time equivalents) and by focusing on man-years of work (without specifying the annual number of full-time equivalent jobs, the time period for the estimate, the wage and salary levels, and whether numbers might fluctuate between years).

The need to make difficult choices

As with other aspects of procurement policy, the issue of alternative industrial policies has been dominated by myths, emotion, and special pleading, especially in relation to the choice between buying from a national firm (national champion) and importing foreign equipment. These myths need to be assessed critically and subjected to empirical testing. Reliable quantitative evidence is needed to assess the benefits and costs of alternative industrial policies. Areas where quantitative evidence is not available need to be identified so that decision makers are clear about the unknowns and the intangible elements when making their choices.

Economic pressures from falling defense budgets and rising equipment costs mean that defense policy makers cannot avoid the need for some difficult choices. One set of choices will require governments to review their traditional procurement policies: will they be willing to continue paying the price of independence through supporting a national defense industry, or are there substantially cheaper ways to acquire defense equipment? Currently, NATO is an inefficient organization for the supply of defense equipment. It is characterized by duplication of costly R & D projects both within Europe and between Europe and the US; and by relatively short production runs, especially in Europe. Within NATO, there are two possible efficiency-improving policy initiatives in weapons procurement: first, the creation of a Single European Market for defense equipment; and second, the possible creation of a NATO free trade area for equipment.

A SINGLE EUROPEAN MARKET FOR DEFENSE EQUIPMENT

The search for efficiency improvements in procurement policy will lead EU nations to review the traditional support for their national defense industries. The inefficiencies of the existing fragmented and national defense

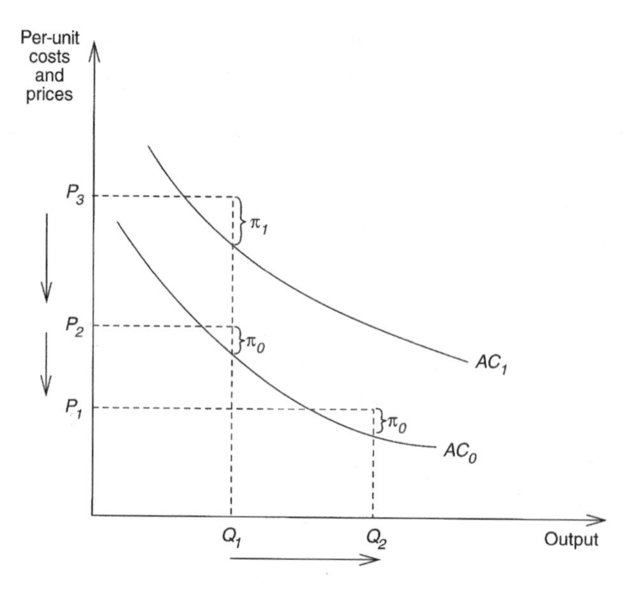

Figure 5.3. Competition and scale effects

markets and industries increase the attractiveness of creating a Single European Market for defense equipment. After all, the economic benefits of the Single Market for *civil* goods and services, namely, competition and scale effects, indicate that similar benefits are likely from extending the Single Market to embrace defense procurement. Article 223 of the Treaty of Rome forms a barrier to extending the Single Market to defense procurement. This article allows member states to take any necessary action for the protection of their essential security interests connected with the production of, or trade in, arms, munitions, and war materiel (e.g., nuclear arms, combat aircraft, missiles, tanks). As a result, member states can use their procurement policies to protect substantial parts of the domestic defense industrial base, leading to inefficiency in EU defense markets.

The economic benefits of creating a Single European Market in defense equipment are expected to result from *savings in R & D costs* (through reduced duplication of costly R & D projects), from *increased competition* (the competition effect) both within and between nations, and from *economies of scale and learning* due to longer production runs (the scale effect). Figure 5.3 shows the impact of the competition and scale effects on unit costs (*AC*), profits (π) and prices (*P*). Competition results in lower-cost suppliers entering the market, leading to lower unit costs, lower profits, and lower prices (P_3 to P_2). The scale effect shows that the successful firms produce a larger output, thus achieving scale and learning economies (reducing prices from P_2 to P_1). There may also be additional *dynamic benefits* from innovations due to competition and the creation of the Single Market. However, dynamic benefits are difficult to measure and give rise to the possibility of double-counting the impacts of competition. One solution is to recognize that if dynamic benefits exist they are a "bonus" to be added to the estimated benefits of competition and greater scale. Nor can it be assumed that a Single Market will end all duplication of costly R & D programs. Some duplication may be required to maintain competition in the development stage and avoid the costs of monopoly (e.g., competitive prototypes).

The Single Market scenarios

There are opportunities for improving the current inefficient arrangements for defense procurement outside Europe. Economists can contribute to policy formulation by estimating the benefits and costs of creating a Single Market for defense equipment. Four scenarios for a Single Market are analyzed, each with a possible role for a future European Armaments Agency. The scenarios were based on a study undertaken for the European Commission, with the scenarios specified by the commission (Hartley and Cox, 1995). For each scenario, there was assumed to be a nondiscriminating liberalized competitive market either restricted to member states or open to the world. This assumption requires the national or centralized purchasing agency to act as a nondiscriminating competitive buyer. The four scenarios are (see Table 5.12):

1. *Scenario 1* comprised a liberalized competitive market with national procurement by national defense ministries and agencies. If the market were restricted to EU member states, firms in each state would be able to bid for defense contracts in other member states. Alternatively, if the market were open to the world, firms in countries outside the EU would be allowed to bid for defense contracts in EU states. Under this scenario, a European Armaments Agency would act as a competition agency ensuring that member states abided by the procurement rules for the opening up of their national defense markets.
2. *Scenario 2* comprised an EU centralized procurement agency buying standardized equipment, with the agency replacing national defense ministries. A European Armaments Agency would have a major role in this scenario, and it would be expected to achieve significant savings

from competitive purchasing, from reduced duplication of R & D, and from large-scale production orders. Effectively, this scenario assumed a single EU army, navy, and air force similar to the US model: hence, this is the most attractive option economically but the most challenging politically (Seidelman, 1997).

3. *Scenario 3* involved limited liberalization. This was a modified version of scenario 1 under which certain categories of equipment were excluded, namely, nuclear systems, anti-toxic radioactive agents, and cryptography. As in scenario 1, a European Armaments Agency would act as a competition agency promoting competition and policing the restrictions.
4. *Scenario 4* was the twin-track model. This involved competition for small and medium-sized projects (e.g., small arms such as rifles and ammunition, artillery, small missiles), with large projects undertaken on a collaborative basis and collaboration extended to major air, land, and sea systems (e.g., aircraft, missiles, tanks, and warships). Two assumptions were applied to collaborative projects – namely, work allocated on the traditional basis of *juste retour* and work awarded on the basis of competition. Under this scenario, a European Armaments Agency would have responsibility for ensuring competition for small and medium scale projects and for developing and managing collaborative programs.

The four scenarios can be ranked in terms of their expected cost savings. Scenario 2 is expected to offer the greatest savings, followed in order by scenarios 4, 1, and 3. There are some overlaps between the scenarios. For example, scenario 1 might involve elements of scenarios 2 and 4. This could arise where two or more nations voluntarily agree to buy the same equipment (standardization) either on a collaborative basis or from a foreign supplier. An example of this occurred in 1975, when four European nations reached a coproduction agreement for the purchase of US F-16 aircraft, thus demonstrating that standardization does not require centralized procurement.

Similarly, the scenarios could be modified. Scenario 2, for example, might involve the creation of a centralized purchasing agency (a European Armaments Agency) which would not replace national defense ministries, which would not impose standardization, and which would operate on a voluntary basis. Such an agency would obtain economies from the use of its large-scale ordering and buying power. It would assemble national orders for equipment, parts, and components and invite firms to bid for large orders and long-term contracts (e.g., national orders for different types of tank track could be offered as one large order over, say, a ten-year period). The agency might also obtain cost savings by aggregating different national orders for the same equipment or components and by identifying products where standardization might be worthwhile (i.e., by acting as an information and education agency).

Estimating the benefits

Estimating the benefits of the four scenarios involved two approaches. The first was a case study approach based on the estimated cost savings from reduced duplication in R & D and from longer production runs for specific weapons. For example, increasing the output of a combat aircraft with a unit production cost of ECU 50 million from 250 to 1,000 units might reduce unit costs by 20 percent to ECU 40 million. This assumes the production of 1,000 units of an identical type of aircraft with no modifications. Such examples provide persuasive illustrations of the cost savings from equipment standardization.

Second, the different scenarios are expected to lead to cost and price savings reflecting the impact of both competition and economies of scale from larger orders. Greater competition from within the EU or from the rest of the world results in alternative estimates of the *competition effect;* while longer production runs lead to lower unit costs and prices, which provide estimates of the *scale effect.* It is assumed that cost savings are reflected in lower prices. The lack of publicly available data required a company interview study to estimate competition and scale effects. The competition effect was estimated at 10% to 20% for the EU-wide market and 15% to 25% for the EU market open to the world. Similarly, the scale effect was estimated at a 12% unit cost reduction for a doubling of output (alternative estimates were used as sensitivity tests). These estimates of competition and scale effects were applied to the EU's total spending on defense equipment and procurement, thus indicating the likely magnitude of the aggregate savings from the various scenarios. There are also possible dynamic benefits which would increase the estimated savings.

The estimated cost savings from the various Single European Market scenarios are summarized in Table 5.12. With all the difficulties and uncertainties involved in this estimation procedure, the reported figures are lower bound estimates and should be regarded as broad orders of magnitude. The estimated budget savings are based on 1990 defense procurement budgets. Disarmament following the end of the Cold War has resulted in lower equipment budgets, but the estimates of the *percentage* competition and

Table 5.12. *Benefits of a single European market*

Scenarios	Annual savings in ECU billion (1990)	Percentage of annual defense procurement
Liberalized market	5.5 to 7.0	8.5% to 11.0%
Centralized procurement	9.4 to 10.9	14.5% to 17.0%
Limited liberalization	5.3 to 6.6	8.0% to 10.0%
Twin track: version A	6.5 to 7.6	10.0% to 12.0%
Twin track: version B	7.4 to 9.3	11.0% to 14.0%

Notes: Figures are for annual aggregate savings based on 1990 total EC defense procurement budgets of ECU 65 billion. Alternative estimates resulted in lower equipment spending figures (i.e., based on Article 223 items and NATO definitions). The original study was based on the EC and the annual total budget savings are for EC member states in 1990.

Twin track A assumes collaboration based on *juste retour;* version B assumes collaboration based on competition for work sharing.

Sources: Hartley and Cox (1995); HCP 333 (1995, p. 100).

scale effects remain unchanged. In fact, budget cuts will increase the intensity of competition in the short to medium term, so that the percentage competition effect is likely to be higher than the lower bound estimates used in the study. Table 5.12 shows that all the scenarios for a Single Market offer substantial cost savings. Centralized procurement (scenario 2) offers the greatest annual savings, reflecting the economies of scale and learning from the large-scale purchase of common and standardized equipment.

The costs of a single market

Creating a Single Market for defense equipment involves costs as well as benefits. Typically, adjustment costs will be incurred in the short to medium term, and the benefits will arise over the longer term. For such a change to be socially desirable, the benefits have to exceed the costs (suitably discounted to a base year). The costs of change will be reflected in job losses, plant closures, and exits from the defense market; and these costs will be in addition to those resulting from disarmament following the end of the Cold War. The most vulnerable sectors include firms in developing defense industries; firms which have not been exposed to competition; and the smaller companies, although some of these might survive through specialization (e.g., in niche markets). It is also likely that the opening up of the EU market, especially to the rest of the world, will shock some firms into improving their efficiency and hence their chances of survival.

Problems remain. Difficulties will arise in creating a level playing field, especially where there is competition between state and privately owned firms. Mergers will result in a smaller number of larger defense contractors and the possibility of cartels, collusive tendering, and monopoly within the EU. As a result, maintaining competition in the EU defense market will require that the market be opened up to firms from the rest of the world. Effectively, this means US competition, with implications for maintaining the EU defense industrial base. However, it has to be recognized that a European defense industrial base does not yet exist; but its creation could be one of the tasks for a European Armaments Agency.

A European Armaments Agency

Defense equipment markets bring together both *buyers* and *sellers* of equipment. Proposals for mergers, industrial restructuring, and rationalization of Europe's defense industries to create European defense firms of a size comparable to that of their US rivals, focus on the *supply side* of the market. However, application of the US model to Europe cannot ignore the *demand side* of the market and its fragmentation into a set of national procurement arrangements. Larger US defense companies benefit from a single large American home market. Proposals for restructuring Europe's defense industries to create larger groups will require the corresponding restructuring of demand to create a larger European market. As a result, supply side changes will be related to the scale and organization of the demand for defense equipment, so that European governments cannot ignore their role in determining appropriate procurement arrangements. The alternatives range from liberalizing or opening up national defense markets in the EU to the creation of a European Armaments Agency.

While a comprehensive European Armaments Agency involving all EU member states remains to be created, a possible start has been made with the formation of the four-nation OCCAR, comprising France, Germany, Italy, and the UK. (OCCAR is the French acronym for Organization Conjointe de Coopération pour l'Armement.) The organization will focus on achieving a more efficient, effective approach to the management of collaborative programs. This is an area where there is considerable potential for efficiency improvements through, for example, the use of competition rather than *juste retour* to allocate work shares. There are, however, other pressures for a "Fortress Europe" policy, with all the worst features of protectionism including the absence of competition, subsidies, and inefficiency (cf. the Common Agricultural Policy). Clearly, producer interest groups likely to lose from greater competition and efficiency improvements will oppose such changes. They will argue that the European DIB is an "infant industry" needing protection from the US; that it is a valuable source of jobs and high technology; that it is vital for European security; and that competition should be managed (see also Chapter 7).

A NATO FREE TRADE AREA

A Single European Market for defense equipment might be viewed by European nations as a precondition for the eventual creation of a NATO free trade area for equipment. The scenarios for such a NATO free trade area could be similar to those outlined in Table 5.12, but with higher estimated cost savings than if the Single Market were restricted to EU member states. A NATO Armaments Agency could be created with the task of promoting both competition and collaboration. Such an agency would be responsible for ensuring free entry into all member nation's markets, for monitoring government contract decisions, for policing cartels and collusive tendering, and for preventing governments from behaving anticompetitively (i.e., favoring their national champions).

A NATO free market will involve both winners and losers. Potential gainers will be US firms which will have open access to all NATO EU markets; such firms are likely to benefit in high technology equipment and where there are significant economies of scale and learning. However, NATO EU firms will benefit from access to the US market, and they are likely to gain for small volume equipment and in specialist (niche) markets. Potential losers will be those NATO EU firms which fail to restructure to match the size of US contractors and those European firms which have operated in protected markets with no experience of competition. But the EU nations can offset their possible losses by combining their orders to create a major buying power to counteract the monopoly power of large US firms (countervailing power).

There is a possible alternative to a NATO free market, namely, managed competition. Such a solution would comprise some limited competition (workable competition) and fair work shares, so that no nation's defense industries would be required to make major adjustments due to the competitive shocks of a free market. Once again, managed competition and fair work shares would be organized by a NATO Armaments Agency. While such a solution is politically attractive to governments and their defense industries, there would be a price to pay in the form of cost penalties, delays, and poor quality resulting from limited competition and work sharing.

CONCLUSIONS

Within the EU, national independence through supporting a domestic defense industrial base is costly. A Single European Market offers opportunities for achieving significant cost savings. However, the long-run trend is toward a smaller number of larger defense firms. By 1998, the US defense industry had reorganized and restructured around three giant companies (Boeing, Lockheed-Martin, Raytheon). By contrast, Europe's defense industries had achieved some restructuring *within* nation states, but there remained considerable scope for international restructuring *among* European nations and between Europe and the United States. This was recognized in December 1997 when the governments of France, Germany, and the UK agreed that their defense industries need to rationalize and merge to survive and achieve international competitiveness in the next century. The governments requested the aerospace and defense electronics industries in their countries to formulate their preferred restructuring solutions by end of March 1998, with the aim of creating European competitors for the US giants.

By the March 1998 deadline, the aerospace industries of the four Airbus partner countries expressed their desire to create a single unified European Aerospace and Defense Company (EADC) comprising initially Aerospatiale (France), British Aerospace (UK), CASA (Spain), and DASA (Germany), but with the opportunity for other firms and nations to join the new group – for example, Alenia (Italy), Saab (Sweden), and the planned merger between Aerospatiale and Dassault (France). In April 1998, these proposals for industry restructuring were supported by the governments of France, Germany, Italy, Spain, and the UK. Further restructuring is likely in other sectors of the European aerospace industry, namely, aero-engines, avionics, missiles, helicopters, and space systems (e.g., missiles involving Matra-BAe Dynamics; helicopters involving Agusta (Italy) and GKN Westland (UK): see Tables 5.7 and 5.11). Elsewhere, the restructuring is likely to embrace other sectors of Europe's defense industries, namely, electronics (e.g., GEC in the UK; Thomson in France), land and sea systems. For the future, the interesting questions are whether the restructuring of Europe's defense industries will involve horizontal, vertical, or conglomerate mergers; whether it will be based on private ownership; and whether nations will sacrifice their national champions and accept the rationalization needed to create competitive European defense companies.

Restructuring through mergers has a price. Efficient scale can be achieved, but at the cost of creating national monopolies in Europe and oligopoly in the US, leading in turn to higher prices, inefficiency, monopoly profits, and reduced incentives to innovate. Competition promotes efficiency, and a NATO free trade area for defense equipment provides the opportunity for ensuring that the American and European defense markets are subject to continuing competitive pressures.

The focus on restructuring and creating giant companies has neglected the continuing challenge of maintaining a market structure which allows opportunities for rivalry. A NATO free trade area provides a framework for maintaining competition. Other possibilities include competitive prototype programs involving international consortia of European and US firms; the funding of rival but cheap technology demonstrators; and the procurement of dual-use technologies and equipment from civil commercial firms outside the traditional defense industries. It also needs to be recognized that genuine competition is a search and discovery process, and that such a process might show that efficient prime contractors do not need to be vertically integrated firms combining development and production units. An efficient industrial structure might comprise prime contractors with development and systems integration capabilities with production work undertaken by subcontractors.

6 NATO challenges on the horizon

In the earlier chapters, NATO has been characterized as facing a host of challenges: identifying its strategic mission; deciding its membership size and composition; procuring the next generation of weapons; and adjusting its defense industrial base. There are myriad other challenges that will confront NATO in the decades ahead. If NATO is to remain relevant, then it must possess the capacity to redesign its forces, doctrines, missions, and institutional structures (see Chapter 8) so as to respond to the most worrisome of the potential threats. Because these challenges differ greatly from one another and involve diverse regions of the world, NATO cannot be expected to respond to *all* of them. Other defense and nondefense arrangements will be required to manage crises that surpass NATO's concerns or capabilities.

Security challenges can be addressed by formal (e.g., treaties, supranational structures) or informal (e.g., discussions) arrangements. Both formal and informal responses can involve a nonmilitary response (e.g., diplomacy, bargaining, economic sanctions) or a military response. The latter can include a variety of actions ranging from a threatened military sanction to an invasion, if all else fails. NATO must possess the means to address security concerns with an appropriately measured response. If the threat is minor and easily addressed, then NATO must show the requisite restraint to keep the crisis from escalating. When the threat affects interests beyond those of the NATO allies, a larger world body would best manage the exigency.

A shorter version of this paper was published by Todd Sandler in *Defence and Peace Economics*, 8, November 1997, 319–353, under the title "The Future Challenges of NATO: An Economic Viewpoint." Part of this article has been reprinted through the kind permission of Harwood Academic Publishers.

Ethnic-based civil wars in Eastern Europe and in the former Soviet republics represent one of the greatest security concerns for NATO allies. Bosnia may be just a taste of what is to come now that the dictatorships – which once kept the ethnically mixed post–World War II nations intact by brute force – are disappearing from Eastern Europe and the former Soviet republics. Transnational terrorism also poses a threat. Because terrorism is often associated with democracy – where the media are free to report incidents, the right of assembly is assured, and governments are expected to protect persons and property[1] – the democratization of Eastern Europe may be associated with an increase in terrorism that may spill over affecting old and new NATO allies.

Another threat may arise from the increasing inequality in the world distribution of income. Between 1960 and 1991 the distribution of income among nations became increasingly more inequitable, despite phenomenal growth in some emerging-market economies (UN Development Programme, 1992, 1994). Increased disparity may breed the revolutions of the next millennium as hopelessness gives rise to violence. Revolutions that can spread among countries create political instabilities that could sever resource supply lines from mineral-rich African and Asian nations. NATO also faces security risks from environmental pollutants that transcend political borders. Norman Myers (1993) characterizes the threat of worldwide environmental degradation from ozone shield depletion, global warming, topsoil erosion, groundwater contamination, expanding populations, acid rain, and tropical deforestation as the "ultimate security" threat, which may call for interventions. One such intervention would be for nations to cooperate both to control their own pollutants and to pressure others into doing the same.

Still other challenges may stem from "rogue" nations that do not ascribe to international norms regarding, say, the spread of democracy or the nonproliferation of weapons of mass destruction (WMD), including nuclear, chemical, and biological weapons. Rogue nations may be run by leaders who are willing to employ terrorism and other intimidating tactics to force the international community to accede to their demands. In some instances, a rogue nation may be willing to invade the territory of another nation to acquire disputed resources, as Iraq did in invading Kuwait in August 1990 to capture oil fields on their common border. In other instances, a rogue nation's single-minded pursuit of WMD places other nations at risk. Iraq's

1. On the relationship between terrorism and democracy, see Crelinsten (1989), Eubank and Weinberg (1994), Sandler (1995), and Schmid (1992). Mickolus, Sandler, and Murdock (1989) record the pattern of transnational terrorism for the 1980s.

repeated refusal to abide by UN-mandated weapons inspections, imposed following its defeat in the Gulf War of 1991, has created episodic crises resulting in numerous buildups of US forces in the region. The latest buildup took place during 1997 and early 1998, following the expulsion of US weapons inspectors from the UN team on 13 November 1997. When it seemed certain in March 1998 that the United States would take military action against Iraq unless it gave UNSCOM inspectors less restricted access, Iraq agreed to this access, with US personnel included on the team.

Yet another threat to world peace stems from some NATO allies' sales of arms to developing countries. As the Gulf War showed, these arms can be deployed at a later date against the supplier and its allies. Such sales present a classic transnational externality problem to the world community, since the seller does not account for the potential costs that the sale may impose on others. Ironically, NATO must maintain larger forces to address potential crises that might arise from these weapons sales.

This chapter is devoted to assessing these potential challenges for NATO, now and into the future. Some of these alleged contingencies (e.g., rogue nations) are shown to be exaggerated, while others (e.g., security of resource supplies and weapon sales) are shown to be understated. We rely on principles of collective action to assess these threats.

CIVIL WARS AT NATO'S DOORSTEP

Bosnia-Herzegovina illustrates the potential for a protracted civil war that could spill over into neighboring states – Croatia, Serbia, Kosovo, Macedonia, Montenegro – and eventually beyond. Much can be learned from the response of the world community to Bosnia. Although this community condemned the ethnic cleansing and conflict in Bosnia, it did little at first to stop it. This inactivity meant that thousands died and that long-standing hatreds were refueled. Once dispatched, UN peacekeepers were, at first, no match for the warring factions and were in constant danger of being taken hostage. On 31 March 1993, the UN Security Council passed Resolution 816, which established a no-fly zone over Bosnia.[2] This resolution was enforced by Operation Deny Flight, which was begun on 12 April 1993 and involved the deployment of NATO aircraft. On 28 February 1994, NATO aircraft shot down four warplanes that had violated the no-fly zone. This

2. The facts reported in this paragraph come from NATO Office of Information and Press (1995).

incident was followed by additional NATO air raids on weapon sites. As outside military pressures mounted on the warring factions, the sides returned to the negotiating table, where the Dayton peace agreement was drafted on 21 November 1995 and later signed in Paris on 14 December 1995.

Both the United States and NATO played a crucial role in getting the sides to accept a cease-fire and to implement the peace agreement. The UN Interim Peace Implementation Forces (IFOR) in Bosnia had real firepower and the permission to use it. Most of the expense and manpower for IFOR was funded by NATO allies.[3] Once the peacemakers demonstrated their resolve to separate the sides even if this required force, the warring sides began to obey the cease-fire. Both the credibility and the capability of the peacekeeping force were necessary ingredients for the success of the operation.

There are at least two views concerning the proper time to intervene in a civil war like the one in Bosnia. One view maintains that swift intervention is needed before bitter animosities are built up, which can make a subsequent peace unstable. If action is quick, then the peacekeeping mission is apt to be simpler, since neither warring side has gained much of a foothold. Furthermore, quicker action means that each side has less chance to grab territory to use as a bargaining advantage at the negotiating table. A second view argues for a waiting period to allow enough time for both sides to deplete their forces and their resolve through a war of attrition. Once opposing forces have been sufficiently weakened, the peacekeepers may be welcomed by both sides. With diminished forces engaged, less peacekeepers are then required, thus making it easier for nations to commit to participating in the mission. Nations are also more willing to assume a peacekeeping role, because risks to their forces are reduced. In Bosnia, the second option was exercised.

Bosnian instability presented the greatest threat to the neighboring countries in the form of spreading ethnic strife. The typical UN member nation had much less to gain from peace in Bosnia than did the typical European NATO ally. Peace in Bosnia gave rise to joint products or multiple outputs that varied in their degree of publicness (Sandler, 1992). For neighboring countries, the reduced conflict had country-specific benefits that did not apply to the world at large. To the extent that a Bosnian peacemaking opera-

3. According to the US GAO (1998, p. 2), the United States spent $2.5 billion in 1996 on Bosnian peacekeeping efforts. It spent $2.3 billion in 1997 and is scheduled to spend $1.6 billion during the first half of 1998. Because US troops are staying beyond the June 1998 withdrawal date, US spending in Bosnia is anticipated to exceed the projected $1.6 billion. For the Stabilization Force (SFOR) deployed in December 1996, the United States provided about a quarter of the troops.

tion reduced the chance of a wider war, a global public good was also produced. Since the primary benefits went to the NATO allies and neighboring countries, NATO was right to assume the lion's share of the operation once risks were deemed acceptable. NATO must be prepared to respond to similar challenges in numerous places throughout Central and Eastern Europe. Hungary, for example, faces potential ethnic problems in three neighboring nations – Slovakia, Romania, Serbia – where concentrations of Hungarians live.[4] Other ethnic conflicts could erupt in Moldavia, Montenegro, Armenia, Slovenia, Georgia, Turkey, and Bulgaria (Klare, 1995; Larrabee, 1997, p. 186; Leech, 1991). In Kosovo, fighting erupted in 1998 between the ruling Serbian minority and the Albanian majority, comprising 90 percent of the population. Conflict could also break out between the Slav population and an Albanian minority in Macedonia, where the United States spent $11.7 million on Task Force Able Sentry during 1997 to avert such a conflict (US GAO, 1998).

To respond to these challenges, NATO must possess a sufficiently large rapid deployment force to deter would-be challengers and to quell conflict quickly once deployed. Such a force must contain state-of-the-art tanks, combat planes, and heavy artillery that can be transported rapidly to flash points. Developing sufficient rapid deployment forces is only part of the problem, since NATO must also have the resolve to use them when necessary. This political dimension is surely the most problematic, because the sovereign allies of NATO do not want to sacrifice their autonomy over their military forces to some organizational body within NATO. In fact, allies are anticipated to hold out for unanimous consent before dispatching these forces. The greater the majority required to reach a decision about deployment, the longer it will take on average to decide, as the form of the decision is altered to please the holdouts (see Chapters 3 and 8).[5] During this lengthy decision process, fighting may escalate as opposing sides seek a territorial bargaining advantage. Opposing factions in a civil war will be less inclined to believe NATO's threats of intervention, because its decision process is apt to be uncertain and drawn out.

As the number of decision makers increases, the possibility of achieving unanimity is apt to decline. Thus, NATO's smaller size compared to the UN

4. The CIA (1995) *World Factbook* has maps showing ethnic concentrations in Central and Eastern Europe. Also see the discussion in Carpenter (1994).
5. Buchanan and Tullock (1962) argued that the constitutional choice of a decision rule must balance, at the margin, the political external costs imposed on a minority with the decision-making costs from having a larger majority (see Chapter 8).

General Assembly means that the former is likely to be quicker to respond to civil wars. If, however, the UN Security Council is the decision-making body and only the five permanent members vote, then this body may, *at times,* respond faster than NATO. With Russia and China as permanent members of the Security Council, tastes for intervention are probably more heterogeneous than in NATO and this factor may, at other times, work against quickly reaching a unanimous decision in the Security Council. The most appropriate decision-making entity for responding to any civil war is expected to vary depending on the conflict and what nations will be influenced by a spread of hostilities. Given that peace preserved by intervention *within the region* provides more localized benefits to NATO, it makes sense for NATO to manage these conflicts itself and not to turn to the United Nations, with its larger agenda and broader viewpoint. Borrowing from the theory of jurisdictional design, local public goods should be provided by a similar-sized political jurisdiction, while more global public goods should be allocated by a global jurisdiction (Olson, 1969).

An increase in NATO's membership will lengthen the anticipated time needed to intervene in a civil war that threatens peace, unless the consensus required for intervention is duly reduced (see Chapter 3). Insofar as the prospective members are either transitional economies or neutral nations, the heterogeneity of tastes among members will increase with expansion, and this heterogeneity will also work against quick and decisive actions.

THE THREAT OF TERRORISM

Terrorism is the premeditated use of, or the threat to use, extra-normal violence or brutality to gain a political objective through intimidation or fear. To qualify as an act of terrorism, the act must be politically motivated. Bombings of NATO infrastructure in Greece by the Revolutionary Organization 17 November during the last twenty years were intended to pressure Greece to leave NATO and, as such, were politically motivated acts of terrorism. Political objectives of terrorists may vary greatly among groups and may be based on nationalism, separatism, Marxism, religious freedoms, anti-capitalism, specific issues, nihilism, or some other political program. Terrorists rely on common modes of attack – skyjackings, kidnappings, assassinations, car bombings – to pressure a government to alter its policies and to concede to their demands. To create an atmosphere of fear, terrorists make their attacks appear to be random so that large numbers of people feel at risk. Even though the true risks of becoming a victim of terrorism is minuscule in most countries, it is human nature to overreact to these low-probability, catastrophic events. To promote this overreaction, terrorists may resort to particularly gruesome acts with high body counts, such as downing a passenger airliner, or placing a powerful bomb in a crowded shopping area.

Terrorist acts are often aimed at innocent victims, not directly involved with the decision makers whom the terrorists really seek to influence (Wilkinson, 1992, p. 289). If terrorists can attack with impunity, then the legitimacy of a democratically elected government, which depends, in part, on its ability to protect life and property, will be called into question. If the government does not respond effectively, it will appear weak and will lose popular support; if, however, the government responds too harshly, it will appear to suppress political dissent and will also lose popular support (Wilkinson, 1986).

Terrorism falls into two primary categories: domestic and transnational. Domestic terrorism is solely directed toward the host country, its institutions, policies, or officials. For domestic terrorism, the terrorists must be citizens of the host country. When a terrorist incident in one country involves victims, targets, institutions, governments, or citizens of another country, terrorism assumes a *transnational* character. Attacks against NATO's or other international organizations' personnel or property are classified as transnational. If a terrorist group is supported (i.e., financed, trained, or armed) by a foreign government seeking to destabilize the target government, then the terrorism is said to be state-sponsored and transnational in character (Mickolus, 1989). Transnational terrorist events lead to instances of *transboundary externalities,* since actions taken in one nation (e.g., fortifying potential targets, securing frontiers) impose uncompensated costs or benefits on the people or property of other targeted countries. If, for example, French airports are made more secure, a terrorist group with a grievance against the French government may merely travel to Italy or elsewhere, where security has not been increased, to hijack an airplane with French nationals on board. Terrorists will simply change their venue based on perceived costs of alternative operations. In consequence, nations acting alone to address a transnational terrorist threat will not allocate an efficient quantity of resources to thwarting terrorism, since these nations are not anticipated to include the impact that their deterrence decision has on other countries. Transnational terrorism has been around from the inception of the nation-state, but there has been a marked increase since 1967 and the Arab-Israeli wars (Mickolus, 1980; Mickolus, Sandler, and Murdock, 1989).

Why might terrorism become more of a concern to NATO and the world in the future? First, WMD may fall into the hands of terrorist groups who are willing to use them. Aum Shinrikyo's sarin attack on a Tokyo subway in the city center on the morning of 20 March 1995, in which twelve people died and over 5,000 were injured, is a case in point (Sopko, 1996/97). This cult had sufficient stockpiles of chemical agents and the means to dispense them throughout Tokyo so as to cause massive casualties. In a different instance, Chenchen rebels planted nuclear waste in some Moscow locations in an unsuccessful attempt to extract concessions from the Russian leadership. Second, terrorism represents a relatively inexpensive way to destabilize a democracy; thus, terrorism may be resource-effective from a sponsor's viewpoint. The emerging democracies in Eastern Europe may be especially prone to terrorist threats owing to their initial weakness. Elements of these countries that want either to return to autocratic rule or to seek their own nation-state may resort to terrorism. Nearby countries that support these movements may view terrorism as an appropriate instrument for change, because they can provide support without necessarily being identified. The cloak of terrorism has its benefits. Third, terrorism remains a concern because it tends to impose a far greater resource cost on the targeted country, which must protect against all means of attack in a variety of venues, than on the terrorists who perpetrate the campaign. In short, terrorism favors the terrorists in terms of resource allocation. Fourth, in the current climate of shrinking defense budgets, terrorism is still an affordable means for a state-sponsor to bring about political change or instability.

In Table 6.1, we report the number of transnational terrorist events for each year for the period 1976–96, as given in the US Department of State (1997), *Patterns of Global Terrorism: 1996.* Since 1976, incident numbers *do not display any marked upward trend,* which has also been established in statistical studies for the 1968–91 period (Enders, Parise, and Sandler, 1992) and the 1970–96 period (Enders and Sandler, 1999). The overall pattern of incidents tends to follow a cycle. One study discerned two regular cycles – one of 7.2 quarters and one of 18 quarters for the worldwide series of transnational terrorist events.[6] The two-year cycle is evident in the data displayed in Table 6.1. Another feature is that the number of attacks have decreased somewhat since the end of the Cold War, thus suggesting that terrorism had been used as a tool during these earlier years by the superpow-

6. See Enders, Parise, and Sandler (1992), which used data from *International Terrorism: Attributes of Terrorist Events* (ITERATE). State Department and ITERATE data totals differ, but display the same overall series shapes. Also see Enders and Sandler (1999) and Im, Cauley, and Sandler (1987).

Table 6.1. *Transnational terrorism, 1976–96*

Year	Number of events[a]	US interests involved[b]	Worldwide fatalities[c]	Worldwide wounded[c]
1996	296	73	311	2,652
1995	440	90	165	6,291
1994	322	66	314	663
1993	431	88	109	1,393
1992	363	142	93	636
1991	565	308	87	233
1990	437	197	193	675
1989	375	193	390	397
1988	605	185	658	1,131
1987	665	149	633	2,272
1986	612	204	604	1,717
1985	635	170	825	1,217
1984	565	133	312	967
1983	497	199	637	1,267
1982	487	208	128	755
1981	489	159	168	804
1980	499	169	507	1,062
1979	434	157	697	542
1978	530	215	435	629
1977	419	158	230	404
1976	457	164	409	806

[a]The incident count in this column comes from US Department of State (1997) and excludes incidents involving Palestinians against other Palestinians within the occupied territory. As such, these numbers do not agree with earlier US Department of State, *Patterns of Global Terrorism* reports which include these figures.
[b]Figures in these columns for 1988–1996 come from US Department of State, *Patterns of Global Terrorism* reports for 1988–96, while figures for 1976–87 come from tables provided to Todd Sandler in 1988 by the US Department of State, Office of the Ambassador at Large for Counterterrorism. As such, these figures correspond to the higher incident counts that the Department of State once reported with all Palestinian incidents included.
[c]US Department of State (various years).

ers. We also list the number of incidents involving US interests in the middle column. Although very few transnational terrorist events took place on US soil, US citizens and property were nevertheless the targets of a sizable share of transnational terrorist acts. This implies that the relatively secure US borders have driven terrorists to attack US interests abroad. In consequence, the United States must rely, in part, on other countries to protect its interests against terrorism. Unless the United States subsidizes these efforts, an undersupply is anticipated.

In Table 6.1, there is no clear pattern reflected in the number of fatalities or injuries associated with international terrorism during the period. Frequently, one or two horrendous incidents are behind a large number of the casualties in any given year. Thus, the downing of Pan American Flight 103 over Lockerbie, Scotland, on 21 December 1988, in which 270 people perished, had a significant influence in making 1988 a deadly year. Similarly, the downing of Air India Flight 182 over the Atlantic Ocean on 23 June 1985, in which 329 people died, made 1985 a deadly year. In 1983, it was the bombing of the US Marine barracks in Beirut, which killed 241 soldiers, that elevated the body count. A few major events can also greatly affect the annual injury total. This is best illustrated by the impact that the Tokyo sarin attack, in which over 5,000 were injured, had on making 1995 the year with the most injuries.

To date, casualty figures do not indicate any trend toward higher body counts or toward the use of WMD. The Tokyo sarin attack represents a warning to NATO allies and others of what could happen if terrorists were to acquire and use chemical or biological weapons to intimidate governments for political concessions. To heed this warning, NATO allies must reevaluate how much of their military and other resources (e.g., police, surveillance equipment) should be allocated to deterring terrorism or to managing crises when they arise (see Wilcox, 1997; Wilkinson, 1996). The potential for terrorist escalation is there, even if the anticipated trend has not *yet* materialized. Furthermore, NATO governments must determine whether or not they have sufficient trained personnel and equipment to deal with chemical or biological attacks so as to minimize the loss of life when they do occur.

On cooperating to address terrorism

As an alliance for mutual defense, NATO must consider the means for cooperating to confront the threat of terrorism. Cooperation is needed when transboundary externalities arising from policy decisions are present, so that some associated costs and/or benefits are not taken into account when resources are allocated without some form of policy coordination among governments. For domestic terrorism, there are no external costs or benefits imposed outside the country's borders unless the terrorism impinges on a country's political stability, so that its status as an ally becomes questionable. If the ally's stability is not a relevant concern, then the allocation of resources to combating terrorism should be solely a domestic concern. For example, West Germany's confrontation with the nihilistic Baader-Meinhof group in the 1970s was a threat only to the West Germans.

A case for cooperation can be made for thwarting transnational terrorism, especially when one or more terrorist influences threaten more than one NATO ally. Suppose that two allies are confronted with a threat from the same group. In the absence of transnational cooperation, each government is apt to allocate resources to limit attacks without accounting for the costs that its decision to augment deterrence imposes on the other country as the terrorists are induced by the heightened risks to stage their acts elsewhere (Enders and Sandler, 1995; Sandler and Lapan, 1988). In particular, each ally is anticipated to overdeter as they try to force the terrorists elsewhere. Much as in the case of an arms race, each targeted country may increase expenditures on security without becoming safer, unless terrorists are deterred from attacking altogether. If a single group targets many allies, then this overexpenditure on deterrence may be particularly acute. Next consider a scenario in which a lone terrorist group threatens two countries – country Alpha and country Beta – but the group's grievance is really only with Alpha. Now, when the terrorists weigh costs after Alpha fortifies and then decide to shift the attack to Beta, they will still target Alpha's interests. If this is the case, and collateral damage to Beta is small, then Beta is apt to spend too little on deterring terrorism, since it is not expected to value fully the benefits that its actions can provide for Alpha. Although numerous scenarios of overdeterrence or underdeterrence are possible, the need for a cooperative response among NATO allies to account for these externalities is clear.[7]

Consider the case of Greece, which has faced a significant amount of transnational terrorism since the early 1970s.[8] For the 1968–91 period, Greece experienced 367 transnational terrorist attacks on its soil involving 64 corporate personnel, 55 private citizens (e.g., tourists), and 155 foreign diplomats (Enders and Sandler, 1996, p. 337). Two small (20–30 members) but effective groups – the Revolutionary Organization 17 November and the Revolutionary Popular Struggle (ELA) – have attacked foreign corporations, NATO, and US officials with impunity. Both groups are anti-imperialist and anticapitalist, and seek to end US and NATO presence in Greece. Since the attacks have been primarily against foreigners with little or no direct collateral damage to Greek property or citizens, Greece would be expected to underdeter this transnational terrorist threat. In over twenty years, not a

7. On recent cooperative efforts in NATO and the European Union to combat terrorism, consult Enders and Sandler (1999) and Wilcox (1997). A list of relevant articles is contained in Enders and Sandler (1999).
8. Greek terrorism and terrorist groups are discussed in Corsun (1991), Enders and Sandler (1996), Enders, Sandler, and Parise (1992), and Kassimeris (1993). The information in this paragraph draws from the study by Enders and Sandler (1996).

single member of the 17 November group has been caught, which strongly suggests underdeterrence. When such attacks are directed against net foreign direct investment (NFDI) or net inflows of new investment from abroad, there may be another form of collateral damage that can have a significant negative economic impact on Greece. This follows because terrorist attacks against NFDI can dissuade foreign capital inflows by creating an atmosphere of intimidation and heightened financial risks. When deciding whether or not to invest in a foreign country, a potential investor is concerned about the expected return and risks associated with a contemplated investment relative to other opportunities at home and abroad. If terrorist attacks are directed at foreign investment and personnel, then perceived risks increase. These risks may also be raised if terrorists attack the military, political officials, the airport, the courts, or other symbols of the establishment.

A measurable and significant impact of terrorism on NFDI was found to exist for Greece by Enders and Sandler (1996) using vector autoregressive (VAR) techniques. The authors showed that, on average, terrorism reduced annual NFDI in Greece by 11.9%. NFDI is an important source of savings, especially in smaller countries. Savings finance investment, which in turn is a prime determinant of economic growth. For 1976–91, real NFDI was large relative to gross fixed capital formation (GFCF) or new investment, since NFDI to GFCF was 72.8% for Greece. Furthermore, NFDI is a vital source of technology transfer, which also supports economic growth (Coe and Helpman, 1995). Enders and Sandler (1996) also found a significant impact of terrorism on NFDI in Spain. For 1975–91, terrorism was shown to reduce annual NFDI in Spain by 13.5%. When the same methods were applied to Portugal, a NATO ally with much less transnational terrorism than either Greece or Spain, a trivial impact of 0.05% decline in NFDI was uncovered.

Large industrial nations should be insulated from any significant impact of terrorism on NFDI, because they draw their foreign investment from a more diversified pool of investor countries. That is, a fall in NFDI, resulting from attacks on one or two investor countries' NFDI, can potentially be made up when nontargetted countries increase their NFDI in response to profit opportunities. Large countries also possess adequate resources to thwart the terrorist threat. Even if terrorism has an effect on NFDI in a large nation, this influence is likely to be relatively small, because the overall size of NFDI is large.

In the case of Greece and Spain, collateral economic damage arises from terrorism even when it is directed against foreign interests. There is, thus, a rationale either to increase anti-terrorist efforts or else to cooperate with other allies to increase these efforts. One means to augment cooperation among allies is to share intelligence – a course of action that is frequently followed. Another is to collaborate on deterrence decisions. For example, allies can develop a common commando force that can be deployed throughout NATO to manage terrorist crises as they occur. To date, most countries finance their own commando squads, which represents duplication of investment. A more efficient course of action for an ally would be to have its own smaller commando squad to manage domestic events and then to contribute manpower and money to support a NATO-wide commando squad for deployment throughout the alliance for NATO-based transnational threats. Nations are, however, reluctant to sacrifice their autonomy over policing terrorism on their own soil, even if the terrorism is spilling in from political struggles abroad. This failure to share deterrence decisions may lead to a paradox, as in the case in which shared intelligence reduces the participating nations' well-being if deterrence is independently chosen. If, that is, the shared information allows a potential target to calculate more accurately how to make its deterrence successful, then greater external costs may result as each nation does more to displace its terrorist threat. As a result, resource allocation becomes less, rather than more, efficient. This outcome demonstrates that a piecemeal approach to cooperation, where some policy decisions are coordinated and others are not, may have undesirable consequences.

NATO still has a long way to go to foster cooperation in combating terrorism that affects NATO allies generally. Depending on the nature of the terrorist challenge, cooperation may not have to involve NATO; some threats against two NATO allies can be best met with an arrangement between the two. Furthermore, there are other forms of international cooperation (e.g., Interpol) that are less formal and need not concern NATO directly. If the terrorist threat were to escalate and involve WMD, then the payoffs from international cooperation would be sure to grow. This growth could then induce greater cooperation than has been seen to date.

On the ineffectiveness of international treaties on thwarting terrorism

Although nations have much to gain from treaties that commit them to a united front against a terrorist threat, treaties have not been an effective tool against terrorism. In many cases, treaties are unsuccessful because the

		Other Three Nations' Strategies			
		Other 3 Nations Abide	2 Others Abide 1 Does Not Abide	1 Other Abides 2 Do Not Abide	3 Others Do Not Abide
Nation *i*	Abide	12	7	2	−3
	Does Not Abide	15	10	5	0

Figure 6.1. Three-nation treaty dilemma

participating nations face what amounts to a Prisoners' Dilemma game. To illustrate this situation, suppose that a four-nation alliance is contemplating signing a treaty that pledges the nations to sanctioning severely any state caught sponsoring terrorism. If warranted for a particularly heinous act, the sanction could even take the form of a retaliatory raid, like the US raid against Libya on the morning of 15 April 1986. Suppose further that each ally that abides by the treaty confers a benefit of 5 on itself *and* on each of the other three allies, but at a cost of 8 to itself. Costs arise because each abiding nation has to expend resources to impose the sanction and then has to assume a risk of retribution. In contrast, benefits stem from the deterrence accomplished and the weakening of a terrorist threat through sanctions. These benefits have the properties of a public good – nonrivalry and nonexcludability. One nation's gain from the treaty does not detract from another's gain, and the benefits go to those who abide by the treaty *and to those who do not.*

In Figure 6.1, we display the associated payoffs for the representative player, nation *i,* in the 2 × 4 matrix. Consider the payoffs in the first column, where nation *i* may abide or not, while the other three nations abide by the treaty. If, say, nation *i* and the other three nations all abide by the treaty, then *each receives* net benefits of 12, equal to gross benefits of 20 (5 times the number of abiders) minus costs of 8. If, however, nation *i* does not abide while the other three nations do abide, then nation *i* receives 15, which equals the number of abiders times the benefits of 5 derived from *each* abider. In the next column, the top payoff of 7 arises when nation *i* and two others abide, so that nation i receives gross benefits of 15 (3 × 5) minus costs of 8 from carrying out the treaty's conditions. The corresponding bottom payoff is the free-rider payoff of 10 when nation *i* does not abide but receives the benefits derived from the two abiders. The four remaining payoffs are computed in an analogous fashion. When nation *i* chooses between abiding or not, it compares the associated payoffs in the two rows. In Figure 6.1, nation *i*'s payoffs from not abiding are higher by 3, or the difference between the benefits and costs of acting alone, regardless of the other nations' strategies. There is a *dominant strategy* to not abide, because the associated payoffs are higher than the corresponding payoffs in the top row from abiding. Nation *i* is expected, therefore, not to abide by the treaty when called upon to act. Because all nations view the game as does nation *i,* none abides when needed. The resulting equilibrium of mutual defection gives each nation a payoff of 0, rather than the net benefit of 12 from mutual cooperation. Herein lies the treaty dilemma: in pursuing its individual best outcome, each nation ends up with the second-worst payoff. As the number of nations increases, the difference between the mutual-cooperative payoff and the noncooperative outcome becomes even greater.

A sixteen-nation NATO alliance would have a large difference between the cooperative and the noncooperative payoffs for the allies. An enlarged NATO would have even greater differences if the underlying game analysis holds. To see the general applicability of the model, consider the US retaliatory raid against the alleged bombing of the LaBelle discotheque in West Berlin on 4 April 1986, which killed three people including two US servicemen, and injured 231 including 62 Americans.[9] Most of those injured were West Germans, Turks, and Arabs. When the United States presented evidence that Libya had sponsored the mission, it could not convince any of its allies to join the raid even though the bombing had injured citizens from other NATO allies. In fact, France and Spain complicated the mission greatly by refusing US permission to fly over their airspace enroute from England to Libya. Only the United Kingdom gave some support by allowing some of the planes in the raid to take off from British bases. Ironically, not until the week of 17 February 1997 did the German government acknowledge that the US case was conclusive and that Libya was behind the discotheque bombing.

Next, suppose that the nations agree to provide an enforcement mechanism to circumvent the free-rider problem posed by the matrix in Figure 6.1. Suppose further that a nation receives a punishment equal to 4 when it does not abide, so that the payoffs in the bottom row of Figure 6.1 are now 11, 6, 1, and –4 (not shown in the figure). Punishment may be in the form of trade sanctions, fines, or diplomatic ostracism. In the resulting game, the dominant strategy is to abide, so that all nations receive a benefit of 12 at

9. For a fuller description of this bombing, see Mickolus, Sandler, and Murdock (1989, vol. 2, pp. 365–7).

the mutual-cooperative equilibrium. Any punishment greater than 3 will produce this outcome. Although this equilibrium gives the desired result, it raises another issue, because the execution of the punishment provides nonrival and nonexcludable benefits to the allies and, as such, is a pure public good with its own free-rider difficulties. Since this punishment must be paid for by the participants, it is conceivable that a second-level Prisoners' Dilemma can characterize the punishment decision, whenever the net benefit from punishing is negative when the enforcer acts alone. Thus, free riding may occur on either of two levels: at the provision level or at the enforcement level. Provision represents a first-order free riding, while enforcement represents a second-order free riding (Heckathorn, 1989). To achieve the treaty outcome, cooperation must circumvent the free-rider problem at both levels.

In terrorism situations, a nation may actually reduce the public good of retaliatory deterrence, achieved by treaty participants, by reaching an accommodation with the terrorists. For example, a safe haven to the terrorists may be offered in return for the terrorists' pledge to attack elsewhere. The Reagan administration once accused the Greek government of a tacit agreement with Arab terrorists, whereby such terrorists agreed not to operate in Greece in exchange for Greek leniency towards terrorists who got in trouble (*The Economist,* 1984, p. 1). When a nation undermines the deterrence provided by others through such a deal, the nation is termed a paid rider (Lee, 1988; Lee and Sandler, 1989). By striking such a deal, the perceived payoffs to the paid rider are anticipated to exceed the free-rider payoffs, since the paid rider gains free-rider benefits and additional payoffs from the terrorists. Paid riding can inhibit treaty adherence to an even greater extent than normal free riding, because the benefits conferred on others by treaty adherence are reduced as the paid rider's accommodation lowers the effective deterrence.

Thus, a lot of strategic considerations work against successful treaties to combat terrorism even among allies confronting a common threat. In addition to the problems just discussed, a time consistency problem may arise when a pledge, made in an earlier period, is viewed in a later period after the true consequences of the pledge are revealed (Lapan and Sandler, 1988). Suppose that two allies agree never to negotiate with terrorists who take hostages. This pledge is made in the hope that it will dissuade would-be kidnappers. If the terrorists are not deterred and capture hostages from one of the allies, this ally must then weigh the cost of reneging on its pledge against the cost of maintaining it. It is conceivable that for the "right" hostages the government will view reneging to be less costly than holding to its pledge, even when its tarnished reputation is considered. Consequently, the government may regret its pledge and renege. The time inconsistency problem arises because uncertainty characterizes the actual costs that the government may later face for a hostage incident. What is needed is an institutional device that denies a treaty participant the right to change its mind at a later date, regardless of the circumstances. Most nations will never agree to be controlled by such a mechanism.

Effective policies against future terrorist threats

If treaty making does not hold much promise to NATO for addressing the heightened threat of terrorism that looms on the horizon, then what types of policies could be expected to work? Past studies show that the application of technology is particularly effective at the national level in thwarting specific types of terrorist events (Enders and Sandler, 1993; Enders, Sandler, and Cauley, 1990). The classic example concerns the installation of metal detectors in US airports to screen airline passengers on 5 January 1973. Shortly thereafter, these devices were deployed in airports worldwide. Prior to January 1973, skyjackings worldwide averaged over sixteen per quarter; after metal detectors were installed, this average dropped to about five per quarter. A similar success followed the fortification of US embassies starting in 1976, which precipitated a dramatic fall in embassy attacks.

There is a pitfall in such applications of technology to address specific types of terrorist events. As technology makes one mode of attack more risky for the terrorists, there is a substitution or transference into related kinds of attacks. Fortification of embassies, while reducing attacks against embassies, was followed by increased assassinations of embassy officials as they left secured grounds. Although metal detectors decreased skyjackings, their introduction was associated with a significant permanent increase in other types of hostage-taking events – kidnappings and barricade-and-hostage-taking events (Enders and Sandler, 1993). This terrorist substitution into less risky modes of attack in response to government efforts to reduce certain types of threat suggests a number of policy insights. First, the authorities must be aware of this possibility and protect against it by fortifying likely substitute targets. Second, given that substitution can be expected, the authorities should try to ensure that the transference is into less costly events from society's viewpoint. This was not the case when embassies were fortified, because the associated increase in assassinations of embassy officials was more costly than attacks against embassy property. Third, efforts to decrease terrorist resources would limit terrorist events of all kinds without resulting in substitution. Any actions that limit the terrorists' general ability to engage in terrorist acts would have this desirable outcome. If, for example, key members of a group are captured, then substitution effects would not be a negative consequence. Intelligence gathered on group activities can also have a positive across-the-board influence on curbing terrorism as planned terrorist missions are prevented. Efforts to infiltrate terrorist groups can effectively curb terrorism as members are discovered and brought to justice.

To date, retaliatory raids appear to have very little long-run impact on terrorism. One study examined the impact that Israeli retaliatory raids had following a number of significant terrorist incidents (Brophy-Baermann and Conybeare, 1994). Retaliations investigated included the raid on Palestine Liberation Organization (PLO) bases in Syria following the Black September massacre of Israeli athletes during the 1972 Olympic Games; the attack on Palestinian guerrilla bases in Lebanon following a March 1978 Haifa bus hijacking; and the bombing of Palestinian bases in Lebanon following a June 1982 assassination attempt against the Israeli ambassador in London. This study found that such raids only temporarily suppressed terrorism: within three quarters, terrorism had returned to its old mean values. Another study showed that the US raid on Libya in April 1986 had the unanticipated consequence of actually raising the level of terrorism in the immediate aftermath as terrorists lashed out against the United States. This was followed by a temporary lull as terrorists tried to accumulate resources recently expended (Enders and Sandler, 1993). Within a matter of months, terrorism was back to its old level. Terrorists merely transferred future planned events into the present as a protest, but no true effect on terrorism was experienced. This suggests that NATO would be better advised to cooperate on efforts to deter terrorists rather than on efforts to stage retaliatory raids.

THE THREAT OF ROGUE STATES: REAL OR IMAGINED?

A great deal of concern has been expressed regarding so-called "rogue states," hostile to the United States and its allies (Gompert and Larrabee, 1997; Khalilzad, 1997; Klare, 1995; Leech, 1991). These states are characterized as acquiring WMD and the means (i.e., ballistic missiles) to deliver them.

In some instances, rogue states are said to sponsor or to condone terrorism as a legitimate means for bringing about political change in other countries. These rogue nations are described by some – especially the US government – as operating outside of the accepted norms of international behavior. The worry for NATO is that these nations will pose a threat to resource supply lines, strategic regions, and emerging democracies.

In the US view, there are five rogue nations: Iran, Iraq, Libya, North Korea, and Syria, all of which have been tied to terrorism in the past and have tried to acquire nuclear, biological, or chemical weapons capable of inflicting massive casualties. Other "possible" rogues include emerging regional powers believed to possess some WMD. These latter nations include some (e.g., China and India) that have had serious disagreements with the West. Other potential rogues represent emerging regional powers that could someday pose a security threat to NATO if relations with the West were to deteriorate. Turkey is an interesting case, since it is a NATO ally with an important strategic position vis-à-vis the Middle East, the Caucasus, and the Balkans (Larrabee, 1997, pp. 188–90). In recent years, relations between Turkey and NATO have been strained over the former's treatment of the Kurds and its continued differences with Greece. Islamic fundamentalism is a powerful political influence in Turkey today. Currently, Western relations with Pakistan and India are problematic because of weapon proliferation concerns. Egypt could pose a problem if Islamic fundamentalist elements were to gain power, while Taiwan could move away from the Western governments if they were to improve relations with mainland China. Even South Korea could present a threat if relations with the West were to change.

If the alleged rogue states were to acquire nuclear weapons, these states could use them as leverage to pressure the West into concessions. Biological weapons can cause massive deaths and, as shown in Table 6.2, may already be in the hands of most rogue nations. US fears are sufficient that it has begun a program to inoculate its troops serving in the Gulf against anthrax. Many NATO allies do not share US concern over these so-called rogues. To put things into perspective, consult Table 6.2, which indicates selective characteristics of the rogue and possible rogue states. Currently, nuclear weapons are under development in Iran and North Korea, while four of the five rogues possess chemical weapons. These same four nations have some form of ballistic missile to deliver WMD to nearby countries. Both Iraq and North Korea allocate very large portions of gross domestic product (GDP) to defense. On average, the world spent about 3 percent of its GDP on defense in 1994, with the greatest percentage in the Middle East, where

Table 6.2. *Rogue and possible rogue states: selective military indicators, 1995*

Country	Nuclear weapons[a]	Chemical weapons[a]	Biological weapons[b]	Ballistic missiles	Active armed forces[c]	Heavy tanks	Combat aircraft	Def/GDP (%)
"Rogues"								
Iran	u.d.	yes	prob	yes	513	1,440	295	3.9
Iraq	no*	no*	yes	?	382.5	2,770	?	14.8
Libya	no	yes	prob	yes	65	2,210	420	5.5
N. Korea	u.d.	yes	prob	yes	1,054	3,400	611	25.2
Syria	no	yes	prob	yes	421	4,600	579	6.8
"Possible rogues"								
China	yes	prob	prob	yes	2,935	8,000+	4,970	5.7
Egypt	no	prob	poss	u.d.	440	3,650	567	4.3
India	yes	prob	prob	yes	1,145	3,500	778	2.5
Pakistan	yes	prob	poss	u.d.	587	2,050	430	6.5
S. Korea	no	prob	poss	yes	660	2,050	461	3.4
Taiwan	no	prob	poss	yes	376	630	392	5.0
Turkey	no	prob	–	no	639	4,280	434	3.6

[a]From Klare (1995, Table 5.1, p. 134).
[b]From Dando (1994, p. 181). Turkey is not listed in this source.
[c]In thousands of men.
*Operation Desert Storm ended this threat temporarily, but Iraq appears determined to develop these weapons.
u.d. = under development
prob = probably
poss = possibly
Source: International Institute for Strategic Studies (1996).

Table 6.3. *Fifteen largest armies in the world, 1995*

Country	Rank	Numbers in armed forces (000)[a]	Military expenditures[b] in millions of US dollars
China	1	2,930.0	31,731
United States	2	1,547.3	277,834
Russia	3	1,520.0	82,000
India	4	1,145.0	8,289
N. Korea	5	1,128.0	5,232
Brazil	6	1,115.0	6,890
S. Korea	7	633.0	14,359
Pakistan	8	587.0	3,642
Vietnam	9	572.0	910
Iran	10	513.0	2,460
Turkey	11	507.8	6,004
Ukraine	12	452.5	1,005
Egypt	13	436.0	2,417
Syria	14	423.0	2,026
France	15	409.0	48,002

[a]Does not include reserves or paramilitary.
[b]In 1995 constant prices.
Source: International Institute for Strategic Studies (1996, Table 1, pp. 306–11).

7.7 percent was spent, down from 14.5 percent in 1992 (Arms Control and Disarmament Agency, 1996, p. 26). Many of the rogues field sizable armed forces and arsenals, as indicated by the numbers of troops, heavy tanks, and combat aircraft in Table 6.2. If these nations continue to acquire military forces and to upgrade them, they may become formidable enemies for NATO or some other regional collective to counter if a crisis were to develop. Given its relatively small armed forces, Libya clearly does not represent the same level of potential threat as the others. Thus, the Reagan and Bush administrations' worry over Libya appears somewhat exaggerated.

Three of the potential rogues – China, India, Pakistan – possess nuclear weapons and probably have biological weapons. China's armed forces, comprising almost 3 million members, is the largest army in the world. As it modernizes its weaponry, China will become a formidable adversary. In Table 6.3, we list the fifteen largest armies for 1995 in descending order. When assessing the true threat that an army presents, we must compare military expenditures with force size, because this comparison indicates something about force readiness, weapon maintenance, weapon sophistication, and troop training. For example, China's defense spending of almost $32 million is about one-ninth that of the United States, while China's army is almost twice the size of the US army. Even though China can pay its soldiers much less than the United States, owing to a lower wage structure, the relatively small Chinese military expenditure level indicates that its military power and preparedness are not comparable to those of the United States. Thus, we should not put too much weight on army size, since military strength and effectiveness are really the issue.

The Gulf War changed US strategic thinking concerning the shape of American post–Cold War military needs. In a major defense budgetary review in 1991, the US Department of Defense (DOD) considered three budgetary options: a two-and-a half-war scenario, a two-war scenario, and a one-and-a-half-war scenario.[10] These scenarios involved being prepared for one or two wars like the one fought against Iraq as well as a smaller operation, such as the one involved with the defeat of Manuel Noriega of Panama in December 1989. The latter constituted the half-war scenario. In May 1997, the DOD announced that its defense needs would be based on the two-war scenario, fought with high-tech weapons. The US military seized on the Gulf War as a means to limit its downsizing by arguing that other rogue nations can pose real threats to US security; hence, the rogue threat served the US military in limiting force cuts. US fears were not necessarily shared by its allies (Khalilzad, 1997, pp. 194–210); thus, the defense burden gap between the US and NATO has widened again.

Any threat posed by a rogue nation raises a number of public good issues. Suppose that a rogue nation were on the brink of developing nuclear weapons. Furthermore, suppose that a preemptive air strike, much like the Israeli air strike on the forty-megawatt Osiraq nuclear reactor on 7 June 1981, could eliminate this threat. Unlike most public goods, where the cumulative contributions or efforts determine the overall good's level, the best-shot or maximal effort of any single ally to neutralize the nuclear threat posed by a rogue determines the safety of everyone. Thus nations are apt to wait for some ally to preempt the threat single-handedly, since they can then reap the benefits without putting their forces in harm's way. Any ally with sufficient interests and enough forces and determination to succeed with a preemptive strike can be the best-shot nation. In a best-shot situation, free riding is anticipated to be even greater than when each individual effort contributes to the outcome, because most nations will do nothing to help. The best shooter is apt to be either the nation with the largest military arsenal or else the nation

10. Klare (1995, chapter 4) provided details about the alternative budget scenarios and the structure of the required armed forces.

most threatened by the nuclear weapons. US action against North Korea during 1994 is an example of the former, while the Israeli attack on the Osiraq power plant is an example of the latter. As long as the NATO alliance includes a member whose military capabilities far exceed those of the other allies, this powerful ally will have to either provide the preemptive attack or else play a leadership role in getting the other allies to join it. Unfortunately, the latter action requires time, which can compromise the secrecy of a preemptive strike. Although Kuwait and Saudi Arabia had much to fear from an Iraqi nuclear capability, Israel acted alone. To counter Iraq's invasion of Kuwait, the United States assumed a leadership role and supplied the lion's share of the coalition's military forces in Operation Desert Storm: 540,000 out of 795,000 combat troops; 165 out of 230 of the warships; and 1,000 out of 2,430 aircraft (Klare, 1995, p. 88).

Perhaps, the best counter to the threat of a rogue nation is to deny it the means to amass a sizable arsenal or to acquire WMD. This obvious fix presents significant coordination problems for the world community. In developing chemical or biological weapons, a nation may buy components and equipment from diverse suppliers. Even if each supplier restricts its firms from selling to a potential rogue everything needed to assemble a weapon, the rogue can circumvent the restrictions by buying from a variety of suppliers. Some of the ingredients and capital required may have dual civilian and military uses, thus making it difficult to know their ultimate application. Consequently, a state of asymmetric information exists: the purchasing nation knows how the components will be used, but the supplier does not. Supplying nations would have to report all of their sales to some central information-gathering agency so that a purchasing nation's intentions could be inferred and, if necessary, key components for WMD denied. Each supplier has *a profit motive* not to report its sales to such an agency and not to withhold sales when requested. This motive works against world security. Coordination on the part of the suppliers is particularly difficult, because it may take only one noncooperating nation to provide a potential rogue nation with the essential ingredients. The weakest-link supplier (i.e., the easiest to buy from) may determine the security risks of everyone. Another problem is that firms within a nation may sell components illegally to a rogue nation, thus creating a collective action problem within nations.

This coordination failure is clear in the case of Iraq. The United States, the United Kingdom, France, and other NATO allies sold Iraq massive amounts of weapons, in part as a counter to Iran prior to August 1990. At the start of the Gulf War, Iraq had amassed an army of a million soldiers with some 5,500 tanks, 3,500 major artillery pieces, 8,000 armored personnel carriers, and 513 combat planes, making it the sixth largest army in the world (Klare, 1995, p. 41–4). It had stockpiles of chemical weapons and possessed the means to deliver them with Soviet-supplied Scud missiles with a 375-mile range. The United States knew of Iraq's development of chemical weapons and their use against the Iranians in 1982 and thereafter. Nevertheless, throughout much of the 1980s, the United States supplied helicopters, computers, and other dual-use items to Iraq (Friedman, 1993; Klare, 1995, pp. 34–64), which furthered Iraqi efforts to acquire WMD.

Table 6.4 lists arms sales to the key nations in the Middle East, North Africa, South Asia, and East Asia for the period 1987–95, in millions of US dollars at constant 1994 prices. Iraq was a major weapon purchaser up until the invasion of Kuwait. Four of the five alleged rogue nations purchased large amounts of armaments until 1990. Some of the potential rogues – India, Egypt, China – engaged in large purchases during the entire period. This suggests that the world community still has not fully learned its lesson from the Iraqi invasion of Kuwait. However, arms sales to the five alleged rogue nations dropped off greatly after 1992, a positive development that can be attributed to caution on the part of arms exporters, a reduction in Russian exports, and economic hardships (e.g., in North Korea).

In Table 6.5, the twenty largest arms exporters for 1994 are listed, along with the twenty largest arms importers. Prior to the end of the Cold War, the Soviet Union had been one of the top two exporters; Russia is now third, well behind the United States and the United Kingdom. Among the top importers are Saudi Arabia, Egypt, the United States, Israel, South Korea, Turkey, and China, in descending order,[11] so that some potential rogues are still being supplied large amounts of arms. This is a myopic policy that occurs because elected leaders often adopt a short time horizon when deciding policies. Table 6.5 also has some important collective action implications regarding the appropriate organization for coordinating arms sales. Since many important arms suppliers – Russia, China, Israel – are not members of NATO, coordination would have to be orchestrated by a different body. If the United Nations were chosen as the arms-trade coordinator, then a choice would have to be made between the General Assembly and Security Council as the appropriate body. The UN Register on Conventional Arms Transfers is a first attempt to coordinate these sales by keeping track of them (also see Congressional Budget Office, 1992). Given that the top five arms exporters are

11. Some of the sales figures differ between Tables 6.4 and 6.5 because two different sources were consulted.

Table 6.4. *Arms sales to Middle East, North Africa, South and East Asia, 1987–95 (in millions of US dollars at constant 1994 prices)*

Middle East and North Africa

Year	Saudi Arabia	Iraq	Iran	Egypt	Israel	Syria	UAE	Libya	Kuwait
1987	8,570	7,310	2,521	2,395	2,521	2,521	189	756	252
1988	7,525	6,796	3,155	1,001	1,335	1,578	146	1,153	316
1989	6,851	2,787	1,742	1,045	1,394	1,277	1,016	1,277	546
1990	8,681	3,116	2,003	890	779	1,057	1,558	412	312
1991	8,039	0	2,251	965	670	884	397	439	515
1992	8,864	0	375	1,147	886	396	375	83	1,043
1993[a]	6,940	0	1,021	1,429	1,123	225	439	0	765
1994[a]	6,900	0	500	1,500	1,200	200	410	0	900
1995[a]	8,100	0	400	1,900	na	200	600	0	1,000
Total	70,470	20,009	13,968	12,272	9,908	8,338	5,130	4,120	5,649

Table 6.4. *(cont.)*

South and East Asia

Year	India	Japan	Taiwan	S. Korea	Vietnam	Pakistan	China	Thailand	N. Korea
1987	3,781	1,386	1,891	882	2,395	416	819	529	529
1988	3,762	1,001	1,092	819	1,820	583	413	698	1,214
1989	3,484	1,974	697	697	1,510	639	453	360	697
1990	2,003	1,336	723	1,224	1,224	890	223	300	223
1991	991	1,501	1,179	724	214	236	214	616	96
1992	678	1,173	886	730	10	469	1,251	386	10
1993[a]	265	2,635	816	1,327	10	536	510	122	5
1994[a]	320	1,900	950	1,000	80	260	130	360	50
1995[a]	450	1,140	1,200	1,100	120	500	480	500	na
Total	15,734	14,046	9,434	8,503	7,383	4,529	4,493	3,871	2,824

[a]1993–95 data are estimates
na = not available
Source: International Institute for Strategic Studies (1996, Tables 6–7, pp. 279–80).

Table 6.5. *Major arms exporters and arms importers, 1994*

Arms exporters			Arms importers		
Country	Rank	Value in millions of dollars	Country	Rank	Value in millions of dollars
United States	1	12,400	Saudi Arabia	1	5,200
United Kingdom	2	3,400	Egypt	2	1,500
Russia	3	1,300	United States	3	1,100
China	4	800	Israel	4	1,000
France	5	800	S. Korea	5	1,000
Germany	6	700	Turkey	6	950
Israel	7	470	China	7	775
Czech Republic	8	300	Japan	8	650
Spain	9	280	Angola	9	600
Canada	10	230	Spain	10	525
Qatar	11	130	Australia	11	430
Netherlands	12	110	Iran	12	390
Switzerland	13	110	Thailand	13	360
Portugal	14	100	Malaysia	14	330
Iran	15	90	Portugal	15	320
Italy	16	80	Greece	16	270
Brazil	17	80	Singapore	17	270
Moldova	18	80	Pakistan	18	260
Sweden	19	60	Kuwait	19	250
Ukraine	20	60	Germany	20	240

Source: Arms Control and Disarmament Agency (1996, p. 43).

the five permanent members of the Security Council, this appears to be an appropriate body to limit arms supplies to rogues or potential rogues. Furthermore, Germany, the sixth largest exporter, may become a permanent member of an expanded Security Council. In contrast, the General Assembly would bring too many diverse views into the decision-making process, many of which are held by nations not involved in the arms trade. The real dilemma with any such arms-limiting body concerns nonmembers, who may increase their arms-producing capacity in order to make up for supply shortfalls to rogue nations. This suggests that the proposed body, initially the Security Council, be allowed to expand over time to subsume other relevant arms suppliers. Additionally, a means for punishing opportunistic nonmembers must be devised, and this presents a tricky collective action problem. Also, there is the ever-present risk that a rogue nation will develop its own defense industrial base, as in North Korea.

Although recent US administrations have appeared to exaggerate the rogue threat as a means for maintaining a large military establishment, there is no question that the world must be vigilant not to arm future Iraqs with even greater capacity for mass destruction. Events of November 1997 and thereafter indicate that nations are still prepared to free ride on US resolve to keep Iraq from acquiring WMD.

ENVIRONMENTAL SECURITY

Traditionally, security has referred to defending against and deterring military invasion. In recent years, nations have had to consider environmentally based threats of two kinds: resource supply blockages and transboundary pollution. Economic activities in one country can create harmful side effects for neighboring nations or for the world at large in the form of transboundary pollutants. For example, the use of a river for irrigation by an upstream country may severely restrict the flow of water for downstream countries, thus jeopardizing crop yields there. The burning of fossil fuels releases sulfur, which in turn leads to acid rain and surface-level ozone that can damage downwind countries. Countries' borders, once made secure by armies, artillery, and demilitarized zones, are now invaded daily by pollutants, unleashed by economic activities abroad. These invaders represent real risks to people and property, which democratically elected governments have the responsibility to protect. Thus, environmental security must now be considered a legitimate security concern (McGuire, 1995, p. 35; Myers, 1993; Sandler, 1997). Surely, the industrial powers would have to find an appropriate response to a nation that played havoc with their economies by severing crucial resource supplies, or that caused the deaths of thousands through the persistent release of a deadly pollutant, whether this release were intentional or not.

The Gulf War of 1991 illustrates that a challenge to the flow of Middle East oil can evoke a military response. The sovereignty of Kuwait was but one factor explaining why the coalition of allies responded so decisively. Interestingly, Japan and Germany, which are both heavily dependent on Middle East oil, made significant contributions, financing about a quarter of Operation Desert Storm (Congressional Budget Office, 1991a, b). The Bush administration clearly expressed its concern about the flow of oil and what a reduced flow would do to world prices and the world's economy (Klare, 1995). Following the Kuwait invasion, the price of oil rose sharply, thereby threatening a worldwide recession and a redistribution of income from the oil importers to the oil exporters, not unlike what happened in the early 1970s. Unchecked price rises brought about by blockades (e.g., the closing of the Straits of Hormuz) could precipitate crises, in which NATO or some other world power may have to take action. If economic sanctions and diplomatic actions fail, then still stronger responses may be necessary. Future crises could involve the supply of strategic metals from Africa used in combat aircraft and satellites (e.g., titanium), or else disputes over water in the Middle East.

As the millennium approaches, global environmental challenges are prevalent, involving both regional and global ecospheres. At the regional level, sulfur and nitrogen oxides (NO_x) emissions from power plants, vehicles, industries, residencies, and other sources combine in the lower atmosphere with water vapor and tropospheric ozone, thus forming sulfuric acid and nitric acid. When these acids later fall with the rain, degradation of lakes, rivers, coastal waters, forests, and man-made structures can result (Mohnen, 1988). These same pollutants can reduce ambient air quality and lead to harmful respiratory effects in humans (Schwartz, 1991).

At the global level, emissions of chlorofluorocarbons (CFCs) and other halocarbons (e.g., carbon tetrachloride, methyl chloroform) have depleted the stratospheric ozone shield, which protect plants and animals from harmful ultraviolet (UV) radiation (deGruijl, 1995). UV radiation is absorbed into the skin of animals and can damage essential molecules, such as DNA, thereby inducing tumors. A thinner ozone layer could cause cataclysmic effects including the mass extinction of species, disruption of the food chain, impairment of the immune system, and the inducement of cataracts. A second global transboundary problem is global warming, which arises from the so-called greenhouse effect: as trapped gases in the Earth's atmosphere let sunlight through but absorb and capture infrared radiation, thereby raising the mean temperature of the Earth. Gases with this property are called greenhouse gases (GHGs) and include carbon dioxide (CO_2), CFCs, methane, and nitrous oxide. Unabated accumulation of GHGs could raise the mean temperature by as much as 2° to 5°C during the next century; estimates differ widely and much uncertainty remains.

If nations can learn to cooperate to address these environmental problems, then stronger actions will be unnecessary. Treaty formation is a logical procedure for internalizing the externality associated with these regional and global transboundary pollution concerns. At the regional level, the Helsinki and Sofia Protocols have set emission reduction targets for sulfur and NO_x, respectively, for Europe.[12] The Helsinki Protocol entered into force on 2 September 1987 and committed ratifiers to reduce sulfur emissions by at least 30 percent from their 1980 levels, while the Sofia Protocol entered into force on 14 February 1991 and committed ratifiers to reduce NO_x emissions to their 1987 levels. For acid rain, the prognosis is good for some form of collective response, since a sizable share of the pollution falls on the emitting country itself, especially in the case of sulfur. Thus, there are strong incentives to act. To date, many of the treaties have merely codified reductions that a majority of nations were already making or else were prepared to make even in the absence of a treaty (Murdoch, Sandler, and Sargent, 1997). The treaties' primary effect has been to impose the largest participants' responses on others.

There are a number of instances where treaties may not work and more drastic measures, even military intervention, may result. Suppose that two neighboring countries have a transboundary pollution problem. Further suppose that the pollution is an unidirectional externality in which water or wind transports the pollutant from nation A to nation B, but not in the reverse direction. Nation A may see little reason to consummate a treaty with its counterpart unless pressured into it. If the damages are sufficiently devastating to nation B, it may resort to force if all diplomatic and nonmilitary means fail.

Another problematic case involves global pollutants when the number of nations contributing to the pollution is very large. In this case, a treaty must include a sufficient number of polluters as participants, or else the nonsigners will be potentially able to undo the efforts of the treaty members to curb pollutants. Global warming is perhaps the best example thus far – an effective treaty must include most nations if the free riders are not to limit drastically the effectiveness of the efforts of the treaty nations. Nonparticipants can serve as "pollution havens," attracting dirty industries that add GHGs to the atmosphere at alarming rates. The industrial countries release GHGs through their industries and vehicles; the agrarian countries add GHGs from their livestock and farming; and the tropical countries release GHGs through their deforestation. Thus, when global warming is considered, there are many major or soon-to-be major polluters, including the transitional economies and the emerging-market economies. Thus far only modest progress

12. Murdoch, Sandler, and Sargent (1997) analyzed the apparent effects of the Helsinki and Sofia Protocols. On the effectiveness of transnational treaties, see Barrett (1993, 1994), Chen (1997), Morisette et al. (1990), Murdoch and Sandler (1997), and Sandler (1997).

has been made with respect to the proposed UN Framework Convention on Climate Change for limiting GHGs. The Kyoto Protocol has select industrial countries in the West agreeing to a cutback in carbon dioxide emissions from 1990 levels. Given the treaty's absence of limits on many large polluters, including China and India, its passage by the US Congress is questionable. If the environmental consequences of global warming *become sufficiently dire and certain,* then nations will be motivated to take action. Even so, there will surely be free riders, who will not go along with the agreed-upon restrictions and may increase GHGs to take advantage of profits. In these instances, the world community will have to decide how to enforce treaty provisions on recalcitrant nations that undo the actions of others, suggesting yet another collective action concern.

Enforcement of transnational environmental treaties

To date, there is no enforcement mechanism for international environmental treaties. A case can only be brought before the World Court, provided that the parties agree to have the dispute heard and to abide by the court's decision. Even when a case is adjudicated and a nation subsequently does not comply with the court's judgment (i.e., a time inconsistency response occurs), there is no effective mechanism for imposing the judgment. After much hand-wringing, the UN Security Council might decide to take some kind of action. Since these global contingencies affect many more nations than those of NATO, any response should be at the UN level. NATO may want to support UN efforts in this regard as a single entity, much as it did in Bosnia. In so doing, NATO allies can pool and economize on scarce nonmilitary and military assets. A multilateral rapid deployment force may be appropriate for such an operation, if force is required as a last resort.

Treaties and diplomatic efforts are clearly the first means for dealing with breaches in environmental security arising from transnational pollutants. These treaties can control pollution through taxes/subsidies, quotas, emission trading, or technological transfer. Even these diplomatic solutions must have an effective enforcement mechanism to convince nations to fulfill treaty pledges. When economic and diplomatic measures fail, strong measures may have to be applied if the environmental consequences of inaction are sufficiently dire.

IMPLICATIONS OF INCREASING WORLD INEQUALITY

Between 1960 and 1991, the richest fifth of all nations had their share of world income rise from 70 percent to 85 percent, while the poorest fifth of all nations had their share fall from 2.3 percent to 1.4 percent (UN Development Programme, 1992; 1994, p. 35). In a UN press release reported by CNN (16 July 1996) income disparity was indicated to have widened both within and among countries in the last few years. There are numerous factors that underlie this increasing inequality:

1. The richest countries have the resources for investing in R & D and developing innovations. This ability means that the wealthiest countries will maintain their control over advanced technologies.
2. The poorest countries must rely on others for technology transfers. Often the capital-intensive technologies being transferred are not suited to the *labor-rich* economies of the poorer countries.
3. The have-not nations experience difficulty when trying to accumulate the savings needed to finance investment. With low saving and investment, growth is retarded and, consequently, the poorest countries' income levels fall ever further behind.
4. The less-developed countries (LDCs) export income-inelastic goods, demand for which increases less proportionately than the rise in world income. The demand for these products, consequently, lags behind that for the income-elastic products sold by the richest nations.
5. Many of the poorest countries are ruled by autocratic regimes that siphon off savings from their people to support the regimes' extravagant lifestyle.
6. The poorest countries are plagued by political instability that results in policing and military buildups that use scarce resources and scare off foreign investment.
7. Population growth in the poorest countries limits their ability to save and invest in growth-promoting activities.
8. Many of the poorest countries are burdened by debts, whose interest payments divert financial assets from investment.

This growing inequality raises possible security concerns for NATO. Poverty breeds despair and discontentment, which, in turn, may lead to revolution. In places in North Africa (e.g., Egypt, Algeria) and the Middle East where NATO has vital interests, Islamic fundamentalists may come to power through revolutions, thereby replacing regimes that currently have good relations with the West. Even Turkey may someday succumb to these revolutionary pressures if living standards are not elevated over time. Abject poverty also leads to externalities that can reduce the well-being of NATO allies. For example, the plagues of the twenty-first century will surely gain a foothold in countries with poor health and sanitary facilities; from these bases, disease could spread worldwide. Environmental disasters may also emanate from these poor countries, which do not have the means to protect their natural assets. Gross inequalities among nations may lead to sudden mass migrations from the poorest countries, with considerable economic and political consequences for the recipient nations, as events during 1996–97 in Zaire demonstrated.

To be prepared for these problems, NATO must develop sufficient capabilities to project power to trouble spots in these poverty-stricken countries, almost all of which are located outside of Europe. The Gulf War of 1991 showed that, except for the United States, NATO allies do not have sufficient means for projecting power rapidly to areas outside of Europe (Khalilzad, 1997; Thomson, 1997). This ability to project power is also required to provide humanitarian aid for poverty-stricken and war-plagued areas. In addition, NATO must reevaluate its foreign aid commitments worldwide. Will increased foreign aid avert security crises in these countries, or will it merely go to corrupt officials or to the military? There is no general answer; each potential recipient must be evaluated individually. Other bodies – the World Bank, the European Union, the IMF – also have a role to play in addressing world inequality.

OUT-OF-AREA CHALLENGES

Another out-of-area threat involves the Pacific Rim and the eventual emergence of China as a major military power. The territorial ambitions of China are difficult to anticipate. Surely, China's growth as an economic and military power will put pressure on Japan to modernize and expand its military forces. Strained relations between the United States and Japan, the subsequent downsizing of Japanese-based US forces, and the Chinese military buildup will mean that Japan will assume a greater defense burden in the future. As Asia continues to expand economically, European NATO allies will have growing interests in the region through trade and other linkages.

The Korean peninsula also poses a threat to world peace, particularly if North Korea maintains its isolation and continues to pursue WMD. North

Korean sale of Scuds and other weapon systems to the Middle East and other areas of instability remains a cause for concern. If war were again to erupt on the Korean peninsula, the United States would be involved, and this implies that other NATO allies could be dragged into the fighting.

At Rome in 1991, NATO acknowledged the need for a rapid deployment force that could be sent to crises outside of Europe.[13] Peacekeeping was added to NATO's missions at Oslo in June 1992. In principle, NATO allies decided at a January 1994 summit to inhibit weapon proliferation worldwide and develop combined joint task forces (CJTFs), drawn from the allies' armies, that can manage crises wherever they arise. To fulfill these out-of-area missions, NATO allies must acquire the ability to move a suitably equipped task force to a crisis in a short period of time. To date, the United States has invested heavily in power projection, while the European allies have focused on territorial defense (Asmus, 1997, p. 45). Even though the United Kingdom and France possess some power projection capabilities, European allies of NATO are not currently sufficiently equipped to respond to these outside challenges without relying on the United States to transport rapid deployment forces. Germany has recently announced plans to acquire some power projection capacity, and France and Britain have also indicated plans to improve their capacity (Asmus, 1997; Thomson, 1997). Currently, the United States is examining options to improve its airlift and sealift capabilities by adding sixty-seven C-17 transport planes and three large roll-on/roll-off ships (Congressional Budget Office, 1997a). These planes and ships would be procured during the 1998–2002 period at a cost of $17 billion, not counting operation and support costs of almost $4 billion.

Development of power projection capabilities presents an interesting strategic dilemma for NATO. Suppose that allies make decisions in two stages: first, they determine their investments in power projection, and second, they decide contributions to a security contingency that arises. Since investment in transport capabilities takes time, this sequence of choices is germane to NATO. By underinvesting in these capabilities in the first period, allies can have more to spend in the earlier period, and then have a good case for relying on their allies' transport facilities capabilities when contingencies later arise.[14] Thus, there is a strategic advantage to being weak in projecting power, insofar as *consumption can be increased in both periods.* To counter this strategic-based behavior, the United States, France, Ger-

13. The facts in this paragraph come in part from Asmus (1997).
14. See Konrad (1994) for a similar argument concerning public good spending in general.

many, and the United Kingdom will have to invest more than their fair share to support these free riders.

To deploy troops to an out-of-area conflict, NATO allies would have to appeal to Article 4 of the NATO treaty, concerning consultations when one or more allies' interests, but not territory, are threatened. Major allies within NATO will continue to augment their own "parallel" rapid deployment forces to be used when their interests are threatened and NATO allies fail to agree to a deployment of the NATO-based CJTFs. These major allies possess private interests beyond Europe that they must be prepared to protect, even if NATO is not convinced of the threat.

DOWNSIZING CHALLENGE

In Chapter 5, we discussed the implications of downsizing on the defense industrial base of the European Union and the United States. To achieve the necessary economies of scale in weapon production, NATO allies may have to sell weapons either to other NATO allies or to non-NATO nations. These latter sales represents a risk to NATO allies as these weapons could end up in the arsenal of an enemy. Military downsizing also implies that NATO allies must become more dependent on one another when taking on conflicts in Europe and beyond. To allocate resources in an economically efficient manner, weapons and other defense costs should be minimized among the allies. This calls for some degree of specialization in activities, so that the marginal or additional costs for each defense operation will be equal for all allies that engage in that operation. For example, submarine hunting should be assigned to those allies with the lowest costs for that operation, while airfield bombing raids should also be allocated to those allies with the lowest costs of operation. NATO allies can address future challenges better if they realize that their home forces should not try to cover all military missions. For allies to accept this realization requires a tremendous amount of trust, which has not typically characterized the NATO alliance.

CONCLUDING REMARKS

Challenges still abound for NATO into the next millennium. Although the new threats may not rival those of the Cold War, when conflict could have resulted in the annihilation of the human race, these new threats can still spell disaster. To meet these challenges, NATO allies have to engage in a greater degree of cooperation than in the past. Forces will have to be restructured to address exigencies within and beyond Europe. To thwart transnational terrorism, allies will have to cooperate with respect to deterrence decisions, the deployment of crises management squads, and intelligence. Both the European Union and the United States will have to assume leadership roles.

Free riding is very much a concern for the post–Cold War NATO. Each new mission creates a new avenue for free riding in terms of projecting power, peacekeeping, countering weapon proliferation, neutralizing rogue nations, and quelling civil wars. If NATO is to survive in the long run, then some of these free-riding opportunities must be addressed adequately, or else the large NATO allies will see little benefit from the alliance unless they place a sufficiently high value on world leadership status.

7 NATO and Europe

The end of the Cold War had major implications for NATO, the European Union, and the United Nations. NATO is basically a voluntary international military club, originally designed to meet a specific Cold War threat, and now seeking to develop new roles. Until the early 1990s, the European Union was a voluntary international economic club with no military activities. Similarly, the United Nations is a voluntary worldwide general club which lacks any military capabilities and which relies on member nations to make voluntary contributions of armed forces for specific UN missions. This chapter analyzes the relationships among these three organizations.

The transatlantic relationship between the United States and the European member states has been a continuing and distinctive feature of NATO. There have been, and continue to be, debates about burden sharing, with the United States concerned that, collectively, the European members are not bearing their fair shares of the alliance defense burden. At the same time, the expansion of the six-nation European Economic Community of 1957 into the fifteen-nation European Union in 1995 created a major economic trading club representing a competitive threat to the United States in world markets and raising concerns about "Fortress Europe" (e.g., protectionism and state support in EU agriculture, public procurement, and aerospace, especially Airbus and its rivalry with Boeing).

The Treaty on European Union, which was signed at Maastricht in 1992 and became effective in late 1993, committed its signatories to the development of a Common Foreign and Security Policy (CFSP) with a long-term objective of creating a common defense policy and eventually a common defense. The European Union Treaty referred to the Western European Union

(WEU, created in 1954) as the defense component of the EU and a means of strengthening the European pillar of NATO. This is a further source of tension both within Europe and between Europe and the United States. Some European states view a defense role for the EU as a necessary *replacement for NATO,* while other states regard such a role as contributing to the development of a European security and defense identity *within NATO.*

These contrasting views about a European defense role and identity partly reflect the uncertainties about the future of NATO following the end of the Cold War. There have been US troop withdrawals from Europe and a European concern about an isolationist United States or of a shift of its interests to the Pacific Rim. Enlargement is also on the agenda for both NATO and the EU, but each club applies different criteria for new entrants so that admission to one neither guarantees nor requires entry to the other. Nevertheless, EU enlargement and its developing defense role raises questions about the continued US leadership role in NATO and whether the Europeans might emerge as equal partners in the alliance rather than as "followers."

The theme of this book is the future of NATO following the end of the Cold War and whether continued membership in the club is worthwhile. Change is inevitable, but NATO and its evolution cannot be considered in isolation. It is one voluntary international club among a population of such clubs whose future evolution will have direct and indirect feedback effects on the future of NATO. This chapter focuses on the European dimension of this evolutionary process and explores the institutional arrangements and linkages between NATO, the EU, the WEU, and the UN. It considers the inefficiencies of NATO as a collective defense organization, including the actual and potential duplication of institutions at the NATO and European levels, and the opportunities for efficiency improvements.

INTERNATIONAL SECURITY ORGANIZATIONS

The member states of NATO and the EU are involved in a variety of interlocking international defense and security organizations. These range from the UN as a world-wide body to involvement in regional groupings, namely, the Organization for Security and Cooperation in Europe (OSCE), the Euro-Atlantic Partnership Council (EAPC, formerly known as the North Atlantic Cooperation Council or NACC), the Partnership for Peace (PFP) and the Western European Union (WEU). Membership differs between NATO, the EU, and the WEU. Most but not all of the European members of NATO are members of the EU; but not all members of the EU are mem-

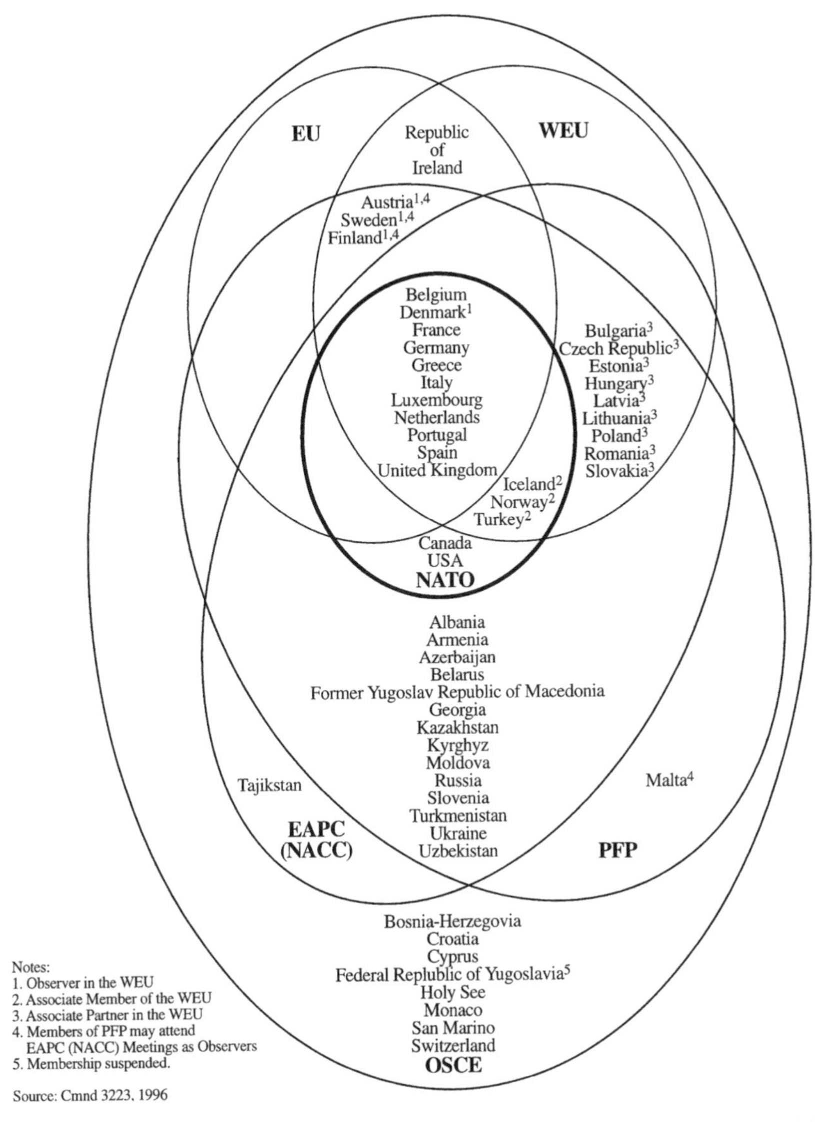

Figure 7.1. Membership of international organizations as of 1 April 1996

bers of NATO. For example, Norway is a member of NATO but not of the EU, while Sweden and Finland are members of the EU but not of NATO. Similarly, all members of the EU are full or associate members or observers in the WEU. The web of interlocking membership for the various international security organizations is shown in Figure 7.1. In this figure, all states are members of the OSCE, but only a subset of these are members of NATO, and all NATO members form part of the membership of both the EAPC and the PFP.

Institutional economics

Economic theory would start to explain the variety of international security organizations as mechanisms for correcting for market failure and improving the operation of markets. In principle, these organizations facilitate and promote opportunities for mutually beneficial trade and exchange of defense goods and services. On this basis, NATO should provide opportunities for international trade based on specialization by comparative advantage. Two implications follow from this simple economic principle. First, international organizations should focus on those activities in which they have a comparative advantage. NATO has a comparative advantage as a specialist military club, so that it might withdraw from its nondefense activities. Similarly, the EU is a specialist economic trading group which might withdraw from efforts to create a duplicate military organization (but see below). Second, economic efficiency requires role specialization within NATO. For example, the United States might specialize in providing high technology and capital-intensive forces such as nuclear forces, large naval aircraft carriers, satellite surveillance, communications, and long-range strategic air transport. Similarly, Germany could specialize in armored forces; the United Kingdom could provide small naval aircraft carriers, antisubmarine forces, and amphibious units; while Turkey might provide labor-intensive forces. National sovereignty, the desire for independence, and the insurance policy of a complete range of air, land, and sea forces is the major barrier to role specialization among member states of NATO.

The analysis can be developed further by regarding each international security organization as a means of minimizing transaction costs and maximizing net transaction benefits. Transaction costs are the costs of running the international collective defense and security system: they are the costs of search, negotiation, agreement, and contracting, together with the policing and monitoring of the contractual agreement. Inevitably, international organizations with different objectives will create different institutional structures to minimize transaction costs and to achieve maximum transaction net benefits (see Chapter 8).

The simple transaction cost explanation of international security organizations has its limitations. Institutions such as NATO and the WEU form the governance framework within which international military transactions are negotiated, agreed upon, and executed. They can be viewed as a framework for formal and informal international contracting. In theory, these institutions are the mechanisms through which "principals" (i.e., governments of member states and ultimately voters) seek to ensure that their objectives are pursued by appointed "agents" (i.e., military commanders, armed forces, and government officials). However, agents are monopoly suppliers of information and experts on military production possibilities, and they are likely to form international coalitions to facilitate collusive behavior and the manipulation of information for the benefit of agents rather than principals. As a result, the actual pattern of international security organizations might not be explained in terms of minimizing transaction costs.

Problems also arise because the transaction cost paradigm is usually applied to commercial transactions and to organizations where there are incentives to minimize transaction costs. International security organizations are nonprofit public sector agencies which are unlikely to be cost-minimizing bodies. They lack the set of incentives, policing, and monitoring mechanisms which are central to efficient behavior in private enterprise economies – namely, the profit motive, the capital market as a takeover threat, and rivalry from alternative suppliers. There is a further analytical complication resulting from the lack of a general equilibrium model of nonprofit organizations, thus necessitating a partial equilibrium approach. This approach analyzes NATO on the assumption that other institutions remain given and unchanged (an unlikely assumption in the light of future developments in the EU and the WEU).

An alternative public choice analysis would explain NATO, the WEU, and other international security organizations in terms of providing opportunities for politicians, civil servants, and armed forces officers to maximize their utility from larger budgets, international travel, international meetings, and the power and prestige associated with international gatherings (see Chapter 5). Such behavior is likely to lead to departures from the simple economic principle of efficiency in NATO.

NATO: AN INEFFICIENT ORGANIZATION?

The Callaghan study

A pioneering contribution in estimating the degree of inefficiency in NATO was published by Thomas Callaghan in 1975. He argued that NATO's defense expenditures were wasted in every phase of the investment process,

Table 7.1. *Callaghan estimates of NATO inefficiency, 1975 (in billions of US dollars, 1975 prices)*

General purpose force expenditures	United States	Europe	Estimated waste
Annual R & D	5.0	2.6	2.6
Annual procurement	12.0	7.0	2.95
Annual support: Europe	4.0	35.0	5.65
Totals	21.0	44.6	11.2+

Source: Callaghan (1975, p. 37).

beginning with the duplication of effort in the development phase, proceding through the loss of scale economies in production, and peaking with a waste of facilities, spares, overheads, and especially manpower in the logistic support phase. It was concluded that the manner in which the Americans and Europeans together converted their substantial annual defense expenditures into NATO conventional fighting units was both "irrational and inefficient" and that "economic necessity requires that all duplication of effort be eliminated" (Callaghan, 1975, p. 15).

The Callaghan study estimated the waste of allied resources at over $10 billion per year in 1975 (and this was a lower bound estimate). The inefficiencies in Europe associated with duplicate R & D programs and the loss of scale economies from short production runs in Europe's defense industries were outlined in Chapter 5. There is further waste in logistic support, with each NATO nation having its own national defense department, its own army, navy, and air force, its separate repair, spares, maintenance, and operational facilities, and its own national training organizations. The Callaghan study estimated waste in NATO's logistic support at some 50 percent of the total annual allied waste. The estimates are shown in Table 7.1.

The estimates in Table 7.1 assume that wasteful duplication comprises all European R&D; plus 10% of US procurement expenditure and 25% of European procurement expenditure; plus 10% of direct US annual NATO cost and 15% of European general purpose force expenditures per year. Overall, Europe accounted for some 85% of the total estimated NATO waste. For NATO as a whole, the estimated waste of $11.2 billion represented some 14% to 17% of NATO's defense budget in 1974–75 (depending on the estimated costs of the US commitment to NATO).

Although these estimates of waste appear attractive, they are based on simple, unsubstantiated assumptions that *all* European R & D and 25 percent of its procurement expenditures are a waste of resources. Such assumptions fail to recognize that the European nations have some comparative advantages in the development and production of defense equipment (e.g., vertical take-off combat aircraft, small missiles, aero-engines, armored fighting vehicles, small aircraft carriers, mine countermeasure vessels). The estimates also assume that in the absence of a competitive threat from Europe's defense industries, US firms would continue to be technically efficient, that prices and profits would be competitive, and that firms would be innovative.

A visitor from Mars would be amazed at the failure of NATO's armed forces to exploit the efficiency savings from greater collective action leading to economies of scale and scope. For example, using the US model, the Department of Defense "managed" 1.62 million personnel in its armed forces in 1995. In NATO Europe, fourteen states each with their defense departments "managed" some three million armed forces personnel in 1995. Applying the US model to NATO Europe suggests that its defense ministries could be reduced to about two defense departments of US size. The solution proposed by Thomas Callaghan was standardization, with defense industry rationalization and specialization throughout NATO. He proposed a North Atlantic common defense market, open government procurement for military and civil goods and services, and the extension of allied cooperation to embrace civil technology.

The 1975 Callaghan study estimated that standardization would increase allied military effectiveness by from 30 to 50 percent for most units and by as much as 300 percent for certain tactical air units. For example, allied tactical air forces operate a variety of different national types of aircraft so that they are constrained to their national airfields, unable to be refueled, repaired, or rearmed at other air bases. The same problems affect allied naval forces, which rely on national replenishment ships for refueling and rearming at sea. Similarly, with the multinational Allied Command Europe (ACE) Mobile Force, standardization both within the force and with the potential host nation for deployment of the force would halve the time required to deploy and become combat ready.

While the case for NATO standardization appears incontrovertible, it can be subject to critical evaluation. The general belief seems to be that all standardization is good, regardless of costs. However, there is likely to be an optimal or socially desirable amount of equipment and force standardization and an associated optimal amount of diversity and differentiation. Indeed, some diversity of weapons and forces is needed as an insurance against the failure of standardized weapons and to meet the variety of future unknown and unknowable threats. The Callaghan analysis was correct in identifying too little NATO standardization and too much diversity, reflecting an emphasis on national or private benefits and costs rather than NATO-wide benefits and costs (the economist's externality problem). Of course, at the NATO level, there is no intergovernmental agency with the legal or fiscal authority to intervene across the alliance and correct for market failure due to such externalities.

There is a further concern about standardization. In the mid-1970s, an idealized model of the Warsaw Pact represented the threat. It was assumed that the Warsaw Pact forces with their standardized Soviet weapons and equipment would be able to operate effectively together. This raises a fundamental methodological issue, namely, the standard of comparison. Were comparisons being made between an existing NATO situation and some ideal, but never achieved, model of standardization (the Warsaw Pact); or were comparisons being made between two ideal alliance and procurement models, neither of which existed? Hindsight is even more revealing. The end of the Cold War suggests that the apparently inefficient NATO was superior to the Warsaw Pact, in that it survived and expanded while the Warsaw Pact collapsed. More generally, doubts were raised about the economic efficiency of centrally planned command economies compared with capitalist, free enterprise market economies. Nonetheless, the success of NATO does not mean that standardization is no longer relevant. Greater standardization might have enabled NATO to be equally successful against the Warsaw Pact, but at a lower resource cost.

NATO standardization

Since its formation, NATO has pursued various initiatives on standardization of equipment, communications, infrastructure, and logistics. There is a NATO common infrastructure program which provides airfields, communications, petroleum facilities and pipelines. NATO air defense is provided through the NATO Air Defense Ground Environment (NADGE); and logistic support in the form of spares supply, maintenance and repair facilities is provided by the NATO Maintenance and Supply Organization (NAMSO).

A *NATO Military Agency for Standardization* was established in 1951 and introduced various Standardization Agreements (STANAGs) for procedures, equipment components, and parts (e.g., the 7.62 mm NATO basic round for small arms). Other early NATO initiatives on cooperation focused on individual collaborative equipment programs. Examples include the selection in 1954 of the Italian G-91 light combat aircraft to meet a NATO requirement; the start in 1957 of the multinational NATO maritime patrol aircraft, known as the Atlantic; and in the late 1950s the European production of US missiles. Efforts to formulate NATO Basic Military Requirements (NBMRs), introduced in 1959, were unsuccessful due to their rigidity, the difficulties of harmonizing the military requirements of different NATO states, and the desire of nations to support their national DIB.

A new procedure to promote armaments cooperation was introduced in 1966 which recognized that countries could not be compelled to cooperate nor be constrained to obey rigid procedural rules. The new focus was on flexibility and the need to make cooperation easy and beneficial; hence, the minimum requirement for a project to be designated a NATO project was the involvement of at least two countries (i.e., NATO-wide agreement was no longer required). Designation as a NATO project allows the partner nations to create a NATO organization for managing collaborative projects. Such a management organization represents the interests of the partner nations and is responsible for the overall control and monitoring of progress on the program as well as its daily management, including the awarding of prime contracts. NATO management arrangements are subject to staffing constraints which require that specific posts be filled by each nation in line with the cost-sharing rules of the program. These NATO management arrangements can be viewed as a set of general rules agreed upon by member states, thus avoiding the need to negotiate a management structure for every new collaborative program and thereby economizing on transaction costs. However, international agreement on general rules might introduce bureaucratic rigidities, so preventing the creation of management organizations which are flexible, responsive to change, and appropriate to specific projects. Similarly, bureaucratic rigidities might not promote the application of modern business practices, nor offer managers incentives and rewards for good performance, nor allow the appointment of managers on merit, requiring instead the appointment of managers on some sharing criteria between the partner nations.

To implement the 1966 armaments cooperation initiatives, the NATO Council created a new high-level body, the *Conference of National Armaments Directors (CNAD).* This group was involved in a number of successful cooperative programs, including the Anglo-French Jaguar strike aircraft, the Franco-German MILAN missile, the Anglo-French helicopter package deal, and the three-nation Tornado combat aircraft. In 1968, the

NATO Industrial Advisory Group (NIAG) was created under the CNAD to provide a forum for exchanging views on the industrial aspects of NATO armaments cooperation (NATO Information Service, 1984). By 1998, both CNAD and NIAG had established formal links with Partnership for Peace countries with the aim of involving PFP states in NATO armaments cooperation.

Yet another NATO standardization initiative was launched in 1995 with the creation of a new *NATO Standardization Organization.* This organization was established "to improve standardization efforts in a structured way, taking into account existing planning disciplines. It is not a duplication of the efforts of the many NATO groups currently involved in this field but provides them with acknowledged and agreed objectives and priorities, thus giving guidance to their programmes of work" (Ferrari, 1995, p. 33). The new approach has created an agreed-upon and recognized organization designed to coordinate overall standardization matters in NATO with components at different levels, involving all parties (i.e., the nations, military and civilian staffs, and major NATO commanders). It also means that standardization issues will be considered at the highest political level in NATO; and that there will be a real coordinating body, which was lacking in the past (the NATO Standardization Liaison Board), together with a dedicated staff (in the Office of NATO Standardization).

Questions have to be asked about the reasons for the variety and number of initiatives on NATO standardization. Is it a management-organizational problem, or is there something more fundamental which cannot be addressed by management changes? The organizational changes can be rationalized as efforts at economizing on transaction costs, and the appointment of dedicated staffs might improve the stock and flow of information on the cost-saving opportunities from further NATO standardization. Nevertheless, nations impose their own barriers to more standardization through their continued preference for, and their willingness to pay for, independence. The result is continued support for independent national armed forces, for "unique" weapons to meet specific and "unique" national requirements, and for the domestic defense industrial base to supply the necessary equipment (thereby providing the preferred amount and type of national insurance).

While it appears attractive, standardization is not problem-free; there are no free lunches. Simplistically, the "grand design" NATO standardization requires all member states to buy the same equipment and to adopt the same operational doctrines, with possible NATO provision of repair, maintenance, supply and training facilities for all member states. This requires most member states to sacrifice national independence and buy foreign equipment. Choices can either be imposed dictatorially (the Warsaw Pact model) or agreed upon voluntarily; but voluntary and complete agreement between all the democratic member states of NATO becomes more difficult as the number of club members increases (see Chapters 3 and 8). Inevitably, there are European concerns about US domination, especially in weapons, with implications for the levels of technology in the United States and Europe (e.g., Europe as a nation of "metal bashers": see Chapter 5). However, economic pressures leading to falling defense budgets will force all member states on both sides of the Atlantic to reevaluate their willingness to pay for nationalism. Already, some of the smaller European states (e.g., Belgium, Denmark, Norway) import much of their high technology equipment (e.g., aircraft, missiles, tanks).

A significant collective choice occurred in late 1978 when NATO defense ministers agreed to the joint purchase of eighteen Boeing Airborne Early Warning and Control System (AWACS) aircraft for low-level radar cover over NATO territory (a nonrival, public good role). This program was managed by the NATO AWACS Program Management Organization, and the aircraft were manned by a multinational force. Interestingly, when the original NATO procurement decision was made, the United Kingdom preferred to buy its national NIMROD Airborne Early Warning aircraft (AEW), which was intended to be interoperable alongside the NATO AWACS force. However, in 1986, the Nimrod AEW aircraft was canceled, and the UK acquired seven Boeing AWACS aircraft. Other recent examples of NATO standardization include the four-nation Eurofighter 2000 combat aircraft and the four-nation NH90 transport helicopter (France, Germany, Italy, and the Netherlands), which is managed on behalf of the partner nations by the NATO Helicopter Management Agency (NAHEMA). These examples confirm the trend toward greater NATO equipment standardization based on agreements between small numbers of nations rather than on the "grand design" of complete agreement between all member states.

A similar example occurred with the introduction of reciprocal defense *memorandums of understanding (MOUs)* between the United States and thirteen European NATO countries. These agreements, signed between 1975 and 1991, were intended by the United States to promote rationalization, standardization, and interoperability of defense equipment by providing competitive opportunities for the signatories' defense industries. For example, the United States met its MOU obligations primarily by waiving the Buy American Act, which allows it to add a 50 percent premium to the price of foreign products when they are competing with US products. Despite the MOUs, the United States continued to place many restrictions on its foreign defense procurements, and the Europeans also reserved the right to award contracts to domestic or other European suppliers. Nevertheless, the MOUs have been associated with a significant change in the balance of defense trade between the United States and its European allies. In the late 1970s, the defense trade ratio (i.e., US defense exports to its European NATO allies compared with US defense imports from these allies) was about 8 to 1 in favor of the United States; by the late 1980s, this ratio had fallen to about 2 to 1 in favor of the United States (US GAO, 1992).

The Combined Joint Task Force

One of NATO's initial reactions to the new security environment following the end of the Cold War was to create a rapid reaction capability. The land component of this capability was the multinational (twelve-nation) Allied Command Europe Rapid Reaction Corps (ARRC). The ARRC headquarters was formed in Germany in 1992 and declared operational in April 1995. It forms the headquarters for IFOR's land forces in the former Yugoslavia.

A new initiative on crisis management known as the Combined Joint Task Force (CJTF) was endorsed at the NATO summit in January 1994. The CJTF is a rapidly deployable multinational, multiservice formation specially designed for specific contingencies in crisis management, humanitarian and disaster relief, peace enforcement, and peacekeeping. It was intended that the CJTF be created from existing assets, so avoiding expensive and potentially divisive duplication of capabilities. This NATO force will also be made available to the WEU, the UN, and the OSCE. It will allow the WEU to conduct operations under its auspices, without having to duplicate the capabilities held collectively by the alliance. As a result, the WEU will be able to mount operations when NATO decides not to act, so supporting a European security and defense identity (on the concept of separable but not separate capabilities, see Cragg, 1996).

Economists can analyze joint forces (i.e., the bringing together of two or more services) as mergers which involve both benefits and costs. Economic benefits take the form of reduced costs resulting from rationalization (less duplication), from greater output leading to scale economies, and from economies of scope reflecting the cost savings from undertaking two or more activities in one firm. The overall effect is to economize on transaction costs by undertaking activities in one firm rather than in a number of firms. But mergers involve costs. They can create monopoly power resulting in higher prices, inefficiency, monopoly profits, and a reduced incentive to innovate. Typically, economists distinguish three types of mergers – horizontal (two or more firms at the same stage of production), vertical (two or more firms at different stages of production), and conglomerate (diversified firms with a variety of activities). Joint forces resemble conglomerate firms. However, joint forces lack the efficiency incentives confronting private sector conglomerate firms, namely, the profit motive, the policing role of the capital market with its threat of takeovers, and the spur of competition. Instead, the armed forces can use joint forces as a means of obtaining funds by persuading politicians of the "vital" contribution of such forces to politically attractive crisis management, humanitarian relief, and peacekeeping operations (Hartley, 1998).

The formation of multinational forces such as the ARRC and the CJTF represents real progress toward the more efficient provision of collective defense in NATO. Nonetheless, there remain significant inefficiencies in the provision of both armed forces and weapons. European states, each with different national preferences, form a major barrier to further NATO standardization. Within Europe, the "big three" of France, Germany, and the United Kingdom represent major constraints: each has a substantial defense industrial base, and France and the United Kingdom retain aspirations to be leading military powers in the world (Hartley, 1997a; Fontanel and Hebert, 1997). As a result, defense and security developments in the European Union and the Western European Union are significant for NATO and for NATO standardization.

A EUROPEAN DEFENSE POLICY?

Until 1991, the European Union did not have any commitment to a common defense and security policy. It focused on creating a customs union and a Single European Market for *civil* goods and services. Article 223 of the Treaty of Rome excluded specialized defense equipment from the rules governing the Single Market. However, since 1991 under arrangements reached at Maastricht, the WEU has been developed in a dual capacity as the defense component of the European Union and the European pillar of NATO. Also, in 1993, the EU introduced its KONVER program, which provides support and assistance to defense-dependent regions experiencing substantial job losses in defense industries or military bases (Hooper and Cox, 1996).

Like NATO, the EU has expanded its membership, and there are plans for further expansion. In 1997, the European Commission published Agenda 2000 setting out its strategy for EU enlargement. Six countries were invited to start accession negotiations in 1998, namely, Hungary, Poland, the Czech Republic (the new NATO members), Estonia, Slovenia, and Cyprus. Other countries on the waiting list for entry include Bulgaria, Latvia, Lithuania, Slovakia, and Romania. As with NATO enlargement, there has been an absence of in-depth, publicly available evaluation of the costs and benefits of EU expansion, including its potential impacts on the Atlantic alliance.

One view welcomes EU expansion as a means of enabling Europe to bear a greater share of the burden of ensuring its own security and freedom. An alternative view of expansion sees the EU becoming a leading world power which might be unwilling to rely on NATO for its defense. Such a view is likely where EU expansion involves nations who are not members of NATO. The EU's commitment to developing a Common Foreign and Security Policy is subject to two major limitations. First, member states have to reach agreement on such a policy or at least on a set of rules which allows effective decision making. Second, the EU lacks the military capability to enforce any agreed Common Foreign and Security Policy and to ensure the military defense of the territory of the EU from armed attack (an adequate military capability is needed for an effective foreign policy). Currently, the countries of the EU have given the WEU the task of developing its defense capability (Seidelman, 1997).

The Western European Union

The WEU had its origins in the Brussels Treaty of 1948 signed by Belgium, France, Luxembourg, the Netherlands, and the UK. Under the Paris Agreement of 1954, the Federal Republic of Germany and Italy acceded to the Brussels Treaty, and the Western Union was renamed the WEU. The WEU has four levels of membership and association – members, associate members, observers, and associate partners. In a 1991 declaration, future members of the EU were invited to accede to the WEU or to become observers, and other European members of NATO were invited to become associate members of the WEU; in 1994, the Kirchberg Declaration gave the nine Central and Eastern European members of the Forum of Consultation the status of associate partners of the WEU. For example, Sweden is not a member of NATO but is a member of the EU and an observer in the WEU; Norway and Turkey, as European members of NATO but not of the EU, are associate members of the WEU; while Bulgaria and Romania are associate partners in the WEU. Full members of the WEU are given defense guarantees which in practice are carried out through NATO (see Figure 7.1).

Following Maastricht, the WEU was designated as the defense component of the EU and its secretariat and planning cell were moved to Brussels. Under the Petersberg Declaration of 1992, the WEU has agreed to categories of tasks on which its military capabilities are to be used. These involve the use of combat forces in crisis management; peacekeeping and peacemaking tasks; and humanitarian and rescue tasks. WEU members have agreed to make available military units from their conventional forces for military tasks conducted under the authority of the WEU. Some of these military tasks could be undertaken in cooperation with the United Nations or the OSCE.

There are a number of other European defense organizations, namely, the Eurogroup, the Independent European Program Group (IEPG) which became the Western European Armaments Group (WEAG), and the European Defense Industry Group (EDIG). *Eurogroup* was formed in November 1968 as an informal association of defense ministers of the European members of NATO, namely, Belgium, Denmark, Germany, Italy, Luxembourg, the Netherlands, Norway, Portugal, Spain, Turkey, and the United Kingdom. (France was not a member.) Its purpose was to make a more effective European contribution to the NATO alliance. Examples of Eurogroup initiatives included the European Defense Improvement Program (EDIP), which provided for substantial investments in infrastructure, the development of an integrated communications network, and the financing of arms procurement and transport aircraft. Eurogroup also coordinated Europe's procurement of US equipment (e.g., F-16 aircraft, Lance missiles) and laid the foundation for equipment standardization (WEU, 1995).

The Independent European Program Group (IEPG) was formed in 1976 and comprised the European members of NATO, including France (but not Iceland). Its aim was to promote European collaboration in defense equipment matters and to expand equipment sales to the US (so creating a "two-way street"). Until 1984, IEPG focused on the exchange of information on national armaments and equipment procurement procedures and on exploring possible models for managing joint projects. In 1984, responsibility for IEPG was transferred from national armaments directors to defense ministers, thereby giving the group a new impetus with a focus on more systematic cooperation in research and procurement and on increasing the effectiveness of the European defense industrial base. The group commissioned the 1986 European Defense Industry Study and accepted all its major recommendations: the creation of a more open and competitive European defense equipment market; a stronger European research effort; and assistance to the Developing Defense Industry nations (the DDIs of Greece, Portugal, and Turkey) to improve their defense industrial base (Vredeling, 1986).

Some limited progress toward an open European defense equipment market has been achieved with arrangements for the dissemination of information through the regular publication of contracts bulletins by IEPG countries and the network of national focal points to promote the exchange of data between governments and potential suppliers. The aim is to provide potential bidders at the prime and subcontract levels the opportunity to learn about and respond to requirements from all IEPG countries. DDI countries were allowed a transitional period before fully opening their markets. In addition, members of IEPG agreed to a government cooperative research and technology program to develop and extend Europe's defense technology base. This was known as the program for European Cooperation for the Long Term in Defense, or EUCLID. By early 1996, a total of fifty-seven Research and Technology Projects (RTPs) worth some $290 million had been approved as part of the EUCLID program. Examples of RTPs involved aspects of modern radar technology, microelectronics, modular avionics, advanced information processing, and satellite surveillance technology. Participation in the EUCLID program was also seen as an opportunity for the DDI countries to improve their capabilities in research and technology (WEU, 1995; 1996).

In 1990, the IEPG structure was joined by the *European Defense Industrial Group* (EDIG). This is a forum created by the national industry trade associations bringing together the defense industries of the IEPG member states. EDIG represents the interests of the European defense industry; it is a source of information and has close working relationships with IEPG governments (e.g., offering advice on improving the EUCLID program). However, while both industries and governments are agreed on the need for greater European defense cooperation, standardization, and collaboration, there are different views on the preferred solutions reflecting national preferences and interests. For example, if European countries are ranked in descending order of defense industrial capability (e.g., based on size of home and export markets, technology base, and scale of defense R & D), two implications follow. First, any country would like all countries ranked below it to operate a free, open, competitive market, because it would be confident of winning any competition with them. Second, wherever a country is in the ranking, it will demand some form of protection from the nations above, whom it will accuse of unfair competition and the absence of a level playing field (McFarlane, 1997).

The 1991 decision to develop the WEU as the defense component of the EU had implications for the other European defense organizations. In December 1992, the IEPG defense ministers decided to transfer the functions of the group to the WEU, and it subsequently became the *Western European Armaments Group* (WEAG, based in Brussels). The change was designed to create a single European authority in this area to avoid any duplication, as well as to ensure continuity of IEPG's work (e.g., EUCLID) and its links with NATO and the EDIG. WEAG is now the WEU agency with the task of pursuing armaments cooperation, joint research and technology programs, the harmonization of operational requirements, and the liberalization and rationalization of the European defense equipment market. In late 1995, a related body known as the Western European Armaments Organization (WEAO) was created as an agency under the WEU which could be the basis for a future European Armaments Agency. To economize and avoid duplication, NATO's Eurogroup, which was disbanded in January 1994, transferred most its activities to the WEU and the remainder to NATO. In addition, in November 1996, four nations – namely, Britain, France, Germany, and Italy – announced the creation of a quadrilateral armaments agency to promote a more efficient and effective approach to the management of collaborative defense programs (OCCAR: see Chapter 5). This agency is outside the framework of the WEU.

Europe's armed forces

There have been a number of bilateral and multinational initiatives among the armed forces of European countries. Examples include the Eurocorps (France, Germany, Belgium, Luxembourg, and Spain); the Multinational Division (Central) comprising the Belgian, British, Dutch, and German components of NATO's ARRC; the UK-Netherlands Amphibious Force; the Belgian-Dutch naval headquarters; the Anglo-French air group; and Eurofor, which is a multinational force of units from France, Italy, Spain, and Portugal designated to implement the WEU's Petersberg missions. In addition, the European members of NATO and the EU can collectively provide significant armed forces. Table 7.2 summarizes the position in 1995.

Table 7.2 shows the magnitude of the European defense effort. In 1995, the aggregate EU defense expenditure was some $185 billion, and its armed

Table 7.2. *Armed forces in NATO and the EU, 1995*

Country	Defense expenditure (millions of US dollars, 1995 prices)	Defense share (D/Y) (%)	GNP per capita (1995, US dollars)	Armed forces (thousands)
Belgium	4449	1.7	26550	47
Denmark	3118	1.8	32540	27
France	47770	3.1	26290	504
Germany	41160	1.9	26190	352
Greece	5056	5.5	8696	213
Italy	19380	1.8	18850	435
Luxembourg	142	0.7	46370	1
Netherlands	8012	2.1	25240	67
Norway	3508	2.7	29350	38
Portugal	2690	2.6	10430	78
Spain	8652	1.6	14160	210
Turkey	6606	4.0	2714	805
United Kingdom	33400	3.0	19020	233
NATO Europe	183900	2.4	18830	3010
Other EU States				
Austria	2106	0.9	28860	45
Finland	2381	2.0	23410	32
Ireland	689	1.3	15250	13
Sweden	6042	2.8	24730	51
USA	277800	3.8	27550	1620
NATO	470800	3.0	22090	4700

Notes: (i) Iceland had no defense expenditure and no armed forces.
(ii) The EU total defense effort is estimated by aggregating for the EU members of NATO and other EU states.
Source: ACDA (1997).

forces totalled 2,308 million personnel. NATO Europe together with the other EU states had an aggregate defense spending of over $195 billion and 3,151 million armed forces personnel; these totals were 70 percent of US defense outlays and almost twice US armed forces numbers. Although the European defense effort is substantial, its allocation across member states means that it lacks the cost-effectiveness of the single-state US defense effort. Europe comprising NATO Europe and the other EU states is also characterized by considerable differences in defense burdens measured by defense shares of GNP. Nations such as Greece, Turkey, France, and the UK had above-average defense efforts for Europe, while Austria, Belgium, Denmark, Germany, and Luxembourg had below-average defense burdens.

Interestingly, the rank correlation between defense shares (D/Y) and per capita income for all European states (i.e., NATO Europe and other EU states) was –0.42, suggesting an inverse relationship between the two variables; but the correlation was only significant at the 10 percent level on a two-tail test.

European scenarios

The 1997 Treaty of Amsterdam modified the Treaty on European Union which was concluded in Maastricht. This 1997 treaty incorporated the Petersberg missions and entrusted the WEU with additional tasks, such as providing the EU with access to operational capability, supporting it in framing the defense aspects of its CFSP, and providing WEU personnel for the EU's policy planning and early warning unit. However, the Treaty of Amsterdam made no provision for a common defense policy, a common defense, or for the WEU's integration into the EU. Many questions remain about the future direction of the EU's defense and security policy (WEU, 1997). A key issue is whether the WEU's activities will be confined to the Petersberg tasks and whether it can ignore the core function of the collective defense of the EU. Some of the issues can be illustrated by considering two scenarios for the possible future development of a European defense policy (Martin and Roper, 1995).

Scenario I adopts a gradual evolutionary approach, building on the existing WEU arrangements. This approach would aim at the efficient provision of forces for achieving the WEU's Petersberg missions. Efficient provision would be achieved by creating an institutional structure which would provide opportunities for voluntary collective action, with WEU members contributing forces on the basis of each nation's comparative advantage. This scenario would allow member states to retain their independent national forces. Nonetheless, the WEU has major deficiencies in its military capabilities needed for rapid deployment. It lacks strategic airlift, modern intelligence systems, and satellite surveillance. These are costly capabilities which might have to be acquired, operated, and financed on a collective basis, with contributions from all members of the EU club and inevitable controversies about burden sharing and free riding. Alternatively, the CJTF concept might be the solution, allowing WEU to use NATO military assets. But such a simple and economically attractive CJTF solution is not without its problems. Questions arise about control of CJTF assets made available to WEU and whether the US would allow command over its military assets to be transferred to the WEU. Similarly, the US might be unwilling to allow WEU to use its military assets in operations involving states which are not members of NATO. There are also questions about the future of the WEU and its relationship with the EU. One option is the eventual integration of the WEU into the EU, which would mean that WEU would cease to exist as an international organization. More fundamental problems arise where different EU members states have to reach agreement on common aims and on joint action, and on whether to use unanimity or majority voting rules for military action.

Scenario II is a long-run option which could be achieved directly or through the development of Scenario I. This scenario involves the creation of a European political union which could take the form of a federation, such as a United States of Europe. This would allow the creation of a single European army, navy, and air force similar to the US model. It would be able to afford a complete range of nuclear and conventional forces, together with strategic airlift and satellite surveillance capabilities. A single European Defense Department would have the buying power to support large EU defense firms able to achieve economies of scale and scope. Scenario II could be the basis for creating a genuine NATO free trade area for defense equipment, thus maintaining competition in both Europe and the US (see Chapter 5). Alternatively, the creation of an EU political union might lead to pressures for an independent and separate EU defense policy, raising questions about the future of NATO.

Implications for the UN

NATO has a recognized and agreed-upon command structure and a proven military capability able to undertake a complete range of peacekeeping and peacemaking functions using forces from a group of major European and North American states. The WEU is developing a limited range of military capabilities, some of which are dependent on the use of NATO military assets. In principle, both organizations could provide military forces for UN operations, so long as the UN lacks its own military forces.

A set of rules might be developed enabling the UN to choose between the deployment of either NATO or WEU forces. These rules might be based on the likely immediate beneficiaries from UN-sanctioned peacekeeping operations. For civil wars in Europe and the adjoining states, the UN might select WEU forces, while conflicts in other areas might require the deployment of US-led NATO forces. Some UN operations might comprise an international coalition based on a core of NATO forces, with members of the coalition drawn from the countries most likely to benefit from peace in their region (see Chapters 4 and 6).

An alternative long-run solution is for the UN to develop its own military forces. This has often been proposed, but its advocates have rarely given much thought to the problems involved. The UN would need a governing body able to make decisions on behalf of its members to use military force (e.g., a world governing body, with implications for the loss of sovereignty by all nation-states). Such a force would have to be created, trained, and based throughout the world; it would need a clear command and accountability structure; and it would need a military capability to enforce UN decisions. Members of the UN would also have to agree on the arrangements for funding its military force. Currently, NATO and WEU forces provide the UN with a cost-effective range of military capabilities, but these capabilities can only be deployed with the consent of member states of NATO and the WEU (Klein and Marwah, 1996; McNamara, 1991).

CONCLUDING REMARKS

Developments in Europe present a challenge and an opportunity for NATO. The challenge is to avoid the creation of duplicate organizations and military capabilities by NATO and the WEU, and to respond to the pressures for a separate EU defense policy and to possible US pressures to withdraw all its armed forces from Europe. At the same time, there is a further challenge to create organizations which are capable of responding to change and uncertainty. Simple economic principles suggest that the various organizations (NATO, the WEU, and the EU) need to specialize in those activities in which they have a comparative advantage.

The opportunity also exists to use the developments in Europe to strengthen NATO by creating a more efficient military alliance both in the provision of armed forces and in the supply of equipment. Europe's defense effort is characterized by major inefficiencies, reflecting duplication as European nations maintain independent armed forces and varying levels of defense industrial base capability. Further potential efficiency improvements are available if the economic principle of specialization by comparative advantage were to be applied to the armed forces and defense industries of NATO as a whole (i.e., Europe and North America). A more efficient NATO would be characterized by more standardization of equipment, greater role specialization of its armed forces, the creation of common training and logistic facilities, and the formation of a NATO free trade area for equipment. Such efficiency improvements would allow NATO to provide collective defense at a lower cost, so releasing resources for alternative uses.

APPENDIX: EUROPEAN CHRONOLOGY

March 1948:	*Treaty of Brussels* establishing the Western Union intended to provide collective security and to encourage cooperation in economic, social, and cultural spheres.
October 1954:	Brussels Treaty modified and *Western European Union (WEU)* established. Treaty signed by Benelux states, France, Italy, the UK and West Germany.
March 1957:	*Treaty of Rome* establishing the European Economic Community (EEC) comprising six states: Belgium, the Netherlands, Luxembourg (Benelux states), France, Italy, and West Germany.
January 1960:	*European Free Trade Area (EFTA)* with seven states: Denmark, Sweden, Norway, Austria, Portugal, Switzerland, and the UK.
April 1965:	Creation of the *European Communities (EC)* incorporating the EEC, Euroatom, and the European Coal and Steel Community (ECSC).
January 1973:	Accession of the UK, Denmark, and Ireland to the EC.
January 1981:	Accession of Greece to the EC.
January 1986:	Accession of Spain and Portugal to the EC.
July 1987:	*Single European Act* comes into effect aiming to complete the internal market by 1992 (i.e., to remove nontariff barriers to the completion of the Single European Market).
August 1987:	Turkey applies for EC membership.
February 1992:	*Treaty on European Union* signed in Maastricht. The treaty aimed at a three-pillar approach to European union based on a reformed EC, a common foreign and security policy, and a common approach to justice and home affairs.
May 1992:	European Court of Justice rules that the EC can proceed with the *European Economic Area* agreement with EFTA states; this agreement came into effect in January 1994.
June 1993:	European Council announced that countries of Central and Eastern Europe which had signed Europe Agreements with the EU would eventually be invited to become EU members.
January 1995:	Austria, Finland, and Sweden become members of the EU, creating a fifteen-nation EU.
March 1995:	Schengen Agreement to abolish internal EU frontiers comes into effect.
November 1996:	Creation of quadrilateral armaments agency known as OCCAR.

8 NATO design

A little-explored issue concerns the design of NATO in terms of the appropriate form of the linkages among allies and the proper organizational structure within NATO itself.[1] The new institutional economics can, however, provide the conceptual framework for an examination of the architecture of NATO based on transaction costs and benefits considerations.[2] Allies belong to NATO because they perceive there to be a net gain from remaining members, despite expenses associated with membership.[3] Article 13 of the North Atlantic Treaty allows any ally to leave the alliance after giving a year's notice, while Article 10 permits other European states to join the alliance if invited (see Chapters 2 and 3). If the alliance is to remain viable, then a proper institutional structure must exist to give the overall membership the greatest possible net gains, while ensuring that each ally also perceives a net advantage over the best nonmembership alternatives. Moreover, the alliance structure must be adjusted over time to respond to developments that alter the configuration of transaction costs and benefits associated with alliance membership. Recent noteworthy changes concerning strategic doctrine, alliance size, and weapon technology may affect the patterns of transaction costs and benefits derived from NATO, and, in so doing, may require changes

1. A notable exception is Sandler and Forbes (1980).
2. The best starting point for gaining a working knowledge of the new institutional economics is Williamson (1975).
3. These net gains may be distributed unevenly within an ally. For example, arms manufacturers may prosper greatly from standardization agreements or from NATO enlargement. To obtain these benefits, potential gainers may lobby vigorously and, in so doing, affect the alliance's organizational structure. While we recognize that the final configuration of an alliance is determined by public choice considerations and lobbying activities, we abstract from these concerns here and focus on the normative aspects of the design of NATO.

in the linkage form among allies as well as in NATO's organizational structure.

With its current linkage structure, NATO is best described as a loose organization in which allies' autonomy is maintained in large part (Sandler, Cauley, and Tschirhart, 1983; Sandler and Forbes, 1980). This follows because alliance decisions must be unanimous; the North Atlantic Council (NAC) meets infrequently at the ministerial level; common funding is relatively modest; decisions are not always binding on allies; and the overwhelming share of defense spending is made independently by the allies (NATO Office of Information and Press, 1995, p. 105). Is this loose structure optimal? If not, how should it be altered to improve efficiency? These and other questions are addressed in this chapter, which has at least four primary purposes. First, a design procedure is put forward that accounts for the trade-offs between ally autonomy and alliance security (see, e.g., Morrow, 1991). This procedure is sufficiently general to include additional trade-offs, as between security and flexibility. Second, NATO's current loose structure is evaluated in terms of potential *net* gains from tightening. Third, the form of NATO's future linkages is considered in light of recent and anticipated changes that affect NATO allies. Fourth, a brief examination of NATO's internal structure – that is, its military and civil organization – is given.

The body of the chapter consists of seven sections. Efficiency gains from linkage are addressed in detail in the first section with the help of some simple game theory. Next, linkage benefits and costs are identified along with the other essential concepts. A design procedure is presented in the third section. Additional aspects are analyzed in the fourth section, followed by an evaluation of the NATO linkage. In the sixth section, the internal structure of NATO is analyzed. Concluding remarks are contained in the last section.

ON EFFICIENCY GAINS

Because of the publicness of shared defense among NATO allies, there is a well-known tendency for allies to undercontribute to defense, thus leading to suboptimal provision (see Chapter 2; Olson and Zeckhauser, 1966; Sandler and Hartley, 1995, chapter 2). When this problem is sufficiently severe, a tighter link among the allies that makes them decide defense spending in closer consultation can achieve resource allocative gains in efficiency. These efficiency gains result if defense resource allocations better reflect the additional (marginal) benefits that defense outlays provide to the ally making the expenditure *as well as to the other allies.* An ally will decide its defense spending so as to equate its anticipated marginal benefits to its marginal costs; however, the public nature of defense spending means that the *sum* of the additional benefits conferred on all allies from an ally's defense spending must also be included on the benefit side. Unless this calculation is made, defense spending is inefficient in the sense that resources could be reallocated to defense spending so as to make at least one ally better off without making any ally worse off.

The standard wisdom, expressed above, simplifies matters considerably when it comes to ascertaining potential efficiency gains from increased cooperation among allies. In particular, the influence of joint products, for which defense activities yield a host of outputs that vary in their degree of publicness, must be taken into account. As explained in Chapter 2, some of these outputs are purely public (e.g., deterrence), others are impurely public, and still others are ally-specific private benefits. Efficiency gains from cooperation or tighter linkages among allies are expected to stem only from the purely public outputs, since markets can allocate private benefits efficiently, and a club arrangement can charge for impure excludable defense outputs (Sandler, 1977; Sandler and Forbes, 1980). The potential for efficiency gains can be related to the ratio of excludable defense benefits to total defense benefits (excludable and nonexcludable) associated with the allies' defense spending. As this ratio approaches 1, so that defense benefits are primarily excludable, there is little suboptimality and, hence, little potential gain from increased cooperation. In contrast, as this ratio nears 0, so that defense benefits are mostly nonexcludable, significant gains in allocative efficiency may result from closer collaboration on defense-spending decisions. Defense technology, strategic doctrine, and alliance composition have a major role to play in determining this ratio. Changes in these contributing factors can thus impact on potential efficiency gains, associated with the manner in which allies reach defense-spending decisions. An alliance is a living entity whose form must be adjusted as warranted in response to internal and external costs.

In order to conceptualize these efficiency gains from cooperation, we shall use some simple game theory notions, introduced previously in Chapter 6, to distinguish between purely public defense outputs and jointly produced defense outputs. In Figure 8.1, three alternative 2×2 game matrices are displayed, complete with alternative strategies, players, and payoffs. To keep matters uncomplicated, we assume a two-country alliance in which ally A and ally B must *independently* decide whether or not to contribute a

A's strategies \ B's strategies	Contributes	Does not contribute
Contributes	*a* 2 , 2	*b* –2 , 4
Does not contribute	*c* 4 , –2	*d* * 0 , 0

a. No joint products, Prisoners' Dilemma

A's strategies \ B's strategies	Contributes	Does not contribute
Contributes	*a* 3 , 3	*b* –1 , 4
Does not contribute	*c* 4 , –1	*d* * 0 , 0

b. Joint products, Prisoners' Dilemma

A's strategies \ B's strategies	Contributes	Does not contribute
Contributes	*a* ** 9 , 4	*b* * 1 , 4
Does not contribute	*c* 4 , 0	*d* 0 , 0

c. Joint products: Asymmetric

Figure 8.1. Game matrices for joint products

unit of a defense activity to the alliance. Additional allies and more complex defense decisions can be easily accommodated within this framework, but are not pursued here since the essential conclusions are the same (see, e.g., Sandler, 1992; Sandler and Hartley, 1995, chapter 2).

In the top matrix of Figure 8.1, a pure public good scenario for defense contributions is presented, which results in a Prisoners' Dilemma. Ally *A*'s two strategies – contribute or do not contribute a unit of defense – are depicted in the rows, while ally *B*'s corresponding strategies are indicated in the columns. In each of the four cells, the first number is the payoff of ally *A* from a particular strategy combination, whereas the second number is the payoff of ally *B* from the same strategy combination. If both allies contribute, each obtains a net payoff of 2. These payoffs and the others listed are based on each unit of defense providing 4 in benefits to each ally at a cost of 6 to the contributing ally. The pure publicness relates to both allies receiving 4 in benefits from a unit provided regardless of whether or not they contributed the unit, so that benefits are nonrival and nonexcludable. Net payoffs are calculated as follows: for cell *a,* each ally receives a net benefit of 2 after its costs of 6 are deducted from its total benefits of 8, which equals the number of units contributed (i.e., 2) times per-unit benefits of 4. If ally *A* contributes and ally *B* free rides (see cell *b*), then the contributor earns a net payoff of –2 after per-unit costs of 6 are subtracted from per-unit benefits of 4. Ally *B* receives the free-rider benefits of 4, since it does not have to pay for defense. In cell *c,* the roles, and consequently the payoffs, are reversed. Each ally receives 0 when neither provides the defense activity, since no costs are incurred and no benefits result (see cell *d*).

The likely outcome of this strategic situation is cell *d,* denoted with an asterisk. Consider ally *A*'s two strategic choices. The payoffs from not contributing are both greater than the corresponding payoffs from contributing: $4 > 2$ and $0 > -2$. This means that ally *A* receives a higher payoff by not contributing to defense regardless of the independent strategic choice of its counterpart. From ally *B*'s viewpoint, the same situation arises because its payoffs from not providing the defense activity exceed the corresponding payoffs from providing it. As each ally chooses its dominant strategy[4] of not contributing, the outcome is the low-level equilibrium at cell *d.* In game theory terminology, this cell is a *Nash equilibrium* because neither ally would unilaterally want to change its strategy, given that the other ally does not contribute. For example, ally *A*'s payoff would drop from 0 to –2 if it alone decided to contribute toward the defense activity once at cell *d.* The payoff pattern in the top matrix is known as a Prisoners' Dilemma,[5] in which each player ends up not cooperating even though mutual cooperation would improve the well-being of both participants as compared with the noncooperative Nash equilibrium. In the top matrix, the payoffs of 2 from mutual cooperation in cell *a* are greater than the 0 payoffs at the noncooperative equilibrium. For a pure public defense good, *efficiency gains* refer to the additional benefits achieved from moving from the independent-action outcome at cell *d* to the cooperative outcome at cell *a.* The greater is this difference in payoffs, the greater are the efficiency gains from cooperating. In the case where each ally determines its own defense contribution, an analogous

4. A dominant strategy yields greater payoffs regardless of the strategic choice of the other player(s).
5. On Prisoners' Dilemma, consult Binmore (1992) or Sandler (1997, chapter 2).

situation arises. That is, the net gains from independent decisions are less than what could be achieved if a cooperative decision were reached accounting for the benefits conferred on all allies (Sandler, 1993).[6]

When defense provision yields joint products, a wider variety of game scenarios can result. Two possibilities and their effects on efficiency gains are now examined. In the middle matrix of Figure 8.1, a unit of the defense activity provides 4 in benefits to each ally and an additional 1 in benefits to just the contributing ally. The 4 represents an alliancewide public benefit, whereas the 1 represents an ally-specific private benefit, so that a joint product situation applies. As before, the defense activity costs 6 to the provider. In cell *a,* the payoffs of 3 follow when the unit costs of 6 are deducted from total benefits of 9 $[(2 \times 4) + 1]$. These benefits correspond to the number of contributors times the per-unit alliancewide benefits of 4, which is then added to the ally-specific benefits of 1. If only one ally contributes as in cells *b* and *c,* then the noncontributor gets a free ride of 4 from the alliancewide benefits, while the contributor receives −1, or the difference between its benefits of 5 (4 + 1) and its costs of 6. The dominant strategy is again to not contribute insofar as $4 > 3$ and $0 > -1$. The resulting matrix is again a Prisoners' Dilemma with a Nash equilibrium at cell *d.*

As compared with the top matrix, there are two noteworthy differences concerning the middle matrix. First, the net gain from reneging on an agreement to contribute (cooperate) is now smaller owing to the private benefits associated with providing the defense activity. In the top matrix, if ally *A* does not contribute while ally *B* contributes, ally *A* gains 2 as compared with its mutual cooperation payoff – i.e., the payoff goes from 2 in cell *a* to 4 in cell *c.* This same gain from reneging is only 1 (4 – 3) in the middle matrix of Figure 8.1. Hence, there is less incentive to free ride for joint products as compared with the cooperative outcome, and this may result in more cooperation even without a tighter link being forged. The ally-specific private benefits motivate action by giving the contributing allies some property rights to the gain from providing defense. The greater are these private benefits, the greater is the motivation. Second, the net efficiency gain from

6. In the one-shot Prisoners' Dilemma game, the Nash equilibrium is clearly suboptimal. But allies often interact repeatedly, so that a more complicated repeated-game analysis may apply, for which allies may use punishment-based tit-for-tat strategies to obtain a cooperative Nash equilibrium (Sandler, 1992). Such repeated games have a plethora of equilibria, some of which still imply noncooperation and the need for a tighter linkage to achieve efficiency gains. When, however, a cooperative outcome results because of threat-based strategies, a looser alliance structure is appropriate. In many ways, an alliance linkage represents an alternative means for achieving efficiency gains without having to threaten one's allies with punishment that could harm everyone.

cooperating, as compared with the noncooperative equilibrium, is greater – mutual payoffs of 3 rather than 2 when payoffs of cell *a* and cell *d* are compared. This also provides an impetus for cooperation even in the absence of a tight link to promote cooperation.

When this analysis is extended to *n* allies, an interesting insight follows. Ally-specific benefits promote collective or cooperative action, which is likely to follow even without a tight linkage. Furthermore, as these ally-specific benefits increase relative to the alliancewide public gains, the resulting gains from cooperation fall. It is as though treaties or linkages can best form when the overall gains from such linkages are relatively small compared with independent responses by the nations, insofar as the proper incentives for nations to act efficiently are already promoting the right kinds of actions (Barrett, 1993, 1994; Murdoch, Sandler, and Sargent, 1997; Sandler, 1997). The troublesome situations are those without these ally-specific gains, and it is these situations where incentives do not motivate nations to behave efficiently unless forced to do so by a tight link. Moreover, these tight linkages are unlikely to form because of the absence of these ally-specific benefits.

A second joint product scenario is illustrated by the bottom matrix of Figure 8.1, where there are asymmetric private benefits for the two allies. In this scenario, a unit of defense gives 4 in alliancewide benefits and an ally-specific benefit of 7 or 2 depending on whether ally *A* or *B*, respectively, does the providing. Per-unit costs are 6, and payoffs are computed as before. For illustration, we shall compute payoffs for cell *a* when both allies contribute. Ally *A* gets 9 when its costs of 6 are subtracted from its gain of 15 [$(2 \times 4) + 7$], equal to the sum of alliancewide benefits and the ally-specific benefit. Ally *A*'s dominant strategy is to contribute. By contrast, ally *B* is indifferent between its strategies, since the two strategies provide the same payoffs. The underlying game is *not* a Prisoners' Dilemma. There are now two Nash equilibria, from which neither ally would gain from unilateral action, at cells *a* and *b*. Of course, cell *a* is the more desirable of the two equilibria, since ally *A* gains and no one loses when there is a movement from cell *b* to cell *a;* hence, the double asterisks indicate that this equilibrium is of "focal" interest. Ally *A* would be wise to take some of its gain from cell *a* and distribute it to ally *B* to motivate it to contribute. This asymmetric scenario, which is applicable to NATO, indicates that independent defense decisions may result in a cooperative outcome even without much explicit linking.

Joint products have one essential impact: they can make independent action achieve near-efficient outcomes, so that efficiency gains from a tighter linkage may be limited. That is, allies may not be too far from optimality when acting with little explicit cooperation. This insight proves instructive when analyzing the appropriate form for linkages among allies in NATO. From the analysis here, we see that the underlying game form and its implications for cooperation depend, in part, on the presence or absence of joint products. If changes in strategy or weapon technology alter the mix of joint products, as shown in Chapter 2, then the underlying game form is affected, thus influencing the appropriate linkages among allies.

LINKAGE BENEFITS AND COSTS

Two questions are crucial when designing any supranational structure. Is the proposed structure justified? If justified, then how should it be configured? One must remember that an inefficient allocation of resources at the transnational level does not necessarily lend support to a nonmarket substitute in the form of a supranational structure that assists nations in providing a public good. Suppose that, in the absence of such a structure, the loss of efficiency is $100 million. Further suppose that, to rectify this misallocation, $110 million must be expended to link nations in order to augment public good contributions. In this scenario, it would make more sense to do nothing and suffer the inefficiency. The key is to identify the transaction benefits and costs, associated with alternative modes of allocations such as a supranational structure.[7] Transaction benefits and costs must be distinguished from production benefits and costs, connected with the production of the public good in the *absence* of a supranational linkage. For example, expenditure on military forces constitutes some of the outlays tied to the production of defense; the expense required to maintain the civil organization of NATO represents a transaction cost, involved with the alliance mode of allocation. If, however, the formation of a supranational structure were to affect production costs in a positive or negative fashion, then this change in costs would constitute a transaction benefit or cost depending on the sign.

In the absence of an alliance, national provision of defense would be the best alternative. Only those transaction benefits and transaction costs that are incurred by the alliance and would not be experienced by independent

7. The following sources contain a discussion of transaction benefits and costs: Arrow (1970), Auster and Silver (1973), and Sandler and Cauley (1977).

Table 8.1. *Primary linkage benefits and costs associated with NATO*

Linkage benefits
• efficiency gains
• economies of scale from larger production levels
• enhanced security from a united stance
• information acquisition
• complementarities
Linkage costs
• decision making (e.g., maintaining NATO's civil structure)
• interdependency costs from loss of autonomy
• enforcement efforts
• monitoring
• infrastructure
• risks

national provision are included.[8] By conceptualizing these transaction benefits and costs in this manner, we can determine the net merits of an alliance and its various structural forms as compared with the best independent alternative. Henceforth, we shall refer to transaction benefits and costs as linkage benefits and costs. There are approximately five categories of linkage benefits and six categories of costs associated with NATO. These are listed in Table 8.1.

A primary linkage benefit is the efficiency gain from a cooperative allocation decision as discussed in the preceding section. If, moreover, an alliance linkage results in larger production runs, which in turn yield economies of scale as per-unit costs are reduced, then cost savings from these larger production runs represent another linkage benefit (see Chapter 5). Yet another linkage benefit could arise if the alliance formation enhances security by creating a united stance. This may be accomplished if, for instance, the formation of an alliance deters aggression because potential enemies may not wish to take on a group of nations. Linkage benefits may also be based on additional information of a strategic nature acquired from pooling intelligence among allies. A final linkage benefit may arise from complementarities derived from the alliance. For example, allies can and do pursue economic, cultural, and political interactions within NATO, which contains a

8. On related models of designing supranational structures, see Cauley, Sandler, and Cornes (1986), Sandler (1997, chapter 5), Sandler, Cauley, and Tschirhart (1983), and Sandler and Cauley (1977).

variety of committees involving a wide range of activities (e.g., arms control, political consultation).

On the linkage cost side, allies must cover decision-making costs as provision, deployment, procurement, financing, strategic, and other common-defense decisions are taken regarding alliance-directed actions. If allies were to meet to decide defense spending levels as a whole for the alliance, then this too would result in decision-making costs. A crucial linkage cost is associated with any loss of national independence or autonomy as an ally agrees to go along with alliance decisions that it may oppose.[9] Many nations take this linkage cost, in particular, very seriously, since national sovereignty is important for a leader and his or her constituency. Enforcement costs may occur when decisions unpopular with some allies are carried out. Linkage expense may also stem from monitoring allies' actions to ascertain whether or not these actions are consistent with alliance mandates and decisions. Another linkage cost involves expenditures to provide a common infrastructure for NATO, including AWACs, pipelines, satellite communication linkages, and airfields. This infrastructure is required to allow the allies to perform more as a single entity than as a group of separate forces. A final linkage cost can arise if additional risks are assumed by allying with nations that suffer from civil strife or else have an enemy not ordinarily hostile to other allies.

Integration within an alliance

A supranational structure, such as an alliance, requires that component governments become fused or linked so as to accomplish common goals. Linkage integration refers to the extent of cooperation among the joined allies. An unintegrated linkage allows for a significant amount of autonomy and flexibility on the part of participants. By contrast, a tightly integrated alliance melds two or more component allied nations so that all defense decisions are made by a decision-making body within the alliance. Allies then sacrifice their autonomy over defense. Although the fifty states of the United States possess autonomy over a wide range of social and economic decisions, they

9. Morrow (1991) indicates that, in an asymmetric alliance containing members of unequal capabilities, the smaller allies may willingly suffer a loss of autonomy in order to be defended by a large partner. In this scenario, the large ally may experience a linkage benefit from enhanced autonomy, as it directs the small allies without being directed by them. That is, the small allies trade off autonomy for security, while the large ally trades off security for autonomy. Our representation is sufficiently general to include more trade-offs than just the one between security and autonomy.

are fully integrated on defense issues as the federal government decides all national defense decisions. A different situation characterizes NATO, since allies still maintain autonomy over the bulk of defense spending (Sandler and Forbes, 1980).

The degree of integration is itself dependent on structural parameters, which are adjustable by the policy makers. Although we shall later focus primarily on only one parameter of integration, potential parameters include the frequency of policy makers' meetings, the extent of common funding, the required majority of the decision rule, the bindingness of the decision, and the scale of communications among the allies' policy makers. If, for example, the policy makers from the allies meet more frequently, then integration is enhanced. As the percent of NATO defense spending that is commonly funded increases, the alliance becomes more integrated insofar as allies lose autonomy over their own defense-spending decisions. When, in addition, the decisions reached by the alliance are binding on all of its members, the structure is integrated. The decision rule adopted by the allies can vary from unanimity to dictatorship by a dominant ally (see Chapter 3). As the decision rule approaches unanimity, the linkage becomes less integrated, since each ally's policy maker remains autonomous, possessing the power of veto. In a dictatorship, however, one ally's policy maker subjugates all others, thereby removing the other allies' autonomy. The last parameter of linkage – the scale of intralinkage communication – is measured by the number of signals generated among policy makers with respect to linkage form, maintenance, and decisions. The relationship between this measure and integration is a direct one: as this communication flow increases, the integration becomes greater.

In practice, the choice of each of these parameters and others not mentioned determines the extent of integration, and consequently the form of the alliance institutional linkage. We shall focus on adjusting the percent of common funding as our solely manipulable parameter of integration. This simplifies discussion considerably, because integration can then be equated with this percentage choice. Moreover, this percentage is readily measured by taking the sum of NATO's common funding on its civil, military, and infrastructure budgets and placing this sum over all allies' defense spending. For the period 1968–78, this percent for NATO was about one percent, thus indicating a loosely integrated structure (Sandler and Forbes, 1980). These figures, although unclassified, are buried in classified documents, thus more current figures are often unavailable. In 1997, the common funding amount was approximately $1.88 billion, which is about 0.4 percent of total defense spending in NATO.[10] This common funding percentage will grow with NATO expansion, but is still expected to remain at less than one percent of NATO total defense spending.

Linkage benefits, linkage costs, and integration

As the degree of integration of an alliance is adjusted, each of the linkage benefits and costs will be affected. Increased integration can raise linkage benefits from efficiency gains, scale economies, enhanced security, information acquisition, and complementaries owing to increased cooperation and the power of the alliance to foster resource allocative efficiency. A tighter alliance will also present a more united set of allies to would-be aggressors, and thus should increase security through deterrence. If allies cooperate to a greater extent, then weapon standardization and interoperability should be fostered as common funding underwrites more weapon procurement. As a result, alliance efficiency, in terms of additional security acquired for a given amount of expenditure, will be promoted. These benefits are, however, subject to diminishing returns; that is, the rate of increase is assumed to decline with increased integration.[11]

On the cost side, tightening most parameters of integration – in particular, the common-funding percentage – will result in larger decision-making costs, interdependency costs, enforcement costs, infrastructure expense, monitoring costs, and risks. These costs are likely to rise at an increasing rate as decisions must be made in consultation with other allies. Thus, there are trade-offs when enhanced cooperation is pursued in an alliance, since both linkage benefits and linkage costs are anticipated to rise. We conceptualize these trade-offs to involve more than just a trade-off between loss of autonomy and enhanced security, in contrast to an earlier treatment by Morrow (1991). In short, there are a host of associated benefits and costs that must be traded off when forming and designing an alliance such as NATO. These design considerations are now presented.

10. The expenditure figure for common funding is inferred from the US share of $470 million given by US GAO (1997c, p. 1). The US contribution represents about 25 percent of NATO's total common funding budget; multiplying the US contributions to this budget by four gives the $1.88 billion reported in the text. In 1997, total NATO defense spending was $465.569 billion, so that the common funding budget amounted to about 0.4 percent of NATO military expenditures.

11. The assumption of diminishing returns is standard to ensure that equating marginal benefits and marginal costs results in a maximum outcome. This assumption means that, for a given linkage (e.g., a linkage on weapon standardization), initial augmentations to tightness from zero values provide greater added benefits than those for subsequent augmentations.

A DESIGN PROCEDURE

Linkage formation

We begin by studying sufficient requirements for an alliance to form. These same conditions would apply if a new linkage – say, for weapon standardization – is being considered for an existing alliance (see, e.g., Hartley, 1991, chapter 7). At least two requirements must be satisfied if an alliance (or a new linkage) is to be instituted. The first requirement is that there must be some linkage form for which net linkage benefits (i.e., the difference between linkage total benefits and linkage total costs) are positive for the set of potential participants as a whole. In other words, there must be some structural form for the contemplated alliance (or link within an established alliance) whereby the efficiency gains and other linkage benefits outweigh the associated linkage costs. Because incremental benefits are anticipated to level out rapidly with increased integration, while incremental costs may accelerate with greater integration, less complex, "loose" alliances and linkages appear to stand a better chance of initial formation. Consider the choice of common funding as the parameter of integration. The gains from the first one or two percent of common funding is likely to be very large as the infrastructure, civil structure, and military structure of the alliance are funded and developed more fully. Thereafter, the increase in payoffs from further common funding is apt to be smaller as less pressing projects are supported. Since, for example, allies' weapon requirements are likely to vary on strategic and political grounds, large common purchases may sacrifice some allies' defense needs, thus offsetting somewhat the gains in efficiency and scale economies and limiting the overall increase of linkage benefits. Linkage costs may go up precipitously, especially because nations vigorously protect their autonomy; that is, incremental interdependency costs may rise rapidly as integration increases. Had the original twelve NATO allies framed a much tighter structure in 1949, NATO might not exist today. Recent attempts to frame tight agreements with respect to biodiversity and the law of the sea have essentially failed by scaring away key participants such as the United States. The tightest proposed linkage for the European Union concerning monetary union has been a big stumbling block so far, because of its implications for national autonomy over fiscal and monetary policy. The formation of an alliance or a linkage may therefore be enhanced if it is started loose, with the autonomy of the allies preserved, and then tightened over time as warranted. Surely, if contingencies arise that increase the threat to allies, they should be more willing to integrate further, provided that this tightening promises significant gains in the effectiveness of the alliance.

A second, more restrictive requirement for linkage formation is that the net linkage gains from cooperating must be distributed in such a way that each ally receives a net benefit from the proposed alliance or linkage. To meet this second condition, some participants may have to be given side payments or concessions, such as the subsidies planned by the United States and other NATO allies to help finance some of the infrastructure needed by the three recently designated entrants to NATO.[12] If an alliance includes heterogeneous allies in terms of national incomes, strategic positions, and risks, then side payments may have to be tailored among potential participants if all allies are to perceive a net gain. This second requirement implies the first, but not vice versa. If each ally experiences a positive net benefit from a contemplated linkage, then surely the sum of these positive net benefits must result in a net positive linkage benefit for the entire alliance. However, net positive linkage gains for the alliance need not imply that, in the absence of side payments, every ally gains. Thus, the second requirement is sufficient on its own for a linkage to form.

Alliance structure or form

Once an alliance or linkage within an alliance, which meets the above conditions, is identified, its degree of integration can be decided so as to achieve the greatest positive difference between linkage benefits and costs. Given that both linkage benefits and costs depend on the extent of integration, net linkage benefits also depend on the integration level. Essentially, the alliance-structure decision requires choosing from among the viable structures the one with the greatest net linkage benefits. Ideally, each parameter of integration can be adjusted to maximize net linkage benefits, while accounting for interdependencies among the parameters. This would result in the design of an optimal alliance structure. But in practice, a discrete choice among a limited number of alternative structures will probably be made so as to choose the structure with the greatest net linkage benefits. Once the desired structure is settled upon, it can be instituted, while making sure that the resulting benefits are distributed so as to satisfy the sufficiency condition that every ally acquires something. The distribution decision is apt to be con-

12. During the period 1995–97, the United States spent $142.7 million on assisting the Czech Republic, Hungary, and Poland to prepare themselves for membership. Assistance included improved air traffic control systems (US GAO, 1997a).

tentious as allies position themselves to achieve the greatest possible gain. Social choice over distribution issues can lead to cyclical voting behavior in which any issue can win, depending on how issues are paired off in a sequence of votes (Kelly, 1988). In NATO, any ally that does not continue to perceive a net gain can, by Article 13, exit the alliance after providing a year's notice. A less drastic action is to leave a particular linkage within NATO, as France and Spain have done with respect to NATO's integrated military command. By allowing allies the right not to participate in selected linkages, NATO has probably held the alliance together when some allies have found fault with some structural aspects. This practice of allowing allies selectively to leave some internal linkages is another indication of NATO looseness.

As technology, the composition of the allies, the alliance's strategic doctrine, and the allies' tastes alter, the linkage benefits and costs of an alliance are sure to change, and with such change the viability of the alliance and its appropriate form must be periodically reevaluated. The important events of the early 1990s – the breakup of the Soviet Union, the dissolution of the Warsaw Pact, NATO's adoption of a new strategic doctrine, the civil war in Bosnia – clearly influenced the net linkage benefits associated with NATO. Some commentators believed that NATO had outlived its usefulness, which is another way of saying that the first sufficiency condition, which requires a net linkage benefit for the alliance, was no longer fulfilled. By contrast, military downsizing could actually increase net benefits derived from NATO if allies were to tighten their linkages and assume tasks according to their comparative advantage (see Chapters 5 and 7). The addition of allies beginning in 1999 will necessitate reevaluation of NATO's structure and, perhaps, alterations in the extent of integration among allies (see Chapter 3).

In Table 8.2, a summary of the three-stage design procedure is given. We have called the first and second sufficiency conditions alliance rationality and ally rationality, respectively, depending on whose net linkage benefits must be positive. These rationality requirements ensure that the alliance is incentive compatible. For the second stage, the two alternatives correspond to choosing either among a finite set of structures or else over a continuum of structures as the parameters of integration are decided. During the third stage, sufficiency conditions are checked before adjusting integration.

If we could translate the different values of the parameters of integration, associated with a particular alliance structure, into a single index of integration, then competing organizational forms for NATO could be placed along a single spectrum, varying from a completely loose alliance to a completely

Table 8.2. *NATO design procedure*

First stage: Formation stage (sufficiency conditions)
- net linkage benefits must be positive for alliance as a whole (alliance rationality)
- net linkage benefits must be distributed so that each ally perceives a net gain (ally rationality)

Second stage: Integration determination
- from alternative feasible structures that satisfy sufficiency conditions, choose the one with the greatest net linkage benefits

or alternatively
- choose linkage parameters to maximize net linkage benefits subject to linkage feasibility

Third stage: Linkage adjustment and periodic review
- determine whether the structure still meets sufficiency requirements
- for viable structures, change parameters of integration to maximize net linkage benefits

tight one. An alliance that uses a majority rule, has frequent meetings at the heads of state level, requires decisions to be binding on all allies, possesses a large share of common funding, and transmits a large share of information among allies, is at the tight end of the spectrum. This example contrasts to today's NATO, which displays much less integrated parameters. A single index of integration is more difficult to conceptualize when an alliance has some loose and some tight parameters. How does one trade off more frequent meetings for, say, less common funding to identify a single degree of integration? This exercise is best avoided, recognizing that in practice alternative structures with varying net benefits can be compared, so that a "best" structure with the greatest net benefits can be distinguished.

FURTHER ASPECTS

International organizations typically perform multiple functions. Although security is NATO's primary function, it also provides for political consultation, economic cooperation, scientific pursuits, treaty verification, traffic control, drug-trafficking interdiction, and others. Why do these large international organizations assume multiple function? The answer lies in the notion of *linkage economies of scope,* which result in a fall in the average cost per linkage as more activities are subsumed within the same supranational structure.[13] Common costs among linkages can give rise to economies of scope. These common costs can stem, for example, from shared communication networks, meeting facilities, administrative offices, and bureaucratic apparatus.

Once an alliance contains multiple linkages among its allies, interlinkage effects must be identified when determining alliance viability and design. As new linkages are added, these interlinkage effects become germane to the periodic reevaluations. Although interlinkage effects may include additional cost savings from economies of scope, they may also include conflicts of interests that could increase costs. For example, a linkage on standardization of weapons would have to coordinate its activities with a linkage on weapon trade or procurement. Communication across linkages must be maintained. Both cost savings and expenditures must be included when judging the desirability of additional linkages within NATO. In Chapter 7, we have seen that NATO has overlapping functions with the United Nations, the European Union, and the Western European Union (also see Carlier, 1995; Leech, 1991; NATO Office of Information and Press, 1995). For example, the Western European Union (WEU) was resurrected in 1984 to promote cooperation among some EU members on security matters. This organization helped direct European efforts during the Desert Shield and Desert Storm operations, and may take a more active role in furthering armament procurement among EU members. The existence of overlapping functions will surely raise linkage costs for NATO, while limiting linkage benefits; consequently, NATO's viability and structural form may be affected.

Some linkage overlap, as in the case of peacekeeping, where NATO interests are more regional than those of the United Nations, may be worth maintaining to allow for alternative jurisdictional decision-making bodies that can better match the interests of those affected by an action (see Chapters 4 and 6). Other linkage overlaps may merely duplicate a linkage in another supranational structure, thus leading to costs without any discernible linkage benefits. Economic principles suggest that these duplicate linkages in parallel supranational structures are best avoided or eliminated. In recent years, there has been a rapid expansion in both the number of these structures and their functions. As a result, overlap is becoming a growing concern.

13. On economies of scope, see Baumol, Panzar, and Willig (1988).

AN EVALUATION OF THE NATO LINKAGE

As mentioned at the outset of this chapter, NATO consists of a loose or unintegrated structure in which sovereign nations maintain both policy independence and discretionary power over the bulk of their military spending. Any action of the primary decision-making body – the NAC – must be unanimous. Furthermore, common-funding percentages have been less than one percent, and even Article 5 leaves unspecified the appropriate action in the event that an ally is attacked.

To analyze whether this looseness is appropriate, we first consider the recent era of flexible response. Efficiency gains from increased integration are apt to be limited because of the large proportion of excludable benefits, including ally-specific private benefits, from the defense activity. In Chapter 2, we saw that during this era, there has been a reasonable matching of benefit shares with cost shares. Moreover, scale economies in weapon production are, essentially, being exploited through markets where large-scale producers sell weapons to allies and nonallies. There are still linkage benefits to be obtained from enhanced security from cooperation, information acquisition, and complementarities, but these may be achieved without much integration. Linkage costs from loss of autonomy, decision making, monitoring, and enforcement are likely to be large. Since allies place such a high value on their autonomy, increased integration is likely to raise interdependency costs greatly. Given the unanimous decision rule of the NAC, agreement is a time-consuming process that keeps decision-making costs high. Any significant augmentation in integration during this era may, consequently, lead to costs outweighing benefits rather quickly, thus justifying NATO's unintegrated structure. To support a more integrated alliance, there must be large efficiency gains, but these gains are modest when *excludable* jointly produced defense outputs prevail, as they have during much of the post-1970 period.

During the MAD era, however, efficiency gains from integration could have been relatively large owing to the publicness of the nuclear deterrent, on which NATO's strategic doctrine then rested. Hence, a "tighter" alliance during this latter period could have been desirable but for the pivotal position of the United States, whose deterrent forces underwrote the alliance's security. Increased integration would have reduced US autonomy in return for a greater collective financing of the defense burden that it carried. US unwillingness at that time to press for a more integrated alliance suggests that US gains in efficiency and other linkage benefits were not sufficient to outweigh the associated costs. Each ally must perceive a net linkage benefit from a change in the alliance structure if the change is to be instituted. While smaller allies may be either cajoled to go along with a disagreeable adjustment or else be bought off with a side payment, the US position in NATO was so dominant during the MAD period that any US side payment would have been prohibitively expensive.

Recent events portend that NATO may become somewhat more integrated in the future. The pronounced downsizing of military forces in the 1990s among the nuclear allies and many of the smaller allies means that the pooling of forces can offset defense cutbacks by utilizing individual allies' particular military strengths – the US strength in the air, for example, or the UK advantage in antisubmarine forces. The proposed development of CJTFs for rapid deployment will mean that integrated *multilateral* forces will be part of the alliance. Weapon standardization, common logistical procedures, and interoperable forces will be promoted as these CJTFs are drawn from the individual allies and as NATO admits new allies. Desert Storm underscored the necessity of interoperable forces if NATO is to be effective in carrying out its new missions of peacekeeping and peace enforcement.

NATO's new missions to limit nuclear proliferation and to address crises that affect its interests produce a large portion of nonexcludable benefits in terms of promoting alliancewide and worldwide stability (see Chapter 4). Thus there is a greater tendency for free riding, particularly among the smaller allies. This implies that efficiency gains from a more integrated alliance may be larger than during the first two decades of the flexible response era. Moreover, scale economies in weapon production are not always being exploited (e.g., the B-2 Stealth Bomber) because of downsizing and the ever-increasing R & D and development costs required by today's high-technology weapons. Since state-of-the-art weapons are typically not sold to nonallies, NATO allies must become one anothers' customers if higher production runs are to bring down unit costs, as discussed in Chapter 5. This in turn requires tighter links in weapons procurement. These greater efficiency gains and economies of scale can justify tighter linkages among NATO allies. Even the imminent increase in NATO's membership can result in a tighter structure. Common funding will surely increase as NATO's civil and military structures are expanded to accommodate the entrants, and infrastructure for these new allies will also raise the common-funding percentage. In addition, downsizing will cause this percentage to increase as the size of the denominator decreases. As the alliance expands, a movement away from unanimity may eventually take place if the alliance missions

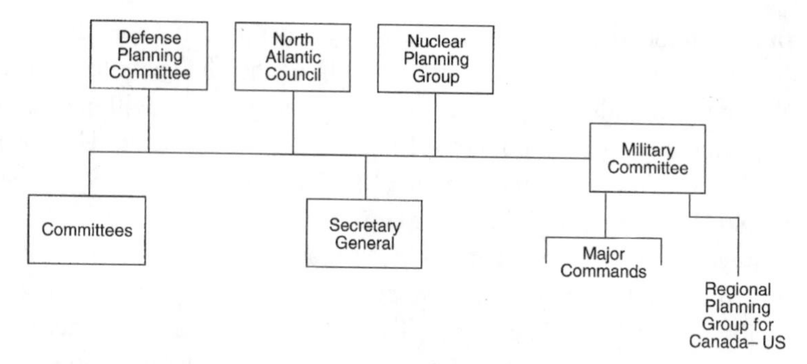

Figure 8.2. NATO's civil and military structure

are to be fulfilled (see Chapter 3). Without a more integrated decision rule, NATO may be endlessly deadlocked owing to the expanding diversity of viewpoints and interests. If this prediction is correct, then a reduced consensus for decision making (e.g., majority rule, weighted majority based on contributions) is consistent with a tighter alliance. Policy-making meetings may also have to be increased in number, which further tightens the alliance, as the first wave of new allies are integrated into NATO.

NATO'S INTERNAL STRUCTURE

Thus far, we have primarily investigated how NATO allies are tied together by the alliance. In particular, our integration measures serve to indicate how much sovereignty NATO allies possess over their defense spending under past and current arrangements. For completeness, we shall now briefly review NATO's internal structure, which coordinates its day-to-day operations and which integrates allies' military forces and assets during an operation. NATO bureaucratic structure is made up of two parts: (1) a *civil structure,* which facilitates cooperation among allies on alliance matters, defense planning, and other areas of concern; and (2) a *military structure,* which provides an organizational framework for defending allies against threats to their territory or interests. Figure 8.2 depicts NATO's civil and military structures in terms of their most basic elements. The civil structure consists of five primary components.

- The secretary general chairs the NAC, the Nuclear Planning Group, and the Defense Planning Committee, and directs decision making and consultation within NATO. The secretary general also serves as the spokesperson of the alliance.
- The North Atlantic Council is the policy-making body of NATO.

Table 8.3. *Areas of responsibility of primary NATO committees*

• Political affairs	• Operations and exercises
• Atlantic policy	• Weapon standardization
• Partnership for Peace steering	• Communications and information
• Weapon proliferation	• Air defense
• Arms control	• European airspace coordination
• Verification coordination	• Science
• Economic affairs	• Civil defense planning
• NATO infrastructure	• NATO security
• Budget (civil and military)	• NATO pipelines
• Defense review	• Environmental concerns
• Information and cultural relations	

Source: NATO Office of Information and Press (1995, pp. 95–7).

- The Defense Planning Committee (DPC) handles most issues regarding collective defense planning.
- The Nuclear Planning Group (NPG) addresses policy and security matters regarding the deployment and possible use of nuclear forces to foster NATO security.
- The numerous committees and working groups address budgetary, economic, political, logistical, environmental, and other concerns and missions of NATO. Some representative committees are displayed in Table 8.3.

Each NATO ally has a permanent representative on the NAC. These representatives hold ambassadorial rank and are supported by a political and military staff or delegation to NATO. Once a week, the permanent representatives of the NAC meet. At the ministerial level, the NAC normally meets twice a year, at which time either the foreign ministers or the heads of state from the allies are in attendance. Decisions of the NAC must be unanimous (NATO Office of Information and Press, 1995, p. 93), thus implying a loose linkage. A similar arrangement holds for the DPC, in which meetings typically involve the permanent representatives of all allies except France. Usually twice a year, the allies' defense ministers attend the DPC meeting. Coinciding with these ministerial level meetings of the DPC, the defense ministers usually conduct a meeting of the NPG. As in the case of the DPC, France does not participate on the NPG. Iceland attends the meeting as an observer. A unanimous decision rule or common accord applies within both the DPC and the NPG. The international staff, drawn from the member nations, work on the NAC and the various committees.[14]

14. A more complete description of NATO's civil and military structure is contained in NATO Office of Information and Press (1995).

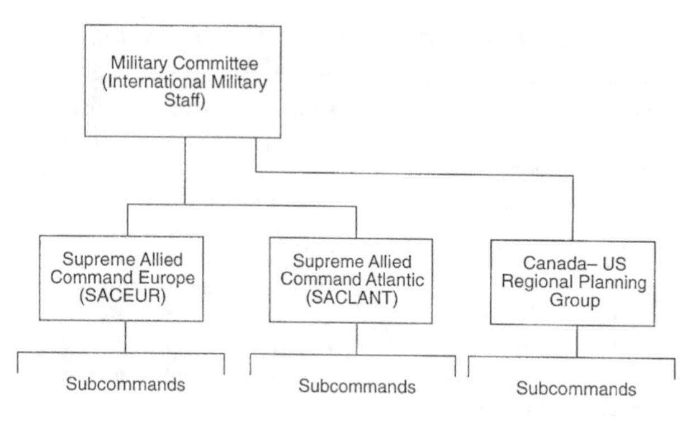

Figure 8.3. NATO's military structure

As the highest authority in NATO's military structure, the Military Committee makes recommendations to the NAC, DPC, and NPG on matters concerning the common defense of NATO allies.[15] The chiefs of staff of the allies and an international military staff constitute the Military Committee, which meets twice a year at the chief of staff level. Except for France, all NATO allies' chiefs of staff are represented on the Military Committee. This committee advises and is politically subordinate to the NAC, DPC, and NPG, depending on the nature of the issue under review. As for other NATO substructures, a unanimous decision rule is used, but the more powerful allies surely exercise a greater ability to influence defense doctrine and decisions. In Figure 8.3, NATO's integrated military structure is displayed.[16] Below the Military Committee are the two major commands – Supreme Allied Command Europe (SACEUR) and Supreme Allied Command Atlantic (SACLANT) – and the Canada-US Regional Planning Group. Each of these three components have a number of subcommands that address either a particular geographical subregion (e.g., Allied Forces North West Europe), or else a particular military function (e.g., crisis management). Subordinate to these subcommands (not shown in Figure 8.3) are still lower subordinate commands involving land, air, and naval forces. These commands, which are under the political control of the NAC, constitute the Integrated Military Structure (IMS), which provides the organizational structure for conducting military operations during times of crisis. The IMS also coordinates military exercises and collaborations when threats are not present. France

15. The NAC directs the Military Committee and, as such, is the true highest level of the combined military and civil structure of NATO.
16. On NATO's military structure, see Jordan (1995), NATO Office of Information and Press (1995), and Thomson (1997).

does not participate in the IMS. Major allies such as the United States and the United Kingdom exercise significant influence by holding key command positions, an indication of greater tightness for the military structure as compared to the civil structure. Surely, this increased tightness and the associated loss of autonomy for many allies are justifiable based on the need for decisive action during crises.

The new institutional economics can, in principle, be applied to determine the appropriate design of NATO's civil and military structures. For example, consider whether or not a linkage for NATO's civil structure should be added – say, in the form of a committee to address a new problem. The introduction of a committee will provide linkage benefits in terms of efficiency gains, information acquisition, and complementaries with other linkages. In addition, there will be linkage costs from decision making, monitoring, information gathering, and enforcement. The set of relevant linkage benefits and costs would depend on the particular linkage considered and would vary among linkages. For example, a linkage on scientific pursuits is unlikely to involve interdependency costs or security risks. If a proposed linkage provides positive net linkage benefits to the alliance as a whole, and if, moreover, each ally stands to gain, then the linkage is viable. Viable linkages can then be formally tailored so as to maximize these net linkage benefits. Any instituted link should be periodically reviewed, and eliminated when it is no longer able to pass the viability tests. Take the case of the Allied Command Channel (ACCHAN), which was disbanded on 1 June 1994. Prior to that date, ACCHAN was one of three military commands. With the end of the Cold War and the subsequent downsizing, having two commands in Europe could no longer be justified, and SACEUR has now assumed ACCHAN's responsibilities. Changes such as this can be inhibited by vested interests.

The various committees in Table 8.3 are associated with diverse configurations of linkage benefits and linkage costs. Consider the Committee on Weapon Standardization, which can provide significant linkage benefits by limiting R & D duplication, promoting scale economies, and furthering gains from trade (see Chapter 5; Callaghan, 1975; Hartley, 1991, chapter 7; Sandler and Hartley, 1995, chapter 9). Given these potentially large gains from integrating, a tighter link may be warranted than for, say, the Information and Cultural Relation Committee, where potential linkage benefits are more modest at a given level of integration. Thus, we are led to the conclusion that committees within NATO should not all display the same degree of integration.

Designing the internal structure of NATO raises some interesting issues, not encountered in the earlier discussion of the form of the alliance linkage among the allied states. NATO's internal structure is hierarchical, with linkages on the same level and on different levels – this arises with respect to both the civil and the military structures. As a consequence, an important issue involves the number of hierarchical levels compared to the number of linkages on the same level. Steep hierarchical structures have many levels and relatively few linkages on a given level; flat hierarchical structures have few levels and relatively many linkages on a given level. What is the optimal number of levels for NATO's civil and military structures? Without giving a precise answer, we shall briefly indicate some crucial considerations. Since the introduction of an additional level creates both stratum benefits and stratum costs, these must be identified and compared when stratification decisions are made. A new level should be added to NATO provided that net stratum benefits are positive for both the alliance and the individual allies. A new level can create stratum benefits in the form of increased division of labor and greater information flows. On the cost side, an important expense is associated with goal conflicts that arise between the Military Committee and any new set of participants associated with the new level. To ameliorate goal conflicts, expenditures must be made to monitor activities and to alter constraints and incentives so that the overall goals of the alliance are pursued by NATO's participants (Williamson, 1975, chapter 8). Other stratum costs concern the infrastructure needed to support a new level. Additionally, Williamson (1967) has stressed the *cost of control loss* due to serial-reproduction difficulties as messages pass among a greater number of intermediaries. A trade-off between information quantity and quality is required whenever an alliance acquires additional levels.

In a recent contribution, Thomson (1997) has raised the stratification issue regarding the CJTFs. According to Thomson (1997, p. 87), the proposed CJTFs are slated to be beneath the regional subcommands of SACEUR and SACLANT. As such, the CJTFs will be an intervening new level of NATO's military hierarchy. With NATO's new strategic doctrine relying on CJTFs to conduct peacekeeping and humanitarian missions, these CJTFs may someday assume paramount importance. Thus, Thomson (1997, pp. 95–6) makes a convincing case for creating a new command within NATO for the CJTFs, on par with SACEUR and SACLANT, so that this new command can be closer in the hierarchy to the Military Committee, the NAC, and the DPC than now proposed. Such an alternative arrangement would reduce control loss, a vital consideration in any military hierarchy. Under Thomson's proposal, two subcommands of the CJTF command would focus on peacekeeping and humanitarian missions. This example shows that changes in a strategic doctrine can have implications for NATO's internal organization. To date, there have been relatively few changes in NATO strategic doctrines – the institution of MAD, the switch to the doctrine of flexible response. Previous alterations have led to the creation of new committees (linkages) and changes in the way that some civil and military linkages were configured.

In a multilevel organization like NATO, the design of the linkages becomes complex, because interlevel and interlinkage costs and benefits must be included when determining viability, the extent of integration, and periodic reevaluations. To adjust for interlevel effects, the stratification step must precede the structural design of the linkages within the alliance. The presence of many levels means that coalitions between lower-level participants may form; such coalitions may gain from hiding information from their superiors. If this is a problem, then incentive-compatible reward systems may have to be instituted that attenuate this motivation. Once stratification is decided, each linkage adjustment and design must then account for the associated marginal net linkage benefits summed over the linkages on any given level *and* then over the number of levels (Sandler, 1980).

Since 1994 and the official launch of the Partnership for Peace (PFP), a number of additional committees or linkages have been added to NATO's civil structure so as to facilitate the cooperation among PFP members.[17] The introduction of Poland, Hungary, and the Czech Republic may necessitate the creation of further committees within NATO. If enough allies are admitted, there will also be a need to consider additional regional subcommands. In short, NATO is expected to increase its complexity at the organizational level, and this augmented complexity may begin to limit NATO's effectiveness (see Chapter 3). The proliferation of committees and other linkages should be periodically reevaluated. In some instances, committees can be combined so as to reduce linkage costs while limiting the complexity of the organization. Complexity not only adds to linkage costs, but it also makes organizational design more arduous owing to interlinkage effects. One must wonder why a military alliance has acquired so many committees and functions, a number of which have nothing to do with the security of the allies. Are economies of scope really strong enough to justify these linkages? Is there a more appropriate international organization to coordinate these activities? These questions must be addressed if NATO is not to tax itself with activities that divert its resources and its focus from the primary

17. These include the Political-Military Steering Committee on Partnership for Peace, the Joint Committee on Proliferation, and a Provisional Policy Coordination Group (NATO Office of Information and Press, 1995, pp. 99–100).

mission of providing security. As in all organizations, there are vested interests among staff and managers in increasing the size of the organization, which must be resisted. Public choice analysis reminds us that the interests of the staff of any nonmarket structure, such as NATO, need not coincide with those of the nations they represent.

CONCLUDING REMARKS

This chapter has used the methods of the new institutional economics to examine the design of NATO. A design procedure was presented for linking nations in an alliance. Next, the design of the internal structure of NATO was addressed. NATO is only viable if it provides positive net linkage benefits to the alliance as a whole. Furthermore, these net linkage benefits must be distributed so that every ally perceives a net gain from its membership. The distribution and size of these net linkage benefits depend on weapon technology, membership size, strategic doctrine, and the mix of excludable and nonexcludable defense benefits. Efficiency gains – a prime linkage benefit – are related to this mixture because a high proportion of excludable defense benefits would limit these potential gains. On the cost side, interdependency costs from the loss of autonomy are arguably the most important linkage expense. Sovereign nations are loathe to sacrifice autonomy, a sacrifice which is required for a more integrated alliance.

Major events as have occurred in the 1990s may require the restructuring of linkages, both among the members *and* within NATO's civil and military structures. As NATO has rationalized its continued existence, the alliance has expanded its missions, starting in 1994. This may eventually present a problem, since the complexity of NATO has grown as a consequence. More involved structures are harder to design and maintain. The expansion of NATO to include new allies will increase this complexity and may inhibit the decision-making ability of the NAC and other bodies, given their unanimous decision rule.

The new institutional economics, with its emphasis on transaction costs and benefits, has provided a conceptual framework for understanding design issues for the NATO alliance. This framework is better for judging among alternative structures than for truly designing an "optimal structure." Nevertheless, the new institutional economics can help us understand why NATO has remained a "loose," unintegrated structure. Moreover, it suggests that recent events may lead to a tightening of the alliance.

9 Conclusions and future scenarios

NATO has weathered momentous changes during the last decade and will confront yet further significant events over the next decade. NATO is at a crossroads: it must adjust to an evolving Europe, prepare for its imminent expansion in 1999, procure the next generation of weapons, refigure its forces to promote mobility, and foster increased allied cooperation to offset defense downsizing. For nearly fifty years, NATO has distinguished itself as an enduring institution that has accepted new members and that has altered it military doctrine in response to changing threats. Despite crises within NATO – for example, the Cyprus invasion, the withdrawal of France and Spain from NATO's integrated military command, socialist governments coming to power in some member states – the alliance has survived the Cold War by outlasting the ex–Warsaw Pact in an arms race of attrition that left the Soviet Union's economy in tatters. Although the outcome of the Cold War has been victory for NATO, its allies have still paid for their protracted arms race in terms of opportunity costs. This arms competition has, for example, given Japan a decided advantage in the past, leading to its success in building a vibrant economy that dominates the world markets in numerous commodities. NATO is a noteworthy institution because of its resilience and flexibility. It has been able to respond to changes in weapon technology, strategic doctrine, membership composition, and perceived threat, because it is a "loose" institution that promotes allies' autonomy, while allowing for the pursuit of common interests. In many ways, NATO has survived and prospered because its members could dissent when the need arose.

The situations in Central and Eastern Europe as well as in the Commonwealth of Independent States (CIS) are sufficiently fluid and unpredictable that NATO's future role is itself subject to much speculation. Will NATO become an international organization that coordinates a host of collective actions or will it again become a counter to a significant eastern threat as during the days of the Cold War? Over time, NATO's relative efforts on defense and nondefense activities (e.g., assisting the transitional economies, verifying arms-control treaties, and coordinating a collective response for an emerging organized crime threat) can alter dramatically depending on external threats within and beyond Europe. These changes will affect the shape and functions of NATO in the years to come.

Although much has been resolved since the end to the Cold War, there is still much to be decided during the coming decade. For example, remaining issues include the nature of future disarmament agreements, the final composition of NATO, the extent of intra-allied arms trade, the ultimate form of the CJTFs, the size of NATO's power-projection capacity, and the structural changes in NATO's civil and military structure. The eventual interface between the Western European Union (WEU) and NATO must be resolved. Will the WEU's development of a common European defense organization, if successful, lead to the eventual withdrawal of the European Union from NATO? This concern has become relevant from the time of the resurrection of the WEU in 1984. A related issue confronting NATO involves its resolution of overlapping functions with other international organizations containing subsets of NATO allies (see Chapter 7). A resolution is needed if scarce resources are to be conserved and if, moreover, competing organizations are to avoid applying inconsistent policies to the same issues. Still another concern relates to how NATO will address nonconventional threats from terrorism, organized crime, and guerrilla warfare throughout Europe, both east and west. The so-called Russian mafia can acquire sufficient resources from its illicit activities at home to branch out westward into neighboring states, including the designated NATO entrants and the NATO allies. To date, NATO has done little to coordinate a collective response to these problems, as is clearly evident in the absence of a single NATO committee promoting such a response. While international terrorism shows no sign of escalating in terms of the number of events, the severity of attacks can increase if biological weapons or nuclear weapons – including the "suitcase bombs" of the former Soviet Union – get into the hands of terrorists or their clandestine state sponsors. Media reports indicate that some of the inventory of nuclear weapons of the former Soviet Union are missing.

This chapter serves three main purposes. First, we review the key conclusions presented in the eight preceding chapters. Second, we speculate on future scenarios for NATO in both the near term and the long run; this latter exercise is, understandably, very speculative. Third, we provide an agenda for future research.

PRIMARY CONCLUSIONS

Conclusions have been collected toward the end of each chapter. Here, we take stock of these conclusions and highlight only the key ones; hence, the interested reader should consult the specific chapters for other conclusions and the analyses from which they follow.

Chapter 1

Insofar as the first chapter was primarily intended to set the stage for the rest of the book, just two main conclusions were presented. One indicated that NATO must redefine itself and demonstrate that it still has a strategic role to perform if it is to survive during the post–Cold War era. That is, NATO must continue to provide greater defense benefits to its members, net of membership costs, than these allies could achieve on their own. An effective alliance sufficiently shifts outward the production possibility frontier for defense versus all other goods by more optimally providing for defense coordination among the allies. In consequence, allies must trade off autonomy for added security (Morrow, 1991). Cooperation must be present to augment the welfare of the allies, so that a sufficient membership surplus is gained to cover the associated costs of being an ally. Another conclusion indicated that NATO security must take on a broader definition in the post–Cold War period to include the protection of the environment, resource supply lines, and informational assets (McGuire, 1995).

Chapter 2

This chapter dealt with the most studied economic issue of alliances to date – burden-sharing behavior. NATO allies were best characterized as sharing a purely public good when under the doctrine of mutual assured destruction (MAD) up through the latter 1960s. Thereafter, these allies began to share defense activities that included alliancewide deterrence, protection, and more localized gains, whose derived benefits varied in their degree of publicness.

As a consequence, defense burden sharing was more disproportionate during the era of MAD than was true during the subsequent era of flexible response, during which there has been a better match between allies' benefits and burdens, thus limiting the need for greater coordination among allies. The mix between ally-specific benefits and alliancewide public benefits was shown to depend on weapon technology, the reigning strategic doctrine, membership composition, and other factors. As these considerations changed over time, the degree of publicness of shared defense altered, and this alteration then had important implications for burden sharing, allocative efficiency, alliance organization, NATO membership, and allies' income distribution. In terms of these factors, NATO has changed significantly at various times during its history.

Although burden-sharing measures often provide a consistent view of burden-sharing behavior over NATO's history, some measures may give a different picture of an individual ally's behavior. As such, different burden-sharing concepts may suggest alternative policy prescriptions to correct for alleged inequities. Before instituting any policy, one must be sure that the prescription is not unique to a single burden-sharing measure, but is consistent with a host of alternative measures. Most studies have relied on the share of GDP devoted to defense as the preferred measure, if only one measure is used. The joint product model remains applicable during the post–Cold War period, during which there has been no significant evidence, thus far, that defense burden sharing is disproportionately carried by the larger allies. In fact, the burden gap has essentially closed over the last twelve years. NATO's new strategic doctrine of crisis management and nonproliferation, adopted in 1994, may eventually reverse this trend by providing for greater opportunities for free riding.

Chapter 3

Actions of the United States and its NATO allies during the 1990s have made the proposed enlargement of NATO, slated for 1999, a virtual certainty, barring some unforeseen events. Benefits and costs associated with NATO expansion must include only those that would not be incurred in the absence of expansion. Thus, for example, a portion of the costs of modernizing the proposed Visegrad entrants is not truly an expansion cost, because these expenditures would have to be made even if NATO did not expand. An entrant should be admitted provided that the resulting net benefits of admission improve the well-being of the entrant and of each of the allies. To date, analyses of NATO expansion have not estimated the resulting membership benefits, focusing instead on the costs under alternative scenarios. In addition, these studies do not clearly distinguish between expansion costs and costs unrelated to expansion (see Asmus, Kugler, and Larrabee, 1996; Bureau of European and Canadian Affairs, 1997; CBO, 1996; NATO, 1995). Given that membership benefit calculations have not been performed, identified costs of expansion can be viewed as representing a minimal level of benefits required to justify admitting a new ally. Thus far, these cost estimates have varied greatly depending on the underlying assumptions regarding threats, power-projection needs, the vintage of upgraded equipment for the entrant, and the size of the reinforcement forces.

The optimal club size for NATO must balance the cost of admitting a new member (e.g., thinning costs, direct expansion costs, increased risks) with the associated benefits. Each prospective ally is expected to be tied to a different configuration of membership benefits and costs. A potential ally with extensive exposed borders or land area creates significant thinning costs and, consequently, would need to bring a large force to the alliance upon joining to offset this thinning. NATO expansion is anticipated to proceed more slowly in the future as many of the remaining applicants present a less favorable combination of costs and benefits as compared to the first three newly designated members. NATO may, consequently, be nearing its optimal size. Membership decisions, based upon the associated pattern of costs and benefits, must account for the entrant's strategic location, its current military assets, and its economic and political stability. NATO structure is apt to require adjustments as further allies are admitted. In particular, NATO's unanimous decision rule may have to be made less stringent if NATO is to be decisive during crises. This change, if eventually instituted, would augment NATO's integration by limiting the autonomy of allies in the minority. If NATO expansion were to result in greater standardization of weapons, increased logistical coordination, and enhanced weapon interoperability, then these other changes would also reinforce a tightening of NATO's institutional structure. By increasing the commonly funded portion of NATO defense spending, NATO expansion would increase yet another parameter of integration. Nevertheless, the common-funding contribution for infrastructure, NATO's civil structure, and its military structure is anticipated to remain a rather modest one percent of NATO's total defense spending. Finally, by increasing the number of conventional weapons, NATO's expansion is apt to have implications for current and future arms-control treaties.

Chapter 4

Although UN-financed peacekeeping missions peaked at $3.5 billion of expenditures in 1994, and have fallen in the last few years, peacekeeping spending will remain many times higher than the level prior to 1988, the start of the big peacekeeping budget increases (Bobrow and Boyer, 1997; Khanna, Sandler, and Shimizu, 1998). In fact, the recent decline in UN-financed peacekeeping missions is not really a reduction in peacekeeping, but rather a substitution of NATO-directed missions (e.g., IFOR, SFOR) for UN-financed operations. When spending on these NATO-directed missions is included with the spending on UN missions, annual peacekeeping spending during the period 1995–98 is still above $3.5 billion. In the past, NATO has been the most important group of nations supporting UN peacekeeping per se. This pivotal support will surely continue into the future. In particular, NATO is poised to assume an even larger share of UN peacekeeping expenditures and operations as NATO pursues its new strategic doctrine of peacekeeping, nonproliferation of WMD, and crisis management. This new doctrine is anticipated to increase the share of purely public benefits in NATO and, by so doing, to eventually result in more disproportionate burden sharing, with the relatively rich NATO nations assuming even greater burdens for maintaining world stability. Nevertheless, relative magnitudes must be kept in perspective. Since peacekeeping is still a relatively small magnitude compared with other defense spending items, burden-sharing patterns are not expected to alter drastically in the near future unless other factors are figured into the calculations. One such influence has to do with the necessary expenditures on power projection and the nations – the United States, France, Germany, the United Kingdom – that are investing billions to acquire this capacity. Unless the United Nations itself invests in these power-projecting ships and airplanes, it will have no choice but to rely on NATO's transport to move its troops and arsenals to contingencies in Africa, Central Europe, Asia, and elsewhere. There is a strategic advantage for the United Nations in being unprepared and letting NATO make the far-sighted preparations, insofar as time is limited when peacekeeping forces are needed. That is, transport capacity cannot materialize overnight. The end result will be that the world's richest nations, and NATO in particular, will assume a disproportionately large share of the burden of peacekeeping and peace-enforcing operations. The share of GDP devoted to the *actual assessed peacekeeping payments* in the United Nations is the most revealing burden-sharing measure concerning UN-financed missions; this was the measure used in Chapter 4.

In the post–Cold War era, there is evidence that the richer NATO allies are, indeed, shouldering for the smaller allies a disproportionately large burden of peacekeeping spending. This disproportionality is tied to the amount of peacekeeping spending; large peacekeeping budgets are typically associated with greater disproportionality. If peacekeeping spending grows, then this disproportionality is expected to worsen. When recent peacekeeping missions, not funded by the United Nations (e.g., Desert Storm, Provide Comfort, Bosnia) are taken into account, the disproportionate burden sharing in the post–Cold War era is even more pronounced, consistent with a greater share of pure public benefits being derived from UN peacekeeping operations. In the future, the United Nations is anticipated to concentrate its peacekeeping efforts in Africa and other places where NATO's direct interests are not as great; while NATO is apt to focus its peacekeeping efforts in Europe, neighboring regions, and the Middle East, where interests are vital to NATO's well-being.

Chapter 5

To achieve the necessary scale economies to lower unit cost, NATO allies may have to sell parts of their production runs to allies and nonallies. As weapon systems become more sophisticated, the share of R & D costs will increase, meaning that large production runs will be required to bring down unit costs during a time when domestic sales are already smaller owing to downsizing. An offset to this need arises from the emerging convergence of some commercial and military production technologies, whereby a military application is associated with a commercial application (Gansler, 1995). The presence of the latter means that R & D fixed costs can be spread over both kinds of applications, thus limiting the need for large production runs for the weapons systems. EU members' support of their own national defense industries has nevertheless resulted in the duplication of costly R & D programs, limited learning economies, modest economies of scope, and relatively small production runs. The rise in R & D and the disarmament of the post–Cold War period have ushered in a period during which NATO allies can no longer afford the luxury of maintaining so large a national defense industrial base. NATO has begun to merge its defense firms into larger-scale operations, resulting in reduced competition.

Efforts by the European Union to create a single market for defense equipment in Europe will lead to less competition in Europe through mergers and buyouts. US defense contractors will eventually compete with their large European counterparts. The associated monopolization of the defense industry, as is being experienced today, will result in higher prices, lack of innovation, skewed income distribution, and other monopoly inefficiencies. A government may become reluctant to punish severely a defense firm caught exploiting its monopoly and asymmetric informational advantages, since the alternative would be to buy weapons abroad or to do without weapons altogether. Inefficiencies abound in the EU defense industries, implying that defense weapons can be considerably more expensive than if purchased from the United States. Within the European Union, an independent domestic defense industrial base is an expensive and inefficient luxury that many European allies can no longer afford.

To obtain the required scale, scope, and learning economies, EU allies must specialize in producing weapons for which they have a comparative advantage. In addition, their markets must be opened to freer trade in weapons within a NATO free trade area (NFTA), which will surely benefit US defense contractors, because they can sell greater quantities of their high-technology equipment in Europe. In the process, European allies will save on procurement costs. Losers from an NFTA will be the EU defense firms that fail to restructure to match the large size of US firms. Mergers within Europe indicate that this matching process is well under way. Other losers will be EU defense firms, which have been previously protected and have virtually no experience with competition. To bolster these firms and to shape their domestic industrial base, governments can use their buying power.

Joint ventures between two or more allies are seen to save on resources, but at the expense of delayed production, compromises regarding weapon specifications, and increased planning and coordination costs. Although these ventures are often desirable, they present limited efficiency gains and are not as efficient as going with a single established producer from the outset. Offsets and licensed agreements present other efficiency concerns that can raise production costs.

Chapter 6

International organizations, such as NATO and the United Nations, should address public good problems whose range of benefits match their political jurisdictions. A large variety of global challenges are creating an increased need for cooperative security arrangements that no longer assume traditional forms (Sandler, 1997). Nations must be as vigilant with respect to their environment borders as they are with respect to their traditional boundaries. Pollution pacts to address a particular problem may have to be tied to security arrangements when dire consequences are suffered at the hands of non-participants.

For some interests, transnational terrorism represents a cost-effective and inexpensive tactic for destabilizing another country. If terrorists were to acquire WMD, then NATO allies would confront even more dangerous potential consequences than in earlier decades. Unfortunately, transnational and domestic terrorism is expected to become an increasing concern for NATO with the democratization of Central and Eastern Europe. There is, consequently, a need for NATO allies to increase their cooperation when confronting the common threats of transnational terrorism. Without this cooperation, efforts to deter terrorism will either be too much or too little, depending in part on whether attacks on foreign citizens and property create significant collateral damage to the host country. When assessing these collateral costs, authorities must be aware that they may take economic forms – losses in tourism and reduced foreign direct investment. Thus far, NATO efforts to coordinate deterrence activities have been modest. Piecemeal policies only to coordinate information concerning terrorists, but not to coordinate deterrence, may worsen a bad situation by stimulating even greater overdeterrence efforts to deflect the threat onto a neighboring country. International treaties on curbing terrorism have been ineffective, because defection may provide sizable short-term gains to the defector when it is called upon to act. Effective means for foreclosing defection as an attractive strategy must be devised; however, many strategic considerations work against nations abiding by treaties when required. An enforcement mechanism is needed, but such a mechanism raises its own collective action conundrum (Heckahorn, 1989). If nations employ technological methods for limiting terrorism, there results mixed success, as terrorists tend to transfer their attacks to relatively less-protected targets. Thus, kidnappings increased once metal detectors secured airports and protected against skyjackings. Authorities can try to direct the terrorists to transfer into less costly activities, or anticipate the likely substitution and protect against it, or limit terrorists' overall resource pools.

Although the threat of rogue states now appears exaggerated, these states have the potential to represent real risks. To limit the arsenals of these rogues, allies must coordinate their trade transactions with these nations on a host of different exchanges. Even the mobility of scientists, technicians, and weapons experts can pose a significant problem. Neutralizing the threat posed by a rogue nation presents a pure public good problem, in which effective action of any single nation may provide a free ride for all others. Perhaps even more disturbing is the realization that once an effective response is made, there is no motivation for further actions. As a consequence, defense burdens for NATO's most powerful allies are apt to increase and become even more disproportionate. Some nations may undo the efforts of others by reaching covert accommodations with a rogue, thereby leading to an outcome even worse than free riding.

Chapter 7

NATO, the European Union, and the United Nations must resolve many of their overlapping functions if scarce resources are to be conserved. The resurrection of the Western European Union creates concerns for the operation of NATO and the European Union. Simple economic principles dictate that these organizations need to pursue functions where they have a comparative advantage; hence, NATO may want to eliminate many of its nondefense committees in light of duplication and the absence of such a comparative advantage. Furthermore, the role of an unintegrated NATO must somehow be resolved with a more integrated European Union. The absence of the United States, Canada, and Turkey in the European Union can present problems as the two organizations pursue different members' interests based on the countries' respective memberships. This rather artificial distinction among allies can create rifts in the alliance, which can worsen as monetary integration and other reforms make some EU nations more seamless. A big push is under way to admit the Czech Republic, Hungary, and Poland to the European Union now that they have been slated for NATO membership. There is also the problem of non-NATO nations – for example, Ireland – which are part of the European Union but not part of NATO.

The inefficiencies in Europe's defense industries are reflected in similar inefficiencies in their provision of armed forces. Each European ally provides independent armed forces with massive duplication of administration (e.g., departments of defense), logistic support, training, and bases. There is a failure to exploit the economies of scale and scope which would be available to European-level armed forces (i.e., a single EU army, navy, and air force comparable in scale to US forces). The inefficiencies are increased by the general failure to use standardized equipment, so that nations have to operate either from their national bases or from national support units deployed overseas. Collaborative programs support standardization, with two or more nations operating identical or similar equipment (e.g., the Eurofighter-2000, operated by four allied nations); but generally the continued desire for autonomy within both the European Union and NATO means major inefficiencies in the provision of armed forces operating nonstandardized equipment.

The economic principle of international trade based on specialization by comparative advantage is conspicuous by its absence in both the European Union and NATO. An application of this principle would result in role specialization within NATO. For example, the United States could specialize in providing high-technology-intensive forces such as the nuclear deterrent, large naval carrier groups, long-range strategic air transport, communications, and satellite surveillance. Similarly, the United Kingdom might provide small naval carriers, with escorts provided by other EU allies such as Belgium and the Netherlands; while allies such as Turkey might provide ground forces. NATO could also apply the principles of comparative advantage to its provision of armed forces to UN peacekeeping and crisis-management missions. Here, the United States might provide long-range strategic air transport and satellite surveillance, while the EU allies might furnish armored forces, ground troops, and combat air forces. National sovereignty is the obvious objection to role specialization; but such objections ignore the fact that the European Monetary Union will involve the sacrifice of sovereignty over national currencies and that independence is costly in terms of the sacrifice of alternative social welfare.

Chapter 8

An alliance is viable when the net linkage gains from formation are positive and distributed among the prospective allies so that each receives a net linkage benefit. When calculating net linkage benefits, a planner must compute the linkage benefits and costs beyond those associated with the best nonalliance alternative. Initial formation of an alliance is enhanced if it is begun loose and then tightened over time as warranted. If an alliance is viable, then its form can be adjusted until marginal linkage benefits equal marginal linkage costs. Often, however, the best structure among a fixed set of alternatives is the one with the greatest net benefits even if the margins are unequal.

Recent changes concerning NATO's strategic doctrine, its membership composition, and its weapon technology are anticipated to affect the patterns of linkage benefits and linkage costs derived from NATO, and, in so doing, to necessitate alterations to NATO's organization. NATO's structure requires periodic evaluation and adjustment. The actual configuration of NATO's internal and external factors influence NATO's ultimate form. For example, economies of scope, resulting from the sharing of common costs, justify NATO's provision of multiple public goods through its committee structure. Vested interests may at some later time resist the shedding of these functions if linkage gains no longer cover the associated linkage costs.

During the MAD period, NATO was loose except for the disproportionate authority of the United States. This structural arrangement was pragmatic, given the US shares of the burden and its underwriting of the security for most NATO allies. NATO's looseness was particularly well suited to much of the era of flexible response, during which efficiency gains were modest since many allies were motivated by private benefits to support defense spending. Recent changes – the downsizing of military forces, the development of CJTFs, the development of NATO's crisis-management doctrine, the threat of WMD proliferation, the augmentation of the membership – support a tighter, more integrated NATO. Weapon standardization, common logistics, and force specialization are just three factors that can support a somewhat more integrated NATO.

NATO IN THE NEAR TERM

In the near term, NATO will continue to be less concerned with guarding its perimeter than in addressing exigencies adversely affecting European and North American economic and security concerns, near and far. NATO is also apt to face a serious threat of terrorism and low-level conflict from both non-state agents and rogue countries, employing the cloak of secrecy to disguise their identities. This increased threat of terrorism is likely to lead eventually to greater policy coordination among NATO allies, which may even result in an allied commando squad, drawn from the individual allies and optimally dispersed throughout Europe and North America. Such dispersion would mean that the squad could reach incidents quickly without necessarily compromising secrecy while enroute.

If NATO continues to exist, it is expected to consist of two approximately equal-sized allies – the United States and the European Union. Thus defense burdens will be shared fairly equally. Both "allies" will contain large-scale producers, specializing in alternative defense systems freely traded among

NATO allies. In the European Union, the smaller allies are apt to be accused of free riding on the three largest allies – the United Kingdom, France, Germany. These burden-sharing concerns could create fractures in NATO, thus causing stresses in both NATO and the European Union. To address these burden-sharing concerns, the EU allies may eventually agree on a common defense policy, thus greatly augmenting the tightness of NATO. Such a policy may assign shares of a common EU defense budget to its members and divide military tasks among allies to take advantage of comparative strengths. Any NATO ally in Europe left out of the European Union (e.g., Turkey) would have a more difficult time integrating into NATO.

Integration within the alliance should not only involve EU members of NATO, but also include Canada and the United States as downsizing and its influence on force strength are addressed. In many ways, NATO makes more *economic sense* now then it did during the Cold War, when budgets were bigger all around. Common funding will increase as a proportion of the defense budget of NATO. With the admittance of the new members, efforts to standardize weapons may be invigorated – it is difficult to insist on entrants having standardized equipment when the rest of the alliance does not. To field a CJTF drawn from the allies, NATO's integration will have to be enhanced as allies increasingly sacrifice autonomy in exchange for a fighting force capable of peace enforcement wherever needed on behalf of the entire alliance. A big question concerns whether or not NATO allies are prepared to move away from unanimous decision making in order to augment the alliance's ability to act quickly. Unless this occurs, NATO will become less decisive, and therefore less effective, as it admits new allies. There is little reason to have the military might if members cannot agree in a timely fashion to deploy it when warranted.

Recent trends in the arms industry are expected to continue over the next five years as the defense industry becomes ever more concentrated both in the United States and Europe. If the profits of the defense firms were to increase greatly, then policy makers on both sides of the Atlantic would have to consider industrial policies to curb monopoly practices and eliminate inefficiency. As this concentration grows, some weapon systems may be produced on just one side of the Atlantic and then traded to allies. To avoid this eventuality, some European governments have resorted to subsidizing home defense industries and to buying from them regardless of price or quality. With shrinking budgets and higher per-unit weapon costs, governments may no longer be able to afford this practice. Free arms trade within NATO is inevitable with such small shares of GDP being devoted to defense. To avoid negative externalities stemming from arms trade to potential enemies, unstable regions, or unstable regimes, NATO is likely to develop a collective sales policy, complete with monitoring and enforcement devices. Economies of scale and falling per-unit costs cannot come at the expense of security as parts of production runs are sold to potential enemies. The Gulf War of 1991 illustrated the downside of selling weapons and dual-use technologies to a regime that represents a threat to its neighbors and to NATO's resource supply lines. In addressing the arms-sales problem, NATO allies must compare the potential costs of war – $61 billion in the case of Iraq – with the expected gains in profits for their defense contractors. If this problem can be viewed from an alliancewide perspective, allies may then constrain their own arms suppliers. Of course, defense contractors will lobby to prevent such constraints.

If free arms trade flourishes in NATO as predicted, then the need to sell to nations outside of NATO will be reduced. Another benefit from this free trade will be increased weapon standardization as NATO allies procure their weapons from the same suppliers. Allies that spend the most on R & D will capture the largest share of this arms trade.

There is yet another factor pushing NATO to becoming more integrated if it survives another decade or more. This has to do with the increasing publicness of NATO's new weapon technologies, its strategic doctrine, and its new defenses. High-technology weapon systems (e.g., spaced-based Strategic Defense Initiative (SDI) weapons, command and control systems, global-positioning systems) can serve additional allies with little or no rivalry. As such, it makes less sense to exclude friendly nations from their benefits. As the degree of publicness increases, allies are more apt to take a free ride unless an integrated alliance can require cost sharing. Crisis-management, peacekeeping, and nonproliferation missions benefit contributors and noncontributors. If a sufficient number of these missions are to be undertaken, NATO will require the means to force members to contribute. Events in late 1997 concerning Iraq's alleged WMD underscore the difficulty of these missions. If NATO remains divided on these missions, the stability of the alliance will be tested. Defensive anti-ballistic missile systems are likely to be perfected during the next decade. Because these systems can possess significant publicness properties, alliance integration again becomes a relevant concern. In short, NATO's future survival will depend on its ability to address a growing list of public good concerns. Unless free riding can be addressed, NATO's cohesion will be challenged.

NATO IN THE LONG RUN

We now take a longer-run perspective on NATO of, say, ten years into the future. Even with this limited time horizon, it is difficult to know how the strategic environment will evolve. There is a possibility that the United States and Canada will have left NATO by then, unless a significant threat to European security has materialized. The US push to develop its own rapid deployment forces and power-projection capabilities foreshadows this possibility. If US troops were completely withdrawn from Europe and if, moreover, the European Union became very integrated, then a European NATO would likely displace the current alliance. Loose ties between the United States and this European NATO could address common security concerns. For example, a US withdrawal from NATO might still carry a commitment to return in an emergency.

To address the threat of rogue nations and the spread of WMD, the technologically sophisticated allies of NATO might rely on Strategic Defense Initiative (SDI) technologies to destroy suspected sites of WMD. Although development of such weapons might run afoul of the treaty banning weapons in outer space, technologically sophisticated allies might still go ahead with these weapons since they would afford worldwide protection without necessarily placing their own soldiers in jeopardy. This technological revolution will carry over onto the battlefield of the twenty-first century, where the ratio of soldiers to programmers, civilians, and support personnel will fall (Cohen, 1996; Stix, 1995). Future battlefields will involve the engagement of "information warriors" who rely on different frequencies along the electromagnetic spectrum to sight, target, and destroy enemy assets. Pilotless airplanes and robotic warriors may increasingly limit the need for traditional soldiers. Military casualties during engagements may be more in terms of assets rather than people. Future armies will spend much of their time in hiding. What can be seen can be targeted, and what can be targeted can be annihilated. As long-range precision-guided munitions are perfected and deployed, large mobile armored forces can be reduced to rubble by an unseen opponent. The Gulf War of 1991 is a taste of things to come, in terms of the use of precision-guided munitions to limit collateral damage among civilians. Moreover, such weapons keep attacking troops during an operation out of harm's way, making such action politically more acceptable.

As the technology embodied in these weapon systems increases in sophistication, R & D costs will drive up unit costs, leading to a number of implications. First, future arms races may be even more wasteful than those of the past, as the acceleration of technology speeds the obsolescence of weapon systems. Second, allies may have to pool their R & D efforts and purchases if these weapons are to be affordable. Third, the pursuit of these high-technology weapons can create burden-sharing difficulties, as only a subset of NATO allies will be able to support the required R & D. Other allies will have to buy from the one or two allies whose defense industries can develop these advanced weapon systems. Fourth, these pivotal supplier allies may demand greater autonomy in NATO as a condition for sharing their technologies. This demand for autonomy, if made by the technology-providing nations, may strain NATO and result in two classes of allies. Unless threats are sufficient to warrant trading away autonomy, NATO's membership may shrink as "second-class" allies exit under Article 13. Fifth, technology developers will probably include just the United States and a coalition of EU nations. Sixth, inventories of high-technology weapons will be minimal owing to the high per-unit expense, thus making future forces more vulnerable to preemption, accidents, and miscalculations. Most allies will not be able to purchase much reinforcement equipment to replace losses on the battlefield or during operations. Seventh, the development of these high-technology weapons provide a first-mover advantage to whichever side acts first to "blind" its opponent, thus increasing instability and threatening world peace.

Another arms race will involve efforts to destroy and to protect information assets – computer networks, satellites, ground-based receptors, transmitters. Insidious agents, such as computer viruses, could play havoc with these information linkages. Since it is difficult to anticipate the kinds of viruses that will be used, allies will have to possess the expertise to deal with novel viruses and to manage quickly to regain control.

The nature of wars in the next decade is likely to involve the protection of scarce natural resources to a greater extent than in the past. As economic systems converge, wars are not apt to be based so much on ideological differences. In January 1991, the Gulf War was sold, in part, to the American people by the Bush administration as a necessary evil to keep oil prices down (Klare, 1995). As population grows, greater demands will be placed on the air, water, and natural resources. These pressures may result in conflicts over the property rights to disputed resources. NATO allies may be drawn in if these conflicts cut off supply lines or put their common interests in jeopardy.

AGENDA FOR RESEARCH

Much effort has been directed toward studying NATO during the last decade in terms of both its economic and political aspects. Despite such efforts, and our own investigation here, many issues remain unresolved. Arguably the most interesting concern is the optimal membership size of NATO under current circumstances. To date, efforts to ascertain this have fallen short because benefits have been ignored when the potential impact of new members is taken into account. A more accurate measurement procedure is needed to identify and measure the incremental benefits *and* costs that new members bring to the alliance.

Although burden sharing has been the most studied aspect of NATO by political economists since the seminal work by Olson and Zeckhauser (1966), many issues remain. For example, there has been little quantitative work done to contrast the policy recommendations that would follow from using alternative burden-sharing measures. Much of the literature has examined whether or not the actual contributions of NATO allies are optimal. More needs to be done in specifying cost-sharing arrangements that would be more optimal from the alliance viewpoint. Furthermore, these arrangements must improve each ally's well-being. Since burden-sharing behavior and NATO's optimal structure are strongly influenced by strategic doctrine, weapons technology, and membership composition, changes in these factors must be continually related to these policy concerns. Thus, a more dynamic theory of burden sharing must be developed to replace current static theories.

With EU integration moving forward, better studies of the emerging defense industrial base of the European Union are required. Is competition between large EU and US defense firms adequate to provide economic efficiency? Clearly, defense industries are becoming more concentrated on both sides of the Atlantic as a result of the disarmament during the post–Cold War years. The effects of this increasing monopolization on profitability, product quality, product variety, and efficiency must be studied. Effective policy for addressing the implications of this monopolization must be devised. Thus far, there are too few studies that use firm-level data to address concerns about the defense industrial base. These data must be generated if political economists are to be sufficiently well-informed about the workings of the defense industrial base to determine its most efficient structure.

As NATO redirects its efforts toward peacekeeping, peace enforcement, and nonproliferation of WMD, the analysis of burden sharing, as presented in Chapter 4, must be expanded. These new strategic missions can have vastly different implications for burden sharing than was the case during the Cold War face-off. The persistence of nations, such as Iraq, in pursuing WMD and delivery devices to dispatch these weapons will pose unacceptable risks to NATO allies. Because some of these allies may their own private gains from normalizing relations with rogue regimes, burdens from curbing these rogues' intentions may fall on a small subset of NATO allies, thus straining the alliance.

Another important area requiring further research, along the lines of that in Chapters 5, 7, and 8, involves determining the proper interface between NATO and other international organizations, such as the European Union, the United Nations, the Western European Union, and the Partnership for Peace. Questions concern the proper extent of overlapping functions, the diversity of memberships, and the form of interorganizational linkages. As these international organizations continue to grow in number, these interlinkage aspects will assume increased importance.

Within NATO, designing the alliance to achieve greater efficiency gains while accounting for linkage costs, as addressed in Chapters 5, 7, and 8, requires further investigation. The actual design of the NATO institution can be improved so as to further its goal of collective security. For example, the trade-off between autonomy and collective security can be made more optimally in light of the other trade-offs within NATO. The scope of NATO, in terms of the number of separate functions performed, needs to be evaluated further. New functions appear to have been added without regard to strains they may create for the alliance.

The analysis and insights developed in this book must be applied to other current alliances – for example, the US-Israeli alliance and the US-Japanese alliance. Alterations in strategic concerns, weapon technology, and nature of threat may necessitate an expansion of some of these alliances. Moreover, updated burden-sharing studies of these alliances should be performed. There are apt to be a growing number of alliances in Asia and Africa among smaller nations intended to counter large regional powers that present a threat to these smaller countries' sovereignty. Arms trade between these emerging alliances and NATO will need to be examined from a security and an economic vantage. Such alliances can substitute for NATO peacekeeping if they represent a sufficient deterrent to aggression by a dominant regional power. Linkages among these new alliances and NATO is worthy of study. This would include the further investigation of defense industrial linkages between NATO and these alliances in terms of licensed production, offsets, and arms trade. For example, there is a need to design an institution for controlling arms trade between allies and non-NATO countries.

Our study has been intended to address the issues of greatest current concern for NATO. With the changes taking place in Europe, NATO's future role and even its existence are by no means certain, despite its success over the last fifty years. As shown in Chapter 6, challenges abound and represent exigencies, including nuclear terrorism and rogue nations, that NATO has had little collective experience in confronting. If NATO is able to alter its organizational structure and its decision-making apparatus to react to such contingencies quickly and decisively, then NATO will have a bright future. Equally important for this future is the ever-present need that allies continue to view membership as providing a positive net benefit.

References

Arms Control and Disarmament Agency (ACDA) (1996), *World Military Expenditures and Arms Transfers 1995* (Washington, DC: US ACDA).

Arms Control and Disarmament Agency (ACDA) (1997), *World Military Expenditures and Arms Transfers, 1996/7* (Washington, DC: US ACDA).

Arrow, Kenneth J. (1970), "The Organization of Economic Activity: Issues Pertinent to the Choice of Market versus Non-market Allocation," in Robert H. Haveman and Julius Margolis (eds.), *Public Expenditures and Policy Analysis* (Chicago: Markham), 59–73.

Asmus, Ronald D. (1997), "Double Enlargement: Redefining the Atlantic Partnership after the Cold War," in David C. Gompert and F. Stephen Larrabee (eds.), *America and Europe: A Partnership for a New Era* (Cambridge: Cambridge University Press), 19–50.

Asmus, Ronald D., Richard L. Kugler, and F. Stephen Larrabee (1995), "NATO Expansion: The Next Steps," *Survival,* 37, 7–33.

Asmus, Ronald D., Richard L. Kugler, and F. Stephen Larrabee (1996), "What Will NATO Enlargement Cost?", *Survival,* 38, 5–26.

Auster, Richard and Morris Silver (1973), "Collective Goods and Collective Decision Mechanisms," *Public Choice,* 14, 1–17.

Barrett, Scott (1993), *Convention on Climate Change: Economic Aspects of Negotiations* (Paris: Organization for Economic Cooperation and Development).

Barrett, Scott (1994), "Self-Enforcing International Environmental Agreements," *Oxford Economic Papers,* 46, 878–94.

Baumol, William J., John C. Panzar, and Robert D. Willig (1988), *Contestable Markets and the Theory of Industry Structure* (New York: Harcourt Brace Jovanovich).

Beer, Francis A. (1972), *The Political Economy of Alliances* (Beverly Hills, CA: Sage).

Binmore, Ken (1992), *Fun and Games* (Lexington, MA: D.C. Heath).

Birkavs, Valdis (1996), "Baltic States and European Security," in Royal United Services Institute for Defence Studies (RUSI) (ed.), *Cooperation and Partnership for Peace: A Contribution to Euro-Atlantic Security into the 21st Century* (London: RUSI), 25–35.

Bobrow, Davis B. and Mark A. Boyer (1997), "Maintaining System Stability: Contributions to Peacekeeping Operations," *Journal of Conflict Resolution,* 41, 723–48.

Boczek, Boleshaw A. (1995), "NATO and the Former Warsaw Pact States," in S. Victor Papacosma and Mary Ann Heiss (eds.), *NATO in the Post-Cold War Era: Does It Have a Future?* (New York: St. Martin's Press), 205–43.

Bogomolov, Oleg T. (1996), "Russia and Europe's Security," in Royal United Services Institute for Defence Studies (RUSI) (ed.), *Cooperation and Partnership for Peace: A Contribution to Euro-Atlantic Security into the 21st Century* (London: RUSI), 17–24.

Bonn International Center for Conversion (BICC) (1997), *Conversion Survey 1997* (Oxford: Oxford University Press).

Brophy-Baermann, Bryan and John A.C. Conybeare (1994), "Retaliating Against Terrorism: Rational Expectations and the Optimality of Rules versus Discretion," *American Journal of Political Economy,* 38, 196–210.

Brown, Michael E. (1995), "The Flawed Logic of NATO Expansion," *Survival,* 37, 34–52.

Bruce, Erika V.C. (1995), "NATO after the January 1994 Summit: The View from Brussels," in S. Victor Papacosma and Mary Ann Heiss (eds.), *NATO in the Post-Cold War Era: Does It Have a Future?* (New York: St. Martin's Press), 229–38.

Buchanan, James M. and Gordon Tullock (1962), *The Calculus of Consent* (Ann Arbor: University of Michigan Press).

Bureau of European and Canadian Affairs (BECA) (1997), *Report to the Congress on the Enlargement of the North Atlantic Treaty Organization: Rationale, Benefits, Costs and Implications* (Washington, DC: US Department of State).

Callaghan, Thomas A., Jr. (1975), *US-European Economic Co-operation in Military and Civil Technology* (Washington, DC: Georgetown University).

Carlier, Claude (1995), "NATO and the European Union," in S. Victor Papacosma and Mary Ann Heiss (eds.), *NATO in the Post-Cold War Era: Does It Have a Future?* (New York: St. Martin's Press), 135–50.

Carlsneaes, Walter and Steve Smith (eds.) (1994), *European Foreign Policy* (Thousand Oaks, CA: Sage).

Carpenter, Ted Galen (1994), *Beyond NATO: Staying out of Europe's Wars* (Washington, DC: Cato Institute).

Cauley, Jon, Todd Sandler, and Richard Cornes (1986), "Nonmarket Institutional Structures: Conjectures, Distribution, and Allocative Efficiency," *Public Finance,* 41, 153–72.

Central Intelligence Agency (1991, 1993, 1995), *World Factbook* (Washington, DC: US Government Printing Office).

Cerjan, Paul (1994), "The United States and Multilateral Peacekeeping: The Challenge of Peace," in Fariborz L. Mokhtari (ed.), *Peacemaking, Peacekeeping and Coalition Warfare: The Future Role of the United Nations* (Washington, DC: National Defense University), 3–7.

Chalmers, Malcolm and Owen Greene (1995), *Taking Stock: The UN Register after Two Years* (Bradford, UK: Westview Press).

Chen, Zhiqi (1997), "Negotiating an Agreement on Global Warming: A Theoretical Analysis," *Journal of Environmental Economics and Management,* 32, 170–88.

Chinworth, Michael (1992), *Inside Japan's Defense* (Washington, DC: Brassey's).

Christopher, Warren (1994), "Opening Statement at the Meeting of the North Atlantic Council," December 1, 1994, gopher://marvin.nc3a.nato.int:70/00/natodata/PRESS/SPEECHES/94/wc 0112.

Cmnd 3223 (1996), *Statement on the Defence Estimates 1996* (London: HMSO).

Coe, David T. and Elhanan Helpman (1995), "International R & D Spillovers," *European Economic Review,* 39, 859–87.

Cohen, Eliot A. (1996), "A Revolution in Warfare," *Foreign Affairs,* 75, 37–54.

Congressional Budget Office (CBO) (1987), *Effects of Weapons Procurement Stretch-Outs on Costs and Schedules* (Washington, DC: US Government Printing Office).

Congressional Budget Office (CBO) (1991a), "Costs of Operation Desert Shield," CBO Staff Memorandum, CBO, Washington, DC.

Congressional Budget Office (CBO) (1991b), "Statement of Robert D. Reischauer, Director of the Congressional Budget Office," CBO Testimony, CBO, Washington, DC.

Congressional Budget Office (CBO) (1992), *Limiting Conventional Arms Exports to the Middle East* (Washington, DC: US Government Printing Office).

Congressional Budget Office (CBO) (1996), "The Costs of Expanding the NATO Alliance," CBO Papers, CBO, Washington, DC.

Congressional Budget Office (CBO) (1997a), *Moving US Forces: Options for Strategic Mobility* (Washington, DC: US Government Printing Office).

Congressional Budget Office (CBO) (1997b), *A Look at Tomorrow's Tactical Air Forces* (Washington, DC: US Government Printing Office).

Conybeare, John A. C., James C. Murdoch, and Todd Sandler (1994), "Alternative Collective-Goods Models of Military Alliances: Theory and Empirics," *Economic Inquiry,* 32, 525–42.

Cornes, Richard and Todd Sandler (1994), "The Comparative Static Properties of the Impure Public Good Model," *Journal of Public Economics,* 54, 403–21.

Cornes, Richard and Todd Sandler (1996), *The Theory of Externalities, Public Goods, and Club Goods,* Second Edition (Cambridge: Cambridge University Press).

Corsun, Andrew (1991), "Group Profile: The Revolutionary Organization 17 November in Greece," *Terrorism,* 14, 77–104.

Cragg, Anthony (1996), "The Combined Joint Task Force Concept: A Key Component of the Alliance's Adaptation," *NATO Review,* 44, July, 7–10.

Crelinsten, Ronald D. (1989), "Terrorism, Counter-Terrorism and Democracy: The Assessment of National Security Threats," *Terrorism and Political Violence,* 1, 242–69.

Dando, Malcolm (1994), *Biological Warfare in the 21st Century* (London: Brassey's).

de Gruijl, Frank R. (1995), "Impacts of a Projected Depletion of the Ozone Layer," *Consequences: The Nature & Implications of Environmental Change,* 1, 13–21.

De Vestel, Pierre (1995), "Defence Markets and Industries in Europe: Time for Political Decisions?", Chaillot Papers 21, Institute for Security Studies, Paris.

Denoon, David B. H. (ed.) (1986), *Constraints on Strategy: The Economics of Western Security* (Washington, DC: Pergamon-Brassey's).

Drown, Jane Davis, Clifford Drown, and Kelly Campbell (eds.) (1990), *A Single European Arms Industry? European Defence Industries in the 1990s* (London: Brassey's).

Dunne, J. Paul (1995), "The Defense Industrial Base," in Keith Hartley and Todd Sandler (eds.), *Handbook of Defense Economics, Vol. 1* (Amsterdam: North-Holland), 399–430.

Durch, William J. (1993), "Paying the Tab: Financial Crisis," in William J. Durch (ed.), *The Evolution of UN Peacekeeping: Case Studies and Comparative Analysis* (New York: St. Martin's Press), 39–55.

The Economist (1984), *Foreign Report,* issue no. 1831 (London: *The Economist* Newspaper Limited).

The Economist (1997a), "A New European Order," *The Economist,* 343, 28 May, 55–6.

The Economist (1997b), "Why Bigger Is Better," *The Economist,* 342, 15 February, 21–3.

The Economist (1997c), "Global Defence Industry," *The Economist,* 343, 14 June, survey.

Enders, Walter, Gerald F. Parise, and Todd Sandler (1992), "A Time-Series Analysis of Transnational Terrorism: Trends and Cycles," *Defence Economics,* 3, 305–20.

Enders, Walter and Todd Sandler (1993), "The Effectiveness of Anti-Terrorism Policies: Vector-Autoregression-Intervention Analysis," *American Political Science Review,* 87, 829–44.

Enders, Walter and Todd Sandler (1995), "Terrorism: Theory and Applications," in Keith Hartley and Todd Sandler (eds.), *Handbook of Defense Economics, Vol. 1* (Amsterdam: North-Holland), 213–49.

Enders, Walter and Todd Sandler (1996), "Terrorism and Foreign Direct Investment in Spain and Greece," *KYKLOS,* 49, 331–52.

Enders, Walter and Todd Sandler (1999), "Transnational Terrorism in the Post-Cold War Era," *International Studies Quarterly,* 43, forthcoming.

Enders, Walter, Todd Sandler, and Jon Cauley (1990), "UN Conventions, Technology and Retaliation in the Fight against Terrorism: An Econometric Evaluation," *Terrorism and Political Violence,* 2, 83–105.

Enders, Walter, Todd Sandler, and Gerald F. Parise (1992), "An Econometric Analysis of the Impact of Terrorism on Tourism," *KYKLOS,* 45, 531–54.

Eubank, William L. and Leonard Weinberg (1994), "Does Democracy Encourage Terrorism?", *Terrorism and Political Violence,* 6, 417–35.

Ferrari, Giovanni (1995), "NATO's New Standardization Organization Tackles an Erstwhile Elusive Goal," *NATO Review,* 43, May, 33–35.

Fetherston, A. B. (1994), *Towards a Theory of United Nations Peacekeeping* (New York: St. Martin's Press).

Flight International (1997), "Military Aircraft of the World," *Flight International,* 152, October, 39–76.

Fontanel, Jacques and Jean-Paul Hebert (1997), "The End of the 'French Grandeur Policy,'" *Defence and Peace Economics,* 8, 37–55.

Friedman, Alann (1993), *Spider's Web: The Secret History of How the White House Illegally Armed Iraq* (New York: Bantam).

Gansler, Jacques S. (1995), *Defense Conversion: Transforming the Arsenal of Democracy* (Cambridge, MA: MIT Press).

Goldgeier, James (1998), "NATO Expansion: The Anatomy of a Decision," *Washington Quarterly,* 21, 85–102.

Goldstein, Avery (1995), "Discounting the Free Ride: Alliances and Security in the Postwar World," *International Organization,* 49, 39–71.

Gompert, David C. and F. Stephen Larrabee (eds.) (1997), *America and Europe: A Partnership for a New Era* (Cambridge: Cambridge University Press).

Gonzales, Rodolfo A. and Stephen L. Mehay (1990), "Publicness, Scale, and Spillover Effects in Defense Spending," *Public Finance Quarterly,* 18, 273–90.

Gummett, Philip and Josephine Anne Stein (eds.) (1997), *European Defence Technology in Transition* (Amsterdam: Harwood).

Hall, G. R. and R. E. Johnson (1967), *Aircraft Co-Production and Procurement Strategy* (Santa Monica: RAND, R-450-PR).

Hansen, Laurna, James C. Murdoch, and Todd Sandler (1990), "On Distinguishing the Behavior of Nuclear and Non-Nuclear Allies in NATO," *Defence Economics,* 1, 37–55.

Hardin, Russell (1982), *Collective Action* (Baltimore, MD: Johns Hopkins University Press).

Hartley, Keith (1983), *NATO Arms Co-Operation* (London: Allen and Unwin).

Hartley, Keith (1991), *The Economics of Defence Policy* (London: Brassey's).

Hartley, Keith (1996), "The Economics of the Peace Dividend," *International Journal of Social Economics,* 24, 28–45.

Hartley, Keith (1997a), "The Cold War, Great-Power Traditions and Military Posture: Determinants of British Defence Expenditure after 1945," *Defence and Peace Economics,* 8, 17–35.

Hartley, Keith (1997b), "National Defence Policy and the International Trade Order," in Horst Siebert (ed.), *Towards a New Global Framework for High-Technology Competition* (Tübingen: JCB Mohr), 165–79.

Hartley, Keith (1998), "Jointery: Just Another Panacea: An Economist's View," *Defense Analysis,* 14, 79–85.

Hartley, Keith and Andrew Cox (1995), "The Cost of Non-Europe in Defence Procurement," unpublished manuscript, European Commission, Brussels.

Hartley, Keith and Nick Hooper (1995), *Study of the Value of the Defence Industry to the UK Economy: A Statistical Analysis* (York, UK: Centre for Defence Economics, University of York).

Hartley, Keith and Stephen Martin (1993), "Evaluating Collaborative Programmes," *Defence Economics,* 4, 195–211.

Hartley, Keith and Todd Sandler (1990), *The Economics of Defence Spending: An International Survey* (London: Routledge).

Hartley, Keith and Todd Sandler (eds.) (1995), *Handbook of Defense Economics, Vol. I* (Amsterdam: North-Holland).

Hartley, Keith and Todd Sandler (1998), "NATO Burden Sharing," unpublished manuscript, University of York, Heslington, York, UK.

HCP 518 (1986), *The Defence Implication of the Future of Westland plc* (London: House of Commons, Defence Committee, HMSO).

HCP 247 (1991), *Ministry of Defence: Collaborative Projects* (London: National Audit Office, HMSO).

HCP 222 (1994), *Progress on the Eurofighter 2000 Programme* (London: House of Commons Defence Committee, HMSO).

HCP 333 (1995), "Aspects of Defence Procurement and Industrial Policy" (London: Defence and Trade and Industry Committees, Memoranda, HMSO).

HCP 724 (1995), *Ministry of Defence: Eurofighter 2000* (London: National Audit Office, HMSO).

HCP 238 (1997), *Ministry of Defence: Major Projects Report* (London: National Audit Office, HMSO).
Heckathorn, Douglas D. (1989), "Collective Action and the Second-Order Free Rider Problem," *Rationality and Society,* 1, 78–100.
Heidenrich, John G. (1994), "Arming the United Nations: Military Considerations and Operational Constraints," in Fariborz L. Mokhtari (ed.), *Peacemaking, Peacekeeping and Coalition Warfare: The Future Role of the United Nations* (Washington, DC: National Defense University), 41–55.
Hill, Stephen M. and Shahin P. Malik (1996), *Peacekeeping and the United Nations* (Aldershot, UK: Dartmouth).
Hilton, Brian and Anh Vu (1991), "The McGuire Model and the Economics of the NATO Alliance," *Defence Economics,* 2, 105–21.
Holder, Stephen (1995), "Support Management – The Weapon Life Cycle," *Air Clues,* 49, 336–41.
Hooper, Nick and Nick Cox (1996), "The European Union KONVER Programme," *Defence and Peace Economics,* 7, 75–94.
Ilke, Fred (1995), "How to Ruin NATO," *New York Times,* 11 January, A-21.
Im, Eric I., Jon Cauley, and Todd Sandler (1987), "Cycles and Substitutions in Terrorist Activities: A Spectral Approach," *KYKLOS,* 40, 238–55.
International Institute for Strategic Studies (1996), *The Military Balance 1995–1996* (London: International Institute for Strategic Studies).
International Monetary Fund (IMF) (1990, 1993, 1994, 1995, 1996), *International Financial Statistics Yearbook* (Washington, DC: IMF).
International Monetary Fund (IMF)(1997), *International Financial Statistics,* April issue, IMF, Washington, DC.
Jordan, Robert S. (1995), "NATO's Structural Changes in the 1990s," in S. Victor Papacosma and Mary Ann Heiss (eds.), *NATO in the Post-Cold War Era: Does It Have a Future?* (New York: St. Martin's Press), 41–69.
Kammler, Hans (1997), "Not for Security Only: The Demand for International Status and Defence Expenditure, An Introduction," *Defence and Peace Economics,* 8, 1–16.
Kaplan, Lawrence S. (1990), *NATO after Forty Years* (Wilmington, DE: SR Books).
Kassimeris, George (1993), "The Greek State Response to Terrorism," *Terrorism and Political Violence,* 5, 288–300.
Kelly, Jerry S. (1988), *Social Choice Theory: An Introduction* (Berlin: Springer-Verlag).
Kennedy, Gavin (1979), *Burden Sharing in NATO* (London: Duckworth).
Kennedy, Gavin (1983), *Defense Economics* (London: Duckworth).
Khalilzad, Zalmay (1997), "Challenges in the Greater Middle East," in David C. Gompert and F. Stephen Larrabee (eds.), *America and Europe: A Partnership for a New Era* (Cambridge: Cambridge University Press), 191–217.
Khanna, Jyoti, Wallace E. Huffman, and Todd Sandler (1994), "Agricultural Research Expenditures in the US: A Public Goods Perspective," *Review of Economics and Statistics,* 76, 267–77.
Khanna, Jyoti and Todd Sandler (1996), "NATO Burden Sharing: 1960–1992," *Defence and Peace Economics,* 7, 115–33.
Khanna, Jyoti and Todd Sandler (1997), "Conscription, Peacekeeping, and Foreign

Assistance: NATO Burden Sharing in the Post-Cold War Era," *Defence and Peace Economics,* 8, 101–21.

Khanna, Jyoti, Todd Sandler, and Hirofumi Shimizu (1998), "Sharing the Financial Burden for UN and NATO Peacekeeping: 1976–1996," *Journal of Conflict Resolution,* 42, 176–95.

Kirby, Stephen and Nick Hooper (eds.) (1991), *The Cost of Peace: Assessing Europe's Security Options* (Reading: Harwood).

Kirkpatrick, David L. I. (1995), "The Rising Unit Costs of Defence – The Reasons and Results," *Defence and Peace Economics,* 6, 263–88.

Kirkpatrick, David L. I. (1997), "Rising Costs, Falling Budgets and Their Implications for Defense Policy," *Economic Affairs,* 17, 10–14.

Klare, Michael (1995), *Rogue States and Nuclear Outlaws: America's Search for a New Foreign Policy* (New York: Hill and Wang).

Klein, Lawrence R. and Kanta Marwah (1996), "Economic Aspects of Peacekeeping Operations," in Nils P. Gleditsch, Olav Bjerkholt, Adne Cappelen, Ron Smith, and John P. Dunne (eds.), *The Peace Dividend* (Amsterdam: Elsevier), 533–53.

Knorr, Klaus (1985), "Burden-Sharing in NATO: Aspects of US Policy," *Orbis,* 29, 517–36.

Kolodziej, Edward A. and Roger E. Kanet (1996), *Coping with Conflict after the Cold War* (Baltimore: Johns Hopkins University Press).

Konrad, Kai A. (1994), "The Strategic Advantage of Being Poor: Private and Public Provision of Public Goods," *Economica,* 61, 79–92.

Kugler, Richard L. (1996), *Enlarging NATO: The Russian Factor* (Santa Monica, CA: RAND).

Lall, Betty G. and John Tepper Marlin (1992), *Building a Peace: Opportunities and Problems of Post-Cold War Defense Cuts* (Boulder, CO: Westview Press).

Lambelet, Jean-Christian (1992), "Do Arms Races Lead to Peace?", in Walter Isard and Charles H. Anderton (eds.), *Economics of Arms Reduction and the Peace Process* (Amsterdam: North-Holland), 249–60.

Lapan, Harvey E. and Todd Sandler (1988), "To Bargain or Not to Bargain: That Is the Question," *American Economic Review Papers and Proceedings,* 78, 16–20.

Larrabee, F. Stephen (1997), "Security Challenges on Europe's Eastern Periphery," in David C. Gompert and F. Stephen Larrabee (eds.), *America and Europe: A Partnership for a New Era* (Cambridge: Cambridge University Press), 166–90.

Latawski, Paul (1996), "Practical Cooperation in Joint Operations, Including Peacekeeping," in Royal United Services Institute for Defence Studies (RUSI) (ed.), *Cooperation and Partnership for Peace: A Contribution to Euro-Atlantic Security into the 21st Century* (London: RUSI), 57–63.

Lee, Dwight R. (1988), "Free Riding and Paid Riding in the Fight Against Terrorism," *American Economic Review Papers and Proceedings,* 78, 22–6.

Lee, Dwight R. (1990), "The Politics and Pitfalls of Reducing Waste in the Military," *Defence Economics,* 1, 129–39.

Lee, Dwight R. and Todd Sandler (1989), "On the Optimal Retaliation Against Terrorists: The Paid-Rider Option," *Public Choice,* 61, 141–52.

Leech, John (1991), *Halt! Who Goes There?: The Future of NATO in the New Europe* (London: Brassey's).

Levine, Paul, Fotis Mouzakis, and Ron Smith (1996), "The Arms Trade: Some Theory and Econometrics," Discussion Paper No. 8/96, University of Surrey, Guildford, UK.

Levine, Robert A. (1988), *NATO, the Subjective Alliance: The Debate over the Future* (Santa Monica, CA: Rand Corporation).

Lorrell, Mark A., Daniel P. Raymer, Michael Kennedy, and Hugh Levaux (1995), *The Gray Threat: Assessing the Next-Generation European Fighters* (Santa Monica: RAND, MR-611-AF).

Markowski, Stefan and Peter Hall (eds.) (1998), "Perspectives on International Defense Procurement," *Defence and Peace Economics,* Special Issue, 9, 1–170.

Martin, Lawrence and John Roper (1995), *Towards a Common Defense Policy* (Paris: Institute for Security Studies, Western European Union).

Martin, Stephen (1996), *The Economics of Offsets* (Reading, UK: Harwood Academic Publishers).

Martin, Stephen and Keith Hartley (1995), "UK Firms' Experience and Perceptions of Defence Offsets," *Defence and Peace Economics,* 6, 123–40.

Martin, Stephen and Keith Hartley (1997), "Comparing Profitability in the Public Utilities, Defence and Pharmaceuticals," *Journal of Public Policy,* 17, 81–105.

McFarlane, Ian (1997), *The European Defense Industry: Perspectives from European Industry* (Brussels: Royal Military Academy Conference on Technology, Defense, and Economy).

McGuire, Martin C. (1990), "Mixed Public-Private Benefit and Public-Good Supply with Application to the NATO Alliance," *Defence Economics,* 1, 17–35.

McGuire, Martin C. (1995), "Defense Economics and International Security," in Keith Hartley and Todd Sandler (eds.), *Handbook of Defense Economics, Vol. 1* (Amsterdam: North-Holland), 13–43.

McNamara, Robert S. (1991), "The Post Cold War World: Implications for Military Expenditure in the Developing Countries," *Proceedings of the World Bank Annual Conference on Development Economics,* supplement to the *World Bank Economic Review* and the *World Bank Research Observer* (Washington, DC: World Bank), 95–125.

Miall, H. (ed.) (1994), *Redefining Europe: New Patterns of Conflict and Cooperation* (London: Pinter, RIIA).

Mickolus, Edward F. (1980), *Transnational Terrorism: A Chronology of Events 1968–1979* (Westport, CT: Greenwood Press).

Mickolus, Edward F. (1989), "What Constitutes State Support to Terrorists?", *Terrorism and Political Violence,* 1, 287–93.

Mickolus, Edward F., Todd Sandler, and Jean M. Murdock (1989), *International Terrorism in the 1980s: A Chronology of Events,* 2 vols. (Ames, IA: Iowa State University).

Mills, Susan R. (1990), "The Financing of UN Peacekeeping Operations: The Need for a Sound Financial Basis," in Indar Jit Rikhye and Kjell Skjelsback (eds.), *The United Nations and Peacekeeping: Results, Limitations and Prospects: The Lessons of 40 Years of Experience* (Houndmills, UK: Macmillan), 91–110.

Mohnen, Volker A. (1988), "The Challenge of Acid Rain," *Scientific American,* 259, 30–8.

Mokhtari, Fariborz L. (ed.) (1994), *Peacemaking, Peacekeeping and Coalition Warfare:*

The Future Role of the United Nations (Washington, DC: National Defense University).

Morrisette, Peter M., Joel Darmstadter, Andrew J. Plantiga, and Michael A. Toman (1990), "Lessons from Other International Agreements for a Global CO_2 Accord," Discussion Paper ENR91-02, Resources for the Future, Washington, DC.

Morrow, James D. (1991), "Alliances and Asymmetry: An Alternative to the Capability Aggregation Model of Alliances," *American Journal of Political Science,* 35, 904–13.

Mueller, Dennis C. (1989), *Public Choice II* (Cambridge: Cambridge University Press).

Murdoch, James C. (1995), "Military Alliances: Theory and Empirics," in Keith Hartley and Todd Sandler (eds.), *Handbook of Defense Economics, Vol. 1* (Amsterdam: North-Holland), 89–108.

Murdoch, James C. and Todd Sandler (1982), "A Theoretical and Empirical Analysis of NATO," *Journal of Conflict Resolution,* 26, 237–63.

Murdoch, James C. and Todd Sandler (1984), "Complementarity, Free Riding, and the Military Expenditures of NATO Allies," *Journal of Public Economics,* 25, 83–101.

Murdoch, James C. and Todd Sandler (1991), "NATO Burden Sharing and the Forces of Change: Further Observations," *International Studies Quarterly,* 25, 109–14.

Murdoch, James C. and Todd Sandler (1997), "The Voluntary Provision of a Pure Public Good: The Case of Reduced CFC Emissions and the Montreal Protocol," *Journal of Public Economics,* 63, 331–49.

Murdoch, James C., Todd Sandler, and Laurna Hansen (1991), "An Econometric Technique for Comparing Median Voter and Oligarchy Choice Models of Collective Action: The Case of the NATO Alliance," *Review of Economics and Statistics,* 73, 624–31.

Murdoch, James C., Todd Sandler, and Keith Sargent (1997), "A Tale of Two Collectives: Sulphur versus Nitrogen Oxides Emission Reduction in Europe," *Economica,* 64, 281–301.

Myers, Kenneth A. (1980), *NATO: The Next Thirty Years: The Changing Political, Economic, and Military Setting* (Boulder, CO: Westview).

Myers, Norman (1993), *Ultimate Security: The Environmental Basis of Political Stability* (New York: Norton).

NATO (1995), "Study on NATO Enlargement," NATO, Brussels.

NATO Information Service (1984), *NATO Facts and Figures* (Brussels: NATO).

NATO Information Service (1989), *NATO Facts and Figures* (Brussels: NATO).

NATO Office of Information and Press (1995), *NATO Handbook* (Brussels: NATO).

NATO Press Release (1996), "Financial and Economic Data Relating to NATO Defence," Press Release (96)168, 17 December, NATO, Brussels.

NATO Press Release (1997a), "Basic Document of the Euro-Atlantic Partnership Council," Press Release M-NACC-EAPC-1(97)66, 30 May, NATO, Brussels.

NATO Press Release (1997b), "Financial and Economic Data Relating to NATO Defence," Press Release M-DPC-2(97)147, 2 December, NATO, Brussels.

Olson, Mancur (1965), *The Logic of Collective Action* (Cambridge, MA: Harvard University Press).

Olson, Mancur (1969), "The Principle of 'Fiscal Equivalence': The Division of Responsibilities among Different Levels of Government," *American Economic Review Papers and Proceedings,* 59, 479–87.

Olson, Mancur and Richard Zeckhauser (1966), "An Economic Theory of Alliances," *Review of Economics and Statistics,* 48, 266–79.

Olson, Mancur and Richard Zeckhauser (1967), "Collective Goods, Comparative Advantage, and Alliance Efficiency," in Roland McKean (ed.), *Issues of Defense Economics* (New York: National Bureau of Economics Research), 25–48.

Oneal, John R. (1990a), "Testing the Theory of Collective Action: NATO Defense Burdens, 1950–1984," *Journal of Conflict Resolution,* 34, 426–48.

Oneal, John R. (1990b), "The Theory of Collective Action and Burden Sharing in NATO," *International Organization,* 44, 379–402.

Oneal, John R. (1992), "Budgetary Savings from Conscription and Burden Sharing in NATO," *Defence Economics,* 3, 113–25.

Oneal, John R. and Mark A. Elrod (1989), "NATO Burden Sharing and the Forces of Change," *International Studies Quarterly,* 33, 435–56.

Palin, Roger H. (1995), *Multinational Military Forces: Problems and Prospects,* Adelphi Paper 294, International Institute for Strategic Studies (Oxford: Oxford University Press).

Palmer, Glenn (1990a), "Alliance Politics and Issue Areas: Determinants of Defense Spending," *American Journal of Political Science,* 34, 190–211.

Palmer, Glenn (1990b), "Corralling the Free Rider: Deterrence and the Western Alliance," *International Studies Quarterly,* 34, 147–64.

Palmer, Glenn (1991), "Deterrence, Defense Spending, and Elasticity: Alliance Contributions to the Public Good," *International Interactions,* 7, 157–69.

Papacosma, S. Victor and Mary Ann Heiss (eds.) (1995), *NATO in the Post-Cold War Era: Does It Have a Future?* (New York: St. Martin's Press).

Partnership for Peace (1996), "Partnership for Peace: What Is It?," NATO, Brussels.

Perlmutter, Amos and Ted Galen Carpenter (1998), "NATO's Expensive Trip East," *Foreign Affairs,* 77, 2–6.

Pryor, Frederic L. (1968), *Public Expenditures in Communist and Capitalist Nations* (Homewood, IL: Irwin).

Pugh, Philip (1986), *The Cost of Sea Power* (London: Conway Press).

Pugh, Philip (1993), "The Procurement Nexus," *Defence and Peace Economics,* 4, 179–94.

Ratner, Steve R. (1995), *The New UN Peacekeeping: Building Peace in Lands of Conflict after the Cold War* (New York: St. Martin's Press).

Rearden, Steven L. (1995), "NATO's Strategy: Past, Present, and Future," in S. Victor Papacosma and Mary Ann Heiss (eds.), *NATO* in *the Post-Cold War Era: Does It Have a Future?* (New York: St. Martin's Press), 71–92.

Reed, Pamela L., J. Matthew Vaccaro, and William J. Durch (1995), "Handbook on United Nations Peace Operations", Handbook No. 3, Henry L. Stimson Center, Washington, DC.

Rich, M., W. Stanley, J. Barker, and M. Hesse (1981), *Multi-National Co-Production of Military Aerospace Systems* (Santa Monica: RAND).

Rikhye, Indar J. (1990), "The Future of Peacekeeping," in Indar J. Rikhye and Kjell Skjelsback (eds.), *The United Nations and Peacekeeping: Results, Limitations, and Prospects: The Lessons of 40 Years of Experience* (Houndmills: Macmillan), 170–99.

Rikhye, Indar J. and Kjell Skjelsback (eds.) (1990), *The United Nations and Peace-*

keeping: Results, Limitations, and Prospects: The Lessons of 40 Years of Experience (Houndmills: Macmillan).
Rogerson, William P. (1990), "Quality and Quantity in Military Procurement," *American Economic Review,* 80, 83–92.
Rogerson, William P. (1991), "Incentives, the Budgetary Process, and Inefficiently Low Production Rates in Defense Procurement," *Defence Economics,* 3, 1–18.
Royal United Services Institute for Defence Studies (RUSI) (ed.) (1996), *Cooperation and Partnership for Peace: A Contribution to Euro-Atlantic Security into the 21st Century* (London: RUSI).
Russett, Bruce M. (1970), *What Price Vigilance?* (New Haven: Yale University Press).
Salmon, Jeffrey (1997), "The US Military Build-Up 1980–1985: What the One Trillion Dollars Purchased," *Defence and Peace Economics,* 8, 101–21.
Sandler, Todd (1977), "Impurity of Defense: An Application to the Economics of Alliances," *KYKLOS,* 30, 443–60.
Sandler, Todd (1980), "A Hierarchical Theory of the Firm," *Scottish Journal of Political Economy,* 27, 17–29.
Sandler, Todd (1987), "NATO Burden Sharing: Rules or Reality?", in Christian Schmidt and Frank Blackaby (eds.), *Peace, Defence, and Economic Analysis* (London: Macmillan), 363–83.
Sandler, Todd (1992), *Collective Action: Theory and Applications* (Ann Arbor: University of Michigan Press).
Sandler, Todd (1993), "The Economic Theory of Alliances: A Survey," *Journal of Conflict Resolution,* 37, 446–83.
Sandler, Todd (1995), "On the Relationship between Democracy and Terrorism," *Terrorism and Political Violence,* 7, 1–9.
Sandler, Todd (1997), *Global Challenges: An Approach to Environmental, Political, and Economic Problems* (Cambridge: Cambridge University Press).
Sandler, Todd and Jon Cauley (1975), "On the Economic Theory of Alliances," *Journal of Conflict Resolution,* 19, 330–48.
Sandler, Todd and Jon Cauley (1977), "The Design of Supranational Structures," *International Studies Quarterly,* 21, 251–76.
Sandler, Todd, Jon Cauley, and John Tschirhart (1983), "Toward a Unified Theory of Nonmarket Institutional Structures," *Australian Economic Papers,* 22, 233–54.
Sandler, Todd and John F. Forbes (1980), "Burden Sharing, Strategy, and the Design of NATO," *Economic Inquiry,* 18, 425–44.
Sandler, Todd and Keith Hartley (1995), *The Economics of Defense* (Cambridge: Cambridge University Press).
Sandler, Todd and Harvey E. Lapan (1988), "The Calculus of Dissent: An Analysis of Terrorists' Choice of Targets," *Synthese,* 76, 245–61.
Sandler, Todd and James C. Murdoch (1990), "Nash-Cournot or Lindahl Behavior?: An Empirical Test for the NATO Allies," *Quarterly Journal of Economics,* 105, 875–94.
Sandler, Todd and John Tschirhart (1980), "The Economic Theory of Clubs: An Evaluative Survey," *Journal of Economic Literature,* 18, 1481–521.
Schelling, Thomas C. (1960), *The Strategy of Conflict* (Cambridge, MA: Harvard University Press).

Schmid, Alex (1992), "Terrorism and Democracy," *Terrorism and Political Violence,* 6, 417–35.

Schwartz, Joel (1991), "Particulate Air Pollution and Daily Mortality: A Synthesis," *Public Health Review,* 19, 39–60.

Seidelmann, Reimund (1997), "Costs, Risks, and Benefits of a Global Military Capability for the European Union," *Defence and Peace Economics,* 8, 123–43.

Seiglie, Carlos (1993), "Technological Progress, Alliance Spillovers, and Economic Growth in a Disaggregated Arms Race Model," *Defence Economics,* 4, 1–13.

Sharp, J. O. (ed.) (1996), *About Turn, Forward March with Europe: New Directions for Defence and Security Policy* (London: IPPR/Rivers Oram Press).

Sloan, Stephen (1993), *Burden Sharing in the Post-Cold War World* (Washington, DC: Congressional Research Services, US Government Printing Office).

Smith, Dan and Ron Smith (1983), *The Economics of Militarism* (London: Pluto Press).

Smith, Ron (1980), "The Demand for Military Expenditures," *Economic Journal,* 90, 811–20.

Smith, Ron (1987), "The Demand for Military Expenditures: A Correction," *Economic Journal,* 97, 989–90.

Smith, Ron (1989), "Models of Military Expenditures," *Journal of Applied Econometrics,* 4, 345–59.

Smith, Ron (1995), "The Demand for Military Expenditures," in Keith Hartley and Todd Sandler (eds.), *Handbook of Defense Economics, Vol. 1* (Amsterdam: North-Holland), 69–87.

Sopko, John F. (1996/97), "The Changing Proliferation Threat," *Foreign Policy,* 105, 3–20.

Starr, Harvey (1974), "A Collective Goods Analysis of the Warsaw Pact after Czechoslovakia," *International Organization,* 28, 521–32.

Stix, Gary (1995), "Fighting Future Wars," *Scientific American,* 273, 92–8.

Stockholm International Peace Research Institute (SIPRI) (1977, 1983, 1994, 1995), *World Armaments and Disarmaments: SIPRI Yearbook* (Stockholm: SIPRI).

Stockholm International Peace Research Institute (SIPRI) (1996), *SIPRI Yearbook 1996: World Armaments and Disarmaments* (Oxford: Oxford University Press).

Stockholm International Peace Research Institute (SIPRI) (1997), *SIPRI Yearbook 1997: Armaments, Disarmaments and International Security* (Oxford: Oxford University Press).

Thomson, James A. (1997), "A New Partnership, New NATO Military Structures," in David C. Gompert and F. Stephen Larrabee (eds.), *America and Europe: A Partnership for a New Era* (Cambridge: Cambridge University Press), 79–103.

Todd, Daniel (1988), *Defence Industries: A Global Perspective* (London: Routledge).

United Nations (1996), *Statistical Yearbook 1994* (New York: United Nations).

United Nations (various years), *Financial Report and Audited Financial Statements for the Biennium Ended 31 December 19_ and Report of the Board of Auditors,* General Assembly (New York: United Nations).

United Nations (1977–97), *Status of Contributions as at 31 December 1976, . . ., 1996,* ST/ADM/SER. B/229, 233, 240, 245, 252, 259, 265, 271, 276, 283, 288, 295, 309, 325, 345, 364, 395, 424, 458, 484, 505 (New York: United Nations Documents).

United Nations Department of Public Information (1995), *The United Nations and Nuclear Non-Proliferation* (New York: United Nations).

United Nations Department of Public Information (1996), *The Blue Helmets: A Review of United Nations Peace-keeping,* Third Edition (New York: United Nations).

United Nations Development Programme (1992), *Human Development Report 1992* (New York: Oxford University Press).

United Nations Development Programme (1994), *Human Development Report 1994* (New York: Oxford University Press).

United States Committee on Armed Services (1988), *Interim Report of the Defense Burdens Sharing Panel,* US House of Representatives, 100th Congress, Second Session, Committee Report No. 23 (Washington, DC: US Government Printing Office).

United States Department of Defense (1992), *Conduct of the Persian Gulf War, Final Report to Congress,* PB92-163674 (Washington, DC: US Department of Defense).

United States Department of Defense (1996), *Report on Allied Contributions to the Common Defense: A Report to the United States Congress by the Secretary of Defense* (Washington, DC: US Department of Defense).

United States Department of State (various years), *Patterns of Global Terrorism* (Washington, DC: US Department of State.

United States General Accounting Office (US GAO) (1992), *International Procurement: NATO and Allies Implementation of Reciprocal Defense Agreements* (Washington, DC: US GAO).

United States General Accounting Office (US GAO) (1997a), "NATO Enlargement: US and International Efforts to Assist Potential New Member," Report to the Chairman, Committee on International Relations, House of Representatives, GAO/NSIAD-97–164, June, US GAO, Washington, DC.

United States General Accounting Office (US GAO) (1997b), "NATO Enlargement: Cost Estimates Developed to Date Are Notional," Letter Report, GAO/NSIAD-97–209, 18 August, US GAO, Washington, DC.

United States General Accounting Office (US GAO) (1997c), "NATO Enlargement: Cost Implications for the United States Remain Unclear," Testimony before the Committee on Appropriations, US Senate, GAO/T-NSIAD-98–50, 23 October, US GAO, Washington, DC.

United States General Accounting Office (US GAO) (1998), "Bosnia: Operational Decisions Needed before Estimating DOD's Costs," Briefing Report to the Chairman, Committee on Foreign Relations, US Senate, GAO/NSIAD-98–77BR, February 1998, US GAO, Washington, DC.

Van Oudenaren, John (1997), "Europe as Partner," in David C. Gompert and F. Stephen Larrabee (eds.), *America and Europe: A Partnership for a New Era* (Cambridge: Cambridge University Press), 104–43.

van Ypersele de Strihou, Jacques (1967), "Sharing the Defence Burden among Western Allies," *Review of Economics and Statistics,* 49, 527–36.

Vredeling, H. (1986), *Towards a Stronger Europe* (Brussels: IEPG).

Weidenbaum, Murray (1992), *Small Wars, Big Defense: Paying for the Military after the Cold War* (New York: Oxford University Press).

Western European Union (WEU) (1995), *WEAG: The Course to Be Followed,* Document 1483 (Paris: Assembly of the Western European Union).

Western European Union (WEU) (1996), *The Euclid Programme and Cooperation between European Defence Electronic Industries,* Document 1524 (Paris: Assembly of the Western European Union).

Western European Union (WEU) (1997), *WEU after Amsterdam,* Document 1584 (Paris: Assembly of the Western European Union).

Wilcox, Philip C., Jr. (1997), "The Western Alliance and the Challenge of Combating Terrorism," *Terrorism and Political Violence,* 9, 1–7.

Wilkinson, Paul (1986), *Terrorism and the Liberal State,* Revised Edition (London: Macmillan).

Wilkinson, Paul (1992), "The European Response to Terrorism: Retrospect and Prospect," *Defence Economics,* 3, 289–304.

Wilkinson, Paul (1996), "The Role of the Military in Combating Terrorism," *Terrorism and Political Violence,* 8, 1–11.

Williamson, Oliver E. (1967), "Hierarchical Control and Optimum Firm Size," *Journal of Political Economy,* 75, 123–38.

Williamson, Oliver E. (1975), *Markets and Hierarchies: Analysis and Antitrust Implications* (New York: The Free Press).

World Bank (1995), *World Data 1995: World Bank Indicators on CD-ROM* (Washington, DC: World Bank).

Author index

Subject index